ACCA

Strategic Professional

Advanced Audit and Assurance – UK (AAA – UK)

Workbook

For exams in September 2023, December 2023, March 2024 and June 2024

Fifth edition 2023

ISBN: 9781 0355 0091 8

Previous ISBN: 9781 5097 4608 8

ISBN (for internal use only): 9781 0355 0137 3

e-ISBN: 9781 0355 0352 0

British Library Cataloguing-in-Publication Data

A catalogue record for this book is available from the British Library

Published by

BPP Learning Media Ltd

BPP House, Aldine Place

142–144 Uxbridge Road

London W12 8AA

learningmedia.bpp.com

Printed in the United Kingdom

Your learning materials, published by BPP Learning Media Ltd, are printed on paper obtained from traceable sustainable sources.

Contents

Helping you to pass

BPP Learning Media – ACCA Approved Content Provider

As an ACCA Approved Content Provider, BPP Learning Media gives you the opportunity to use study materials reviewed by the ACCA examining team. By incorporating the examining team's comments and suggestions regarding the depth and breadth of syllabus coverage, the BPP Learning Media Workbook provides excellent, ACCA-approved support for your studies.

These materials are reviewed by the ACCA examining team. The objective of the review is to ensure that the material properly covers the syllabus and study guide outcomes, used by the examining team in setting the exams, in the appropriate breadth and depth. The review does not ensure that every eventuality, combination or application of examinable topics is addressed by the ACCA Approved Content. Nor does the review comprise a detailed technical check of the content as the Approved Content Provider has its own quality assurance processes in place in this respect.

BPP Learning Media do everything possible to ensure the material is accurate and up to date when sending to print. In the event that any errors are found after the print date, they are uploaded to the following website: https://learningmedia.bpp.com/catalog?pagename=Errata

The PER alert

Before you can qualify as an ACCA member, you not only have to pass all your exams but also fulfil a three-year practical experience requirement (PER). To help you to recognise areas of the syllabus that you might be able to apply in the workplace to achieve different performance objectives, we have introduced the 'PER alert' feature (see the next section). You will find this feature throughout the Workbook to remind you that what you are learning to pass your ACCA exams is equally useful to the fulfilment of the PER requirement. Your achievement of the PER should be recorded in your online My Experience record.

Chapter features

Studying can be a daunting prospect, particularly when you have lots of other commitments. This Workbook is full of useful features, explained in the key below, designed to help you to get the most out of your studies and maximise your chances of exam success.

Key term

Central concepts are highlighted and clearly defined in the Key terms feature. Key terms are also listed in bold in the Index, for quick and easy reference.

Formula to learn

This boxed feature will highlight important formula which you need to learn for your exam.

PER alert

This feature identifies when something you are reading will also be useful for your PER requirement (see 'The PER alert' section above for more details).

Real world examples

These will give real examples to help demonstrate the concepts you are reading about.

Illustration

Illustrations walk through how to apply key knowledge and techniques step by step.

Activity

Activities give you essential practice of techniques covered in the chapter.

Essential reading

Links to the Essential reading are given throughout the chapter. The Essential reading is included in the free eBook, accessed via the Exam Success Site (see inside cover for details on how to access this).

Figure 1.1: Key to icons

At the end of each chapter you will find a Knowledge diagnostic, which is a summary of the main learning points from the chapter to allow you to check you have understood the key concepts. You will also find a Further study guidance which contains suggestions for ways in which you can continue your learning and enhance your understanding. This can include: recommendations for question practice from the Further question practice and solutions (available in the digital edition of the Workbook), to test your understanding of the topics in the Chapter; suggestions for further reading which can be done, such as technical articles, and ideas for your own research.

Introduction to the Essential reading

The electronic version of the Workbook contains additional content, selected to enhance your studies. Consisting of revision materials and further explanations of complex areas including illustrations and activities, as well as practice questions and solutions and background reading, it is designed to aid your understanding of key topics which are covered in the main printed chapters of the Workbook.

A summary of the content of the Essential reading is given below.

Chapter		Summary of Essential reading content
1	International regulatory environments for audit and assurance services	• Legal and professional framework in place (uses the UK as an illustrative example) • Corporate governance and audit committees (again, using UK examples as illustrations)
2	Code of ethics and conduct	• An overview of the various ethical threats and how the firm should respond to them using the ACCA and IESBA Codes • Specific guidance on confidentiality and conflicts of interest
3	Fraud and professional liability	• A summary of the relevant legal cases used to determine auditor liability • Advantages and disadvantages of different structures for firms
4	Quality management	• Guidance from the FRC on how to display professional judgement when making decisions in a variety of situations
5	Obtaining and accepting professional appointments	• Ethical requirements from AA and acceptance/continuance factors from ISQM 1 plus money laundering and PEPs and their impact on acceptance decisions • Contents of an engagement letter
6	Planning and risk assessment	• Business risks related to emerging trends in IT and e-commerce • Planning issues: risks of material misstatement, documentation, materiality, initial audits and audit risk • Professional scepticism and additional information required • Analytical procedures as substantive procedures
7	Evidence	• Various additional elements of evidence: external confirmations; opening balances; documentation • Further detail on the auditor's responses to risks presented by related parties, the use of experts and the use of internal audit by the external auditor
8	Evaluation and review – matters relating to specific accounting issues	• A revision of the accounting and financial reporting issues associated with relevant IAS/IFRS from SBR plus suggested auditing issues relevant to each area covered

Chapter		Summary of Essential reading content
9	Group audits and transnational audits	• A recap on group accounting including associates and joint ventures, plus an overview of consolidation problems and procedures • Communication with the component auditor
10	Completion	• Further reading on ISA 220 (revised) and quality management for audits • Additional details on how to apply ISA 560 Subsequent Events
11	Reporting	• Discussion documents from the IAASB on the auditor's report, including the use of KAMs • Illustrations of unmodified and modified auditor's reports • Further considerations when reporting to those charged with governance and management • FAQ publication from IAASB that is designed to clarify the relationship between material uncertainty related to going concern, KAMs and EoM paragraphs when addressing going concern disclosures in the auditor's report
12	Audit-related services and other assurance services	• Examples of various assurance and audit-related reports for information • Further detail on how to apply the various assurance and audit-related services standards
14	Forensic audits	• Further detail on how to plan and conduct a forensic audit engagement
15	Social, environmental and public sector auditing	• A summary of how the public sector is considering the best way to improve its sustainability reporting • An overview of the difficulties encountered by firms when measuring social and environmental performance • A reminder of the capitals used in the Integrated Reporting framework as well as some practical issues from their use
16	Current issues	• Topical issues relevant to the audit profession, including reforms to the regulation of auditing, big data and data analytics, professional scepticism, ethics and audit quality

Introduction to Advanced Audit and Assurance – UK (AAA – UK)

Overall aim of the syllabus

To analyse, evaluate and conclude on the assurance engagement and other audit and assurance issues in the context of best practice and current developments.

Brought forward knowledge

The AAA syllabus uses a lot of content that you will have already seen in Audit and Assurance (AA) and Strategic Business Reporting (SBR) but the crucial difference here is that it is all tested in the context of more detailed scenarios and requires higher level skills to pass. There are also some new areas of content that you will need to learn, so you should treat AAA as an exercise in itself, rather than an extension of AA.

The syllabus

The broad syllabus headings are:

A	Regulatory environment
B	Professional and ethical considerations
C	Quality management and practice management
D	Planning and conducting an audit of historical financial information
E	Completion, review and reporting
F	Other assignments
G	Current issues and developments
H	Professional skills
I	Employability and technology skills

Main capabilities

On successful completion of this exam, you should be able to:

A	Recognise the legal and regulatory environment and its impact on audit and assurance practice
B	Demonstrate the ability to work effectively on an assurance or other service engagement within a professional and ethical framework
C	Assess and recommend appropriate quality management policies and procedures in practice management and recognise the auditor's position in relation to the acceptance and retention of professional appointments
D	Identify and formulate the work required to meet the objectives of audit assignments and apply the International Standards on Auditing (UK)
E	Evaluate findings and the results of work performed and draft suitable reports on assignments
F	Identify and formulate the work required to meet the objectives of non-audit assignments
G	Understand the current issues and developments relating to the provision of audit-related and assurance services

H	Apply a range of professional skills in addressing requirements within the Advanced Audit and Assurance exam, and in preparation for, or to support current work experience
I	Demonstrate employability and technology skills

Links to other exams

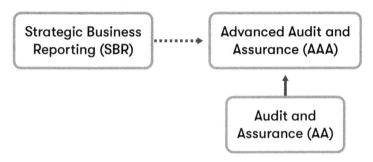

This diagram shows where direct (solid line arrows) and indirect (dashed line arrows) links exist between this exam and others that may precede or follow it.

The Advanced Audit and Assurance syllabus assumes auditing knowledge acquired in Audit and Assurance and develops and applies this further in greater depth. AAA also assumes accounting knowledge from SBR.

Achieving ACCA's Study Guide Outcomes

This BPP Workbook covers all the AAA – UK syllabus learning outcomes. The tables below show in which chapter(s) each area of the syllabus is covered.

A	Regulatory environment	
A1	International regulatory frameworks for audit and assurance services	Chapter 1
A2	Money laundering	Chapter 1
A3	Laws and regulations	Chapter 1

B	Professional and ethical considerations	
B1	Code of Ethics and Conduct	Chapter 2
B2	Fraud and error	Chapter 3
B3	Professional liability	Chapter 3

C	Quality management and practice management	
C1	Quality management (firm-wide)	Chapter 4
C2	Advertising, tendering and obtaining professional work and fees	Chapter 5
C3	Professional appointments	Chapter 5

D	Planning and conducting an audit of historical financial information	

D1	Planning, materiality and assessing the risk of material misstatement	Chapter 6
D2	Evidence and testing considerations	Chapter 7
D3	Audit procedures and obtaining evidence	Chapter 8
D4	Using the work of others	Chapter 7
D5	Group audits	Chapter 9

E	**Completion, review and reporting**	
E1	Subsequent events and going concern	Chapter 10
E2	Completion and final review	Chapter 10
E3	Auditor's reports	Chapter 11
E4	Reports to those charged with governance and management	Chapter 11

F	**Other assignments**	
F1	Audit-related and assurance services	Chapter 12
F2	Specific assignments: • Due diligence • Review of interim financial information • Prospective financial information • Forensic audits	Chapter 12 Chapter 12 Chapter 13 Chapter 14
F3	The audit of social, environmental, sustainability and integrated reporting	Chapter 15
F4	Auditing aspects of insolvency (and similar procedures)	Chapter 15
F5	Reporting on other assignments	Chapters 12 and 13

G	**Current issues and developments**	
G1	Professional and ethical developments	Chapters 1 and 2
G2	Other current issues	Chapter 16

H	**Professional skills**	
H1	Communication	You will find more guidance on how to achieve these learning outcomes within the professional skills checkpoints.
H2	Analysis and evaluation	
H3	Professional scepticism and judgement	
H4	Commercial acumen	

I	**Employability and technology skills**	

I1	Use computer technology to efficiently access and manipulate relevant information	You will find more guidance on how to achieve these learning outcomes within the professional skills checkpoints.
I2	Work on relevant response options, using available functions and technology, as required by the workspace	
I3	Navigate windows and computer screens to create and amend responses to exam requirements, using the appropriate tools	
I4	Present data and information effectively, using the appropriate tools	

The complete syllabus and study guide can be found by visiting the exam resource finder on the ACCA website: www.accaglobal.com/gb/en.html.

The exam

Computer-based exams

Strategic Professional exams are all computer-based exams (CBE).

Approach to examining the syllabus

The exam lasts 3 hours and 15 minutes and consists of two sections. Questions will be adapted to have a UK focus and will require no more than basic calculations at most (for example, to assess materiality and calculate relevant ratios where appropriate) so candidates should always aim to have a calculator handy when attempting any study for AAA.

35% Knowledge   65% Application

Format of the exam		Marks
	Question 1 will comprise a Case Study, worth 50 marks, set at the planning stage of the audit, for a single company, a group of companies or potentially several audit clients.	50 (incl. 10 professional marks)
	Candidates will be provided with detailed information, which will vary between examinations, but is likely to include extracts of financial information, strategic, operational and other relevant financial information for a client business, as well as extracts from audit working papers, including results of analytical procedures. The 50 marks will comprise 40 technical marks and 10 professional skills marks. All professional skills with be examined in Question 1.	
	Candidates will be required to address a range of requirements, predominantly from syllabus Sections A, B, C and D, thereby tackling a real-world situation where candidates may have to address a range of issues simultaneously in relation to planning, risk assessment, evidence gathering and ethical and professional considerations. Other syllabus areas, excluding Section E, may also be drawn on as part of the Case Study.	
	Ten professional marks will be available in Question 1 and will be awarded based on the demonstration of all four professional skills in candidates' answers.	
	The remainder of the exam will contain two compulsory 25-mark questions, with each being predominately based around a short scenario which may relate to more than one client.	50 (incl. 10 professional marks)
	One question will always predominantly come from syllabus Section E, and consequently candidates should be prepared to answer a question relating to completion, review and reporting. There are a number of formats this question could adopt, including, but not limited to, requiring candidates to assess going concern, the impact of subsequent events, evaluating identified misstatements and the corresponding effect on the auditor's report. Candidates may also be asked to critique an auditor's report or evaluate the matters to be included in a report which is to be provided to management or those charged with governance.	

Format of the exam		Marks
	The other 25-mark question can be drawn from the remaining areas of the syllabus, including Sections A, B, C, D and F. In each question, the 25 marks will comprise 20 technical marks and 5 professional skills marks. These questions will examine a combination of professional skills appropriate to the question. Each question will examine a minimum of two professional skills: analysis and evaluation plus professional scepticism and judgement and/or commercial acumen.	
Quality management and ethics	The auditor's assessment of effective quality management procedures and consideration of ethical issues are fundamental to all stages of the audit and therefore these concepts could be examined in any section of the exam.	
Current issues	Content from Section G on current issues is unlikely to form the basis of any question on its own but instead will be incorporated into any of the three questions, dependent on that question's content and the topical issues affecting the profession at the time of writing.	
		100

Remote invigilated exams

In certain geographical areas it may be possible for you to take your exam remotely. This option, which is subject to strict conditions, can offer increased flexibility and convenience under certain circumstances. Further guidance, including the detailed requirements and conditions for taking the exam by this method, is contained on ACCA's website at https://www.accaglobal.com/an/en/student/exam-entry-and-administration/about-our-exams/remote-exams/remote-session-exams.html.

Analysis of past exams

The table below provides details of when each element of the syllabus has been examined in the ten most recent sittings and the section in which each element was examined.

* Covered in Workbook chapter

*		Sept 2022	Mar/Jun 2022	Sep/Dec 2021	Mar/Jun 2021	Sep/Dec 2020	Mar 2020	Sep/Dec 2019	Mar/Jun 2019	Dec 2018	Sept 2018
	REGULATORY ENVIRONMENT										
1	International regulatory frameworks for audit and assurance services										
1	Money laundering		1(c)							3(a)	
1	Laws and regulations	1(d)									
	PROFESSIONAL AND ETHICAL CONSIDERATIONS										
2	Code of Ethics and Conduct		2(b)	1(d)	1(d)	2(a)	3(b)	1(d)	1(d)	3(b)	1(d), 2(b), 3(b)
3	Fraud and error						2(a)	3(c)		1	
3	Professional liability										

*		Sept 2022	Mar/Jun 2022	Sep/Dec 2021	Mar/Jun 2021	Sep/Dec 2020	Mar 2020	Sep/Dec 2019	Mar/Jun 2019	Dec 2018	Sept 2018
	QUALITY MANAGEMENT										
4	Quality management (firm-wide)	2			2, 3(a)	2(a)					
5	Advertising, tendering, obtaining professional work and fees					1(c)					
5	Professional appointments		1(d)			2(b)	3(a)			1	
	ASSIGNMENTS										
6, 7, 8	The audit of historical financial information including: Planning, materiality and assessing the risk of misstatement Evidence	1(a), 1(b), 1(c)	1, 2(a)	1	1	1	1, 2	1	1, 3	1	1
9	Group audits						1				
	COMPLETION, REVIEW AND REPORTING										
10	Completion	3(c)	3	3	3(a)	3		2(a)		2(a), 2(b)	2(a)
11	Auditor's reports		3(b)	3(b)	3(b)	3	2(b)	2(b)	2(a)	2(c)	2(a)
11	Communications to management								2(b)		
11	Other reports										
	OTHER ASSIGNMENTS										
12	Audit-related services									1(e)	
12	Assurance services										
13	Prospective financial information	3(a), 3(b)		2			3(a)				
14	Forensic audits							3(a), 3(b)			
15	Social and environmental auditing					1(c)					
15	Auditing aspects of insolvency						3(b)				3(b)
	CURRENT ISSUES AND DEVELOPMENTS										
1, 2, 3	Professional, ethical and corporate governance						1(c)				
16	Other current issues					1(d)			3(a)		

IMPORTANT!

The table above gives a broad idea of how frequently major topics in the syllabus are examined. It should not be used to question spot and predict for example that Topic X will not be examined because it came up two sittings ago. The examining team's reports indicate that the examining team is well aware some students try to question spot. The examining team avoid predictable patterns and may, for example, examine the same topic two sittings in a row.

Understanding the question verbs

Verbs that are likely to be frequently used in this exam are listed below, together with their intellectual levels and guidance on their meaning. Bold text denotes verbs used most frequently in AAA.

Intellectual level		
3	**Evaluate/critically evaluate**	Determine the value of, in the light of the arguments for and against (critically evaluate means weighting the answer towards criticisms/arguments against)
3	**Design**	To devise in order to execute a plan
3	Assess	Determine the strengths/weaknesses/importance/significance/ability to contribute
3	Examine	Critically review in detail
3	**Discuss**	Examine by using arguments for and against
3	Explore	Examine or discuss in a wide-ranging manner
3	**Criticize**	Present the weaknesses of/problems with the actions taken or viewpoint expressed, supported by evidence
3	Construct the case	Present the arguments in favour or against, supported by evidence
3	**Recommend**	Advise the appropriate actions to pursue in terms the recipient will understand
2	Distinguish	Define two different terms, viewpoints or concepts on the basis of the differences between them
2	Compare and contrast	Explain the similarities and differences between two different terms, viewpoints or concepts
2	Contrast	Explain the differences between two different terms, viewpoints or concepts
2	**Analyse**	Give reasons for the current situation or what has happened
1	Define	Give the meaning of
1	Explain	Make clear
1	Identify	Recognise or select
1	Describe	Give the key features

A lower-level verb such as define will require a more **descriptive answer**. A higher-level verb such as evaluate will require a more **applied, critical answer**. The examining team has stressed that **higher-level requirements and verbs** will be most significant in this exam, such as critically evaluating a statement and arguing for or against a given idea or position. The examining team is looking to set questions that provide evidence of student understanding.

Note. Answers that can address higher level requirements and verbs will be more likely to attract professional skills marks (for example, when providing a balanced answer in response to 'discuss' and displaying appropriate levels of challenge or judgement when asked to 'evaluate' risks or other factors presented in a scenario).

Certain verbs have given students particular problems.

(a) Identify and explain

Although these verbs are both Level 1, the examining team sees them as requiring different things. You have to go into more depth if you are asked to explain than if you are asked to identify. An explanation means giving more detail about the problem or factor identified, normally meaning that you have to indicate why it's significant. If you were asked to:

- Identify the main problem with the same person acting as chief executive and chair – you would briefly say excessive power is exercised by one person.

- Explain the main problem with the same person acting as chief executive and chair – you would say excessive power is exercised by one person and then go on to say it would mean that the same person was running the board and the company. As the board is meant to monitor the chief executive, it can't do this effectively if the chief executive is running the board. Also, you may be asked to explain or describe something complex, abstract or philosophical in nature.

(b) Evaluate

Evaluate is a verb that the examining team uses frequently. Its meaning may be different from the way that you have seen it used in other exams. The examining team expects to see arguments for and against, or pros and cons for what you are asked to evaluate.

Thus, for example, if a question asked you to:

'Evaluate the contribution made by non-executive directors to good corporate governance in companies'

You would not only have to write about the factors that help non-executive directors make a worthwhile contribution (independent viewpoint, experience of other industries), you would also have to discuss the factors that limit or undermine the contribution non-executive directors make (lack of time, putting pressure on board unity).

If the examining team asks you to critically evaluate, you will have to consider both viewpoints. However, you will concentrate on the view that you are asked to critically evaluate, as the mark scheme will be weighted towards that view.

The examining team has stated that 'Evaluate' is likely to be used for risk-based questions, ie Question 1.

Examinable documents

Knowledge of new examinable regulations issued by 31 August will be examinable in examination sessions being held in the following exam year. Documents may be examinable even if the effective date is in the future. This means that all regulations issued by 31 August 2022 will be examinable in the September 2023 to June 2024 examinations.

The Workbook offers more detailed guidance on the depth and level at which the examinable documents should be examined. The Workbook should therefore be read in conjunction with the examinable documents list.

Accounting standards

All questions set will be based on IFRS© Accounting Standards.

The accounting knowledge that is assumed for Advanced Audit and Assurance (AAA) is the same as that examined in Strategic Business Reporting (SBR). Therefore, candidates studying for AAA should refer to the IFRS Accounting Standards listed under SBR.

Note. AAA will only expect knowledge of accounting standards and financial reporting standards from SBR. Knowledge of exposure drafts and discussion papers will not be expected.

Auditing standards

	Title
	International Standards on Auditing (ISAs) (UK)
	Glossary of terms (ethics and auditing) December 2019
	Scope and Authority of Audit and Assurance pronouncements
ISA (UK) 200 (Revised June 2016)	Overall Objectives of the Independent Auditor and the Conduct of an Audit in Accordance with ISAs (UK)
ISA (UK) 210 (Revised June 2016)	Agreeing the Terms of Audit Engagements
ISA (UK) 220 (Revised July 2021)	Quality Management for an Audit of Financial Statements
ISA (UK) 230 (Revised June 2016)	Audit Documentation
ISA (UK) 240 (Revised May 2021)	The Auditor's Responsibilities Relating to Fraud in an Audit of Financial Statements
ISA (UK) 250A (Revised November 2019)	Consideration of Laws and Regulations in an Audit of Financial Statements
ISA (UK) 260 (Revised November 2019)	Communication With Those Charged With Governance
ISA (UK) 265	Communicating Deficiencies in Internal Control to Those Charged with Governance and Management
ISA (UK) 300 (Revised June 2016)	Planning an Audit of Financial Statements
ISA (UK) 315 (Revised July 2020)	Identifying and Assessing the Risks of Material Misstatement
ISA (UK) 320 (Revised June 2016)	Materiality in Planning and Performing an Audit
ISA (UK) 330 (Revised July 2017)	The Auditor's Responses to Assessed Risks
ISA (UK) 402	Audit Considerations Relating to an Entity Using a Service Organisation
ISA (UK) 450 (Revised June 2016)	Evaluation of Misstatements Identified During the Audit
ISA (UK) 500	Audit Evidence
ISA (UK) 501	Audit Evidence – Specific Considerations for Selected Items
ISA (UK) 505	External Confirmations
ISA (UK) 510 (Revised June 2016)	Initial Audit Engagements – Opening Balances
ISA (UK) 520	Analytical Procedures
ISA (UK) 530	Audit Sampling

	Title
ISA (UK) 540 (Revised December 2018)	Auditing Accounting Estimates and Related Disclosures
ISA (UK) 550	Related Parties
ISA (UK) 560	Subsequent Events
ISA (UK) 570 (Revised September 2019)	Going Concern
ISA (UK) 580	Written Representations
ISA (UK) 600 (Revised November 2019)	Special Considerations – Audits of Group Financial Statements (Including the Work of Component Auditors)
ISA (UK) 610 (Revised June 2013)	Using the Work of Internal Auditors
ISA (UK) 620 (Revised November 2019)	Using the Work of an Auditor's Expert
ISA (UK) 700 (Revised November 2019)	Forming an Opinion and Reporting on Financial Statements
ISA (UK) 701 (Revised November 2019)	Communicating Key Audit Matters in the Independent Auditor's Report
ISA (UK) 705 (Revised June 2016)	Modifications to the Opinion in the Independent Auditor's Report
ISA (UK) 706 (Revised June 2016)	Emphasis of Matter Paragraphs and Other Matter Paragraphs in the Independent Auditor's Report
ISA (UK) 710	Comparative Information – Corresponding Figures and Comparative Financial Statements
ISA (UK) 720 (Revised November 2019)	The Auditor's Responsibilities Relating to Other Information
	International Standards on Quality Management (ISQM)
ISQM (UK) 1	Quality Management for Firms that Perform Audits or Reviews of Financial Statements, or Other Assurance or Related Services Engagements
ISQM (UK) 2	Engagement Quality Reviews
	Conforming and consequential amendments to the IAASB's other standards as a result of the new and revised quality management standards (January 2022)
	International Standards on Assurance Engagements (ISAEs)
ISAE (UK) 3000 (July 2020)	Assurance Engagements other than Audits or Reviews of Historical Financial Information
	IAASB Non-authoritative guidance on applying ISAE 3000 (Revised) to extended

	Title
	external reporting assurance engagements (April 2021)
ISAE 3400	IAASB: The Examination of Prospective Financial Information
	Practice Notes (PNs)
PN 23	Special Considerations in Auditing Financial Instruments
	Ethical Standards (ESs)
ES	Revised Ethical Standard December 2019
	Bulletins
2009/4	Developments in corporate governance affecting the responsibilities of auditors of UK companies
Bulletin	Illustrative auditor's reports on United Kingdom private sector financial statements (August 2021)
	Statement of Standards for Reporting Accountants (SSRAs)
ISRE (UK) 2410 (Revised May 2021)	Review of Interim Financial Information Performed by the Independent Auditor of the Entity
	Exposure Drafts (EDs)
	FRC – Proposed International Standard on Auditing (UK) 600 (Revised), Special Considerations - Audits of Group Financial Statements (Including the Work of Component Auditors) (May 2022)
	Other Documents – Ethical guidelines
	ACCA's Code of Ethics and Conduct (January 2022)
	IESBA's International Code of Ethics for Professional Accountants (Revised 2021)
	IESBA – Quality Management Related Conforming Amendments to the Code (April 2022)
	IESBA – Revisions to the definitions of listed entity and public interest entity in the Code (April 2022)
	Other documents – ACCA
	ACCA's Anti-money laundering guidance for the accountancy profession
	Other Documents – FRC

	Title
	The UK Corporate Governance Code (Revised July 2018)
	Guidance on Audit Committees (Revised April 2016)
	Audit Quality – Practice aid for audit committees (December 2019)
	Staff Guidance: Auditor responsibilities under ISA (UK) 720 in respect of climate related reporting by companies required by the Financial Conduct Authority (February 2022)
	Audit Quality Thematic Review – The Use of Technology on the Audit of Financial Statements (March 2020)
	Audit Quality Thematic Review – Other Information in the Annual Report (December 2018)
	Climate Thematic: Audit (November 2020)
	Extended auditor's reports – A further review of experience (January 2016)
	Professional Judgement Guidance (June 2022)
	Other documents – IAASB
	Discussion Paper: Fraud and Going Concern in an Audit of Financial Statements (October 2020)
	Frequently Asked Questions: Reporting Going Concern Matters in the Auditors Report (August 2022)
	IAASB Toward Enhanced Professional Skepticism (August 2017)
	IAASB Feedback Statement – Exploring the Growing Use of Technology in the Audit with a Focus on Data Analytics (January 2018)
	IAASB Support Material Related to Technology: Audit Documentation when using Automated Tools and Techniques (April 2020)
	Integrated Reporting Working Group: Supporting Credibility and Trust in Emerging Forms of External Reporting: Ten Key Challenges for Assurance Engagements (January 2018)
	IAASB Support material: Using Automated Tools and Techniques in Performing Audit Procedures (September 2020)

	Title
	IAASB Auditor Considerations Regarding Significant Unusual or Highly Complex Transactions (September 2010)
	IAASB The consideration of climate related risks in an audit of financial statement (October 2020)
	IAASB Support material: Using Automated Tools and Techniques when Identifying Risks of Material Misstatement in Accordance with ISA 315 (Revised) (November 2020)
	IAASB Addressing risk of overreliance on technology arising from the use of automated tools and techniques and from information produced by an entity's system (March 2021)

Note. Topics of exposure drafts are examinable to the extent that relevant articles about them are published in *Student Accountant*.

Essential skills areas to be successful in Advanced Audit and Assurance – UK (AAA – UK)

We think there are three areas you should develop in order to achieve exam success in AAA – UK:

(a) Knowledge application

(b) Professional skills

(c) Exam success skills

Knowledge application

In the September 2022 examiner's report, the need for students to be **specific** in their answers and **tailor them to the scenario** was emphasised. This continues to be something that should be emphasised for students attempting the AAA exam. The examiner's report included the following:

> Some candidates continued to produce very vague answers which were not tailored to the specific scenario and, therefore, did not achieve high technical or professional skills marks. This exam requires candidates to demonstrate both technical knowledge but also, they need to be able to **apply this knowledge** to a specific scenario. Generic responses with speculative risks not evident from the detail provided in the scenario will gain little credit. Candidates should **use the specific information provided within the scenario** demonstrating both knowledge and application of skills to pass each requirement.

You should take note of this advice about applying your knowledge when considering how to answer AAA questions. Let's now think about the **skills** you will need to display, which are shown in the diagram below.

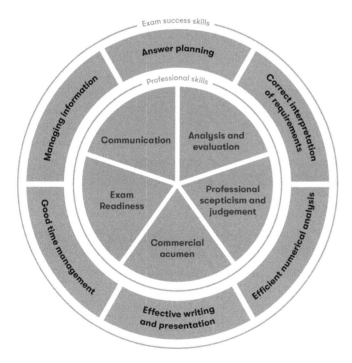

Professional Skills

From the September 2022 exam onwards, 20 marks will be available for demonstrating 'professional skills' that would be expected from a proficient senior financial professional.

There are four professional skills, which are introduced gradually in a series of skills checkpoints. The fifth skills checkpoint will bring these professional and exam success skills together and consider them in the context of the CBE where you can also demonstrate employability and technology skills.

The four professional skills are:

(a) Analysis and evaluation (covered in skills checkpoint 1)

(b) Communication (covered in skills checkpoint 2)

(c) Professional scepticism and judgement (covered in skills checkpoint 3)

(d) Commercial acumen (covered in skills checkpoint 4)

In section A of the exam, which is a single 50-mark case study, 10 of the 50 marks will be allocated to demonstrating professional skills. All of the professional skills will be examined in Section A.

Section B will consist of two compulsory scenario-based 25-mark questions. Each Section B question will allocate five marks to professional skills, so 10 marks in total will be available for professional skills marks in Section B.

Each Section B question will contain a minimum of two professional skills: Analysis and Evaluation plus Professional scepticism and judgement and/or Commercial acumen. Professional skills will apply to the whole question and not to any of the individual requirements. Just like the technical marks available for each question, you can also expect a certain amount of headroom in the marking scheme for the demonstration of professional skills. In Section A, Question 1 will include 10 professional skills marks but the mark scheme will have up to 14 marks available for demonstrating professional skill in all four categories, although the weighting of marks across each skill will not always be the same. Each Section B question worth 25 marks will have up to seven professional skills marks available, this time split across two or three of the professional skills, depending on the question, and will be capped at five marks in line with the requirement.

The following table introduces these skills briefly with some examples of each:

ACCA professional skill: Definition	Three aspects of each professional skill
Analysis and evaluation To appraise information objectively and to draw logical conclusions from both quantitative and qualitative information, recognising the impact on relevant stakeholders and prioritising issues appropriately.	Consider the meaning of data Assess impact on stakeholders Apply analysis to the company in the question
Communication To express yourself clearly, concisely and convincingly through an appropriate medium, while being sensitive to the needs of the intended audience.	Inform target audience using clear format Persuade with logical argument Appropriate use of technology
Professional scepticism and judgement To probe, question and challenge information and views presented to you, in order to fully understand business issues, establish facts objectively and reach appropriate conclusions, based on ethical values and professional standards.	Question the validity of approaches Challenge opinions Make informed decisions in the context of the engagement
Commercial acumen To show awareness of the wider business and external factors affecting business and use commercially sound judgement and insight to resolve issues and exploit opportunities.	Practical considerations Recognise constraints Awareness of alternative opportunities to those suggested

You should refer to each of the Skills Checkpoints for more information on how to apply each skill and earn the professional marks on offer.

Note. You will also find a number of interactive and audio-visual resources on the ACCA website that explain how professional skills marks can be earned. Within the 'Students' section of accaglobal.com, select 'Study resources', 'ACCA qualification' and then 'Advanced Audit and

Assurance (AAA)' and as well as a host of other important resources, you will also find content on professional skills.

Exam success skills

Passing the AAA exam requires more than applying syllabus knowledge and demonstrating the specific AAA skills; it also requires the development of excellent exam technique through question practice.

We consider the following six skills to be vital for exam success. The Skills Checkpoints show how each of these skills can be applied specifically to the AAA exam. You will also find details on how to apply these skills in the context of the CBE and Syllabus Area H 'Employability and technology skills'.

Exam success skill 1

Managing information

Questions in the exam will present you with a lot of information. The skill is how you handle this information to make the best use of your time. The key is determining how you will approach the exam and then actively reading the questions.

Advice on developing managing information

Approach

The exam is 3 hours 15 minutes long. There is no designated 'reading' time at the start of the exam, however, one approach that can work well is to start the exam by spending time carefully reading through all of the questions to familiarise yourself with the exam.

Once you feel familiar with the exam, consider the order in which you will attempt the questions; always attempt them in your order of preference. For example, you may want to leave to last the question you consider to be the most difficult.

If you do take this approach, remember to adjust the time available for each question appropriately – see Exam success skill 6: Good time management.

If you find that this approach doesn't work for you, don't worry – you can develop your own technique.

Active reading

You must take an active approach to reading each question. Focus on the requirement first, highlighting key verbs such as 'prepare', 'comment', 'explain', 'discuss', to ensure you answer the question properly. Then read the rest of the question, highlighting and using the scratch pad for important and relevant information, and making notes of any relevant technical information you think you will need.

The CBE

At first glance, the CBE is quite daunting as the screenshot of the workspace below illustrates:

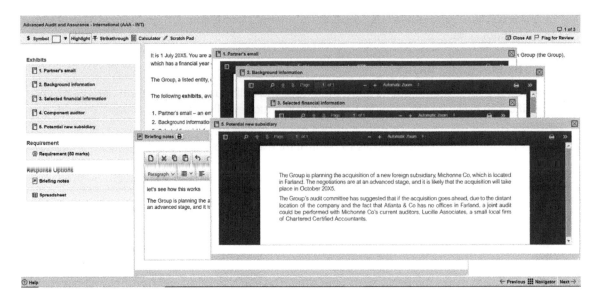

Managing this information is quite a challenge – however, on the left-hand side of the screen is all the information you need:

- The exhibits (for Question 1 of the AAA exam, the partner's email will usually outline the requirements so is a good place to start)
- The requirement (for other questions, you will find the requirements here)
- The response options (in most cases you will just need the word processing document but if presented with more complex financial statements extracts, the spreadsheet option may be of use)

You will also note that the various windows can be re-sized and moved around the screen to help you navigate each of the exhibits as you make sense of the question.

Note. There are resources on the ACCA website that will help you apply sound exam technique in the CBE – within the 'study support resources' for AAA, select the section marked 'CBE exam technique – how to apply your knowledge and maximise marks in the exam'.

Exam success skill 2

Correct interpretation of the requirements

The active verb used often dictates the approach that written answers should take (eg 'explain', 'discuss', 'evaluate'). It is important you identify and use the verb to define your approach. The **correct interpretation of the requirements** skill means correctly producing only what is being asked for by a requirement. Anything not required will not earn marks.

Advice on developing correct interpretation of the requirements

This skill can be developed by analysing question requirements and applying this process:

Step 1 Read the requirement

Firstly, read the requirement a couple of times slowly and carefully and highlight the active verbs. Use the active verbs to define what you plan to do. Make sure you identify any sub-requirements.

Step 2 Read the rest of the question

By reading the requirement first, you will have an idea of what you are looking out for as you read through the case overview and exhibits. This is a great time saver and means you don't end up having to read the whole question in full twice. You should do this in an active way – see Exam success skill 1: Managing Information.

Step 3 Read the requirement again

Read the requirement again to remind yourself of the exact wording before starting to produce your answer. This will capture any misinterpretation of the requirements or any missed requirements entirely. This should become a habit in your approach and, with repeated practice, you will find the focus, relevance and depth of your answer plan will improve.

The CBE

The workspace allows you to copy and paste as you would normally do within any word processing package – you could copy the requirement into your response option (such as the briefing note shown in the screenshot) and it will then be there to remind you what the question is asking for.

There is a 'flag for review' function within the CBE which can be used to highlight areas that you may wish to revisit later in the exam.

Exam success skill 3

Answer planning: Priorities, structure and logic

This skill requires the planning of the key aspects of an answer which accurately and completely responds to the requirement.

Advice on developing answer planning: priorities, structure and logic

Everyone will have a preferred style for an answer plan. For example, it may be a mind map, bullet-pointed lists or simply annotating the question. Choose the approach that you feel most comfortable with, or, if you are not sure, try out different approaches for different questions until you have found your preferred style.

For a discussion question, annotating the question is likely to be insufficient. It would be better to draw up a separate answer plan in the format of your choosing (eg a mind map or bullet-pointed lists). For a risk question, you should annotate the scenario noting which areas present the type of risk being examined and explain why. Remember that you can use the scratch pad for any of these planning activities.

The CBE

In the screenshot below, you can see that some of the text has been highlighted:

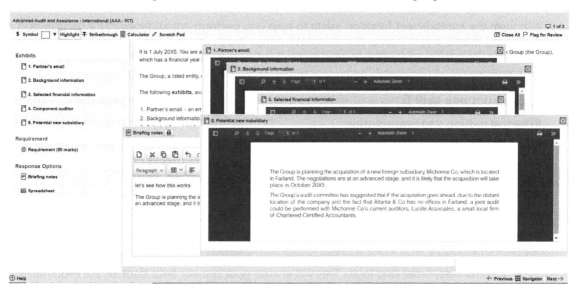

You can use a variety of colours to highlight different parts of the exhibits to address separate aspects of the requirements.

There is a 'scratch pad' that you can also use to organise your thoughts and make rough workings. You can copy and paste content from the scratch pad into your response option, but the scratch pad itself is not submitted for marking at the end of the exam. The answer space can also be used for rough workings.

Exam success skill 4

Efficient numerical analysis

- Typing time for part (b): 8 x 1.95 minutes per mark = 16 minutes

Keep a note of when you started each part and when you should aim to finish so you don't lose track of time.

Keep an eye on the clock

Aim to attempt all requirements, but be ready to be ruthless and move on if your answer is not going as planned. The challenge for many is sticking to planned timings. Be aware this is difficult to achieve in the early stages of your studies and be ready to let this skill develop over time.

If you find yourself running short on time and know that a full answer is not possible in the time you have, consider recreating your plan in overview form and then add key terms and details as time allows. Remember, some marks may be available, for example, simply stating a conclusion which you don't have time to justify in full.

The CBE

Sitting this exam as a computer-based exam and practising as many exam-style questions as possible in the ACCA CBE **Practice Platform** will be the key to passing this exam. You should attempt questions under timed conditions and ensure you produce full answers to the discussion parts as well as doing the calculations. Also ensure that you attempt all mock exams under exam conditions.

ACCA have launched a free on-demand resource designed to mirror the live exam experience helping you to become more familiar with the exam format. You can access the Platform via the Study Support Resources section of the ACCA website navigating to the CBE question practice section and logging in with your myACCA credentials.

Question practice

Question practice is a core part of learning new topic areas. When you practise questions, you should focus on improving the Exam success skills – personal to your needs – by obtaining feedback or through a process of self-assessment.

repeated practice, you will find the focus, relevance and depth of your answer plan will improve.

The CBE

The workspace allows you to copy and paste as you would normally do within any word processing package – you could copy the requirement into your response option (such as the briefing note shown in the screenshot) and it will then be there to remind you what the question is asking for.

There is a 'flag for review' function within the CBE which can be used to highlight areas that you may wish to revisit later in the exam.

Exam success skill 3

Answer planning: Priorities, structure and logic

This skill requires the planning of the key aspects of an answer which accurately and completely responds to the requirement.

Advice on developing answer planning: priorities, structure and logic

Everyone will have a preferred style for an answer plan. For example, it may be a mind map, bullet-pointed lists or simply annotating the question. Choose the approach that you feel most comfortable with, or, if you are not sure, try out different approaches for different questions until you have found your preferred style.

For a discussion question, annotating the question is likely to be insufficient. It would be better to draw up a separate answer plan in the format of your choosing (eg a mind map or bullet-pointed lists). For a risk question, you should annotate the scenario noting which areas present the type of risk being examined and explain why. Remember that you can use the scratch pad for any of these planning activities.

The CBE

In the screenshot below, you can see that some of the text has been highlighted:

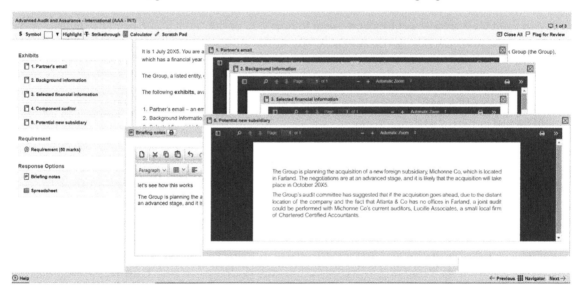

You can use a variety of colours to highlight different parts of the exhibits to address separate aspects of the requirements.

There is a 'scratch pad' that you can also use to organise your thoughts and make rough workings. You can copy and paste content from the scratch pad into your response option, but the scratch pad itself is not submitted for marking at the end of the exam. The answer space can also be used for rough workings.

Exam success skill 4

Efficient numerical analysis

This skill aims to maximise the marks awarded by making clear to the marker the process of arriving at your answer. This is achieved by laying out an answer such that, even if you make a few errors, you can still get some credit for your calculations. It is vital that you do not lose marks purely because the marker cannot follow what you have done.

Advice on developing efficient numerical analysis

This skill can be developed by applying the following process:

Step 1   Explain your workings where relevant

Materiality calculations or other forms of analytical procedure should have a brief explanation of their purpose so the examining team can understand what your calculations are trying to tell them. Remember, for AAA, calculations are just a way of quantifying a part of your answer (such as a form of risk assessment or when considering going concern indicators). Remember that explaining and justifying your materiality assessment will also earn professional skills marks.

Step 2   Show your workings

Keep your workings as clear and simple as possible and ensure they are cross-referenced to the main part of your answer. Where it helps, provide brief narrative explanations to help the marker understand the steps in the calculation. This means that if a mistake is made you should not lose any subsequent marks for follow-on calculations.

Step 3   Keep moving!

It is important to remember that, in an exam situation, it is difficult to get every number 100% correct. The key is therefore ensuring you do not spend too long on any single calculation. If you are struggling with a solution then make a sensible assumption, state it and move on. It's also important to remember that for AAA, you will not be expected to generate a large number of calculations; usually, only key ratios or calculations will be required.

The CBE

Although the spreadsheet function exists to help you perform calculations more quickly and efficiently than using the onscreen calculator, there may not always be enough of them to merit using the spreadsheet function. It is probably best to practise using the CBE software as part of your revision so you can settle on a style that you feel comfortable with.

Exam success skill 5

Effective writing and presentation

Answers should be presented so that the marker can clearly see the points you are making, presented in the format specified in the question. The skill is to provide efficient type-written answers with sufficient breadth of points that answer the question, in the right depth, in the time available.

Advice on developing effective writing and presentation

Step 1   Use headings

Using the headings and sub-headings from your answer plan will give your answer structure, order and logic. This will ensure your answer links back to the requirement and is clearly signposted, making it easier for the marker to understand the different points you are making. Underlining your headings will also help the marker.

Step 2   Write your answer in short, but full, sentences

Use short, punchy sentences with the aim that every sentence should say something different and generate marks. Write in full sentences, ensuring your style is professional.

Step 3   Do your calculations first and explanation second

Questions often ask for an explanation with suitable calculations, such as materiality. The best approach is to prepare the calculation first but present it on the bottom half of the page of your answer, or on the next page. Then add the explanation before the calculation. Performing the calculation first should enable you to explain what you have done.

The CBE

Within the workspace, the response option does allow you to format your answer as you would in any word processing package: eg **bold**, <u>underline</u> or *italics*. These will help you provide emphasis on different parts of your answer (and in the case of Question 1, will help you earn the communication professional marks by use of sub-headings etc).

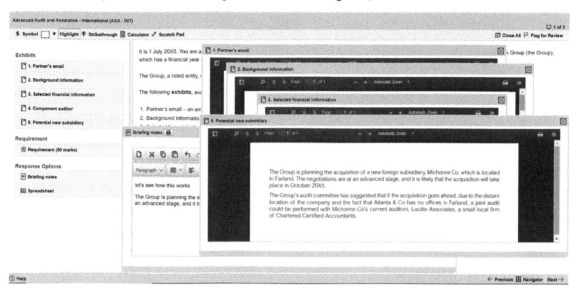

Tables and bullets can also be introduced into your response (although you should only be using these if you feel it still helps you to address the requirement fully).

Exam success skill 6

Good time management

This skill means planning your time across all the requirements so that all tasks have been attempted by the end of the 3 hours 15 minutes available and actively checking on time during your exam. This is so that you can flex your approach and prioritise requirements which, in your judgment, will generate the maximum marks in the available time remaining.

Advice on developing Good time management

The exam lasts for 195 minutes, this equates to 1.95 minutes per mark.

Approximately 20% of your time should be allocated to planning (including reading and thinking) to ensure that you are able to assimilate the key features of the scenario before starting to write or type.

- For a 50-mark question, planning time should be 50 marks × 1.95 × 20% = approximately 20 minutes.
- For a 25-mark question, planning time would be 25 marks × 1.95 × 20% = approximately 10 minutes per question.

The time spent **typing your answer** should reflect the number of technical marks for each requirement. Typing time can be calculated by multiplying the technical mark allocation for each requirement by 1.95 minutes – you could think of it as having already spent the time for professional marks on your plan, leaving the rest of the time for producing the technical requirements of your answer.

So, time management for a 25-mark question with 12 marks for part (a) and 8 marks for part (b) plus the 5 professional skills marks should be as follows:

- Total time: 25 marks x 1.95 minutes per mark = 49 minutes
- Planning time: 49 minutes x 20% = 10 minutes
- Typing time for part (a): 12 x 1.95 minutes per mark = 23 minutes

- Typing time for part (b): 8 x 1.95 minutes per mark = 16 minutes

Keep a note of when you started each part and when you should aim to finish so you don't lose track of time.

Keep an eye on the clock

Aim to attempt all requirements, but be ready to be ruthless and move on if your answer is not going as planned. The challenge for many is sticking to planned timings. Be aware this is difficult to achieve in the early stages of your studies and be ready to let this skill develop over time.

If you find yourself running short on time and know that a full answer is not possible in the time you have, consider recreating your plan in overview form and then add key terms and details as time allows. Remember, some marks may be available, for example, simply stating a conclusion which you don't have time to justify in full.

The CBE

Sitting this exam as a computer-based exam and practising as many exam-style questions as possible in the ACCA CBE **Practice Platform** will be the key to passing this exam. You should attempt questions under timed conditions and ensure you produce full answers to the discussion parts as well as doing the calculations. Also ensure that you attempt all mock exams under exam conditions.

ACCA have launched a free on-demand resource designed to mirror the live exam experience helping you to become more familiar with the exam format. You can access the Platform via the Study Support Resources section of the ACCA website navigating to the CBE question practice section and logging in with your myACCA credentials.

Question practice

Question practice is a core part of learning new topic areas. When you practise questions, you should focus on improving the Exam success skills – personal to your needs – by obtaining feedback or through a process of self-assessment.

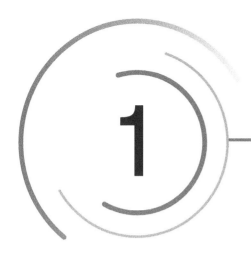

International regulatory environments for audit and assurance services

Learning objectives

On completion of this chapter, you should be able to:

	Syllabus reference no.
Explain the need for laws, regulations, standards and other guidance relating to audit, assurance and related services.	A1(a)
Outline and explain the need for the legal and professional framework including: (i) Public oversight of audit and assurance practice (ii) The impact of the UK Corporate Governance Code on audit and assurance practice	A1(b)
Discuss the role of the audit committee and its impact on audit and assurance practice in relation to: (i) The relationship with the external auditor, including the appointment, removal and monitoring of effectiveness; and (ii) The oversight and approval of the provision of non-audit services	A1(c)
Define 'money laundering' and discuss international methods for combatting money laundering.	A2(a)
Explain the scope of criminal offences of money laundering and how professional accountants may be protected from criminal and civil liability.	A2(b)
Explain the need for ethical guidance in this area.	A2(c)
Describe how accountants meet their obligations to help prevent and detect money laundering including record keeping and reporting of suspicion to the appropriate regulatory body.	A2(d)
Explain the importance of customer due diligence (CDD), also referred to as know your customer (KYC), and recommend the information that should be gathered as part of CDD/KYC.	A2(e)
Recognise potentially suspicious transactions and assess their impact on reporting duties.	A2(f)
Describe with reasons the basic elements of an anti-money laundering program.	A2(g)
Compare and contrast the respective responsibilities of management and auditors concerning compliance with laws and regulations in an audit of	A3(a)

	Syllabus reference no.
financial statements.	
Describe the auditors' considerations of compliance with laws and regulations and plan audit procedures when possible non-compliance is discovered.	A3(b)
Discuss how and to whom non-compliance should be reported.	A3(c)
Recognise and recommend when withdrawal from an engagement is necessary.	A3(d)

Business and exam context

This chapter covers a wide range of regulations that affect the work of audit and assurance professionals. You need to be aware of the international nature of the audit and assurance market and the main issues driving the development of regulatory frameworks.

The detailed requirements relating to money laundering are then discussed. You should be prepared to explain the responsibilities of professional accountants in this area and to outline the procedures that audit firms should implement.

The final section looks at the auditor's responsibilities in respect of laws and regulations that apply to an audit client. This is a topic that could be built into a practical case study question. The technical content of this part of the syllabus is mainly drawn from your earlier studies. Questions in this exam are unlikely to ask for simple repetition of this knowledge, but are more likely to require explanation or discussion of the reasons behind the regulations.

Chapter overview

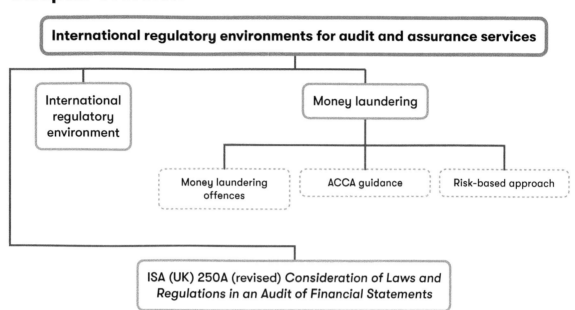

1 International regulatory environment

Activity 1: Regulating the audit profession

What factors have led to the growth in regulation of the audit profession?

Solution

PER alert

One of the competencies you require to fulfil **Performance Objective 18** of the PER is the ability to use up to date auditing standards and legal and ethical frameworks. You can apply the knowledge you obtain from this section of the Workbook to help you demonstrate this competency.

Essential reading

See Chapter 1 of the Essential reading for more detail on the legal and professional framework (including the role of regulators, standard setters and those responsible for oversight, as well as a recap of corporate governance and the audit committee).

The Essential reading is available as an Appendix of the digital edition of the Workbook.

2 Money laundering

KEY TERM

Money laundering: The **process** by which criminals attempt to **conceal the true origin** and ownership of **the proceeds of their criminal activity**, allowing them to maintain control over the proceeds and, ultimately, providing a cover for their sources of income.

Money laundering usually consists of **three stages:**

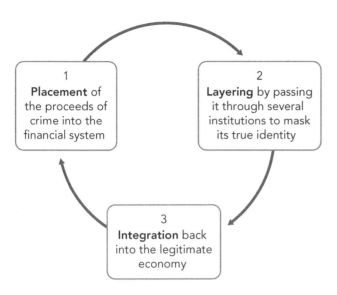

2.1 Money laundering offences

The **Financial Action Task Force (FATF)** has clarified a number of criminal offences relating to money laundering. Many of these have a **significant impact** on the auditor and it is therefore **imperative** that firms are aware of them and consider the risk that they may be committing an offence. The key offences are as follows:

(a) **Acquiring, using, possessing or concealing criminal property** (this includes arranging, or becoming involved in an arrangement which might facilitate the acquisition of criminal property).

(b) **Failing to report** knowledge or suspicion of money laundering to the appropriate authority. For example, in the UK, the National Crime Agency (NCA) receives over 300,000 suspicious activity reports each year.

(c) **Tipping off** a client of suspicions relating to money laundering or disclosing any information that may prejudice an investigation.

2.1.1 International efforts to combat money laundering

Since 1989, FATF has acted as an intergovernmental body to set standards and develop policies to combat money laundering and terrorist financing.

FATF has made **40 recommendations** designed to combat money laundering and these have been adopted across the world.

2.2 ACCA guidance

In order to assist members, the ACCA has included **guidance on anti-money laundering** within the ACCA Rulebook (2022) alongside the Code of Ethics and Conduct.

2.2.1 The key elements of the guidance:

Internal controls and policies	Members should ensure their staff receive **regular training** to ensure that **client identification procedures** are carried out correctly and that knowledge and suspicions of money laundering or terrorist financing are reported. Firms should identify to their staff a clear procedure for reporting suspected money laundering and appoint an individual through whom reports of suspicions can be channelled to the relevant authority (Money Laundering Reporting Officer (MLRO)); in the UK this role can also be fulfilled by a separate officer known as a Money Laundering Compliance Principal (MLCP), although one person can fulfil both roles if sufficiently senior within the firm).
Client identification	Before any work is undertaken, members should verify the identity of the potential client – this is known as either **'know your client' (KYC)** or

	'customer due diligence' (CDD) and requires awareness of the client's identity, their ownership structure and their operating cash flows. This is discussed in more detail in Section 2.2.2.
Record keeping	Members should retain all client identification records for at least five years after the end of the client relationship. Records of all transactions and other work carried out, in a full audit trail form, should be retained for at least five years after the conclusion of the transaction.
Recognition of suspicion	Suspicion can be described as being more than speculation but falling short of proof based on firm evidence. The key to recognising a suspicious transaction or situation is for members to have sufficient understanding of clients and their activities. Special attention should be paid to any transactions without any visible lawful or economic purpose.
Reporting suspicious transactions	Where members know or suspect that funds are the proceeds of crime or relate to terrorist financing, they should request that their MLRO promptly report their suspicions to the relevant authority (such as the NCA in the UK).
Tipping off	Members should not 'tip off' a client that a report has been made. If a suspicion has arisen during the course of client identification procedures, members should take extra care that carrying out those procedures will not tip off the client. However, attempts to discourage a client from breaking the law will not be seen as tipping off.

Activity 2: Ethics and money laundering

Why is there a need for ethical guidance for accountants in respect of money laundering?

(4 marks)

Solution

2.2.2 Client identification

The guidance on members' responsibilities mentions the requirement to gather CDD/KYC information. This includes:

Who the client is (company or individual?)	Who controls it	The purpose and intended nature of the business relationship
The nature of the client	The client's source of funds	The client's business and economic purpose

KYC enables the audit firm to understand its client's business well enough to spot any **unusual** business activity. This assists the firm in identifying **suspicions** of money laundering.

In the UK, the Money Laundering Regulations (2017) extended the circumstances under which CDD must be carried out for new and existing clients.

CDD is the term used in the money laundering regulations for the steps that businesses must take.

(a) They must **identify the customer** and verify their identity using documents, data or information obtained from a reliable and independent source: for individuals, this could be a passport and proof of address; for a company, obtaining proof of incorporation or similar.

(b) They must **identify any beneficial owner who is not the customer**. This is the individual (or individuals) behind the customer who ultimately owns or controls the customer or on whose behalf a transaction or activity is being conducted.

(c) Where a business relationship is established, they must understand the **purpose and intended nature of the relationship**, such as details of the customer's business or the source of the funds.

Businesses must also conduct ongoing monitoring to identify large, unusual or suspicious transactions as part of CDD. The requirement to confirm the identity of customers and other individuals clearly links to the concept of KYC described above.

If a potential client's identity cannot be established, no work should be done by the professional accountant.

2.3 Risk-based approach

On any assignment, the auditor should assess the risk of money laundering activities. Clearly, every circumstance is different, but the following diagram illustrates some key risk factors.

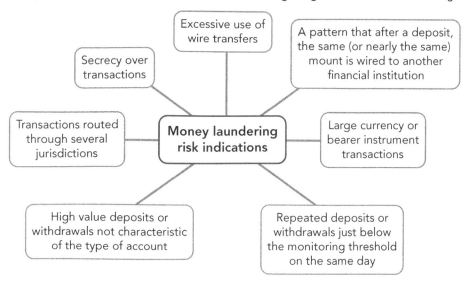

Investigation by a **regulatory organisation** or **government department** or payment of fines or penalties
Payments for **unspecified services** or loans to consultants, related parties, employees or government employees
Sales commissions or agents' fees that appear excessive in relation to those normally paid by the entity or in its industry or to the services actually received
Purchasing at prices significantly above or below market price
Unusual payments in **cash**, purchases in the form of cashiers' cheques payable to bearer or transfers to numbered bank accounts
Unusual transactions with companies registered in **tax havens**
Payments for goods or services made other than to the country from which the goods or services **originated**
Payments without proper exchange control documentation
Existence of an **information system** that **fails**, whether by design or by accident, to **provide an adequate audit trail** or sufficient evidence
Unauthorised transactions or improperly recorded transactions
Adverse media comment

(ISA (UK) 250A (revised): para. A13)

When evaluating the possible effect on the financial statements, the auditor should consider:

The **potential financial consequences**, such as fines, penalties, damages, threat of expropriation of assets, enforced discontinuation of operations and litigation
Whether the **potential financial consequences** require **disclosure**
Whether the potential financial consequences are so serious as to call into question the **fair presentation** given by the financial statements, or otherwise make the financial statements misleading

(ISA (UK) 250A (revised): para. A14)

The auditor should also **report** any cases of NOCLAR to the appropriate level of **management** and, where appropriate, to **those charged with governance**. However, ISA (UK) 250A (revised) does also state that if there are laws and regulations that **prohibit** this (for example, where reporting to either management or those charged with governance would constitute 'tipping off') or if the auditor suspects that **management or those charged with governance are involved in NOCLAR**, then the auditor should communicate the matter to the next higher level of authority (such as an audit committee or regulator), usually after seeking suitable legal or professional advice to confirm who this is.

In extreme cases, the auditor may feel compelled to make disclosures about NOCLAR in the **public interest** (for example, if a client is wilfully polluting public land) but is still bound by the fundamental ethical duty of **confidentiality**. Both ISA (UK) 250A (revised) and the IESBA Code of Ethics specifically encourage auditors to seek legal advice before deciding on how to proceed in such cases.

3.4 Withdrawal from the engagement

The auditor may conclude that withdrawal from the engagement is necessary when the **entity does not take the remedial action that the auditor considers necessary** in the circumstances, even when NOCLAR is not material to the financial statements. However, ISA (UK) 250A (revised) and the IESBA code also emphasise that **withdrawal should not be used by firms as a substitute**

KYC enables the audit firm to understand its client's business well enough to spot any **unusual** business activity. This assists the firm in identifying **suspicions** of money laundering.

In the UK, the Money Laundering Regulations (2017) extended the circumstances under which CDD must be carried out for new and existing clients.

CDD is the term used in the money laundering regulations for the steps that businesses must take.

(a) They must **identify the customer** and verify their identity using documents, data or information obtained from a reliable and independent source: for individuals, this could be a passport and proof of address; for a company, obtaining proof of incorporation or similar.

(b) They must **identify any beneficial owner who is not the customer**. This is the individual (or individuals) behind the customer who ultimately owns or controls the customer or on whose behalf a transaction or activity is being conducted.

(c) Where a business relationship is established, they must understand the **purpose and intended nature of the relationship,** such as details of the customer's business or the source of the funds.

Businesses must also conduct ongoing monitoring to identify large, unusual or suspicious transactions as part of CDD. The requirement to confirm the identity of customers and other individuals clearly links to the concept of KYC described above.

If a potential client's identity cannot be established, no work should be done by the professional accountant.

2.3 Risk-based approach

On any assignment, the auditor should assess the risk of money laundering activities. Clearly, every circumstance is different, but the following diagram illustrates some key risk factors.

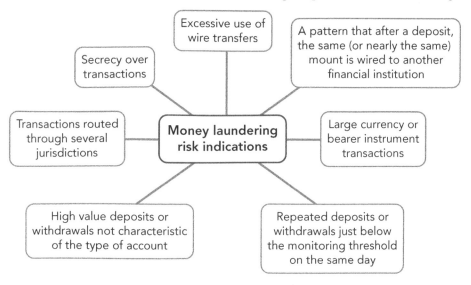

3 ISA (UK) 250 A (revised) *Consideration of Laws and Regulations in an Audit of Financial Statements*

Companies are increasingly subject to laws and regulations with which they must comply. Here are some examples:

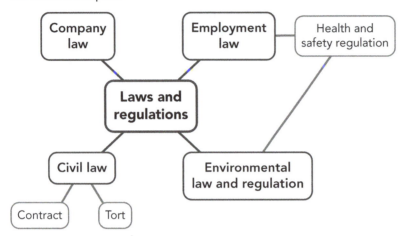

When designing and performing audit procedures and in evaluating and reporting the results thereof, the auditor should recognise that **non-compliance** by the entity with law or regulations may **materially affect the financial statements**.

> **Non-compliance:** Refers to acts of omission or commission, intentional or unintentional, committed by the entity, or by those charged with governance, by management or by other individuals working for or under the direction of the entity, which are contrary to the prevailing laws or regulations. Non-compliance does not include personal misconduct unrelated to the business activities of the entity.
>
> (ISA (UK) 250A (revised): para. 12)
>
> Non-compliance with laws and regulations is sometimes referred to as **NOCLAR**.

3.1 Responsibilities of management

It is management's responsibility to ensure that the **entity's operations** are conducted in accordance with laws and regulations. The responsibility for the **prevention** and **detection** of non-compliance also rests with management.

The following policies and procedures, among others, may assist management in discharging its responsibilities for the prevention and detection of non-compliance:

Monitoring legal requirements and any changes therein and ensuring that operating procedures are designed to meet these requirements	Instituting and operating appropriate systems of **internal control**	Developing, publicising and following a **Code of Conduct**, and ensuring employees are properly trained and understand the Code of Conduct
Monitoring **compliance** with the Code of Conduct and acting appropriately to discipline employees who fail to comply with it	Engaging **legal advisers** to assist in monitoring legal requirements	Maintaining a **register of significant laws and regulations** with which the entity has to comply within its particular industry and a record of complaints

In **larger entities**, these policies and procedures may be supplemented by assigning appropriate responsibilities to:

- An internal audit function

- An audit committee
- A compliance function

3.2 The auditor's consideration of compliance with laws and regulations

The auditor is not, and cannot be, held responsible for preventing NOCLAR. The fact that an audit is carried out may, however, act as a deterrent. The auditor needs to consider the **impact** of any non-compliance on the financial statements, and assess the risk of material misstatement by considering the various laws and regulations which clients must comply with and how the auditor should **respond**.

- Those that have a **direct effect** on determining material amounts in the financial statements (such as tax laws) require the auditor to obtain evidence of **compliance**.
- Those that are fundamental to the operating aspects of the client which have a **material (but not direct) effect** on the financial statements (such as compliance with an operating licence) require the auditor to undertake procedures to identify any **non-compliance**.

The auditor has no formal responsibility for NOCLAR that has neither a direct nor a material effect on the financial statements, but should respond appropriately should such cases be detected. Maintaining an **awareness** of such laws and regulations for clients is obviously a challenge for auditors, especially if clients attempt to deliberately **conceal** NOCLAR.

Examples of laws and regulations that may have either a direct or material effect on the financial statements include those that relate to:

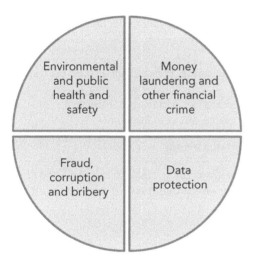

In order to determine whether NOCLAR has occurred, the auditor needs to obtain a **general understanding** of the **legal** and **regulatory framework** and whether the client is **complying** with this framework. This takes the form of **enquiries** of management and **reviews** of correspondence with the appropriate regulatory and/or licensing authorities (although ISA (UK) 250A (revised) points out that **other testing** during the audit might provide valuable evidence of non-compliance, so the team needs to be alert throughout the audit).

3.3 Audit procedures when possible NOCLAR is discovered

When the auditor becomes aware of information concerning a possible instance of non-compliance, the auditor should obtain an **understanding** of the **nature** of the act and the **circumstances** in which it has occurred, and seek **further information** to **evaluate** the possible effect on the financial statements. This may require **amendments** to both **amounts** and **disclosures** (as well as casting doubt on the entity's **going concern status** if sufficiently serious). All such information and evaluations should be fully **documented**.

ISA (UK) 250A (revised) sets out examples of the type of information that might come to the auditor's attention that may indicate non-compliance.

Investigation by a regulatory organisation or government department or payment of fines or penalties
Payments for unspecified services or loans to consultants, related parties, employees or government employees
Sales commissions or agents' fees that appear excessive in relation to those normally paid by the entity or in its industry or to the services actually received
Purchasing at prices significantly above or below market price
Unusual payments in cash, purchases in the form of cashiers' cheques payable to bearer or transfers to numbered bank accounts
Unusual transactions with companies registered in tax havens
Payments for goods or services made other than to the country from which the goods or services originated
Payments without proper exchange control documentation
Existence of an information system that fails, whether by design or by accident, to provide an adequate audit trail or sufficient evidence
Unauthorised transactions or improperly recorded transactions
Adverse media comment

(ISA (UK) 250A (revised): para. A13)

When evaluating the possible effect on the financial statements, the auditor should consider:

The potential financial consequences, such as fines, penalties, damages, threat of expropriation of assets, enforced discontinuation of operations and litigation
Whether the potential financial consequences require disclosure
Whether the potential financial consequences are so serious as to call into question the fair presentation given by the financial statements, or otherwise make the financial statements misleading

(ISA (UK) 250A (revised): para. A14)

The auditor should also **report** any cases of NOCLAR to the appropriate level of **management** and, where appropriate, to **those charged with governance**. However, ISA (UK) 250A (revised) does also state that if there are laws and regulations that **prohibit** this (for example, where reporting to either management or those charged with governance would constitute 'tipping off') or if the auditor suspects that **management or those charged with governance are involved in NOCLAR**, then the auditor should communicate the matter to the next higher level of authority (such as an audit committee or regulator), usually after seeking suitable legal or professional advice to confirm who this is.

In extreme cases, the auditor may feel compelled to make disclosures about NOCLAR in the **public interest** (for example, if a client is wilfully polluting public land) but is still bound by the fundamental ethical duty of **confidentiality**. Both ISA (UK) 250A (revised) and the IESBA Code of Ethics specifically encourage auditors to seek legal advice before deciding on how to proceed in such cases.

3.4 Withdrawal from the engagement

The auditor may conclude that withdrawal from the engagement is necessary when the **entity does not take the remedial action that the auditor considers necessary** in the circumstances, even when NOCLAR is not material to the financial statements. However, ISA (UK) 250A (revised) and the IESBA code also emphasise that **withdrawal should not be used by firms as a substitute**

for responding appropriately to any NOCLAR at a client (in other words, the auditor cannot just keep quiet about any NOCLAR they discover, regardless of how difficult it may be for them to do so).

The process for dealing with laws and regulations can be summarised for auditors like this:

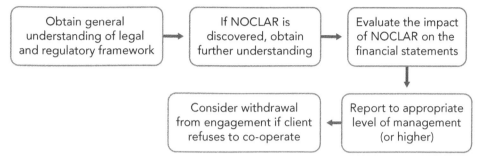

3.5 The auditor's report

3.5.1 Material misstatement

Where the auditor concludes that the non-compliance (**such as failing to disclose certain items within the financial statements**) has a material effect on the financial statements which have not been amended, they should express a **qualified** or **adverse opinion**.

3.5.2 Insufficient or inappropriate audit evidence

Where adequate information about compliance or suspected non-compliance cannot be obtained (either due to **obstruction by the client** or **any other circumstance**), the auditor may need to express a **qualified opinion** or **disclaimer of opinion** due to inability to obtain sufficient appropriate audit evidence.

Chapter summary

International regulatory environments for audit and assurance services

International regulatory environment

- International Federation of Accountants (IFAC)
- International Auditing and Assurance Standards Board
  - ISAs
  - ISREs
  - ISAEs
  - ISRSs

Money laundering

Money laundering offences

- Acquiring, using, possessing, dealing with or concealing criminal property
- Failure to report knowledge or suspicion
- Tipping off
- Concealing the true origin and ownership of the proceeds of crime
- Consists of three stages:
  - Placement
  - Layering
  - Integration
- Financial Action Task Force role

ACCA guidance

- Internal controls and policies, including Money Laundering Reporting Officer (MLRO) role (Money Laundering Compliance Principal or MLCP in the UK) and training
- Client identification (identity, ownership and cash flows) via CDD or KYC
- Record keeping – at least five years
- Recognition of suspicion – more than speculation but falling short of firm proof
- Reporting suspicious transactions
- Tipping off should not be done, even by accident

Risk-based approach

- Secrecy over transactions
- Transfers via several jurisdictions
- High value transactions not in line with business model
- Excessive use of wire transfers
- Patterns between deposits and transfers
- Transactions of great value
- Repeated transactions below monitoring threshold on same day

ISA (UK) 250A (revised) *Consideration of Laws and Regulations in an Audit of Financial Statements*

- Non-compliance with laws and regulations (omission, commission, deliberate, accidental) is sometimes referred to as **NOCLAR**
- Management is responsible for **operational compliance** and also for prevention and **detection** of **non-compliance**
- Auditors are responsible for the **impact** of any non-compliance on the financial statements, and for assessing the **risk of material misstatement** due to the following:
  - Those that have a **direct effect** on the financial statements (eg compliance with enacted laws) require evidence of compliance
  - Those that have a **material (but not direct) effect** on the financial statements (eg compliance with an operating licence) require evidence of any non-compliance
  - Those that have **neither a direct nor material effect** on the financial statements require an awareness of any NOCLAR and an appropriate response
- Auditors need a **general understanding** of the legal and regulatory framework in place (see ISA (UK) 315) including environmental/public health and safety, fraud, corruption, bribery, data protection or other financial crime (such as money laundering)

- If NOCLAR is discovered, the following steps should take place:
  - The auditor must **understand** the matter fully and document their findings
  - They must **report** cases of NOCLAR to the appropriate level of management or those charged with governance (TCWG) unless prohibited by law
  - If management and/or TCWG are suspected of involvement in NOCLAR, the auditor **may report to next most higher level of authority** (eg audit committee or regulator)
  - They may need to **disclose** to others in the **public interest**
  - In all cases, especially when reporting or disclosing NOCLAR, **legal advice** should be sought due to the need for confidentiality
- If NOCLAR has not been addressed by a client, the auditor may **withdraw** from the engagement, but this should not be seen by auditors as a suitable way of responding to NOCLAR without any further action being taken
- Material NOCLAR can lead to a **modified audit opinion**:
  - Failure to comply with a requirement could lead to a **misstatement**
  - An obstruction by the client or poor record keeping could lead to **insufficient or inappropriate audit evidence**

Knowledge diagnostic

1. Regulatory framework

The various **laws, standards, governance structures** and **regulations** in place within the financial community are essential to protect and enhance the **reputation** of the profession within the society it serves.

2. Money laundering offences

A key area where guidance and regulations exist is **money laundering**. Auditors are at risk of committing various **criminal offences** regarding money laundering, for example **not reporting** suspicious transactions and/or **tipping off** the client that suspicion has arisen – as such they must know the requirements before acting in any engagement.

3. Client due diligence

There are **three key areas** that need to be covered when performing customer due diligence (CDD) or know your client (KYC) procedures: the **identity** of the customer; the **ownership** of the customer's business; and the likely **cash flows** of the business.

4. NOCLAR

Auditors must also know how to **respond** to such cases of **NOCLAR**, including the need to **disclose** to an appropriate level of authority.

Further study guidance

Question practice

Now try the following from the Further question practice bank (available in the digital edition of the Workbook):

- Question 1 'Mr Roy and Mr Fox' is an opportunity to practise some of the theory discussed in this chapter in an applied situation.

Further reading

There are technical articles on the ACCA website written by members of the AAA examining team which are relevant to some of the topics covered in this chapter that you should read:

- *Laws and regulations*
- *Corporate governance and its impact on audit practice*

Own research

Consider your own organisation or one that you are familiar with – what can you learn from the following to help you with topics from this chapter?

- Which laws and regulations matter most? Why do you think this is?
- How does an audit committee actually work? Are you aware of its impact?
- Have you received training on anti-money laundering procedures? If so, what did it include and are you aware of any instances of reports that needed to be made to the appropriate authority?

Activity answers

Activity 1: Regulating the audit profession

> ### Approach
>
> This question is designed to get you thinking about why there is so much regulation within the audit profession. Your answer needs to have considered the reasons why people rely on auditors; however, you also need to consider why people may find their trust in auditors has been damaged in recent years and how the profession has responded.
>
> This type of requirement is possible within a larger question, especially if it relates to the content of an ACCA examining team technical article. The AAA UK specimen exam (available on the ACCA website) contains an illustration of how a subject like this could be examined.

Suggested solution

- The reputation of the audit profession has, in recent years, suffered due to high profile audit failures (eg Carillion, BHS, Patisserie Valerie, Autonomy, the financial crisis of 2008 – and of course the classic examples of Enron, Parmalat and WorldCom) and somehow the public's trust needs to be re-established.

- The existence of auditing standards and other regulations should protect/enhance the reputation of the profession amongst all stakeholders by ensuring a consistently high level of work across all firms.

- Businesses have become more complex and global, and firms have expanded their range of services beyond traditional assurance and tax advice. This has led to a great deal of re-examination of regulatory and standard-setting structures both nationally and internationally in recent years.

- The competitiveness in the UK audit sector (or lack thereof, especially in FTSE 350 audits for example) has led to downward pressure on fees and a consequent impact on quality, which has led some to consider the regulatory role of ethical codes as key (eg stopping firms from offering non-audit services to their audit clients).

Activity 2: Ethics and money laundering

> ### Approach
>
> As with the activity on regulation, there is a balance to be struck here between the duty of care owed by auditors to their clients (and to themselves, as they are not charities!) and the duty to society overall, to demonstrate that they can be trusted to act in the public interest.
>
> Requirements of this type are seen in the AAA exam but usually in the context of something topical.

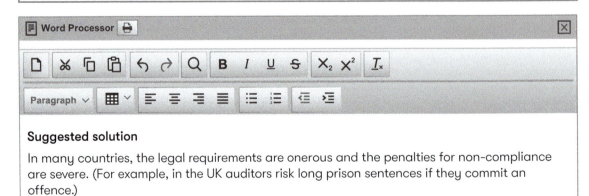

Suggested solution

In many countries, the legal requirements are onerous and the penalties for non-compliance are severe. (For example, in the UK auditors risk long prison sentences if they commit an offence.)

Money laundering is widely defined and it is not always obvious that an offence has been committed, so without the guidance in issue, accountants may be used unwittingly to launder criminal funds.

In many countries, the law creates a conflict between the ethical duty of confidentiality to the client and the legal duty to report money laundering offences. The guidance helps to clarify the members' professional duty to report offences.

The reputation of accountants is poor, leading many in society to question whether they are acting in their own (or their clients') best interests, rather than those of society as a whole. For example, if accountants are to be paid for tax advice that reduces the liability of the client, is this in the best interests of society? Ethical guidance is vital for accountants to maintain their reputation.

2

Code of ethics and conduct

Learning objectives

On completion of this chapter, you should be able to:

	Syllabus reference no.
Explain the fundamental principles and the conceptual framework approach.	B1(a)
Identify, evaluate and respond to threats to compliance with the fundamental principles.	B1(b)
Discuss and evaluate the effectiveness of available safeguards.	B1(c)
Recognise and advise on conflicts in the application of fundamental principles.	B1(d)
Discuss the importance of professional scepticism in planning and performing an audit.	B1(e)
Consider the ethical implications of the external auditor providing non-audit services to a client including an internal audit service.	B1(f)
Assess whether an engagement has been planned and performed with an attitude of professional scepticism, and evaluate the implications.	B1(g)
Discuss emerging ethical issues and evaluate the potential impact on the profession, firms and auditors.	G1(a)
Discuss the content and impact of exposure drafts, consultations and other pronouncements issued by FRC and IFAC and its supporting bodies (including IAASB, IESBA and TAC).	G1(b)

Business and exam context

You have already learnt about ethical principles for auditors in your earlier studies. We will examine the issues in more detail and consider some of the complex ethical issues that auditors may face.

We also refer to the ethical guidance of the International Federation of Accountants. This is similar to the ACCA's guidance. Both approach issues of ethics in a conceptual manner.

Some of this chapter is likely to be revision, but that does not mean you should ignore it. Ethics is a key syllabus area. Complex ethical issues are introduced in this chapter. You particularly need to work through the questions given so that you practise applying ethical guidelines in given scenarios, as this is how this topic will be tested in the exam.

Professional ethics are of vital importance to the auditing and assurance profession and a major area of the syllabus, so this is likely to be a regular feature of the exam. Ethics can be tested in either Section A or Section B.

Questions are likely to be practical, giving scenarios where you are required to assess whether the situations presented are acceptable. Some of these can be answered by reference to specific guidance in the IESBA International Code of Ethics and the FRC Ethical Standard but others may require you to apply your understanding of the fundamental principles underlying the Code. Ethics may be examined alongside other areas within scenarios; commonly, practice management.

Chapter overview

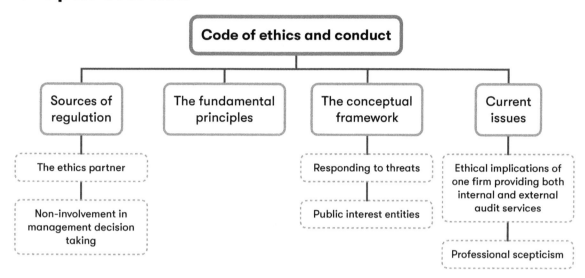

1 Sources of regulation

The IESBA's International Code of Ethics for Professional Accountants gives the key reason why accountancy bodies produce ethical guidance: the **public interest**.

'A distinguishing mark of the accountancy profession is its acceptance of the responsibility to act in the public interest. A professional accountant's responsibility is not exclusively to satisfy the needs of an individual client or employing organisation.' (IESBA Code: para. 100.1 A1)

> **Public interest:** Considered to be the collective wellbeing of the community of people and institutions the professional accountant serves, including clients, lenders, governments, employers, employees, investors, the business and financial community, and others who rely on the work of professional accountants.

The key reason **why** accountants need to have an ethical code is that people **rely** on them and their expertise. Accountants deal with a range of issues **on behalf of clients**. They often have access to confidential and sensitive information. Auditors also claim to give an **independent** opinion. It is therefore critical that accountants and particularly auditors are, and are seen to be, independent.

As the auditor is required to be, and seen to be, ethical in their dealings with clients, the **ACCA** publishes guidance for its members in its **Code of Ethics and Conduct**. This guidance is given in the form of fundamental principles, guidance and explanatory notes. (This guidance is contained within the ACCA Rulebook, which can be found on the ACCA website and which is of crucial importance for ACCA members.)

The **IESBA** (International Ethics Standards Board for Accountants), a body of IFAC, also lays down fundamental principles in its **International Code of Ethics for Professional Accountants**. The fundamental principles of the two associations are extremely similar (much of the ACCA Code is drawn directly from the IESBA Code). The IAASB also issues quality management standards and auditing standards (ISAs (UK)), which work together to promote auditor independence and audit quality.

In the UK, auditors are bound by the **FRC Ethical Standard** (ES) which either matches or exceeds the requirements of both ACCA and IESBA Codes on ethical matters. Independence is considered an overarching principle by the FRC.

> **Independence:** Freedom from conditions and relationships which, in the context of an engagement, would compromise the integrity or objectivity of the firm or covered persons.
>
> (FRC Ethical Standard: para. I21)

1.1 The ethics partner

All firms must appoint an ethics partner (ES: para. 1.12). The partner must be a **senior partner** with **a good deal of authority within the firm,** who will be available for **consultation** on ethical matters for engagement partners and other matters of judgement that arise. The ethics partner should not undertake another role within the firm that conflicts with their responsibilities as ethics partner.

(ES: paras. 1.13, 1.16 and 1.17)

The ethics partner should be **consulted** when judgements are being taken about whether the **safeguards** in place in the firm are sufficient to counter potential threats. Any **actual** or **suspect breaches** are reported to the engagement partner, and the ethics partner if appropriate.

(ES: para. 1.21)

The **very smallest firms** are **exempt** from this requirement. For firms with three partners or fewer, this function is expected to be covered by regular discussions between the partners.

(ES: para. 1.19)

1.2 Non-involvement in management decision taking

A key supporting provision for independence is **not taking management decisions**. The Ethical Standard states that these typically involve **leading** and **directing** the entity, including making **significant judgements** and taking **decisions** regarding the acquisition, deployment and control of human, financial, physical and intangible resources.

Consequently, the FRC Ethical Standard adds the **management threat** to the five threats used by both ACCA and IESBA, which we will cover in Section 3. It also defines the threats slightly differently from the Code because it uses the term 'covered person'.

Covered person: A person in a position to influence the conduct or outcome of the engagement.

(FRC Glossary of Terms, 2019c)

PER alert

One of the competencies you require to fulfil **Performance Objective 1** of the PER is the ability to act diligently and honestly, following codes of conduct, taking legislation into account and keeping up to date with legislation. You can apply the knowledge you have obtained from this chapter of the Workbook to help demonstrate this competency.

2 The fundamental principles

Integrity: Members should be **straightforward** and **honest** in all professional and business relationships (so **truth** is fundamental).

Objectivity: Members should not allow **bias, conflicts of interest or undue influence of others** to override professional or business judgement (therefore **fairness** is also fundamental).

Professional competence and due care: Members have a continuing duty to **attain and maintain** professional **knowledge and skill** at the level required to ensure that a client or employing organisation receives **competent** professional service, based on **current technical and professional standards** and **relevant legislation**. Members should also act **diligently** and in accordance with applicable **technical** and **professional standards**.

Confidentiality: Members should respect the confidentiality of **information acquired** as a result of professional and business relationships and **should not disclose** any such information to third parties without proper and specific authority, unless there is a legal or professional right or duty to disclose. Confidential information acquired as a result of professional and business relationships should not be used for the **personal advantage** of members or third parties.

Professional behaviour: Members should comply with relevant laws and regulations and should avoid any action that **discredits** the profession. (ACCA Code: para 110.1 A1)

3 The conceptual framework

Activity 1: Ethical threats

The FRC identifies six circumstances which have the potential to threaten a member or professional accountant's compliance with the fundamental principles. These are:

- The self-interest threat
- The self-review threat

- The management threat
- The advocacy threat
- The familiarity threat
- The intimidation threat

Required

What real-world situations could lead to the above threats to compliance with the fundamental principles?

Solution

3.1 Responding to threats

Having identified threats to compliance with the fundamental principles, the IESBA Code goes on to give guidance as to appropriate conditions, policies and procedures that may be relevant in **evaluating** the level of threats – examples of these include the following:

- Corporate governance requirements
- Education, training and experience requirements for the profession
- Effective complaint systems which enable the professional accountant and the general public to draw attention to unethical behaviour
- An explicitly stated duty to report breaches of ethics requirements
- Professional or regulatory monitoring and disciplinary procedures

(IESBA Code: para. 120.8 A2)

Addressing these threats requires the professional accountant to either eliminate them or reduce them to an acceptable level – this is achieved by one of the following actions:

Eliminating the circumstances, including interests or relationships, that are creating the threats	Applying safeguards, where available and capable of being applied, to reduce the threats to an acceptable level	Declining or ending the specific professional activity

(IESBA Code: para. R120.10–11)

Factors that are relevant in responding appropriately include **reviews** of significant **judgements** made or **conclusions** reached and the use of '**the reasonable and informed third party test**'

 BPP

(asking if the conclusion reached by the professional accountant would also have been reached by an independent and informed third party if faced with the same set of circumstances).

The use of **professional scepticism** (see Section 4.2) is also reinforced as being 'inter-related' with the fundamental ethical principles (IESBA Code: para. 120.13 A1).

Activity 2: Ethical responses

Discuss the ethical issues raised by the following scenarios and recommend suitable responses that the auditor should take in each case.

1   An audit partner has recently been asked by the finance director of the firm's longest-standing client to be her son's godfather.

2   A partner of the firm, who is a qualified actuary, wishes to provide valuation services to the firm's audit clients.

Solution

Essential reading

See Chapter 2 of the Essential reading for more detail on the various ethical threats and responses given by the ACCA Rulebook, the IESBA Code and the FRC Ethical Standard. You can assume that unless you are told otherwise, the guidance is aligned across ACCA, IESBA and FRC. You should learn this content.

The Essential reading is available as an Appendix of the digital edition of the Workbook.

3.2 Public interest entities

The previous activity required you to consider whether any of the firm's clients were public interest entities. The IESBA Code distinguishes between 'public interest entities' and other entities because the ethical requirements applicable to public interest entities are frequently stricter than for other entities. At this level of your studies, you must be able to **recognise** a public interest entity in a question and **adapt** your answer accordingly.

The term 'public interest entity' is defined as follows.

> **Public interest entities:**
>
> (a) A **publicly traded entity** ie one that issues financial instruments that are transferrable and traded through a publicly accessible market mechanism, including through listing on a stock exchange (in other words, a listed entity)
>
> (b) An entity one of whose main functions is to **take deposits from the public** (clearly this means banks, but there may be other financial institutions that do not fall into the above category, such as pension funds or other investment companies)
>
> (c) An entity one of whose main functions is to provide **insurance to the public**
>
> (d) An entity specified as a public interest entity by law, regulation or professional standards due to the **significance of the public interest in its financial condition** and which consequently will mean stakeholders have **higher expectations** regarding the **independence** of any firm performing its audit.
>
> (IESBA Code: Section 400 and Glossary)

This final definition is perhaps the most important to professional firms as the IESBA Code now requires an **active decision** on what is considered a public interest entity so the appropriate level of independence can be applied and **formally disclosed** by the firm if acting for such a client.

4 Current issues

4.1 Ethical implications of one firm providing both internal and external audit services

It stands to reason that a **good working relationship** should exist in order to facilitate the external auditor being able to place reliance on the work of internal auditors. Following this through to its logical conclusion, surely the **best** form of relationship would be one in which **two separate teams** from the **same firm** (with the same methodology, systems, knowledge sharing etc) carry out both internal and external audit work simultaneously.

Obviously, this has one major **drawback** – working for the same firm dramatically increases the risk of a **self-review threat** to the external auditor's objectivity. Following the 2019 update to the FRC Ethical Standard, the provision of internal audit services to any audit client in the UK is now **prohibited** (ES: para. 5.44).

Essential reading

You can read what the IESBA Code says about the provision of internal audit services to audit clients within the section on self-review threats. You should be prepared to consider the risk of the external auditor assuming a management responsibility and how the firm's ability to deliver this work varies between public interest entity and other clients.

The Essential reading is available as an Appendix of the digital edition of the Workbook.

4.2 Professional scepticism

The IESBA Code explains that in order to follow best practice, all professional accountants (including auditors) are required to exercise professional scepticism when planning and performing audits, reviews and other assurance engagements in order to scrutinise and challenge what is placed before them. The Code cites three categories where this can be applied:

Integrity	'Integrity requires the professional accountant to be straightforward and honest. For example, the accountant complies with the principle of integrity by: (a)

	(a) Being straightforward and honest when raising concerns about a position taken by a client; and
	(b) Pursuing inquiries about inconsistent information and seeking further audit evidence to address concerns about statements that might be materially false or misleading in order to make informed decisions about the appropriate course of action in the circumstances.
	In doing so, the accountant demonstrates the critical assessment of audit evidence that contributes to the exercise of professional scepticism.'
Objectivity	'Objectivity requires the professional accountant not to compromise professional or business judgment because of bias, conflict of interest or the undue influence of others. For example, the accountant complies with the principle of objectivity by:
	(a) Recognising circumstances or relationships such as familiarity with the client, that might compromise the accountant's professional or business judgment; and
	(b) Considering the impact of such circumstances and relationships on the accountant's judgment when evaluating the sufficiency and appropriateness of audit evidence related to a matter material to the client's financial statements.
	In doing so, the accountant behaves in a manner that contributes to the exercise of professional scepticism.'
Professional competence and due care	'Professional competence and due care requires the professional accountant to have professional knowledge and skill at the level required to ensure the provision of competent professional service, and to act diligently in accordance with applicable standards, laws and regulations. For example, the accountant complies with the principle of professional competence and due care by:
	(a) Applying knowledge that is relevant to a particular client's industry and business activities in order to properly identify risks of material misstatement;
	(b) Designing and performing appropriate audit procedures; and
	(c) Applying relevant knowledge when critically assessing whether audit evidence is sufficient and appropriate in the circumstances.
	In doing so, the accountant behaves in a manner that contributes to the exercise of professional scepticism.'

(IESBA Code: para. 120.13 A2)

ISA (UK) 200 *Overall Objectives of the Independent Auditor and the Conduct of an Audit in Accordance with International Standards on Auditing (UK)* lists the following examples of risks that may arise from a lack of professional scepticism.

'Maintaining professional scepticism throughout the audit is necessary if the auditor is, for example, to reduce the risks of:

- Overlooking unusual circumstances
- Over generalizing when drawing conclusions from audit observations
- Using inappropriate assumptions in determining the nature, timing and extent of the audit procedures and evaluating the results thereof.' (ISA (UK) 200: para. A21)

In the UK, the **FRC's Audit Quality Review team has found a lack of professional scepticism to be a significant problem in every year since at least 2010–11.** The 2014–15 report stated that a common issue was '…insufficient skepticism in challenging the appropriateness of assumptions in key areas of audit judgment such as impairment testing and property valuations…' (FRC 2015b: s2.3).

This links with the question of independence generally, and the risk that the audit is not conducted with **professional competence and due care** as a result of a lack of scepticism.

In the end, the auditor must balance being sceptical with being trusting, and the concept of 'professional scepticism' is an attempt to convey this. It has also been observed in practice that the auditor should not only trust, but also verify what the client tells them.

Activity 3: Aventura International

Aventura International, a listed company, manufactures and wholesales a wide variety of products including fashion clothes and audio-video equipment. The company is audited by Voest, a firm of Chartered Certified Accountants, and the Audit Manager is Darius Harken. The following matters have arisen during the audit of the group's financial statements for the year to 31 December 20X7 which is nearing completion:

(1)   During the annual inventory count of fashion clothes at the company's principal warehouse, the audit staff attending the count were invited to purchase any items of clothing or equipment at 30% of their recommended retail prices.

(2)   The Chief Executive of Aventura International, Armando Thyolo, owns a private jet. Armando invoices the company, on a monthly basis, for that proportion of the operating costs which reflects business use. One of these invoices shows that Darius Harken was flown to Florida in March 20X7 and flown back two weeks later. Neither Aventura nor Voest have any offices or associates in Florida.

(3)   Last week Armando announced his engagement to be married to his personal assistant, Kirsten Fennimore. Before joining Aventura in September 20X7, Kirsten had been Voest's senior in charge of the audit of Aventura.

Required

Discuss the ethical, professional and quality issues raised and the actions which might be taken by the auditor in relation to these matters.   **(15 marks)**

Note. Assume it is 6 March 20X8.

Solution

Chapter summary

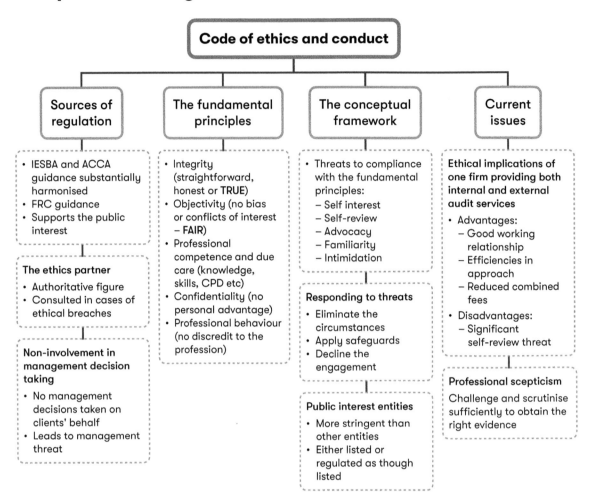

Code of ethics and conduct

Sources of regulation

- IESBA and ACCA guidance substantially harmonised
- FRC guidance
- Supports the public interest

The ethics partner
- Authoritative figure
- Consulted in cases of ethical breaches

Non-involvement in management decision taking
- No management decisions taken on clients' behalf
- Leads to management threat

The fundamental principles

- Integrity (straightforward, honest or **TRUE**)
- Objectivity (no bias or conflicts of interest – **FAIR**)
- Professional competence and due care (knowledge, skills, CPD etc)
- Confidentiality (no personal advantage)
- Professional behaviour (no discredit to the profession)

The conceptual framework

- Threats to compliance with the fundamental principles:
  - Self interest
  - Self-review
  - Advocacy
  - Familiarity
  - Intimidation

Responding to threats
- Eliminate the circumstances
- Apply safeguards
- Decline the engagement

Public interest entities
- More stringent than other entities
- Either listed or regulated as though listed

Current issues

Ethical implications of one firm providing both internal and external audit services
- Advantages:
  - Good working relationship
  - Efficiencies in approach
  - Reduced combined fees
- Disadvantages:
  - Significant self-review threat

Professional scepticism
Challenge and scrutinise sufficiently to obtain the right evidence

 BPP

Knowledge diagnostic

1. Codes of ethics

The **ACCA Code of Ethics and Conduct, IESBA International Code of Ethics for Professional Accountants** and **FRC Ethical Standard** explain how accountants should act in the public interest.

2. Fundamental principles

ACCA, IESBA and FRC guidance are based on **five fundamental principles** which govern the general behaviour and characteristics of members: integrity; objectivity; professional competence and due care; confidentiality; and professional behaviour.

3. Conceptual framework

The fundamental principles are themselves underpinned by a **conceptual framework** which identifies **threats** to compliance with the fundamental principles (self-interest, self-review, management, advocacy, familiarity and intimidation).

4. Responses

Responses to ethical threats require them to be **evaluated** and suitable **responses** adopted: removing the circumstances leading to the threat; applying safeguards to reduce the threats to an acceptable level; and declining the activity that leads to the ethical threat.

5. Professional scepticism

Professional scepticism is used to challenge and scrutinise the subject matter placed before the auditor to ensure engagements are undertaken using best practice. You should also refer to the Essential Reading for Chapter 16 where you will find more on the ways that professional scepticism is influencing how assurance engagements are conducted.

6. Combined internal and external audit?

Provision of combined 'internal and external' audit by the same firm can deliver **savings** and provide a more '**joined-up**' service, but does present **threats to audit objectivity**.

Further study guidance

Question practice

Now try the following from the Further question practice bank (available in the digital edition of the Workbook):

- Question 2 'Fundamental principles' is an opportunity to practise some of the theory discussed in this chapter in an applied situation.
- Question 3 'Business assurance' is a discussion question that tests how well you have understood the theory regarding certain non-audit services.

Further reading

There are technical articles on the ACCA website written by members of the AAA examining team which are relevant to some of the topics covered in this chapter that you should read:

- *Professional scepticism*
- *Exposure draft: Proposed revisions to the code to promote the role and mindset expected of professional accountants*

Own research

Consider your own organisation or one that you are familiar with – what can you learn from the following to help you with topics from this chapter?

- Do you have a Code of Ethics that you are expected to follow? If so, obtain a copy and see how closely it matches the content presented here.
- Start to keep a diary of events where you believe you needed to consider the ethical implications of your actions – in each case, do you think you behaved as you should have done? If not, why do you think this was?

You may find the **ACCA Rulebook** helpful to refer to. The Rulebook is updated periodically to reflect changes in policy, regulation, standards and legislation. The most recent update took effect from **September 2022**. Should you wish to access the ACCA Rulebook at any time, it is available on the **ACCA website**: www.accaglobal.com/lk/en/about-us/regulation/rulebook.html

Activity answers

Activity 1: Ethical threats

> **Approach**
>
> This activity serves as something of a refresher for you, as you should have seen the ethical threats in your earlier studies. The only new one for you might be the management threat which is only used in the UK. Use this activity as a way of reminding yourself what each threat means and how it could be present from the situations you suggest.
>
> Note that in the real exam, you are likely to consider this from the opposite direction: a scenario will present a set of circumstances that you will need to analyse in order to find the appropriate ethical threat.

Suggested solution

Self-interest threat

This would arise in situations where the audit firm or a member of the engagement team has some financial or other interest in the audit client. For example:

- Providing a loan to a client
- Earning fees on a contingent basis, ie profit related
- Owning shares in a client
- Undue dependence on fees from a client

Self-review threat

The self-review threat occurs when a previous judgement needs to be re-evaluated by members responsible for that judgement. The situation tends to arise when the auditor has provided other services to a client. Key examples would be:

- The auditor providing a specialist valuation (eg pension liabilities)
- The audit firm providing internal audit services and subsequently relying on the work for the external audit
- Reporting on the operation of financial systems after being involved in their design or implementation

Management threat

While this threat is only formally defined by the FRC Ethical Standard in the UK, its existence is commonplace throughout any relationship between a firm and its clients. The IESBA Code prohibits firms from accepting any management responsibilities for an audit client due to the creation of self-interest, self-review, advocacy and familiarity threats (IESBA Code: paras. R400.13, 400.13 A2). Some activities that may be undertaken by the firm or its staff may give rise to a threat of being involved in making decisions that should be the responsibility of the client's management. Key examples of management decisions, which the auditor must not be involved in, include:

- Setting policies and strategic direction
- Directing and taking responsibility for the actions of the entity's employees
- Authorising transactions
- Deciding which recommendations of the firm or other third parties should be implemented, recognising that a greater threat exists where management are considering recommendations made by the firm, where this no alternative course of action
- Taking responsibility for the preparation and fair presentation of financial statements in accordance with the applicable financial reporting framework
- Taking responsibility for the preparation and presentation of subject matter information in the case of another public interest assurance engagement

 BPP

- Taking responsibility for designing, implementing and maintaining internal control

(FRC ES: para. 1.25)

A threat to integrity, objectivity and independence also arises where the firm provides non-audit/additional services and, based on that work, management is required to make judgements and take decisions.

Advocacy threat

The advocacy threat occurs when members promote a position or opinion to the point that subsequent objectivity may be compromised. Specific examples would be:

- Acting as an advocate on behalf of an assurance client in litigation or disputes with third parties
- Promoting shares in a listed entity when that entity is a financial statement audit client

Familiarity threat

The familiarity threat occurs when, because of a close relationship, members become too sympathetic to the interest of others. Circumstances which would create a familiarity threat would include:

- Long association with a client
- Acceptance of gifts or preferential treatment unless the value is clearly insignificant
- Overfamiliarity with the management of the organisation such that judgement could be compromised

Intimidation threat

The intimidation threat occurs when members are deterred from acting objectively by threats, actual or perceived. Such a threat will occur in the following circumstances:

- The threat of dismissal or replacement of the member, or a close or immediate family member, over a disagreement about the application of an accounting principle or the way in which financial and performance information is to be reported
- A dominant personality attempting to influence the decision-making process or controlling relations with auditors
- Being threatened with litigation
- Being pressured to reduce inappropriately the extent of work performed in order to reduce fees

Activity 2: Ethical responses

Approach

This is similar to the way that such content would be examined in the AAA exam, albeit with slightly less detail than an exam-standard scenario would present. The approach you should follow needs to cover two things: firstly, the **threat(s)** presented by the scenario with **reasons** why this represents the threat(s) identified; and secondly, the **response(s)** that should be taken, along with **justifications**.

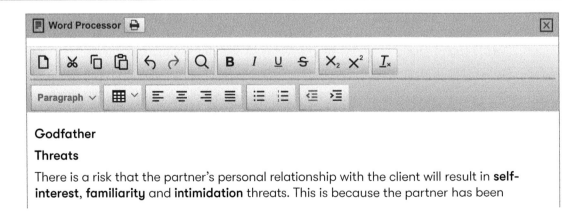

Godfather

Threats

There is a risk that the partner's personal relationship with the client will result in **self-interest, familiarity** and **intimidation** threats. This is because the partner has been

 BPP

involved with the client for many years and evidently has a **personal relationship** with a senior member of client staff, despite the fact that this should be an independent audit assignment. We are not told whether or not the partner involved is the engagement partner for this client, so our responses will need to consider both possibilities, but any partner would be able to exert significant influence on the conduct of the audit.

Responses

The risk arising here is **significant**, because both the engagement partner of the firm and the finance director of the client are in senior positions, meaning that any lack of objectivity could affect the financial statements. The firm should therefore implement **safeguards** to mitigate against these threats. If it is the engagement partner who has been asked to be godfather, that partner should be **rotated** away from this engagement immediately. If it is not the engagement partner who has been asked to be godfather, an independent partner should provide an **engagement quality review** (sometimes called a 'hot review' or pre-issuance review) of the audit to ensure there has been no undue influence on conduct of the audit. Consultation with the firm's **ethics partner** would also be considered appropriate here.

(IESBA Code: section 521; FRC ES: paras. 2.59–2.64)

Actuarial services

Threats

Actuarial services are covered by **valuation services** in the IESBA Code and **actuarial valuation services** under the FRC Ethical Standard, which state that the provision of such services may give rise to a **self-review** or **advocacy** threat. For clients that are not public interest entities, if the service involves evaluating matters that are **material** to the financial statements and the valuation involves a **significant degree of subjectivity**, then the threat to objectivity and independence **cannot be reduced to an acceptable level by appropriate safeguards** and the service should not, therefore, be provided.

For public interest entities, under the IESBA Code, should the valuation services lead to the existence of a **self-review threat** for the firm, the work is prohibited. Should an **advocacy threat** be present, the use of separate teams might be a suitable safeguard to mitigate this threat. Under the FRC Ethical Standard in the UK, this work can only be undertaken when it would have an 'inconsequential' effect on the audited financial statements.

Responses

Undertaking this service for an audit client that is not a public interest entity, for amounts that are neither separately, nor in aggregate, material to the financial statements, or that do not involve a significant degree of subjectivity, could still create a **self-review** or **advocacy** threat. However, safeguards could be applied, such as the involvement of informed management or an **additional accountant** who is not a member of the assurance team to review the work done, and ensuring that **members** doing the valuation work **do not also undertake the audit work for that client**.

For public interest entities, under the IESBA Code, should the valuation services lead to the existence of a **self-review threat** for the firm, the work is prohibited. Should an **advocacy threat** be present, the use of separate teams might be a suitable safeguard to mitigate this threat. Under the FRC Ethical Standard in the UK, this work can only be undertaken when it would have an 'inconsequential' effect on the audited financial statements.

(IESBA Code: section 603; FRC ES: paras. 5.59)

Activity 3: Aventura International

Suggested solution

Ethical situations arising in connection with the audit of Aventura International

(1) **Offer of goods**

At the inventory count, the auditors attending were invited to purchase inventory at 30% of RRP, that is, at a 70% discount.

ACCA's guidance on accepting goods states that such benefits should only be accepted on 'normal commercial terms' or if the value is 'trivial and inconsequential' (ACCA Code: section 250.11 A2; IESBA Code: para. R906.3; FRC ES: para. 4.40). What constitutes trivial and inconsequential will be a matter of judgement for the auditor.

Benefit

It is possible that this offer does approximate to offers made to staff at Aventura, as clothes commonly retail at prices with a substantial mark-up on cost. It would not be unreasonable for a clothes retailer to give staff a 'cost' benefit. The auditor should determine whether such a benefit is made available to staff. If it is not made to staff it should not be accepted by the auditor. The ethical threat most likely to be relevant here is **self-interest**, although enjoying a discount that client staff may also have access to could introduce a **familiarity** threat too.

The term 'trivial and inconsequential' should be considered in terms of materiality to both the auditor and the company. The offer is not material to Aventura, for whom clothes retail is only one division. However, the offer of unlimited fashion at a 70% discount is extremely likely to be material to junior audit staff (who are the grade most likely to be allocated to the inventory count). In this context, the benefit is clearly not inconsequential.

Timing

It would be inappropriate to take up the offer at the inventory count, not least because this would constitute movement of inventory during the count, which would be wrong.

Also, the junior staff members should not accept such goods without having first discussed the matter with the audit partner (it is assumed in this answer that this is the first time such an offer has been made).

Lastly, if mistakes were to be made on the inventory count, the audit might be open to charges of negligence if it appeared its staff members indulged in a shopping trip when they should have been auditing.

Action to be taken

The audit staff members should not take up the offer at the inventory count.

The audit partner should discuss the matter with management, ascertain whether a similar benefit is offered to Aventura staff and decide whether he feels it is appropriate for his staff to take up the offer. It may be inappropriate as Aventura might become perceived to be a 'reward' job by audit staff. Alternatively, it might be appropriate if the audit firm imposed a financial limit to the benefits their staff could accept.

FRC ES paragraph 4.42 requires established policies on gifts, favours and hospitality and reminds firms that they should issue guidance to staff on how to comply with such a policy.

(2) **Hospitality**

An invoice to the company for business use of the Chief Executive's jet shows that the Audit Manager was flown to Florida and back for a stay of two weeks.

Issues arising

(i) If the invoice was ostensibly for 'business use', what was the business? (Neither the client nor the auditor have offices in Florida.)

(ii) If the invoice was not for business, the Chief Executive is wrong to invoice it to the company. Is this common practice?

(iii) If it was for business, the cost of the auditor's flight should not have been charged directly to the company, but to the audit firm instead, which could then have recharged it. Was Darius Harken working for the weeks in question, or is it recorded as holiday in the audit firm's records?

(iv) Does the invoice actually represent a significant example of hospitality being accepted by the Audit Manager?

(v) Did the Audit Manager travel alone, with family, or even with the Chief Executive? Does this indicate that the audit manager has a close personal relationship with the Chief Executive?

Hospitality/close personal relationship

It is possible that points (iv) and (v) above may be indicated by the invoice.

In terms of accepting hospitality, the guidance from ACCA, IESBA and FRC is the same as was discussed above in relation to accepting goods. It is unlikely that paying for an auditor's flight would be considered to be on normal commercial terms, because it would be traditional for the audit firm simply to recharge the cost of a business trip. Taking steps such as these would help to reduce the suggestion that something inappropriate has occurred, if the trip was genuinely business related.

If the trip was for pleasure (a) it should not have been charged to the company, which raises several auditing issues in its own right, and (b) it does not come within the definition of 'trivial and inconsequential'. Ethical threats of **self-interest** and **familiarity** are evidently possible here.

In terms of close business or personal relationships, ACCA's guidance states that these might adversely affect, or appear to affect, the objectivity of the auditor. The FRC requires firms to consider the cumulative effect if such hospitality has been offered more than once (FRC ES: para. 4.44).

It therefore seems likely that in this instance, if the Chief Executive and the Audit Manager have been on holiday together, or at least a business 'jolly', then as a minimum, objectivity will **appear** to be threatened.

Action to be taken

(i) The audit firm should review its personnel records and confirm whether Darius Harken was working or holidaying at the relevant time.

(ii) If the trip was business related, the audit partner should establish why the cost has been invoiced to the company by the Chief Executive and not by the audit firm.

(iii) If the trip was personal, then the Audit Manager appears to have threatened the objectivity of the audit and, indeed, given that the trip appears to have been taken around the time the prior year audit was taking place, that audit is also adversely affected.

(iv) The prior year audit files should be subjected to a 'post-issuance' or 'cold' review and the Audit Manager should be replaced on this year's audit, which should also be subject to a quality management review.

(v) All invoices rendered to the company in respect of the jet should be scrutinised by the audit team, for further evidence of personal expenses being charged to the company.

 BPP

(3) **The impending marriage of the Chief Executive**

The Chief Executive's assistant is the former accountant in charge of the audit of Aventura, who is likely to have been involved with the audit of the previous year end. She has just announced her engagement to the Chief Executive.

Issues arising

(i)   Current year audit – there is a risk of loss of independence as the Chief Executive's assistant is aware of the firm's auditing methods.

(ii) Prior year audit – there is a suggestion that the accountant in charge of the audit may have been in a personal relationship with the Chief Executive which may have adversely affected her objectivity.

Movement of audit staff

Ethical guidance states that where a member of the audit team gains employment with an audit client, then **familiarity** and **intimidation** threats may arise. Where a 'significant connection' remains, then no safeguards could reduce the risk to an acceptable level.

If there is no significant connection, then the IESBA Code suggests a number of safeguards in this situation, such as:

-   Considering the appropriateness of modifying the plan for the engagement

-   Assigning the audit team to someone of sufficient experience in relation to the person who has left

-   Involving an additional accountant not previously associated with the audit to review

In the UK, the FRC Ethical Standard states that if a significant connection exists, the following factors should be considered:

(i)   The position the individual had in the engagement team or firm

(ii)   The position the individual has taken at the audit client

(iii) The amount of involvement the individual will have with the engagement team (especially where it includes former colleagues)

(iv)   The length of time since the individual was a member of the engagement team or employed by the audit firm

(FRC ES: para. 2.41)

Following the assessment of such threats, appropriate safeguards should be applied where necessary.

Action to be taken

Although the accountant in charge was not the most senior staff member on the audit, it would have been prudent to modify the audit plan before this year's audit. However, this does not appear to have been done, and the audit is nearing completion.

Therefore, it is important that Voest conducts an engagement quality review of this audit.

In relation to the suspicion that Ms Fennimore's objectivity may have been affected last year, it might also be a good idea to conduct a similar review of last year's audit work, evidence obtained and conclusions drawn. However, as the work should have been reviewed by an audit manager and partner after Ms Fennimore's involvement, the risk of a problem on last year's audit appears to be slight.

3

Fraud and professional liability

Learning objectives

On completion of this chapter, you should be able to:

	Syllabus reference no.
Identify and develop an appropriate response to circumstances which indicate a high risk of error, irregularity, fraud or misstatement in the financial statements or a given situation.	B2(a)
Compare and contrast the respective responsibilities of management and auditors for fraud and error.	B2(b)
Describe the matters to be considered and recommend procedures to be carried out to investigate actual and/or potential misstatements in a given situation.	B2(c)
Explain how, why, when and to whom fraud and error should be reported and the circumstances in which an auditor should withdraw from an engagement.	B2(d)
Consider the current and possible future role of auditors in preventing, detecting and reporting error and fraud.	B2(e)
Recognise circumstances in which professional accountants may have legal liability and the criteria that need to be satisfied for legal liability to be recognised.	B3(a)
Describe the factors to determine whether or not an auditor is negligent and discuss the auditor's potential liability in given situations.	B3(b)
Compare and contrast liability owed to a client with liability owed to third parties (ie contract vs establishing a duty of care).	B3(c)
Evaluate the practicability and effectiveness of ways in which liability may be restricted including the use of liability limitation agreements.	B3(d)
Discuss and appraise the principal causes of audit failure and other factors that contribute to the 'expectation gap' (eg responsibilities for fraud and error) and recommend ways in which that gap may be bridged.	B3(e)

Business and exam context

Auditors have responsibilities to several parties. This chapter explores the various **responsibilities** and the **liability that can arise** in respect of each of them. It also looks at ways of restricting liability, including professional indemnity insurance.

The auditors' responsibility to members and other readers of the financial statements in tort and contract can give rise to some form of **liability**, particularly in the event of **negligence**. Case law on this matter is complex and not wholly satisfactory. It results in auditors being liable to some parties and not others. However, **auditors' liability** is a dynamic issue in that it **evolves as cases are brought to court**.

There are some interesting issues for auditors with regard to liability, for example **limited liability partnerships**. The reasons for **audit failure** and other factors contributing to the 'expectation gap' are also covered here.

Critically, and contrary to widespread public belief, **auditors do not have a responsibility to detect and prevent fraud**. The responsibilities that auditors do have with regard to fraud and error are outlined here as well. Auditors are required to follow the guidance of ISA (UK) 240 (revised) *The Auditor's Responsibilities Relating to Fraud in an Audit of Financial Statements*.

Auditor liability is a key issue facing the profession globally, and is linked in with ongoing debate about the role of audit in the future. This area can be examined in topical **discussion** questions, or in **practical** scenarios considering whether an auditor may be held to have been negligent in specific circumstances. It can be tested in either Section A or Section B.

The extent of the auditor's responsibilities in relation to fraud and error is a critical element of the public's perception of the auditor's role. The requirements of ISA (UK) 240 in this respect are core knowledge for this exam and may have to be applied in practical scenarios.

Chapter overview

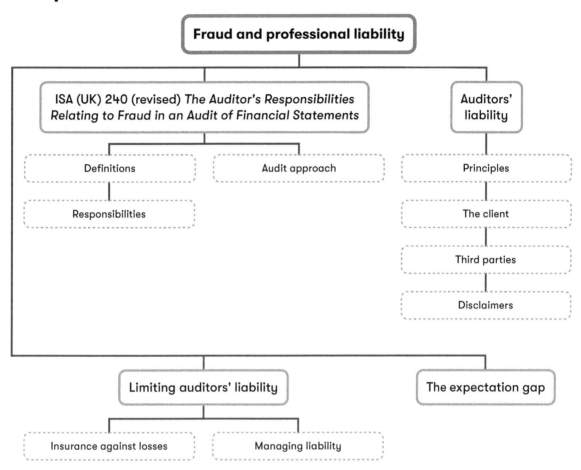

1 ISA (UK) 240 (revised) *The Auditor's Responsibilities Relating to Fraud in an Audit of Financial Statements*

1.1 Definitions

KEY TERM

> **Fraud:** An **intentional** act by one or more individuals among management, those charged with governance [management fraud], employees [employee fraud] or third parties involving the use of deception to obtain an unjust or illegal advantage. (ISA (UK) 240: para. 11)
>
> Fraud may be perpetrated by an individual, or in collusion with people internal or external to the business.

Two types of **misstatements** caused by fraud are relevant to the auditor (ISA (UK) 240: paras. 3, A3, A5):

Misstatements resulting from **fraudulent financial reporting** (such as those used to **manipulate** financial results, artificially improving an entity's true position – revenue recognition is often tested as it is the most common form of this type of fraud)

Misstatements resulting from **misappropriation of assets** (such as **stealing cash** from fictitious payments or **inventory** for personal use or sale)

1.2 Responsibilities

'The **primary responsibility** for the prevention and detection of fraud rests both with those charged with governance of the entity and management. It is important that **management**, with the oversight of those charged with governance, place a strong emphasis on fraud prevention... and fraud deterrence... **this** involves a **commitment** to creating a **culture** of honesty and ethical behaviour which can be reinforced by an active oversight by those charged with governance .... considering the potential for override of controls or other inappropriate influence over the financial reporting process, such as efforts by management to manage earnings in order to influence the perceptions of analysts as to the entity's performance and profitability.' (ISA (UK) 240 (Revised): para. 4)

However, the **auditor** should obtain **reasonable assurance** that the financial statements as a whole are free from **material misstatement**, whether caused by **fraud or error**. The deliberate nature of fraud creates a higher risk of misstatement which the auditor needs to factor into the audit approach. In the UK, the auditor may also have **additional responsibilities** under law, regulation or relevant ethical requirements regarding NOCLAR, including fraud, which may go beyond these auditing standards:

Responding to identified or suspected NOCLAR	Communicating identified or suspected NOCLAR to other auditors	Documentation of any identified or suspected NOCLAR

(ISA (UK) 240 (revised): paras. 5-8a)

Specific **objectives** for achieving this **reasonable assurance** are:

- To **identify** and **assess** the **risks of material misstatement** due to fraud
- To obtain **sufficient appropriate evidence** regarding the assessed risks of material misstatement due to fraud, through designing and implementing appropriate responses; and
- To **respond** appropriately to fraud or suspected fraud identified during the audit

(ISA (UK) 240: para.10)

1.3 Audit approach

Members of the engagement team should discuss the **susceptibility** of the entity's financial statements to material misstatement due to fraud. An overriding requirement of the ISA (UK) is

 BPP

that auditors are aware of the possibility of there being misstatements due to fraud. The mindset of **professional scepticism** is important here, with the auditor always being alert to the possibility that things may not be as they seem, and that the management who have always appeared honest may not really be. The UK version of the ISA specifically mentions the importance of complying with ISA (UK) 550 *Related parties* which reinforced the need to be aware of the wide reach of fraud (ISA (UK) 240: paras. 12–14-1).

The auditor should make **enquiries of management** regarding **management's assessment** of the risk that the financial statements may be materially misstated due to fraud and management's process for identifying and responding to the risks of fraud in the entity.

The auditor should also **determine management's process** for identifying and responding to the risks of fraud and how such a process is communicated, both to those charged with governance and to staff. The auditor should also enquire about any **actual, suspected or alleged fraud** affecting the entity, including discussions about fraud with Internal Audit.

The auditor should obtain an understanding of how those charged with governance exercise oversight of **management's processes for identifying and responding** to the risks of fraud and the internal control that management has established to mitigate these risks as part of its ongoing risk management procedures.

1.3.1 Examples of fraud risk factors

In determining an **approach** to fraud, auditors could consider the **conditions** that lead to fraud:

(a) An incentive or pressure to commit fraud (Motive)

(b) A perceived opportunity to commit fraud (Opportunity)

(c) An ability or attitude to rationalise the fraudulent action (Dishonesty)

(ISA (UK) 240: para. A1)

```
                          ┌──────────────────────────────────┐
                          │  Fraudulent financial reporting    │
                          └──────────────────────────────────┘
```

Incentives/pressures	Opportunities	Attitudes/rationalisations
• Financial stability/ profitability is threatened	• Significant related-party transactions	• Ineffective communication or enforcement of the entity's values or ethical standards by management
• Pressure on management to meet the expectations of third parties	• Assets, liabilities, revenues or expenses based on significant estimates	• Known history of violations of securities laws or other laws and regulations
• Personal financial situation of management threatened by the entity's financial performance	• Domination of management by a single person or small group	• A practice by management of committing to achieve aggressive or unrealistic forecasts
• Excessive pressure on management or operating personnel to meet financial targets	• Complex or unstable organisational structure	• Low morale among senior management
	• Internal control components are deficient	• Relationship between management and the current or predecessor auditor is strained

```
                            ┌─────────────────────────────┐
                            │ Misappropriation of assets  │
                            └─────────────────────────────┘
        ┌───────────────────────────┬───────────────────────────┐
        │                           │                           │
┌──────────────────┐    ┌──────────────────┐    ┌──────────────────┐
│Incentives/pressures│    │   Opportunities  │    │Attitudes/rationalisations│
└──────────────────┘    └──────────────────┘    └──────────────────┘
```

Incentives/pressures
- Personal financial obligations
- Adverse relationships between the entity and employees with access to cash or other assets susceptible to theft

Opportunities
- Large amounts of cash on hand or processed
- Inventory items that are small in size, of high value, or in high demand
- Easily convertible assets, such as bearer bonds, diamonds, or computer chips
- Inadequate internal control over assets

Attitudes/rationalisations
- Overriding existing controls
- Failing to correct known internal control deficiencies
- Behaviour indicating displeasure or dissatisfaction with the entity
- Changes in behaviour or lifestyle

In accordance with ISA (UK) 330 (covered in Chapter 6) the auditor shall determine **overall responses** to address the **assessed risks of material misstatement due to fraud at the financial statement level** by performing the following:

(a) Consider the assignment and supervision of personnel

(b) Consider the selection and application of accounting policies used by the entity

(c) Incorporate an element of unpredictability in the selection of the nature, timing and extent of audit procedures ISA (UK) 240: paras. 28–29)

Similarly, the auditor may have to **amend** the **nature, timing or extent** of planned audit procedures to address assessed risks of material misstatement due to fraud at the **assertion level**. The Revised ISA (UK) also refers auditors to ISA (UK) 540 (Revised) in relation to the risk of management bias arising from accounting estimates.

Consequently, the auditor should also consider the following.

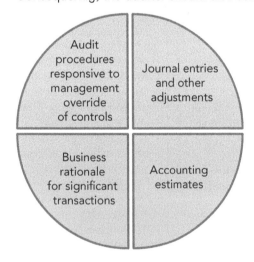

(ISA (UK) 240: paras. 30, A41–48)

1.3.2 Procedures when misstatements are discovered

The auditor **evaluates** the audit evidence obtained to ensure it is consistent and that it achieves its aim of answering the risks of fraud. This will include a consideration of results of analytical procedures and any misstatements found.

The auditor must obtain **written representations** that management accepts its responsibility for the prevention and detection of fraud and has made all relevant disclosures to the auditors. However, when there is a misstatement indicative of fraud, the auditor should consider its implications in relation to other aspects of the audit, particularly the reliability of those written representations.

 BPP

The auditor must also document:

The significant decisions reached as a result of the team's discussion of fraud
The fraud risk factors and the identified and assessed risks of material misstatement due to fraud
The overall responses to assessed risks
Results of specific audit tests
Any communications with management

(ISA (UK) 240: paras. 44–46)

1.3.3 Communication

When the auditor identifies fraud or suspected fraud, they should communicate it to the **appropriate level of management** as soon as practicable, unless **prohibited** by **laws** or **regulation**.

Fraud should be communicated to **those charged with governance** where it involves:

(a) Management;

(b) Employees who have significant roles in internal control; and

(c) Others where the fraud results in a material misstatement in the financial statements.

The auditor should communicate to management, and those charged with governance, any material deficiencies in the design or implementation of internal control to prevent and detect fraud which have come to the auditor's attention. (ISA (UK) 240: paras. 40–42)

The auditor may have a **statutory duty** to report fraudulent behaviour to **regulators** outside the entity. If no such legal duty arises, the auditor must consider whether to do so would breach their **professional duty of confidence**. In either event, the auditor should take **legal advice** (ISA (UK) 240: paras. A65–66).

1.3.4 Auditor's report

When the auditor confirms that, or is unable to conclude whether, the financial statements are materially misstated as a result of fraud, the auditor should consider the implications for the auditor's report:

1.3.5 Withdrawal from an engagement

The auditor should consider the need to withdraw from the engagement if they uncover **exceptional** circumstances with regard to fraud (ISA (UK) 240: para. 38).

If this becomes necessary, it will be necessary to discuss the reasons with management and those charged with governance, and it may be necessary to make a report to **regulators**. However, remember the **confidentiality** and **tipping-off issues** from earlier chapters: whenever you are considering whether to make a public interest disclosure, you should always bear this in mind.

2 Auditors' liability

2.1 Principles

Auditors could be found guilty of financial market abuse offences, such as **insider dealing**, since they are privy to inside information and may use this information for their own gain. Auditors could also be found guilty of a **criminal offence** if they knew or suspected a person was

laundering money and they either 'tipped off' or failed to report their suspicions to the proper authority.

The auditor has a **contractual relationship** with their client. If they breach the contract, then they can be sued. In addition to this, auditors have a duty to carry out their work with reasonable skill and care. **Negligence** is a common law concept under English law. It seeks to provide compensation to a person who has suffered loss due to another person's wrongful neglect. To succeed in an action for negligence, **an injured party must prove four things**:

(a) A **duty of care** exists which is enforceable by law;

(b) This duty of care was **breached**;

(c) The breach caused the injured party **loss**. In the case of negligence in relation to financial advisers/auditors, this loss must be pecuniary (ie financial) loss; and

(d) The harm was **not too remote** a consequence of the breach.

2.2 The client

The **company** has a **contract** with the audit firm. In English law, a contract for the supply of a service such as an audit has a duty of reasonable care implied into it by statute.

Client	
Duty of care exists?	Automatic
Breached?	Must be proved
Loss arising?	Must be proved
Not too remote?	Must be proved

In order to prove whether a duty of care has been breached, the court has to give further consideration to what the duty of **reasonable care** means in practice. A number of judgements made in **case law** show how the auditor's duty of care has been gauged at various points in time because legislation often does not state clearly the manner in which the auditors should discharge their duty of care. It is also not likely that this would be clearly spelt out in any contract setting out the terms of an auditor's appointment.

As a basic rule though, demonstrating that the firm **followed auditing standards** would probably be seen as strong defence against claims of negligence from audit clients.

2.3 Third parties

'Third parties' in this context means **anyone other than the company (audit client) who wished to make a claim for negligence**. Clearly, this could be many people.

The key **difference** between third parties and the company is that third parties have **no contract** with the audit firm. There is therefore no implied duty of care, but the circumstances of the relationship between the audit firm and any third party might **create** a duty of care. The situation is therefore as follows.

Third parties	
Duty of care exists?	**Must be proved**
Breached?	Must be proved
Loss arising?	Must be proved
Not too remote?	Must be proved

Essential reading

See Chapter 3 of the Essential reading for more detail on the various cases that have been used to understand the extent of the auditor's professional liability. You are not expected to know all the precise details of the relevant cases for your exam, however; you will be tested on your ability to apply the basic principles to specific scenarios. It is vital that you use the right kind of **language** when answering questions in this area. Your correct use of such terms as **duty of care**, **liability**, **negligence**, **proximity** and **third party** can help to demonstrate to the marker that you are familiar with the subject matter, and that you are simply **applying** it to the circumstances in the question.

The Essential reading is available as an Appendix of the digital edition of the Workbook.

2.4 Disclaimers

The cases discussed suggest that a duty of care to a third party may arise when an accountant does not know that their work will be relied on by a third party, but only knows that it is work of a kind which is liable in the ordinary course of events to be relied on by a third party.

Conversely, an accountant may sometimes be informed or be aware, before they carry out certain work, that a third party will rely on the results. An example is a report on the business of a client which the accountant has been instructed to prepare for the purpose of being shown to a potential purchaser or potential creditor of that business. In such a case, an accountant should assume that they will be held to owe the same duty to the third party as to their client. The Bannerman case suggests this will also be necessary for **audit work**. Since the Bannerman case, many audit firms have included a **disclaimer paragraph** in their auditor's report.

When ACCA's Council considered the use of such disclaimers, its view was that:

Standard disclaimers are not an appropriate or proportionate response to the Bannerman decision. Their incorporation as a standard feature of the auditor's report could have the effect of devaluing that report.

(ACCA 2008: para. 20)

Activity 1: Moorland

Your firm of Certified Accountants, in common with many other firms of accountants and auditors, issues to its staff an audit manual which contains, amongst other matters, recommended procedures to be adopted in carrying out audits. A number of these recommended procedures relate to physical observation of inventory counts and review of inventory counting instructions. Owing to pressure of work, you neglected to arrange for the physical observation of inventories at the premises of Moorland, a limited liability company audit client, at 31 March 20X3, but your review of inventory counting instructions indicated that company procedures appeared to be in order. You decided to accept the amount at which inventories were stated in the financial statements at 31 March 20X3 on the grounds that:

(1)   The inventory counting instructions appeared to be satisfactory

(2)   No problems had arisen in determining physical inventory quantities in previous years

(3)   The figures in the financial statements generally 'made sense'

You issued your auditor's report with an unmodified opinion on 28 May 20X3 and unbeknown to you, Moorland used the financial statements and the auditor's report for the purpose of obtaining material additional finance from a third party in the form of an unsecured long-term loan. Unfortunately, in October 20X3, the company ran into financial difficulties and was forced into liquidation, as a result of which, the long-term loan holder lost the amount of their loan. During the liquidation proceedings, it became clear that inventory quantities at 31 March 20X3 had been considerably overstated.

 BPP

Required

1   Explain the probable legal position (under English law) of your firm in respect of the above matter, commenting specifically on the following:

   (1)   The possibility of demonstrating your firm was negligent

   (2)   The fact that the inventories figure in the financial statements apparently 'made sense'

   (3)   The fact that you were not informed that the financial statements and your auditor's report were to be used to obtain additional finance

2   Describe the reasonable steps your firm should take to avoid a recurrence of a matter such as that described above.

(Total = 10 marks)

Solution

3 Limiting auditors' liability

The auditing profession is concerned about the extent of their liability to third parties. They argue that although they are required to have insurance, they are unable to get **sufficient** insurance cover to meet the potential level of claims. Also, even if other parties, such as directors, share an element of responsibility for misleading financial statements, audit firms argue that they still bear the burden of giving financial compensation while trying to act in good faith.

3.1 Insurance against losses

> **Professional indemnity insurance (PII):** Insurance against civil claims made by clients and third parties arising from work undertaken by the firm.
>
> **Fidelity guarantee insurance:** Insurance against liability arising through any acts of fraud or dishonesty by any partner, director or employee in respect of money or goods held in trust by the firm.

These types of insurance do not actually restrict the auditor's liability, but rather provide compensation to the auditor for liabilities that are incurred.

It is important that auditors have insurance so that if negligence occurs:

- The audit firm does not find itself with a liability that is **too big** for it to pay; and
- The client can be **compensated** for the error. An insurance policy would enable this to happen, even where the compensation is greater than the resources of the firm.

ACCA requires that all firms which hold practising and auditing certificates have PII with a reputable insurance company (ACCA *Rulebook*: s2.2.9(1)). If the firm has employees, it must also have fidelity guarantee insurance (ACCA *Rulebook*: s2.2.9(1)).

The insurance must cover 'all civil liability incurred in connection with the conduct of the firm's business by the partners, directors or employees' (ACCA *Rulebook*: s2.2.9(2)). The cover must continue to exist for **six years** after a member ceases to engage in public practice (ACCA *Rulebook*: s2.2.9(5)).

Remember that accountants usually trade as **partnerships**, so all the partners are jointly and severally liable to claims made against individual partners. However, insurance could be seen to encourage auditors to take **less care** than they should, knowing that they are covered for any potential liability, so it is not the only way of addressing auditors' liability.

3.2 Managing liability

Auditors may reduce the chances of litigation by ensuring they have good procedures over:

The following courses of action have been put forward as possible methods of reducing liability:

Incorporation

This would protect the partners from personal bankruptcy. However, the firm itself could be forced into liquidation. Further, there could be adverse tax implications and the firm would need to publish accounts and be subject to an audit, which might be unacceptable to partners. Despite these issues, many of the world's largest professional firms have incorporated in some way.

Limited Liability Partnerships (LLPs)

The Limited Liability Partnership Act 2000 enabled UK firms to establish limited liability partnerships as separate legal entities. These combine the flexibility and tax status of a partnership with limited liability for members.

The effect of this is that **the partnership, but not its members, will be liable to third parties**. However, the personal assets of **negligent** partners will still be at risk.

Several prominent professional partnerships are incorporated as LLPs.

Limited liability partnerships are set up by similar procedures to those for incorporating a company. An incorporation document is sent to the Registrar of Companies. The Registrar will issue a certificate of incorporation to confirm that all statutory requirements have been fulfilled.

In a similar way to traditional partnerships, relations between partners will be governed by internal partner agreements, or by future statutory regulations. Each member of the partnership will still be an agent of the partnership, unless they have no authority to act and an outside party is aware of this lack of authority.

Liability limitations

Even with PII and other means of restricting liability, there has been great concern throughout the audit profession globally about the remaining risks to firms' survival in the face of claims which still might exceed their insurance cover. One protection against these is to control the liability itself via agreements between auditors and their clients.

KEY TERM

Proportionate liability: Allows claims arising from successful negligence claims to be split between the auditors and the directors of the client company, the split being determined by a judge on the basis of where the fault was seen to lie. This would require the approval of shareholders.

Capping liability: Sets a maximum limit on the amount that the auditor would have to pay out under any claim.

Essential reading

See Chapter 3 of the Essential reading for more detail on the advantages and disadvantages of different structures for firms to adopt.

The Essential reading is available as an Appendix of the digital edition of the Workbook.

4 The expectation gap

KEY TERM

Expectation gap: This term is used to describe the difference between the expectations of those who rely upon auditor's reports concerning audit work performed and the actual work performed.

The expectation gap arises due to a general **misunderstanding** by the **public** of the respective **responsibilities of both management** and the auditor, and a **misunderstanding** of the **scope of an audit**. Such misunderstandings might include the following perceptions:

That it is the auditor's duty to prevent and detect fraud

That the auditor is liable for any errors in the financial statements

Clearly, there is still a **debate** to be had and the continuing occurrence of financial **scandals** where fraud was present, despite an audit being conducted, means that this debate is not about to go away. Logically, the expectations gap could be narrowed in two ways.

(a) **Educating users**

The auditor's report, as outlined in ISA (UK) 700 *Forming an Opinion and Reporting on Financial Statements*, now includes an explanation of both the auditor's and management's responsibilities, but also quite extensive discussions of the key matters arising from the audit.

Additionally, the audit firm will reiterate the respective responsibilities of management and the auditor, and the nature, scope and purpose of an audit, in the **engagement letter**.

(b) **Extending the auditor's responsibilities**

Research indicates that extra work by auditors, with the inevitable extra costs, is **likely to make little difference to the detection of fraud** because:

- Most material frauds involve management
- More than half of frauds involve misstated financial reporting but do not include diversion of funds from the company
- Management fraud is unlikely to be found in a financial statement audit
- Far more is spent on investigating and prosecuting fraud in a company than on its audit

Suggestions for expanding the auditor's role have included:

- Requiring auditors to **report** to boards and audit committees on the adequacy of controls to prevent and detect **fraud**
- Encouraging the use of **targeted forensic fraud reviews** (see Chapter 14)
- **Increasing** the requirement to report **suspected frauds**

However, the adoption (in the UK for example) of **caps on auditors' liability** has been seen as a **retrograde step in 'building bridges'** between the audit profession and those members of the public who remain sceptical of the auditor's benefits to society and their apparent reluctance to stop future Enron-style scandals.

In an attempt to redress the balance following audit firm **Andersen's** involvement in the **Enron** collapse, the **UK Companies Act 2006** includes an **offence** aimed at punishing audit firms that knowingly or recklessly cause an auditor's report to be misleading, false or deceptive. Committing such an offence would lead to a fine.

The many different forms of assurance report that we will see in AAA all seem full of **disclaimers** that appear to protect the auditor and reduce the amount of reliance that users can place on these reports. However, without any protection from **potentially unscrupulous clients**, auditors are continually exposed to the threat of liability and without protection, auditors would not consider accepting any such engagement. If this were to happen, who would perform the audit?

Chapter summary

Fraud and professional liability

ISA (UK) 240 (revised) *The Auditor's Responsibilities Relating to Fraud in an Audit of Financial Statements*

Definitions
- An **intentional** act involving the use of deception to obtain an unjust or illegal advantage
- Two main types:
  - Fraudulent financial reporting (eg Enron)
  - Misappropriation of assets (eg security guard stealing from warehouse)

Responsibilities
- **Primary** responsibility for prevention and detection rests with management
- Auditor should obtain **reasonable assurance** that the F/S are free from material misstatement whether caused by fraud or error

Audit approach
- Act with professional scepticism
- Assess risks due to fraud
- Fraud risk factors
  - An incentive or pressure to commit fraud (motive)
  - Opportunity to commit fraud
  - Ability to rationalise such actions (dishonesty)
- Respond to risk at F/S level (assignment and supervision; accounting policies; introduce unpredictability; reviewing nature, timing and extent of audit procedures)
- Respond to risk at assertion level (sensitive controls; journals; estimates; significant transactions)
- Reporting or withdrawing if necessary

Auditors' liability

Principles
- Duty of care exists
- Duty of care was breached
- Loss arose from that breach
- Not too remote

The client
Following auditing standards will support automatic duty of reasonable care to clients

Third parties
Not guaranteed but may be present from situations in the scenario – need to know case law

Disclaimers
- Bannerman connection
- Need to be used if felt it will protect auditor's liability
- Discouraged by ACCA as seen to devalue the auditor's report

Limiting auditors' liability

Insurance against losses
- Professional indemnity insurance (PII) for civil claims from clients and 3rd parties
- Fidelity guarantee insurance (FGI) for losses due to fraud by firm employees

Managing liability
- Avoid litigation by performing quality audits
- Incorporation
- Limited liability Partnerships (LLPs)
- Proportionate and capping liability (UK CA 2006)

The expectation gap
- Due to misunderstanding of auditor's responsibilities
- Educate users – auditor's report wording seeks to close the expectation gap
- Extend auditor's responsibilities
- Caps vs 'reckless knowledge' offence

 BPP

Knowledge diagnostic

1. Fraud

Fraud is a risk that auditors must be aware of. However, the primary **responsibility** for prevention and detection lies with the **directors** of the entity. Auditors have a variety of issues to consider when fraud is either discovered or suspected and should act appropriately.

2. Professional liability

Auditors take a considerable risk when signing the auditor's report, since many third parties rely on the opinion given. If the opinion is proven to have been negligently provided, the **auditor** may be **liable** for financial losses suffered. This leads to the risk of **litigation**.

3. Negligence

Case history has determined that auditors are currently only likely to be **liable** to the **client** itself and the **shareholders as a body**. Any other third party would have to demonstrate sufficient **proximity**, and therefore a **duty of care**, to be successful in a claim of negligence.

4. Limiting liability

The profession has taken many steps recently to try to **limit liability** to third parties via **caps**; many major firms have changed their **legal structure** as a result (eg **LLPs** or **limited companies**). All firms hold insurance as part of the requirements for holding a practising certificate: **PII** is mandatory for all ACCA firms alongside **FGI**.

5. Expectation gap

The expectation gap refers to the difference between what the **public perceives** the role of the audit to be and the **actual responsibilities** that the auditor is prepared to accept. This is very contentious.

Further study guidance

Question practice

Now try the following from the Further question practice bank (available in the digital edition of the Workbook):

- Question 4 'Professional responsibilities' is an opportunity to display your overall knowledge of the auditor's responsibilities in the areas covered by this chapter.
- Question 5 'Mobile Sales' is approaching exam standard and tests how well you can apply this knowledge to a scenario.

Further reading

There are technical articles on the ACCA website written by members of the AAA examining team which are relevant to some of the topics covered in this chapter that you should read:

- *Auditor liability*
- *Professional scepticism*

www.accaglobal.com/africa/en/student/exam-support-resources/professional-exams-study-resources/p7/technical-articles.html

Own research

Consider your own organisation or one that you are familiar with – what can you learn from the following to help you with topics from this chapter:

- Consider the current 'width' that you believe the expectations gap is currently at – is it getting wider or narrower? Do you think recent corporate failures (for example, such as BHS and Carillion in the UK) are helping the auditor's case that they are doing as much as they can?
- Can you find an example of an auditor's report that includes a disclaimer paragraph?
- Find some examples of frauds online and see if you can determine what caused them – if you had been the external auditor in each case, what might you have done to try and uncover the fraud yourself?

Activity answers

Activity 1: Moorland

Approach

While based on an exam-standard question, this activity is really all about seeing how well you can apply your knowledge of liability issues to a specific set of circumstances. Use the Essential reading (available in the digital edition of the Workbook) to refresh your knowledge if required and consider how each requirement is testing the various factors associated with liability.

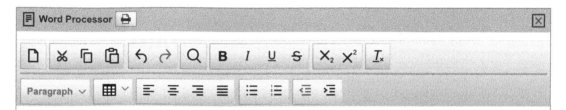

Suggested solution

There were a number of interesting developments in the area of auditors' liability to third parties in the 1980s and 1990s. The most significant recent case decision is the Caparo case (1990).

Prior to the Caparo case, the position was that auditors' liability depended on a qualified test of reasonable foresight, that is to say, liability depended on a principle whereby negligent accountants owed a duty of care to those who can be foreseen as likely to sustain damage if carelessness exists. However, this came with the important qualification that any prospective plaintiff, to succeed in their action, must establish that it was reasonable in the circumstances for them to rely on the audited accounts.

However, the Caparo case narrowed those who can successfully sue the auditors for negligence to the company or the shareholders as a group. It is unlikely that an individual shareholder will be able to successfully sue an auditor. However, the case has not yet been tested in the UK courts.

The possibility of demonstrating negligence

It is worth noting the comments of the UK's Auditing Practices Committee at the time (now the Financial Reporting Council), in the preface to the auditing standards and guidelines on the relationship of standards and guidelines to the law:

Members are advised that a court of law may, when considering the adequacy of the work of an auditor, take into account any pronouncements or publications which it thinks may be indicative of good practice. Auditing standards and guidelines are likely to be so regarded.

The Littlejohn case demonstrated this principle: following auditing standards and documenting the approach is a good defence against possible third-party action.

In the case of Moorland, the auditors seem to have laid themselves open to a possible charge of negligence in that they did not observe the company's physical inventory counting procedures as recommended by ISA (UK) 501 Audit Evidence – Specific Considerations for Selected Items. Much would depend on whether or not the auditors could satisfy the court as to whether there were good practical reasons for non-attendance and the other audit work which they carried out in relation to inventories provided sufficient, relevant and reliable audit evidence on which to base the audit opinion.

The fact that the inventories figure in the financial statements apparently 'made sense'

This seems to suggest that the main audit evidence on which the auditors based their opinion, in relation to the inventories figure, was the result of analytical review work in this area. As the auditors seem, through pressure of work, to have neglected to attend the inventory count, then one would expect them to have carried out more extensive analytical review procedures than would perhaps normally have been the case for that client. If it appeared that the auditors had only carried out a minimal amount of review tests, then they would be very likely to be open to a charge of negligence.

The fact that the auditor was not informed that the financial statements and auditor's report were to be used to obtain additional finance

If the person who provided the unsecured long-term loan to Moorland were to be able to recover damages against the auditors, then the court would need to be satisfied, on the evidence before it, that:

1. The auditors had been negligent;

2. The third party had suffered loss in consequence of that negligence on the part of the auditors; and

3. The auditors should reasonably have foreseen that the third party might wish to place reliance on the audited accounts.

As a result of the Caparo case, it would appear that the third party would not succeed in an action against the company: the plaintiff would need to prove that the auditors knew that the financial statements would be used specifically to obtain finance from this third party, which is not the case here.

However, this can only be decided by the courts.

Reasonable steps your firm should take to avoid recurrence

From the above it may be seen that the issue of auditor's liability will always be dependent on the facts of an individual case. However, there are steps that any firm of auditors/accountants should take to minimise the risk of successful litigation against them on the part of clients and/or third parties. Such steps would include:

1. Adhering at all times to International Standards on Auditing relevant to the client

2. Adequate training of all audit staff to ensure that they are fully aware of how the audit procedures considered necessary by the firm are to be carried out

3. Ensuring that there are adequate review procedures which are constantly applied within the firm to see that laid-down standards are being properly applied in practice

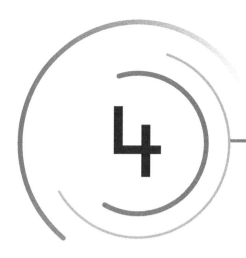

Quality management

Learning objectives

On completion of this chapter, you should be able to:

	Syllabus reference no.
Explain the principles and purpose of quality management of audit and other assurance engagements.	C1(a)
Describe the elements of a system of quality management relevant to a given firm.	C1(b)
Evaluate the firm's system of quality management (SoQM) and whether this is effective in the proactive prevention and identification of deficiencies.	C1(c)

Business and exam context

The role performed by auditors represents an activity of significant public interest. Quality independent audit is crucial, both to users and to the audit profession as a whole. Poor audit quality damages the reputation of the firm and may lead to loss of clients and thus fees, as well as an increased risk of litigation and associated professional insurance costs.

Although there are specific standards giving guidance on how auditors should perform their work with satisfactory quality, these can never cater for every situation. Quality at a general level is dealt with by ISQM (UK) 1 *Quality Management for Firms that Perform Audits or Reviews of Financial Statements, or Other Assurance or Related Services Engagements.*

The UK version of ISQM (UK) 1 provides more detail on the types of engagement that a firm operating in compliance with ISQM (UK) 1 might undertake, including those where the FRC has issued guidance (for example, audits using ISAs (UK), investment circulars and reviews of interim financial information).

Issues relating to firm-wide quality management link best with professional and ethical considerations and should be distinguished from quality management issues on an individual audit, which are more likely to be examined at the completion stage (Chapter 10) under ISA (UK) 220 (Revised).

You could be asked to suggest quality management procedures that a firm should implement in specific circumstances, or to review a firm's procedures and assess their adequacy. Firm-wide quality management can be tested in either Section A or Section B.

Chapter overview

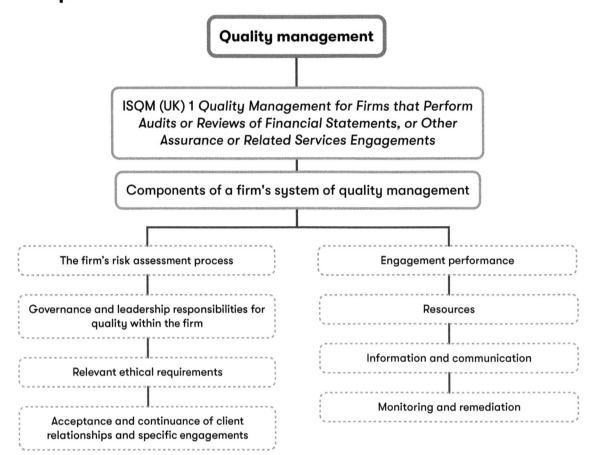

1 ISQM (UK) 1 Quality Management for Firms that Perform Audits or Reviews of Financial Statements, or Other Assurance or Related Services Engagements

Activity 1: Does quality matter?

Quality management is a key issue for all audit firms. Why do firms want or need good quality management?

Solution

---

2 Components of a firm's system of quality management

The firm's system of quality management shall include policies and procedures addressing each of the following components:

(a) The firm's risk assessment process

(b) Governance and leadership

(c) Relevant ethical requirements

(d) Acceptance and continuance of client relationships and specific engagements

(e) Engagement performance

(f) Resources

(g) Information and communication

(h) The monitoring and remediation process

(ISQM (UK) 1: para. 6)

In the UK, firms are expected under ISQM (UK) 1 to adopt strong internal control policies and procedures that support quality (ISQM (UK) 1: para 19-1).

Essential reading

The FRC has published non-authoritative guidance on how auditors can improve their professional judgement by means of a framework that is designed to demonstrate best practice in this area. Given the number of standards that require the adoption of suitable levels of professional judgement, this is relevant throughout all stages of the engagement but should be considered at this point in the context of building professional judgement into a firm's system of quality management. You can find an overview of this FRC guidance within Chapter 4 of the Essential reading.

The Essential reading is available as an Appendix of the digital edition of the Workbook.

2.1 The firm's risk assessment process

ISQM (UK) 1 para. 23 explains the risk assessment process undertaken by the firm for managing quality, which is broadly similar to the way that risk is assessed and managed within any entity:

- Quality objectives are established in relation to each of the components in the system of quality management
- Quality risks that jeopardise the achievement of these objectives are then identified and assessed
- Responses that address each of these quality risks are designed and implemented, usually leading to policies and procedures that make up the system of quality management

The **quality objectives** adopted by the firm shall not only include those from ISQM (UK) 1 but also any that the firm feels are necessary for the achievement of the objectives of its system of quality management.

When identifying suitable **quality risks**, the firm shall consider anything that could adversely affect the achievement of these quality objectives, including:

- Those relating to the nature and circumstances of the **firm** (such as complexity, leadership style, resources and ownership)
- Those relating to the nature and circumstances of the **engagements performed by the firm** (such as the type of engagement, the type of entity and the reports required)

In some cases, **other risks** that are not immediately considered to be quality risks may still affect quality objectives; for example, the firm may be pursuing a business strategy where its financial goals are driven by providing services to clients that are not within the scope of the quality management standard. This might mean that the firm's resources are prioritised for these services, leading to a negative impact on the quality of engagements that are included under ISQM (UK) 1. As a result, the process of risk assessment needs to be thorough enough to consider all appropriate risks (this is one such example of **scalability**: risk assessment will vary depending on the structure and organisation of the firm).

Responses are then developed on the assessment of each risk and suitable policies and procedures are implemented. Should additional information be identified in relation to quality objectives, risks or responses as a result of this process, suitable action shall be taken (either to amend those already assessed or to assess new risks). (ISQM (UK) 1: paras. 23-27, A39, A46)

We will cover responses in the context of each of the remaining elements of the system of quality management, but ISQM (UK) 1: para. 34 lists some **specific responses** that require the following policies and procedures:

- Identifying and addressing both threats to, and breaches of, the relevant **ethical requirements**
- Annual confirmation that personnel comply with **independence requirements**
- Resolution of any complaints or allegations about any **non-compliance with laws, regulations** or firm **policies and procedures**
- Managing information about **relationships with clients** that becomes known once the engagement has been accepted
- Communication protocols with **external parties** (such as confirming with those charged with governance for a listed entity that the firm's system of quality management has contributed to a quality audit)
- The identification of those engagements that require an **engagement quality review** under ISQM (UK) 2 *Engagement Quality Reviews* (we will cover this in more detail in the section on engagement performance)

2.2 Governance and leadership

The firm shall design, implement and operate a system of quality management, exercising the application of professional judgement. This is achieved by the allocation of **specific responsibilities for quality management** among certain members of staff:

- **Ultimate responsibility** and accountability for quality management rests with the firm's chief executive officer, managing partner or managing board of partners, whichever is most applicable

- **Operational responsibilities** are assigned to separate personnel, including specific aspects that include compliance with independence and remediation and monitoring

It is expected that all roles are assigned to individuals who possess appropriate levels of experience, knowledge, influence and authority, that they understand their role and are accountable for fulfilling it, and that they are given sufficient time to fulfil their responsibility. In the UK, firms that perform audits shall ensure that at least one individual who is eligible to perform the role of statutory auditor is assigned both ultimate and operational responsibility for the firm's system of quality management (ISQM (UK) 1: paras.20-22).

Quality management is not considered a separate function of the firm: it is considered to be a **cultural factor** that combines all aspects of the firm's strategy, activities and processes into a commitment to quality that runs through the whole firm (ISQM (UK) 1: para. A30).

The firm shall establish quality objectives that address governance and leadership and which support the system of quality management through a **culture** that recognises and enforces the following:

- The importance of quality as part of the firm's role to serve the public interest
- The importance of ethics, values and attitudes
- The perception that quality is the responsibility of all personnel in the firm
- The importance of quality within the firm's strategic, financial and operational priorities (the standard goes on to say that resources, including financial resources, should be deployed in order to support the system of quality management in the firm, reinforcing the fact that quality is integral to the firm's DNA)

(ISQM (UK) 1: para. 28)

Note. In the UK, the term **key audit partner** is used to indicate the individual assigned overall responsibility for carrying out the statutory audit on behalf of the firm. It is a term that is defined in UK legislation and so is separate from engagement partners of other non-audit engagements, but in terms of the overall responsibility for quality on an engagement, the meaning is the same.

2.3 Relevant ethical requirements

The firm shall establish quality objectives designed to provide it with reasonable assurance that the firm and its personnel both **understand** and **fulfil their responsibilities** in relation to the relevant ethical requirements that apply to the firm (as covered in Chapter 2).

The firm's quality objectives should emphasise the fundamental principles of the IESBA Code of Ethics (or others, such as the FRC's Revised Ethical Standard in the UK for example). The standard also explains that it may be possible for the firm's system of quality management to go beyond the provisions of the relevant ethical guidance – for example:

- Accepting all gifts and hospitality, no matter what their value or significance, is prohibited
- Rotation requirements on certain engagements may extend beyond the engagement partner and include senior engagement team members

(ISQM (UK) 1: paras. 29, A63)

In the UK, there are other ethical matters that need to be addressed: the UK version of the standard prohibits the appointment of anyone to an engagement where it would create a threat to independence and objectivity and requires a process for dealing with both actual and potential incidents of an ethical nature (ISQM (UK) 1: paras. 34-1(a) and (b)).

2.4 Acceptance and continuance of client relationships and specific engagements

The firm shall establish quality objectives for the acceptance and continuance of client relationships and specific engagements that address the following points:

- Information obtained about the integrity and ethical values of the client, their management and, where appropriate, those charged with governance, supports the judgement to accept or continue that engagement (this could include factors such as the client's expectations of low fees or an indication that they may be indications of money laundering)

- Other information about the nature of the engagement may affect the decision to accept or continue, for example, if it is an integrated report requiring specialist expertise
- The firm is able to perform the engagement in accordance with applicable laws, regulations and professional standards (such as whether the firm possesses appropriate levels of resource and expertise, the need for additional expertise or technology and whether an engagement quality review will be required)
- Acceptance and continuance decisions are not based purely on financial or operational priorities

In the UK, there are more specific requirements that reinforce the need for compliance with the **FRC Ethical Standard** during acceptance and continuance, including the provision of appropriate information to the incoming auditor after ceasing to hold office.

The final point on financial and operational priorities makes quite interesting reading and the supporting information from ISQM (UK) 1 is a reflection of the real-world issues facing professional firms today. It may suit the firm's business strategy or support the firm's profitability targets to accept or continue a specific engagement, but if the client lacks integrity, the engagement should not be accepted or continued. Should a fee be set which is below what the engagement would likely cost to perform, that would affect the firm's ability to adhere to professional standards, which would also compromise quality. ISQM (UK) 1 evidently expects firms to consider quality management in a holistic manner.

(ISQM (UK) 1: paras. 30, 34-1(c)-(e), A67-74)

2.5 Engagement performance

The firm shall establish the following quality objectives that address the performance of quality engagements:

- All members of the engagement team (including the engagement partner) understand and fulfil their responsibilities for managing and achieving quality on the engagement
- Direction, supervision and review responsibilities are allocated and performed appropriate to the engagement and the resources made available
- Appropriate levels of professional judgement and scepticism are displayed
- Consultation on difficult or contentious matters is undertaken and suitable responses implemented
- Differences of opinion between engagement personnel and any others involved in the engagement (for example, the engagement quality reviewer) are addressed satisfactorily by the firm
- Engagement documentation is promptly assembled, maintained and retained in line with laws, regulations, professional and ethical requirements (ISQM (UK) 1: para 31)

2.5.1 ISQM (UK) 2 *Engagement Quality Reviews*

Engagement quality reviews have been mentioned in the context of the firm's risk assessment process for identifying specific responses to quality risks. Let's confirm the **definition** of an engagement quality review by reference to the standard, ISQM (UK) 2 *Engagement Quality Reviews*:

'An engagement quality review is an objective evaluation of the significant judgments made by the engagement team and the conclusions reached thereon. The engagement quality reviewer's evaluation of significant judgments is performed in the context of professional standards and applicable legal and regulatory requirements. However, an engagement quality review is not intended to be an evaluation of whether the entire engagement complies with professional standards and applicable legal and regulatory requirements, or with the firm's policies or procedures.'

ISQM (UK) 2 contains a scalability point: 'The engagement quality reviewer's procedures would likely be less extensive for engagements involving fewer significant judgments made by the engagement team'.

(ISQM (UK) 2: paras. 4, 8)

ISQM (UK) 2 has one **objective** that explains what the standard is designed to support:

'The objective of the firm, through appointing an eligible engagement quality reviewer, is to perform an objective evaluation of the significant judgments made by the engagement team and the conclusions reached thereon.'

(ISQM (UK) 2: para. 12)

Engagement quality reviews are required by law or regulation for the following **engagements** (ISQM (UK) 1: paras. 34(f), A133):

- Listed or public interest entities

- In the UK, certain types of investments might also be subject to an engagement quality review (including those carried out under the Standards of Investment Reporting or where client assets need to comply with standards laid down by the Financial Conduct Authority)

- Entities that operate in the public sector or who receive government funding or have public accountability

- Entities that operate in certain industries (including financial, such as banking, insurance or pension funds)

- Entities that meet a specified asset threshold or which are under some form of judicial control (such as liquidation)

Engagement quality reviews are also required in situations where it is considered that it would be a suitable response to one or more quality risks (ISQM (UK) 1: para. A134). Engagements that would fall into this category include:

- Those in an industry displaying high levels of complexity, skill or judgement, such as a mining entity or an entity experiencing going concern problems

- Engagements experiencing issues such as significant deficiencies in internal control or material restatements of comparative information in the financial statements

- Engagements where acceptance and continuance procedures have been unusual (such as a disagreement with a previous auditor)

- Entities in emerging industries, those in communication with a regulator and any others that have a public interest aspect to them

The objective of ISQM (UK) 2 mentions an **eligible engagement quality reviewer** so let's consider who that might be. The standard explains that the individual shall possess competence and capabilities, including sufficient time, and the appropriate authority to perform the engagement quality review but that they shall also comply with relevant ethical requirements (such as a two-year cooling-off period between serving as engagement partner and assuming the role of engagement quality reviewer). In the UK, the engagement quality reviewer for audits of public interest entities must be of sufficient calibre to be able to be appointed as statutory auditor, nut obviously not be appointed to that audit! (ISQM (UK) 2: paras. 17-19).

The **performance** of the engagement quality review will occur throughout the engagement and will follow policies and procedures agreed by the firm that include the following:

- Obtaining an understanding of the information shared between the firm and the engagement team about the conduct of the engagement as part of monitoring and remediation procedures

- Discussions with the engagement partner and others in the engagement team about the significant matters and significant judgements made while planning, performing and reporting on the engagement

- Review of selected documentation related to significant judgements made by the engagement team for evidence of professional scepticism, consistency with the conclusion reached and whether suitable conclusions have been drawn

- Evaluation that independence requirements have been fulfilled and appropriate consultation on difficult or contentious decisions has taken place (in the UK, the engagement quality reviewer must also evaluate compliance with relevant ethical requirements, especially if non-audit services are performed for an audit client, conclude on the appropriateness of safeguards used and assess the appropriateness of the engagement partner's documentation of these ethical matters)

- Reports and underlying subject matter have been reviewed

- For audit engagements, an evaluation of whether the engagement partner's involvement has been sufficient and appropriate

The engagement partner is **precluded** from dating the engagement report until notification has been received from the engagement quality reviewer that the engagement quality review is complete.

The UK version of the standard also requires that for audits of **public interest entities**, the firm shall ensure that engagement quality reviews have been conducted in line with ISQM (UK) 1, that all key audit partners agree with the outcome of the review and that a mechanism for resolving disagreements exists.

However, should there be **concerns** that significant judgements made by the engagement team or conclusions based thereon are inappropriate, the engagement quality reviewer will inform the engagement partner of this and expect their concerns to be resolved. If they remain **unresolved**, the engagement quality reviewer will notify an appropriate individual in the firm that the engagement quality review cannot be completed. In some instances, this may require consultation with an external party (such as a regulator or professional body).

Finally, in the UK, **engagement quality reviews of public interest entity audits** should consider the following:

- The firm's independence from the audited entity
- How the key audit partner(s) identified and managed significant risks relevant to the audit
- The reasoning used by the key audit partners in areas such as risk assessment and materiality
- The appropriateness of the use of any external expertise
- Any corrected and uncorrected misstatements in the financial statements identified during the course of the audit
- Discussions with outside parties (such as audit committees or regulators)
- Whether the audit documentation supports the proposed audit opinion

The engagement quality reviewer will discuss all these matters with the key audit partners (including any that are relevant to components in the context of a **group audit**).

Documentation related to the engagement quality review shall also record all the results and conclusions of their review, including information obtained from the key audit partner(s) relevant to their own judgements and conclusions, including the draft opinion expressed under their reporting responsibilities.

(ISQM (UK) 2: paras. 24-27, 30-1-2)

2.6 Resources

'The firm shall establish ... quality objectives that address appropriately obtaining, developing, using, maintaining, allocating and assigning resources in a timely manner to enable the design, implementation and operation of the system of quality management.' (ISQM (UK) 1: para. 32)

The resources that the firm will have at its disposal include the following:

- Human resources
- Technological resources
- Intellectual resources
- Service providers

Let's focus on **human resources** first, as there are many quality objectives that apply to all personnel who are assigned to work on an engagement, including those that relate to competence, capabilities, knowledge and experience. Personnel are also required to demonstrate their commitment to quality through their actions and are to be held accountable through various mechanisms such as evaluation, compensation, promotion and other incentives (although, should personnel's behaviour adversely affect quality, suitable responses might have an impact on these same mechanisms, or consist of training or even disciplinary action). Personnel should be given sufficient time to perform in line with the expectations of the firm's system of quality management. Should the firm have insufficient human resource, they may source it from outside of the firm, provided they possess the appropriate level of capabilities and competence.

In the UK, the appointment of the key audit partner for any audit of financial statements must recognise their importance in adhering to quality standards, plus their independence and competence. The firm must also ensure that the key audit partner is actively involved in the audit (ISQM (UK) 1: paras. 34-1(j)-(k)).

Activity 2: Capabilities and competence

List examples of appropriate quality management procedures to ensure the firm's personnel have the necessary capabilities and competence.

Solution

2.6.1 Technological and intellectual resources

According to ISQM (UK) 1: para. 32(f) and (g) appropriate technological and intellectual resources are obtained or developed, implemented, maintained, and used, to enable the operation of the firm's system of quality management and the performance of engagements.

We need to understand what these resources actually mean in order to understand the policies and procedures that the firm needs to put in place to address the necessary quality objectives.

Activity 3: Technological and intellectual resources

What do you think technological and intellectual resources are and how do they form part of the operation of the firm's system of quality management and the performance of engagements?

Solution

2.6.2 Service providers

It is possible that the firm may decide to source human, technological and intellectual resources from a service provider, usually due to possessing inadequate levels of these resources. However, the responsibility for maintaining appropriate levels of quality when such external resources are used remains with the firm using these resources.

Examples of the types of resources available from a service provider:

- Individuals providing monitoring, review or technical consultation services

- Commercial IT applications used in certain engagements
- Individuals performing procedures on an engagement, such as a component auditor or someone working on an inventory count in a remote location
- An expert used by the auditor

Just like any other risk to achieving audit quality, the firm needs to evaluate the potential impact of using a service provider. This will include consideration of the nature of the work itself and the extent that it will be relied upon by the firm, often by reference to other sources of information such as the service provider's experience and reputation, how up to date their methodology is and the security of any IT applications used.

2.7 Information and communication

'The firm shall establish ... quality objectives that address obtaining, generating or using information regarding the system of quality management, and communicating information within the firm and to external parties on a timely basis to enable the design, implementation and operation of the system of quality management' (ISQM (UK) 1: para. 33).

The standard relates to the way that technology works and its critical role in the system of quality management, plus it also has some cultural aspects to it:

- How IT systems support the system of quality management with information for decision-making that is accurate, complete, timely and valid
- How personnel use and share information within the firm (this includes how the firm informs personnel about changes to the systems of quality management that they need to know)
- Information that is both relevant and reliable to the delivery of quality flows appropriately from the firm to the engagement teams and back again (including any changes to the client that personnel need to know)
- Communication with network firms is appropriate to allow the fulfilment of their responsibilities (this might consist of understanding the independence requirements of a particular engagement)
- Confidentiality permitting, information is communicated externally when required by law, regulation or professional standards (such as in cases of suspected non-compliance) or to support external parties' understanding of the system of quality management

We have seen the terms **network** and **network firms** used in this chapter. These terms need to be defined to make sure you understand the impact that networks can have on the firm's system of quality management.

2.7.1 Networks

ISQM (UK) 1: para. 16 contains the following definitions:

- **Network** – a larger structure that is aimed at cooperation and that is clearly aimed at profit or cost-sharing or shares common ownership, control or management, common quality management policies or procedures, common business strategy, the use of a common brand name, or a significant part of professional resources
- **Network firm** – a firm or entity that belongs to the firm's network

The term **network services** is also relevant here as it describes the use by the firm of services provided to them by another network firm.

The standard expects that the system of quality management adopted by the network (and consequently adopted by all associated network firms) complies with the requirements of ISQM (UK) 1.

2.8 Monitoring and remediation

The firm shall establish a monitoring and remediation process to:

- Provide relevant, reliable and timely information about the design, implementation and operation of the system of quality management
- Take appropriate actions to respond to identified deficiencies such that deficiencies are remediated on a timely basis

In the UK, for audits of financial statements, the firm shall monitor and evaluate the adequacy and effectiveness of the firm's systems, internal quality control mechanisms and arrangements established in accordance with ISQM (UK) 1 and take appropriate measures to address any deficiencies (ISQM (UK) 1: para. 35).

The **monitoring process** is designed to identify **deficiencies** in the system of quality management and will consider issues such as risk, change, previous monitoring activities and complaints or allegations about quality failures when determining the nature, timing and extent of its monitoring activities. The standard states that this process should facilitate the **proactive and continual improvement of engagement quality** and the system of quality management.

The monitoring process will focus on completed engagements and consider other monitoring activities when deciding on which engagements to select (however, this will include at least one completed engagement for each engagement partner, selected on a cyclical basis). Other factors, such as listed entities, those in emerging industries and the experience of engagement partners, may also be relevant in selecting engagements for monitoring.

Those individuals performing this monitoring activity should have sufficient competence, capability and time to perform the activity effectively and not be part of the engagement team under inspection. The information needs of the monitoring and remediation process may vary depending on the complexity of the firm.

(ISQM (UK) 1: paras. 37-39, A138, A144, A151)

Where the monitoring process identifies deficiencies in an engagement, the firm needs to understand their severity and pervasiveness. This will require investigation of the frequency of any deficiencies, any root causes and their effect on the firm's system of quality management.

Remedial actions will then be designed and implemented such that the deficiency is addressed.

Should the process of monitoring identify engagements where procedures required by laws, regulations or professional standards were not completed or the auditor's report issued was inappropriate, the firm must take appropriate action to comply with the necessary deficiency and consider the implications for the firm, including whether to obtain legal advice.

(ISQM (UK) 1: paras. 40-45, A163)

The outputs of any monitoring and remediation are communicated to the individual with overall responsibility and accountability for the firm's system of quality management. Engagement teams are also informed of matters arising from this process in order to ensure they adhere to the firm's system of quality management.

(ISQM (UK) 1: paras. 46-47)

Evaluating the System of Quality Management

The individual with overall responsibility and accountability for the firm's system of quality management is required to undertake an **annual evaluation of the system**. This evaluation is designed to conclude one of the following:

- Reasonable assurance that the objectives of the system of quality management are being achieved;

- Deficiencies that have a severe but not pervasive effect on the design, implementation and operation of the system of quality management exist, but otherwise, reasonable assurance that the objectives of the system are being achieved; or

- The system of quality management does not provide reasonable assurance that the firm's quality objectives are being achieved

Should either of the last two options apply, the firm needs to take **prompt and appropriate action** and **communicate** these conclusions to engagement teams and external parties as required.

The difference between severe and pervasive is down to judgement, but in general, pervasiveness is displayed when deficiencies:

- affect several parts of the system of quality management;

- are confined to one part but have a fundamental effect on the system of quality management;

- affect several locations or functions of the firm;

- are confined to one location or function but have a fundamental effect on that location or function; or

- affects a substantial portion of engagements of a specific type or nature.

The individuals with overall responsibility and accountability for, and operational responsibility for, the firm's system of quality management should be subject to a periodic **performance evaluation.**

(ISQM (UK) 1: paras. 53-56, A192)

Documentation

Within the UK, ISQM (UK) 1 requires the retention of all documentation that demonstrates the firm's compliance with both the standard and any other legal requirements. Factors that should be included in the documentation for **audits of financial statements:**

- Compliance with relevant ethical requirements and any threats to the firm's independence

- The appropriateness of personnel appointed to the engagement (including the suitability of the key audit partner) and whether the right time and resources have been deployed

- Key details of any audits carried out (such as the entity's name and address, the identity of the kay audit partner(s) and the fees charged)

- Records of any complaints against the firm and how any breaches of standards, laws or regulations have been addressed

An annual report of any measures that should be taken to address these matters should be created and shared internally. Documentation should be retained for a period of time that satisfies all legal and regulatory requirements, but as a minimum, this should be at least six years after the date of the auditor's report (ISQM (UK) 1: paras. 58-1, 60-1).

Activity 4: VBMC

Varley, Bell, Murphy and Cobbitt (VBMC) is a small four-partner independent audit firm with a single office in a regional location. Clients include businesses and companies mainly in the retail and financial services industries. Two of the firm's biggest clients are listed. VBMC operates in a regime which has adopted IAASB audit, assurance, quality management and ethical standards as its national standards.

Leadership for quality within the firm

The firm considers quality management very important and endeavours to comply with international guidance. Mickey Murphy is the partner in charge of quality. He is also Marketing Partner of the firm due to his commercial awareness. There is no specific quality management department, but Mickey gives an annual update on the firm's quality management procedures in August when he is not busy.

Annual quality reviews of audits are not undertaken due to the firm's size: the partners are in daily contact and discuss quality at their monthly meetings. However, as part of Mickey's annual marketing review of clients, he identifies any clients perceived as risky due to their size or the firm's dependence on them.

Human resources

New joiners to the firm are generally accounting graduates from the local university to minimise training costs. They all attend final interviews with the Senior Partner, Roger Varley. Selection is based on their exam marks, the ability to speak fluent English, presentation and confidence. Annual appraisals of all professional staff are conducted by the Senior Partner. He feels that the firm which, although growing, is still small enough to appraise staff personally.

Promotion is based on a 'balanced scorecard' of four criteria:

- Marketing events attended

- Completion of audit work on time

- Feedback from clients (based on an assessment after each audit)

- Punctuality of arrival in the mornings (staff should arrive by 8am, but can leave once their work is complete)

Audit process

All audit work is reviewed by the auditor in charge (AIC) before presentation of the files to the engagement partner. The AIC highlights the key risk areas for the partner to perform a second review on. Files are created and delivered for review entirely electronically. Due to the firm's scanning facility being oversubscribed, less important physical evidence is discarded at the end of the audit. The firm is too small to have industry units, so clients are spread across the four partners based on their location.

Technical matters

An ethical helpdesk is staffed by one of the partners, Janine Bell (when she's in the office), who is respected in the firm for her technical knowledge. Staff are encouraged to seek help where they consider it appropriate. All audit staff are provided annually with a memory stick containing PDFs of the latest IFAC Pronouncements for reference while conducting audits. Any necessary 'library' data – exchange rates, share prices etc – are obtained directly by audit staff from the internet. Technical issues are resolved by the engagement partner on the relevant audit.

Required

Identify and comment on the quality management issues arising from the scenario.   **(10 marks)**

Solution

Chapter summary

```
┌─────────────────────────────┐
│     Quality management      │
└─────────────────────────────┘
              │
┌─────────────────────────────────────────┐
│ ISQM (UK) 1 *Quality Management for Firms that Perform* │
│ *Audits or Reviews of Financial Statements, or Other*  │
│ *Assurance or Related Services Engagements*            │
└─────────────────────────────────────────┘
              │
┌─────────────────────────────────────────┐
│ Components of a firm's system of quality management │
└─────────────────────────────────────────┘
```

The firm's risk assessment process

- Manages the link between quality objectives, risks to their achievement and appropriate responses
- Quality risks are driven by factors relating to both the firm and its engagements

Governance and leadership responsibilities for quality within the firm

- Assign management responsibility so that commercial considerations do not override quality
- Ultimate responsibility for quality from senior management down
- Quality to be a cultural factor within the firm

Relevant ethical requirements

- Firm's policy shall emphasise the fundamental principles:
  - Leadership
  - Education & Training
  - Monitoring
  - Dealing with non-compliance
- Annual confirmation by staff of independence compliance

Acceptance and continuance of client relationships and specific engagements

- Consider:
  - Integrity of client
  - Firm's ability to perform the engagement in accordance with applicable laws, regulations and professional standards
  - Firm's ethical compliance

Engagement performance

- All engagement personnel understand their responsibilities for quality
- Direction, supervision and review, plus suitable application of professional judgement and scepticism
- Policies and procedures on consultation, differences of opinion and documentation
- Engagement quality reviews of appropriateness of significant judgements and conclusions for listed and other risky entities undertaken by suitable individual as per ISQM (UK) 2 *Engagement Quality Reviews*

Resources

- Firms shall ensure they have sufficient personnel with the capabilities, competence and commitment to ethical principles
- Technological resources (eg data analytics software) and intellectual resources (eg methodologies for undertaking certain types of engagement)
- Service providers who may provide human, technological or intellectual resources for the firm

Information and communication

- The use of suitable information technology to allow communication within the firm to support appropriate levels of quality
- Any networks, network firms or networks services must also comply with ISQM (UK) 1

Monitoring and remediation

- Aim is to ensure that professional standards have been adhered to and that quality management systems have worked
- 'Cold ("post-issuance") reviews' carried out to identify any deficiencies in the firm's system of quality management once the audit is completed

Knowledge diagnostic

1. Principles of quality for firms

Quality management is a **fundamental issue** for all audit firms. The main source of guidance for firms in relation to quality management comes from **ISQM (UK) 1** which details the specific components of a system of quality management for a **professional firm** to adopt. **Engagement quality reviews** are supported by **ISQM (UK) 2**.

2. Quality management elements

Sound systems of quality include the following:

- The firm's **risk assessment process**
- **Governance and leadership** responsibilities for quality within the firm
- **Ethical requirements** including any independence issues
- **Acceptance and continuance** of client relationships and specific engagements
- **Resources** including the assignment of personnel to engagements, technological and intellectual resources and the use of service providers
- **Engagement performance** including procedures over adequate consultation if required and specific quality reviews
- **Information and communication** within and without the firm
- **Monitoring** to ensure compliance with the standard and **remediation** if necessary

Further study guidance

Question practice

Now try the following from the Further question practice bank (available in the digital edition of the Workbook):

- Question 6 'Osbourne plc' tests how well you have remembered quality management from AA and that you can apply the theory to an applied scenario.

Further reading

There are technical articles on the ACCA website written by members of the AAA examining team which are relevant to some of the topics covered in this chapter that you should read:

- *International Standards on Quality Management - part 1 (ISQM 1)*
- *International Standards on Quality Management - part 2 (ISQM 2 and ISA 220 (Revised))*

You may find it helpful to read alongside the article on 'Professional scepticism' as this supports the importance of quality auditing.

Own research

If you want to understand the way that regulators are attempting to enhance the quality of audit, you could research this using resources available where you are studying – for example:

- In the UK, the FRC undertakes a series of quality inspections which you may find of use: www.frc.org.uk/auditors/audit-quality-review/thematic-inspections
- The IAASB also regularly consults on quality issues: www.iaasb.org/focus-areas/focus-audit-quality

Activity answers

Activity 1: Does quality matter?

> **Approach**
>
> This is a brief discussion question – remember that you could always be asked for something like this in the exam, so you need to have something to say about everything! The introduction of a new suite of quality management standards (including ISQM (UK) 1) in 2021 does make this a topical current issue.

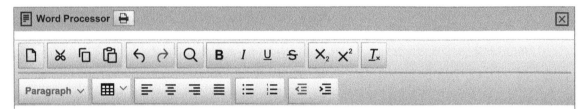

During 2021, the IAASB adopted a new suite of quality standards and introduced us to a new term: quality management. While it sounds like it's the same as quality control (which you might have learned about in your previous studies), it is actually a response to the ongoing issues surrounding audit quality and the failure of high-profile clients. A system of quality management is designed to be continual and iterative, but not necessarily linear, and should proactively manage the risks of poor quality as the firm and its engagements change over time (ISQM (UK) 1: paras 6-7). So why do firms want or need it then? We can answer this by reference to ISQM (UK) 1 (which explains the need) and a few other points (more related to what firms want):

- To provide reasonable assurance that the firm and its personnel fulfil their responsibilities in accordance with professional standards and applicable legal and regulatory requirements and conduct engagements in accordance with such standards and requirements (ISQM (UK) 1: para. 14a)

- To provide reasonable assurance that engagement reports issued by the firm or engagement partners are appropriate in the circumstances (ISQM (UK) 1: para. 14b)

- To protect the reputation of the firm

- To protect the reputation of the profession (ie to narrow the expectation gap) as part of working to serve the public interest (ISQM (UK) 1: para.15)

- To reduce the risk of legal action against the firm for negligence

> **Tutorial note.** It is worth noting that not every firm will require the same type of quality management systems as described in the standard; ISQM (UK) 1 para. A29 cites the example of a sole practitioner where assigning roles and undertaking direction, supervision and review activities may not be relevant. This concept of scalability (in other words, a response that is appropriate under the circumstances) is revisited often within ISQM (UK) 1 – the key message is to proactively manage those risks that lead to poor audit quality.

Activity 2: Capabilities and competence

> **Approach**
>
> Sometimes the answer is just what the standard says – get used to being able to summarise some of the key elements of each one – fortunately in this case, much of this is common sense.

Suggested solution

ISQM (UK) 1: paras. A88-89 define competence as 'the ability of the individual to perform a role and goes beyond knowledge of principles, standards, concepts, facts, and procedures; it is the integration and application of technical competence, professional skills, and professional ethics, values and attitudes. Competence can be developed through a variety of methods, including professional education, continuing professional development, training, work experience or coaching of less experienced engagement team members by more experienced engagement team members.

'Law, regulation or professional standards may establish requirements addressing competence and capabilities, such as requirements for the professional licensing of engagement partners, including requirements regarding their professional education and continuing professional development.'

Summarising this in a list might deliver the following quality management procedures which the firm could focus on:

- Use **technical knowledge** obtained from accounting studies and continuing professional development (CPD)
- Refer to **training** which has been obtained from the employer (both current and any previous)
- Consult **ethical guidance** available by the employer (both internal and from ACCA)
- Reflect on **work experience** from current and previous employment
- Support staff via **coaching** (and being coached) within the engagement team
- Confirm **accreditation** required in order to meet the competence and capabilities required by legal, professional or other standards

Activity 3: Technological and intellectual resources

> **Approach**
>
> You can probably take a guess at this, and in some instances, you would be right. However, there are other areas that are included in these categories that you need to know about, hence the reason why they have been flagged for inclusion in this activity. As with any such task, you need to think of the context: what resources might the firm use on an engagement that isn't a human resource? Why might those resources be required?

Suggested solution

Technology will typically include information technology (IT) environment, usually consisting of IT applications that operate within an IT infrastructure and that are supported by specific IT processes. Here are some examples of these terms:

- IT applications might include data analytics software or packages that monitor independence
- IT infrastructure usually includes the hardware and software on a network
- IT processes include controls (both IT and human) that manage access, updates, security or development of the IT environment

Not all technology used within the firm will be connected to the system of quality management, but those that are will include resources such as those described above which are essential in either the delivery or performance of an engagement or to support that delivery or performance.

The nature of any technology used may vary depending on the complexity of the firm (in other words, the standard assumes that technology needs will be scalable) so smaller firms may operate 'off the shelf' IT solutions while larger firms might create their own 'bespoke' applications, infrastructure and processes.

Examples of **intellectual resources** from the standard: 'Written policies or procedures, a methodology, industry or subject matter-specific guides, accounting guides, standardized documentation or access to information sources (e.g., subscriptions to websites that provide in-depth information about entities or other information that is typically used in the performance of engagements)'.

 BPP

Access to intellectual resources could require certain technological resources: for example, the firm may have a specific audit methodology that is operated for planning and performance purposes that runs on a specific IT application. The firm must allow for adequate levels of resource to exist to allow them to support the work done on the engagement and ensure all personnel have adequate levels of access and training.

Any system of quality management is set up to ensure that the firm follows laws, regulations and professional and ethical standards when producing their reports for an engagement. Technology allows access to faster and more efficient processing of data, while intellectual resources support personnel with both information and approach to plan and perform engagements in line with policies and procedures that deliver quality.

(ISQM (UK) 1: paras. A98-104)

Activity 4: VBMC

> **Approach**
>
> From a quick read of the scenario, it appears that VBMC do not take quality as seriously as ISQMs (UK) 1 and 2 require, so you have plenty to write about here! The good news is that when this is tested in the exam, quality management and other professional issues frequently appear as described here (clearly wrong). However, the challenge is to present your assessment by explaining why they are wrong in the context of ISQMs (UK) 1 and 2. You can assume at least one mark for each well-explained point, so you should have come up with at least ten points – fortunately, that would not have been a struggle here!

Suggested solution

- There is no evidence of any **risk assessment process** for quality management being conducted at the firm. Indeed, it is questionable whether a system of quality management that reflects ISQM (UK) 1 exists at the firm.

- Mickey's role as Marketing Partner, managing the growth of the business, is in direct conflict with his role as Quality Partner – it should be allocated to one of the other partners. This goes against the **governance and leadership** aspects of ISQM (UK) 1.

- It is also possible that this conflict of interests between Mickey's commercial and ethical roles might obstruct the necessary **acceptance and continuance** procedures that the firm should have in place – there is no mention of any screening procedures for determining client integrity or to ascertain the availability of time and resources for any of the firm's engagements.

- The approach to quality updates is inadequate to meet ISQM (UK) 1's **resources** requirements; a more formalised programme is needed. Training should be conducted at a time when staff are not likely to be on holiday (or on alternative dates).

- Ongoing **monitoring and remediation** of compliance with the firm's system of quality management is required but the necessary inspections do not appear to be present. The partner cannot argue that the firm is too small if working under IAASB standards. Indeed, an engagement quality review for the firm's two listed clients is required before the auditor's report can be issued.

- New joiners should be trained in the firm's **resources** principles and methodology. The firm cannot rely on their university degree.

- It is not sufficient to provide staff with standards on a memory stick. Typically, a staff manual would be produced, backed up by training and updates (the potential issues with regard to data confidentiality and cyber security may also not be compliant under the **information and communication** aspects of ISQM (UK) 1).

- In addition to the above points on **resources**, the appraisal criteria are not consistent with quality management objectives; for example, a 'quality' audit may overrun due to investigation of emerging issues.

- The review process undertaken as part of **engagement performance** is inadequate to ensure quality. Areas undertaken by the AIC not highlighted as important would not be reviewed by anyone. Typically, a manager review would cover the AIC's work and a second review of work undertaken by more junior staff.

- Documentation is key to quality when assessing **engagement performance**. Audit evidence required to support the file should not be destroyed.

- Allocation of audits to partners based on location does not foster quality. Industry units may not be practical in a small firm, but the retail and financial clients could be divided between the partners to develop specialisms (and foster efficiency). This approach to **resources** is a particular concern for the financial services clients which are subject to complex regulation, which could open up VBMC to liability if not suitably competent and experienced with the requirements of such work.

- Facilities should be available for technical consultation when assessing **engagement performance** (beyond simply ethical issues) both within and outside the firm. A facility for second opinions should be put into place between the partners. Consultation would be better allocated to a technical manager (or group of staff) to make them more accessible to audit team members.

- Additionally, **ethical** compliance should not be left to members of staff. At least annually, written confirmation of independence is required from professional staff by ISQM (UK) 1 to ensure there are no individual conflicts of interest (such as shareholdings or other connections).

- Data can be obtained from the internet, but staff should be provided with guidance as to where to source data from (**information and communication**) to ensure accuracy and consistency of approach during **engagement performance**.

Skills checkpoint 1

Analysis and evaluation

Chapter overview

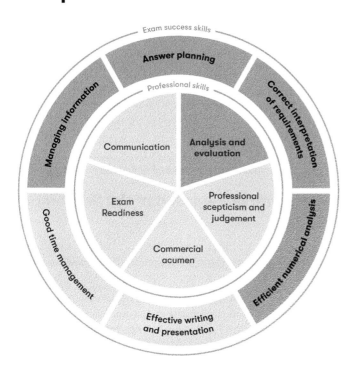

Skills checkpoint 1 – Analysis and evaluation

'Analysis and evaluation' is one of the four professional skills that have been introduced by ACCA into the AAA exam. This professional skill will be examined in Section A of the exam as part of the compulsory 50-mark question which will test all four of the professional skills for 10 marks in total. This professional skill will also be examined in Section B, which consists of two compulsory scenario-based 25-mark questions, each of which allocates five marks to professional skills.

Each Section B question will contain a minimum of two professional skills: 'analysis and evaluation' plus 'professional scepticism and judgement' and/or 'commercial acumen'. Section B questions will state which of these professional skills are being tested. No professional skill will ever be worth more than five marks in a question.

Syllabus learning outcomes

This is how the AAA syllabus expects candidates to demonstrate the professional skill of 'analysis and evaluation':

- Investigate relevant information from a range of sources, using appropriate analytical techniques to establish reasons and causes of issues, connections between different sources of information and to determine significant risks and appropriate responses.

- Consider information, evidence and findings carefully, reflecting on their implications and how they impact the engagement, audit firm or audit client.
- Assess and apply appropriate judgement when considering ethical and professional issues, audit matters and when making conclusions or recommendations, taking into account the implications of such decisions on the audit firm, engagement and audit client.
- Appraise information objectively, in order to effectively prioritise audit issues, explore suitable audit responses and when making decisions, devising courses of action or determining audit conclusions.

How to demonstrate professional skill in 'analysis and evaluation'

How could you demonstrate 'analysis and evaluation' when attempting the Specimen exam?

In Question 1, the marks for this professional skill came from appropriate use of relevant information to determine suitable calculations and to support balanced discussions and draw appropriate conclusions, including effective prioritisation and consideration of the impact of contradictory or unusual events.

This continued in Questions 2 and 3 where the professional skills marks for 'analysis and evaluation' were awarded for appropriate appraisal of information in the scenario, including the identification of any omissions, using examples where relevant to support overall comments, draw appropriate conclusions and make suitable recommendations for appropriate courses of action.

How were 'analysis and evaluation' marks awarded in the September 2022 exam?

This was the **first time** that the exam was split into 80 technical marks and 20 professional skills marks. From an analysis of the solutions and the examining team's feedback, the following **additional points** should be noted:

- In **Question 1**, both business risks and risk of material misstatement were required, but only those that were considered **significant** and for risks of material misstatement, they also needed to be **prioritised**, which the solutions stated should have been in terms of their **magnitude** and **likelihood**.
- In order to **prioritise** these risks, candidates needed to **calculate a materiality threshold** to **quantify magnitude.** (This will be discussed in Skills Checkpoint 3 as it is considered part of demonstrating skill in 'professional scepticism and judgement'.)
- Once a threshold was set, answers needed to **demonstrate this prioritisation** somehow, either by their **positioning** within candidates' answers or via a **conclusion paragraph** within the briefing notes. (It is unlikely that there will ever be only one right answer in such cases, so as long as you can justify your decisions on which risks are prioritised, you should be given credit.)

What can you do to demonstrate 'analysis and evaluation' when answering other questions?

It is vital that you read the data in the scenario and then consider the requirements of the question in that context. All too often, candidates read the requirements and then produce an answer to the question they think has been asked or the question they think they can answer, not the actual question itself. The **process** of analysing and evaluating the data in the scenario (including all the **Exhibits**) and the requirement should help you lock down what you are going to put in your answer.

Here is a screenshot from Question 1 of the AAA exam:

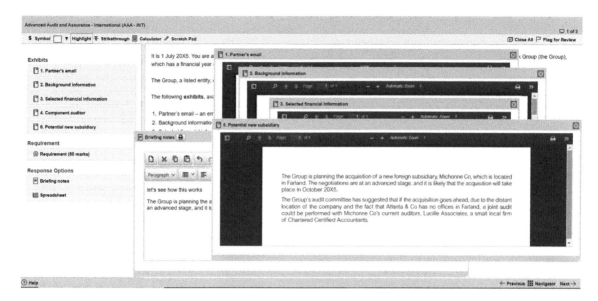

For you to demonstrate 'analysis and evaluation' you will need to make sure that you have read the requirement and understood what it is asking you to do. In the screenshot above, you will need to open Exhibit 1 to access the instructions so you know what you are being asked to produce and then use the remaining Exhibits to analyse the rest of the scenario, including the financial data provided in Exhibit 3. To help you perform 'analysis and evaluation' there is also a **spreadsheet** response option which will allow you to perform calculations such as trends, ratios and materiality using the data in Exhibit 3.

You should start to familiarise yourself with the CBE software as soon as possible using the ACCA's Practice Platform where you will find a number of questions that are presented in the same CBE software as the real AAA exam. Attempting questions will also help you practise the exam success skills of **managing information, correct interpretation of requirements** and **efficient numerical analysis.**

'Analysis and evaluation' are also an important part of **answer planning,** another one of the six exam success skills. In order to help you tailor your answer to include the correct number of points to address the requirement, a form of 'scaffolding' to construct an answer plan might help when you are performing your analysis and evaluation.

Let's consider a recent exam question.

For each of the three matters described above:

(a) **Explain the matters which should be discussed with management in relation to each of the uncorrected misstatements, and**

(b) **Assuming that management does not adjust the misstatements identified, evaluate the effect of each on the audit opinion.**

Note. The total marks will be split equally between each matter.   **(15 marks)**

With 195 minutes to find 100 marks, that works out as 1.95 minutes per mark, meaning this 15-mark requirement should take no more than 29 minutes in total. Assuming that we want to spend 20% of this time on our plan, that would mean six minutes for reading, thinking and planning, leaving you 23 minutes to type your answer. What will you need to produce for each of the three matters mentioned in the requirement?

	(1) Matters to be discussed	**(2) Effect on the opinion**	**Marks for each matter**
Matter 1	1) 2) 3)	1) 2) 3)	5 marks
Matter 2	1)	1)	5 marks

	(1) Matters to be discussed	(2) Effect on the opinion	Marks for each matter
	2) 3)	2) 3)	
Matter 3	1) 2) 3)	1) 2) 3)	5 marks

During your six minutes of reading, thinking and planning time, you should devise something like this and use it as a form of scaffolding to support your answer. We are told in the requirement that the 15 marks are split equally between the three matters, so each should score 5 marks, and for each matter, there are two tasks: (1) the matters to be considered and (2) the impact on the audit opinion. In general, well-explained points score 1 mark, so to score 5 marks for each matter, you will need two or three points for each task. By filling in as many of the gaps in the middle two columns of the scaffolding above as you can, you are giving yourself the best chance of tailoring your answer to the requirements.

This approach may seem like a lot to do in only six minutes, but it should help you make the most of your valuable reading, thinking and planning time.

Skills practice

To help you develop your use of the professional skill 'analysis and evaluation' you should attempt Question 6 'Osbourne plc' from the 'Further question practice' section at the back of the digital edition of the Workbook. It is a question that tests quality management and requires an evaluation of the issues facing the firm, the engagement and the client in a scenario.

You should also attempt Question 32 'Grissom Group' which reflects how Question 1 in the AAA exam will look. As it covers all of the professional skills and technical content up to and including group audits, you may wish to leave this question until you have covered all chapters in the Workbook.

 BPP

Obtaining and accepting professional appointments

Learning objectives

On completion of this chapter, you should be able to:

	Syllabus reference no.
Evaluate the appropriateness of publicity material including the use of the ACCA logo and reference to fees.	C2(a)
Outline the determinants of fee-setting and justify the bases on which fees and commissions may and may not be charged for services.	C2(b)
Discuss the ethical and other professional problems, for example, lowballing, involved in establishing and negotiating fees for a specified assignment.	C2(c)
Recognise and explain the matters to be considered prior to tendering for an audit or other professional engagement and explain the information to be included in the proposal.	C2(d)
Explain the professional and ethical matters to be considered and the procedures that an audit firm/professional accountant should carry out before accepting a specified new client/engagement or continuing with an existing engagement, including: (a) Client acceptance (b) Engagement acceptance (new and existing engagements) (c) Establish whether the preconditions for an audit are present (d) Agreeing the terms of engagement	C3(a)
Recognise the key issues that underlie the agreement of the scope and terms of an engagement with a client.	C3(b)

Business and exam context

It is a commercial fact that companies change their auditors. The question that firms of auditors need to understand the answer to is 'Why do companies change their auditors?' We shall examine some of the common reasons here.

Related to the fact that entities change their auditors is the fact that many auditing firms advertise their services. ACCA has set out rules for professional accountants who advertise their services which we shall also examine.

The audit fee can be a key consideration for an entity when it makes decisions about its auditors. Determining the price to offer to potential clients can be difficult, but it is just one part of the whole process that is tendering. Audits are often put out to tender by companies. We shall examine all the matters firms consider when tendering for an audit.

Linked in with tendering is the process of determining whether to accept the audit engagement if it is offered. ISQM (UK) 1 *Quality Management for Firms that Perform Audits or Reviews of Financial Statements, or Other Assurance or Related Services Engagements* sets out some basic requirements for all audit firms accepting engagements. Finally, ISA (UK) 210 *Agreeing the Terms of Audit Engagements* sets out the agreement necessary when an audit is accepted.

Many of the issues in this chapter are ethical. You could be faced with a change in auditor scenario in the exam. The issues surrounding a change in auditor have often been examined in the past, with scenarios featuring tendering and practical issues around audit planning. This area could be examined in either Section A or Section B.

Chapter overview

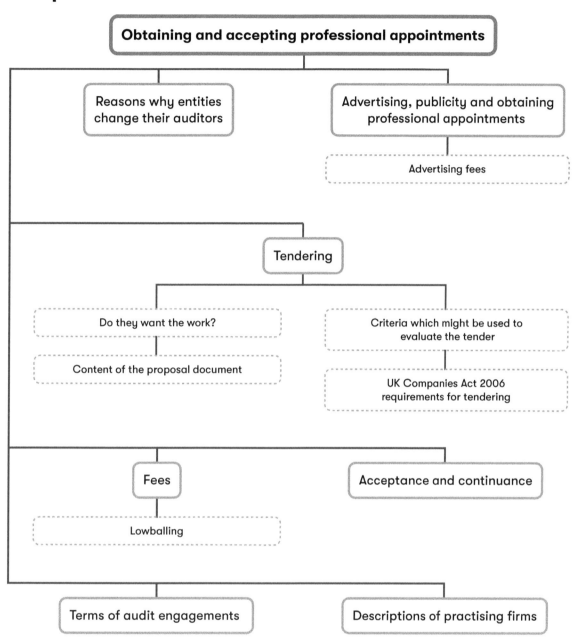

1 Reasons why entities change their auditors

The focus of this topic is on issues surrounding the change of auditors by an entity. It is important that you are aware of the circumstances that may lead to a need for the auditors to be replaced.

Activity 1: Changing auditors

Can you think of reasons why an entity may need to replace its auditors?

Solution

2 Advertising, publicity and obtaining professional appointments

Audit firms are allowed to advertise. The ACCA Code states that any advertisements or promotional material shall not reflect adversely on the professional accountant, ACCA or the accountancy profession (Section B13 para. 1).

Advertisements and promotional material should not:

- Bring ACCA into **disrepute** or bring **discredit** to the professional accountant, firm or the accountancy profession;
- **Discredit** the **services** offered by others whether by claiming superiority for the professional accountant's or firm's own services or otherwise;
- Be **misleading**, either directly or by implication; and
- **Fall short of any local regulatory or legislative requirements**, such as the requirements of the United Kingdom Advertising Standards Authority's Code of Advertising and Sales Promotion, notably as to legality, decency, clarity, honesty and truthfulness.

(ACCA Code: Section B13 para. 2)

2.1 Advertising fees

It is difficult to explain the service represented by a single fee in the context of an advertisement and **confusion may arise as to what a potential client might expect to receive in return for that fee** (ACCA Code: Section B13 para. 5). This means that it is risky for an accountant to refer to fees in advertising.

In longer advertisements, where reference is made to fees in promotional material, the **basis** on which those fees are calculated (hourly and other charging rates etc) **should be clearly stated** (ACCA Code: Section B13 para. 4).

The key issue to remember with regard to advertising fees is that the **greatest care should be taken not to mislead potential clients, particularly if comparing fees with those of competitors** (ACCA Code: Section B13 para. 6). Any reference to fees must be **factual**, and the accountant **must be able to justify it**. It should not make 'unflattering' references to competitors (ACCA Code: Section B13 para. 10). It is appropriate to advertise free consultations to discuss fee issues (ACCA Code: Section B13 para. 9). This free consultation will allow fees to be explained, thus avoiding the risk of confusion.

We will look at how firms should set their fees in Section 4.

3 Tendering

A firm puts together a tender either in response to an **open invitation to tender** or if it has been **approached** by a prospective client and the partners have decided that they are capable of doing the work for a reasonable fee.

When an audit firm is approached by a prospective client, the first question it has to ask itself is whether or not it wants the work.

3.1 Do they want the work?

The **risk** attaching to the client must be considered. The audit firm would wish to consider the following:

Why has the approach arisen – first year of audit or a desire to change auditors?	What the future plans of the entity are – growth, survival, change etc?	What the client requires from the audit firm (for example, audit, number of visits, tax work?)
Can the firm afford to spend time on the proposal?	Does the proposed timetable for the work fit with the current work plan?	Does the firm have suitable personnel available?
Where will the work be performed and is it accessible/cost effective?	Are (non-accounting) specialist skills necessary?	Will staff need further training to do the work and if so, what is the cost of that further training?

Activity 2: Risks from prospective clients

What work would you perform in order to assess the risk attached to a prospective client?

Solution

3.2 Content of the proposal document

Assuming a firm is happy that it can manage the risks discussed above, the basic format of the tender proposal will depend on the **circumstances** and the **prospective client's requirements**. The principal objective is to convince the client to appoint the audit firm. The firm will therefore want to demonstrate that it has **understood** the **unique** features and requirements of the business and has considered how best it can **meet** those.

The following matters will usually need to be covered:

- The fee and details of how it has been calculated (discussed in Section 4)

- An assessment of the requirements of the prospective client
- An outline of how the firm proposes to address those requirements for the fee
- The assumptions made, for example, regarding deadlines or availability of information
- The proposed approach to the engagement
- An outline of the firm and the staff involved

If the tender is being submitted to an **existing client**, some of those details will be unnecessary. However, if it is a competitive tender, the firm should ensure they submit a comparable tender, even if some of the details are already known to the client. This is because the tender must be **comparable** to competitors and must appear professional.

3.3 Criteria which might be used to evaluate the tender

Academic research has shown that proposals are often won on the quality of service offered, value for money and the chemistry with the client, rather than simply on fees. The following criteria are likely to be used by prospective clients to evaluate the tender.

- Location
- Personal knowledge of the partners and staff
- Prior experience of the industry or of a similar sized business
- Matching the service offered to the specific needs of the business
- Communication, including prior agreement of the impact on fees before any additional work is undertaken
- The development of an effective relationship between the client and the key members of the audit teams

3.4 UK Companies Act 2006 requirements for tendering

As an **example**, the UK Companies Act 2006 requires some companies to put the audit out to tender after ten years, with mandatory rotation after 20 years.

The tender will not always result in a change in auditor – it is possible that the current auditor will win the tender. But it means that management will have to consider whether the audit meets its needs, as discussed above.

Under the UK Companies Act 2006, for a quoted (listed) company, an auditor must always submit a **statement of circumstances** when they cease to be auditor, even where there are no matters which the auditor believes should be brought to the attention of members or creditors (Companies Act 2006: s.519).

In the case of a **private company** (or an **unlisted** public company), the auditor does not need to submit a statement if they are leaving because their term of office has come to an end. If they are leaving before this, then a statement must be submitted, unless the reasons for leaving are 'exempt reasons' (eg the auditor is ceasing to practise as an auditor, or the company is now exempt from audit), and there is nothing that needs to be communicated (*Companies Act 2006*: s. 519(1)–(3)).

4 Fees

The ACCA *Code of Ethics and Conduct* states that fees should be '**fair and reasonable**'. They recommend that the basis of charging fees should be mentioned in the engagement letter (para. 330.3 A7).

Fees should not be charged on a **contingency**, **percentage** or similar basis, save where that course of action is generally accepted practice for certain specialised work (ACCA Code: para 330.4 A5). **Commission paid and received** (known as referral fees) as a result of recommendations from and to clients respectively can be accepted, as long as adequate safeguards exist (usually full disclosure will suffice) (ACCA Code: para 330.5 A2).

Fee disputes may arise when the client believes that the fee charged is excessive. If a firm is about to issue a fee note which is higher than previous fees, it is good practice to explain the reasons for the variation to the client concerned (ACCA Code: para 330.7).

Assuming there is no dramatic change in the size or complexity of an audit client, it is reasonable to expect that the audit fee should fall over time. Some reasons why this would be the case are as follows:

(a) Time spent on the audit should reduce as the **auditors' knowledge** of the business improves over time, allowing the work to be completed **more efficiently**.

(b) The **client's systems and procedures** should be **fully documented** in the first year. This is very time consuming; in subsequent years, this information only needs updating if there have been any major changes.

(c) The **first year** of an audit is generally **high risk** due to a lack of knowledge of the business; the firm is likely to respond to this risk by assigning more senior staff to the audit, which will drive the fee up. In **subsequent years**, this **risk should fall** and more junior, and therefore cheaper, staff can be assigned to the audit.

4.1 Lowballing

> **Lowballing:** This refers to the practice of setting the initial audit fee low in order to win the client.

The ACCA's guidance on quotations states that it is **not improper** to secure work by **quoting a lower fee**, so long as the **client has not been misled** about the level of work that the fee represents, and as long as audit quality is not compromised (ACCA 2012: p4 'Fees').

Section 410 of the ACCA Code also discusses fee levels. The **ethical implications** of this practice are:

(a) Because the fee is set low, the audit firm needs to **retain** the client for a number of years in order to recover its initial losses; therefore, independence will be impaired via a **self-interest threat** as the audit firm will not wish to lose the client in the short term.

(b) **Professional competence and due care** may not be applied if the fee is so low that adequate levels of quality management cannot be displayed on the engagement.

(c) This can be seen as unprofessional because it means that **smaller practices** cannot compete.

5 Acceptance and continuance

There are a number of **issues** that auditors should consider when their tender proposal has been accepted by a prospective client:

- Does the firm have the necessary **technical competence** to perform the work?
- Does the firm have **sufficient resources** to perform the work?
- Are there any **ethical or independence issues** if the firm decides to proceed with the work?
- Has the firm considered the risks associated with **new clients**, such as **money laundering** or the potential for them becoming a **Politically Exposed Person**? Such people (known as PEPs) are usually in the public eye and as such become a target for extortion, blackmail or simple human frailties such as corruption – this makes any association with them a possible threat to a firm's reputation.
- Has the auditor obtained **references** for the entity's directors?
- Has the auditor obtained **professional clearance** from the **outgoing auditors**?

    Has the **outgoing auditor** communicated information regarding **NOCLAR** that they are aware of that might affect acceptance by the firm?

- Have the **terms of engagement** (covered in Section 6) been discussed and agreed prior to accepting the appointment?

Note that this list is not exhaustive and that many of these relate to questions asked at the tendering stage.

Why might the firm be offered an engagement that it has submitted a tender for, but then choose not to proceed with the engagement?

Consider this in the context of a **graduate** looking for work – they may submit a number of job applications (like tender proposals) and some of them may lead to interviews and even job offers from prospective employers (like offers of acceptance by the client). However, in the **time** between submission and job offer, **factors may have emerged** that might mean the graduate is less keen to work at this particular employer and if they have a number of options available, the graduate may decide to go with the best one that fits their circumstances at that time.

Essential reading

See Chapter 5 of the Essential reading for more detail on acceptance and continuance procedures. This includes an awareness of the ethical and professional matters required for consideration and the requirements of ISQM (UK) 1.

The Essential reading is available as an Appendix of the digital edition of the Workbook.

Activity 3: Albion and Baggie

Albert Albion and Chris Baggie are partners in a successful firm of certified accountants. Total fee income for the firm is £5 million.

Last year, a branch of the large national firm Anders Arthurson opened up in the same town and since that time, Albion & Baggie Certified Accountants have been losing business.

Albert has therefore launched an advertising campaign, of which he is very proud, to try to win clients away from Anders Arthurson. The campaign has consisted of the following quarter-page advert being placed in the local newspaper every day for three weeks.

ALBION & BAGGIE
CERTIFIED ACCOUNTANTS

Audit fee too high?
Lack of personal service?
Problems with your audit?

Anders Arthurson's service is not as high as their price.

Fixed audit fee of £1,000 for revenue up to £750,000.

CALL US NOW ON 0800 555 H-A-P-P-Y

Albert has also organised a door-to-door leaflet drop, paying his nephew £3.00 to deliver 500 leaflets to local businesses and personal addresses.

Chris has been reviewing outstanding fee income. He has noticed that one of the partnership's clients, Virgo, owned by Dick Branston, has still not paid the previous year's audit fee. Virgo has tendered for a contract to run the National Lottery which has left the company with cash flow problems. Dick and Chris are very good friends; Chris is sure that Dick would not default on the fee.

In reply to the advertising campaign, a lottery company called Rolling Balls has approached Albion & Baggie, requesting the firm to act as its auditor. Rolling Balls is a large company which currently runs the Florida lottery and is also tendering for the National Lottery contract. Albert is immensely excited about this opportunity, as the audit fee is likely to be in the region of £500,000. As well as the audit, Rolling Balls would like Albion & Baggie to supply other services including accounts preparation and compliance monitoring (which would involve ensuring that Rolling Balls is complying with all lottery regulations).

Chris Baggie has two adult daughters, who both work for Albion & Baggie. Sophie, who has worked for the partnership for seven years, has recently taken out a £500,000 mortgage with Midwest bank, which is an audit client of the partnership.

Maggie, Chris's other daughter, has only recently joined the partnership. Up until three months ago, she was the financial accountant at Nibbles Pet Foods, which is also an audit client. Chris feels that Maggie's knowledge of this client will be a great help and is intending to use her as the manager on this year's audit of Nibbles. Maggie's husband Sid owns £100,000 worth of shares in this company.

Required

Comment on the practice management and ethical issues presented by the above scenario.

Solution

6 Terms of audit engagements

ISA (UK) 210 *Agreeing the Terms of Audit Engagements* sets out best practice concerning this issue.

The objective of the auditor is to accept or continue an audit engagement only when the basis on which it is to be performed has been agreed, through:

(a) Establishing whether the **preconditions for an audit** are present, and

(b) Confirming that there is a **common understanding** between the auditor and management and, where appropriate, those charged with governance of the terms of the audit engagement. (ISA (UK) 210: para. 3)

KEY TERM

> **Preconditions for an audit:** The use by management of an acceptable financial reporting framework in the preparation of the financial statements and the agreement of management and, where appropriate, those charged with governance to the premise on which an audit is conducted.
>
> To determine if these preconditions exist, the auditor will assess whether the applicable financial reporting framework is acceptable, ensuring fair presentation of the financial statements, sufficient internal control to address material misstatements due to fraud or error and that the auditor has been provided with access to all the evidence they require for their opinion. (ISA (UK) 210: paras. 4–6)

This will all be confirmed in the **engagement letter**.

Essential reading

See Chapter 5 of the Essential reading for a reminder of the contents of an engagement letter.

The Essential reading is available as an Appendix of the digital edition of the Workbook.

If any of these conditions do not exist (eg the framework used is unacceptable or management does not acknowledge its responsibilities) or those charged with governance impose **a limitation on the scope of the auditor's work** which is likely to result in a disclaimer of opinion, then the auditor should **not accept the engagement**, unless legally required to do so (ISA (UK) 210: para. 7).

In a **recurring or continuing audit**, the auditor must assess whether circumstances have changed so that the engagement terms need to be changed. The auditor must also assess whether the entity needs to be reminded of the existing terms (ISA (UK) 210: para. 13). There is no need to send a new letter for each audit unless there is evidence of misunderstanding by the client.

7 Descriptions of practising firms

Members of the ACCA may be either associates or fellows, in which case they are allowed to use the designatory letters ACCA or FCCA after their names (ACCA Code: Section B4 paras. 5–6).

A firm may describe itself as a firm of 'Chartered Certified Accountants' where:

- At least half the partners are ACCA members
- Those partners hold at least 51% of voting rights under the partnership agreement

(ACCA Code: Section B4 para. 15)

Such a firm may use the ACCA logo on its stationery and website.

A firm which holds a firm's auditing certificate from ACCA may **describe** itself as 'Registered Auditors' and a firm in which all the partners are Chartered Certified Accountants may use the description 'Members of the Association of Chartered Certified Accountants'.

However, a firm must not use this term as part of its **registered practice name** (ACCA Code: Section B4 para. 19) which should be consistent with the dignity of the profession in the sense that it should not project an image inconsistent with that of a professional bound by high ethical and technical standards (ACCA Code: Section B4 para. 32).

Chapter summary

Obtaining and accepting professional appointments

Reasons why entities change their auditors

- Fee is too high or audit is no longer value for money
- Auditor no longer large enough to service a growing client
- Auditor may resign due to not making enough profit or independence issues
- Breakdown in relationship

Advertising, publicity and obtaining professional appointments

- Firms are allowed to advertise...
- ...but should comply with advertising standards and not discredit the work of another member, firm or the profession
- Fees must not be misleading

Advertising fees

Needs to explain fees clearly and what clients will get in return

Tendering

Do they want the work?

- Risks – what could change?
- Enough time and staffing?
- Logistics and expertise?
- Nature of work?
- Why approached?
- Cost effective and deadlines?

Content of the proposal document

- Fee
- Client requirements
- How firm will address requirements
- Assumptions
- Proposed approach
- Outline of firm and staff

Criteria which might be used to evaluate the tender

- Location
- Knowledge of partners and staff
- Prior experience of industry
- Matching service offered to needs of business
- Communication
- Development of effective relationship

UK Companies Act 2006 requirements for tendering

Statement of circumstances

Fees

- Should be fair and reasonable
- Commission OK only if disclosed
- No contingent fees for audits

Lowballing

- Practice of setting the initial fee low in order to win the client
- Not unethical but may affect quality and competition
- Auditor may need to retain the client in subsequent years in order to recover initial losses (self-interest threat)

Acceptance and continuance

- Necessary technical competence?
- Sufficient resources to complete the work?
- Ethical or independence issues?
- Obtained references for entity directors (PEPs?)
- Obtained clearance from outgoing auditors?
- Agreed and discussed the terms of the engagement prior to acceptance?

ISQM (UK) 1 has further details (Essential reading found in the digital edition of this Workbook)

Terms of audit engagements

- Contractual terms and conditions in engagement letter (ISA (UK) 210)
- Pre-conditions for an audit present?

Descriptions of practising firms

At least 50% of partners are ACCA and have at least 51% of voting rights

Knowledge diagnostic

1. Changing auditors

There is nothing unusual about an entity **changing** its **auditors** and there are a number of reasons why it would wish to do so: fees; client fit; rotation due to independence issues; disputes etc.

2. Advertising

Advertising by audit firms is perfectly acceptable; however, firms should be aware of their responsibility to the profession and do nothing to bring it into disrepute.

3. Tendering

Tendering is a very common way for businesses to select auditors and requires the following questions to be considered: do we want the work and can we do it profitably? If so, the content of the tender and how it is likely to be assessed is considered.

4. Fees

Auditors have a professional responsibility to charge **fees** that are fair and reasonable: all things being equal, we can expect audit fees for a client to fall over time. Fees must not be so low to adversely affect audit quality though – this is the practice known as '**lowballing**'.

5. Acceptance

There are a number of considerations the auditor needs to assess before officially **accepting** a new engagement: quality management and professional issues are often the most important.

6. Engagement letters

The terms of audit engagements are agreed and recorded in the **engagement letter** and act as defined terms of reference for both client and auditor, provided the pre-conditions for an audit are present.

7. Practising firms

A firm may only call itself 'certified' if it has **at least half its partners as ACCA members** and those partners own **at least 51%** of the **voting rights** in the firm.

Further study guidance

Question practice

Now try the following from the Further question practice bank (available in the digital edition of the Workbook):

- Question 7 'PLD Associates'
- Question 8 'Scenarios'

Both are excellent practice for applying this knowledge about acceptance and continuance in a scenario-based question – remember to justify your answer with reasons if asked to discuss or comment on anything.

Further reading

At the time of writing, there are no relevant technical articles on the ACCA website for this chapter but you should check regularly to make sure there are no recent additions from the examining team.

Own research

- In the UK, the FRC has conducted research into the current state of the audit market – as an example, you can see how issues you have studied so far interact in the real world by accessing their reports

  www.frc.org.uk/auditors/report-on-developments-in-audit

Activity answers

Activity 1: Changing auditors

> **Approach**
>
> As this is just an idea generation exercise, you should only spend a few minutes thinking about the various reasons that an entity might change its auditor:
>
> - Who might be keen for it to happen?
> - Why might this be?
> - Is it a choice or an obligation?

Suggested solution

- The client may perceive the audit fee to be too high or poor value for money.
- The 'fit' between the auditor and the client may no longer be appropriate. For example, a company experiencing rapid growth may become too large and complex relative to the capabilities of its auditors.
- The audit firm may not seek re-election or resign. This could be for a number of reasons. For example, the auditor may have independence issues with the client or the auditor may have doubts about the integrity of the client staff. There may also be an insurmountable conflict of interest with another client. There may also just be a routine need to rotate or re-tender the audit due to the legal and regulatory framework in place.
- The reason could be due to a breakdown in the working relationship between the auditor and the client; this is especially likely with small clients who value a fairly close relationship with their auditors.

Activity 2: Risks from prospective clients

> **Approach**
>
> This is getting closer to an exam-standard question as it requires some lateral thinking. However, in the exam, you will have to consider this kind of request in the context of a scenario, so consideration of the factors presented will help you generate ideas.

Suggested solution

The following work would be performed in order to assess the risk attached to a prospective client:

- Perform a company search to ascertain shareholders, directors, security granted and whether or not annual returns are filed on a timely basis.
- Consult a credit reference agency to review solvency and consider whether the firm's fees are likely to be paid promptly.
- Review the most recent published financial statements for solvency, adequacy of disclosure and to determine whether or not the accounting policies adopted are acceptable to the firm.

- Examine background information to identify industry-specific problems, issues, legislation and trends.
- Less 'technical' methods such as looking at business and other media or finding out about the company's location and reputation in that area may also be productive.
- The firm may make use of contacts with knowledge of the company to assess its reputation and that of its owners and managers. Useful sources of information may include trade associations and local chambers of commerce.

Activity 3: Albion and Baggie

Approach

You could view this as a progress test as it covers material from previous chapters as well as content on fees and advertising. This is very much exam standard, and so you can start to get into good habits right now:

- Always start with the issue, explaining why it is an issue.
- Justify the issue using the FRC, ACCA or IESBA Code if possible.
- Recommend suitable responses, acknowledging that there may be outstanding information which is required before you can respond.
- Consider the 'bigger picture' of events that could change from what's presented in the scenario, as these may be relevant to the firm's consideration.
- Format your answer using sub-headings and separate paragraphs.

Suggested solution

Advertisement

Albion & Baggie has clearly broken the ACCA's ethical guidance on 'Marketing professional services' (ACCA Code: Section B13 para. 2) by **discrediting** the services offered by another firm.

The **leaflet drop** itself is acceptable as long as it abides by advertising rules – Section B13 paragraph 11 of the ACCA Code states:

'Professional accountants in public practice are reminded that any promotional activity shall be carried out in accordance with any relevant legislation. For example, a professional accountant in public practice shall comply with legislation relating to the making of unsolicited telephone calls or other communication to a non-client with a view to obtaining professional work.'

The **fixed fee** is acceptable. However, fixed fees are not generally wise as the auditor is unable to assess the amount of work required until discussion with the client has taken place - fixed fees may reduce service and quality, if insufficient time can be devoted to the audit and losses may be made if problems occur that cannot be covered by increasing fees. An alternative basis may need to be considered by the firm to maintain quality and manage clients' expectations.

Outstanding fee income from Virgo

The outstanding fee income is similar to **making a loan to a client** – it may create a **self-interest threat** as the firm may choose to ignore issues relevant to the audit until it has received its own overdue fees. IESBA Code para. 410.7 A1 says that you would expect the fee to be settled before the auditor's report is issued, and if fees are overdue and not considered trivial, FRC ES para. 4.11 says that the firm should consider whether to continue; prompt payment should therefore be encouraged.

There is an implied **familiarity threat** to objectivity presented by the friendship between Dick and Chris. However, this is neither immediate nor close family, so could be addressed by applying safeguards such as an independent review of the Virgo audit.

Virgo and Rolling balls

The lottery company tendering for the same contract as Virgo would constitute a **conflict of interest** for the firm if it wishes to act for both clients, as this is a major contract and they are competitors. This could also present confidentiality issues regarding any sensitive information about tenders for either client.

The Rolling Balls appointment could be accepted providing:

- Both parties are informed that you are acting for the other;

- Both parties are in agreement that this situation is acceptable;

- Different audit teams should be used on each audit and information should not be transferred between teams (safeguards such as the use of confidentiality agreements and information barriers would be required); and

- Reviews are carried out by different partners to those involved in each audit.

Rolling balls fee income

The ACCA and IESBA only set fee thresholds for public interest entities (PIEs) and in this case, the threshold is 15% of the firm's total fees for 2 consecutive years (IESBA Code: para. R410.18) before a **self-interest threat** starts to emerge. However, guidance in the UK states that the maximum fee income from any one client should not exceed 15% of gross recurring practice income, but this is reduced to 10% if the company is a listed or other public interest client (FRC ES: paras. 4.23 and 4.24).

The Rolling Balls fee currently only represents 10% of recurring income. However, two issues arise:

(1) We need to determine whether Rolling Balls is a PIE due to being a lottery company and not just because of its size or status; **and**

(2) Other services are required (presumably on a regular basis) which are likely to push the fee percentage closer to 15% for future years.

Although there is no imminent self-interest threat, it is necessary to take extra precautions, such as disclosing this issue to those charged with governance at Rolling Balls and performing an external review of the engagement.

Additional services for Rolling Balls

In addition to the fee limit issue, the auditor should consider:

- The amount of fee generated from Rolling Balls compared to the audit fee could create a **self-interest threat** (ie would Albion & Baggie be inclined to not modify the auditor's report in order to 'please' the client and retain lucrative other services?).

- Whether Albion & Baggie have adequate **resources** and **expertise** required to perform the additional services (for example, do they know enough about lottery regulations?). The fundamental principle of **professional competence and due care** is the key issue here.

Sophie and Maggie

The issue here is close, but not immediate, family connections that could create a **familiarity threat**. The risk is that the auditor may not be willing to issue a modified audit opinion to someone they are closely attached to, either in business or personally.

The issue is **perceived independence** – whether the public would perceive that the auditor has done a 'proper audit' on the financial statements of a party where such a connection exists or whether independence and objectivity have been compromised.

Under the ACCA Code (para. R511.5) there appears to be **no self-interest threat** regarding Sophie's **£500,000 mortgage**, as long as the loan from Midwest is on normal commercial terms.

Maggie cannot be manager on the audit of **Nibbles** until two years have elapsed since leaving the company, otherwise she may be auditing her own work and **no safeguards** could reduce the familiarity, self-interest and self-review threats to acceptable levels.

Despite Sid and Maggie being immediate family members, **Sid's shares** should not present a **self-interest threat** and do not require disposal because she is not to be involved in the audit. However, should Maggie subsequently be involved in the Nibbles audit, then Sid should **dispose** of his shares.

Planning and risk assessment

Learning objectives

On completion of this chapter, you should be able to:

	Syllabus reference no.
Define materiality and performance materiality and demonstrate how it should be applied in financial reporting and auditing.	D1(a)
Discuss and demonstrate the use of analytical procedures in the planning of an assignment.	D1(b)
Evaluate and prioritise business risks, audit risks and risks of material misstatement for a given assignment.	D1(c)
Interpret the results of analytical procedures, in an unbiased manner and apply professional scepticism to support the identification of contradictory information and assessment of risks of material misstatement.	D1(d)
Evaluate the results of planning and risk assessment procedures to determine the relevant audit strategy including the auditor's responses.	D1(e)
Recommend additional information which may be required to effectively carry out a planned engagement or a specific aspect of an engagement.	D2(d)
Discuss the importance of the auditor gaining an understanding of the entity including the applicable financial reporting framework, its accounting policies, its significant classes of transactions, balances and disclosures and the entity's system of internal control and recommend additional information which may be required in gaining that understanding.	D1(g)
Recognise matters that are not relevant to the planning of an assignment.	D1(i)

Business and exam context

The issue of audit planning should not be new to you. You learnt how to plan an audit in your previous auditing studies. Why is this chapter here? There are three key reasons:

- To provide you with a technical update
- To **revise** the details that should be included in an **audit plan** and the general considerations included in planning
- To consider some of the **finer points of planning** from the point of view of the engagement partner, specifically to consider the issue of the **risk associated with the assignment** (which is a personal risk to the partner in the event of litigation arising)

Risk is an important factor in the audit. It falls into two categories:

- Specific **assignment risk** (which could be either audit risk or risk of material misstatement), both of which you have studied previously
- **Business risk** associated with the client, which may form a part of inherent risk and therefore impacts on the audit

Risk is a key issue in an audit, and most auditors take a risk-based approach to auditing.

Section A of the exam will feature a case study set in the context of audit planning, identifying risk areas and planning procedures to audit them. These questions will also draw from other parts of the syllabus (Sections A–D).

Chapter overview

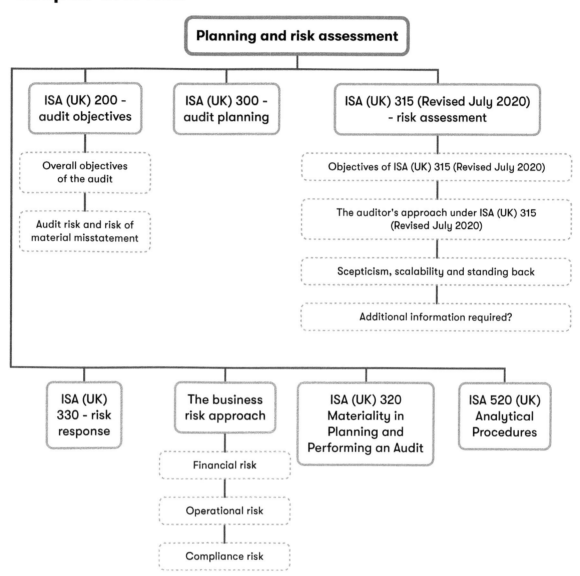

1 ISA (UK) 200 – audit objectives

1.1 Overall objectives of the audit

ISA (UK) 200 *Overall Objectives of the Independent Auditor and the Conduct of an Audit in Accordance with International Standards on Auditing (UK)* states that in conducting an audit of financial statements, the overall objectives of the auditor are:

(a) 'To obtain reasonable assurance about whether the financial statements as a whole are free from material misstatement, whether due to fraud or error, thereby enabling the auditor to express an opinion on whether the financial statements are prepared, in all material respects, in accordance with an applicable financial reporting framework; and

(b) To report on the financial statements, and communicate as required by the ISAs (UK), in accordance with the auditor's findings.' (ISA (UK) 200: para. 11)

ISA (UK) 200 states that the key requirements for the auditor to obtain reasonable assurance and to express an opinion are:

- **Ethics**: Comply with relevant ethical requirements (ISA (UK) 200: para. 14)
- **Professional scepticism**: Plan and perform an audit with professional scepticism, recognising that circumstances may exist that cause the financial statements to be materially misstated. In the UK, auditors are advised to stay alert to such situations regardless of their past experience of the client (ISA (UK) 200: para. 15)
- **Professional judgement**: Exercise professional judgement in planning and performing an audit (ISA (UK) 200: para. 16)
- **Sufficient appropriate audit evidence and audit risk**: Obtain sufficient appropriate audit evidence to **reduce audit risk to an acceptably low level** thereby enabling reasonable conclusions to be drawn by the auditor for their audit opinion (ISA (UK) 200: para. 17)

Managing audit risk allows the auditor to **express an audit opinion** and is therefore central to audit planning and risk assessment.

Essential reading

See Chapter 6 of the Essential reading for more detail on professional scepticism.

The Essential reading is available as an Appendix of the digital edition of the Workbook.

1.2 Audit risk and risk of material misstatement

You will remember this formula from your earlier studies:

> **Formula to learn**
>
> Audit Risk = (Inherent Risk × Control Risk) × Detection Risk

Let's remind you of what each part of the formula relates to, so you know what to look for: you won't be rewarded for stating these definitions in the exam – you only get marks for evaluating specific risks that are relevant to the scenario (ISA (UK) 200: para. 13):

> **Audit risk:** The risk that the **auditor** expresses an **inappropriate opinion** when the financial statements are materially misstated. Audit risk is a function of the **risk of material misstatement** and **detection risk**.
>
> **Risk of material misstatement:** The risk that the **financial statements are materially misstated prior to audit**. This consists of **inherent risk** and **control risk**. For the purposes of the ISAs (UK), a risk of material misstatement exists when there is a reasonable possibility of a misstatement occurring (ie its **likelihood**) and being material if it were to occur (ie its **magnitude**).

> **Inherent risk:** The **susceptibility of an assertion** about a **class of transaction, account balance or disclosure** to a **misstatement** that could be **material**, either individually or when aggregated with other misstatements, before consideration of any related controls.
>
> **Control risk:** The risk that a **misstatement that could occur in an assertion** about a **class of transactions, account balance or disclosure** and that could be **material**, either individually or when aggregated with other misstatements, **will not be prevented, or detected and corrected**, on a timely basis by the entity's controls.
>
> **Detection risk:** The risk that **the procedures performed by the auditor to reduce audit risk to an acceptably low level will not detect a misstatement** that exists and that could be material, either individually or when aggregated with other misstatements.

These are concepts that you will have already met in your earlier studies. However, for AAA, you will need to consider in greater detail the approach that auditors use when meeting their overall objectives regarding audit risk. This requires you to consider the following ISAs (UK):

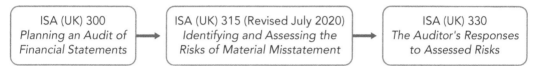

ISA (UK) 300
Planning an Audit of Financial Statements → ISA (UK) 315 (Revised July 2020) *Identifying and Assessing the Risks of Material Misstatement* → ISA (UK) 330 *The Auditor's Responses to Assessed Risks*

2 ISA (UK) 300 – audit planning

The **objective** of ISA (UK) 300 *Planning an Audit of Financial Statements* is to help the auditor **plan the audit** so it will be performed in an **effective manner** (ISA (UK) 300: para. 4). This is done by the adoption of two complementary items:

An **audit strategy** (characteristics of the engagement that define its scope, for example, as well as those factors that might be felt to be significant in carrying out the engagement) which then leads to...

An **audit plan** (more specific risk assessment procedures via ISA 315, responses to such risks via ISA 330 and any other work required to comply with all other relevant ISAs).

The **specific reasons** for planning are to:

Ensure that appropriate attention is devoted to **important areas** of the audit.
Ensure that **potential problems** are identified and resolved on a timely basis.
Ensure that the engagement is **properly organised** and **managed** in order to be performed in an effective and efficient manner.
Assist in the **proper assignment of work** to engagement team members.
Facilitate the **direction, supervision and review** of engagement team members.
Assist in **co-ordination** of work done by auditors of components and experts.

The **nature of the audit** might change during the term of the engagement for a variety of reasons, so all such changes and reasons shall be **documented**. The auditor shall also address as part of planning those ethical issues under ISA (UK) 220 (Revised) *Quality Management for an Audit of Financial Statements* for **initial audit engagements**, such as acceptance and communication with previous auditors.

Planning shall not be a one-off process only carried out at the start of the engagement – it is **iterative** and so the need for any **additional procedures** should be **constantly reviewed**.

PER alert

One of the competencies you require to fulfil **Performance Objective 18** of the PER is the ability to determine the level of audit risk and risk areas, including considering any internal or external information that may have implications for the audit, and to use this to document the audit plan, designing audit programmes and planning audit tests for an internal or external audit. You can apply the knowledge you gain from this chapter of the Workbook to help demonstrate this competency.

Activity 1: Johnson plc

You are the audit manager planning the audit of Johnson plc, a listed multinational food and drinks manufacturer. Johnson has plants all over the world and its head office is based in London.

Required

What general matters would you consider when planning the engagement?

Solution

Essential reading

See Chapter 6 of the Essential reading for more detail on planning documentation and planning an initial audit engagement.

The Essential reading is available as an Appendix of the digital edition of the Workbook.

3 ISA (UK) 315 (Revised July 2020) – risk assessment

3.1 Objectives of ISA (UK) 315 (Revised July 2020)

The **objective** of the auditor from ISA (UK) 315 (Revised July 2020) *Identifying and Assessing the Risks of Material Misstatement* is to **identify** and **assess** the **risks of material misstatement**, whether due to **fraud** or **error**, at the **financial statement** and **assertion levels**, thereby providing a basis for designing and implementing **responses** to the assessed risks of material misstatement (ISA (UK) 315 (Revised July 2020): para. 11).

3.1.1 Risks of material misstatement at the financial statement level

These risks relate to the **entire financial statements** and could affect **many assertions**. The auditor therefore determines the impact of such risks and designs suitable responses.

Examples of these risks and their impact on the financial statements could include the following:

Financial statement level risk	Impact on the financial statements
Operating losses and cash flow problems.	Doubt over the appropriateness of continuing to adopt the **going concern** basis of accounting, which could lead to restatement of the financial statements affecting all assertions.
The client's information systems are assessed as poor.	Poor internal controls may lead the auditor to conclude that there are misstatements within the **accounting records** that could affect all assertions.
Concerns are raised about the integrity of management at the client.	Evidence of a weak control environment may lead the auditor to be sceptical about the quality of **representations** and other judgemental evidence from management, which could affect all assertions.
Increased risk of fraud at the financial statement level (for example, if the client is attempting to secure additional finance).	Fraud of this nature can lead to **manipulation** of the financial statements, which could affect all assertions.

Clearly, any of these **financial statement level risks** could also be considered in more specific terms when assessing risks of material misstatement at the **assertion level**.

(ISA (UK) 315 (Revised July 2020): paras. 28(a), 30, A195–198)

3.1.2 Risks of material misstatement at the assertion level

When assessing risks of material misstatement at the **assertion level**, the auditor focuses on assertions about a **class of transactions**, an **account balance** or a **disclosure** and considers these assertions **separately** in the context of the two key components of the risk of material misstatement:

Inherent risk assessment	Control risk assessment
The **susceptibility** of an assertion to any form of misstatement (both fraud and error) varies and will therefore sit on what is known as a **spectrum of inherent risk**, which the auditor assesses in terms of **likelihood** and **magnitude** (supplemented by any financial statement level risks of material misstatement as appropriate). Assessed risks of material misstatement that sit towards the **higher end of the spectrum of inherent risk** are considered to be **significant risks** and will therefore demand **more** of the auditor's attention and will therefore be **prioritised**. Unless specifically required by a separate ISA (UK), the determination of significant risks will be a matter of the auditor's **professional judgement**.	This is the risk that a misstatement is not prevented, detected or corrected by internal controls. The assessment of control risk is supported by the auditor **testing the operating effectiveness of controls**. However, if such testing is not undertaken, the overall risk of material misstatement is considered to be the same as the auditor's assessment of inherent risk. When considering controls, the auditor will need to differentiate between: • **Direct controls** (those that are precise enough to address risks of material misstatement at the assertion level); and

Inherent risk assessment	Control risk assessment
Should assertion-level risks be considered to have a **pervasive** effect on the financial statements, they may be classified as financial statement level risks.	• **Indirect controls** (those that support direct controls)

(ISA (UK) 315 (Revised July 2020): paras. 4–6, 12, A5, A218–220)

Spectrum of inherent risk

The assessment of inherent risk requires **professional judgement** by the auditor when determining both **likelihood** (how likely a misstatement is to occur) and **magnitude** (the misstatement itself, which could be expressed in either qualitative or quantitative terms) by reference to the **nature, size and complexity** of an audited entity. The resulting combination of likelihood and magnitude is then evaluated and the higher it gets, the higher the assessment of inherent risk. The ISA points out that for an assessment to be considered high, it does not necessarily require **both** likelihood and magnitude to be assessed as high (ISA 315 (Revised 2019): paras. A208–216).

Significant risks

Clearly, significant risks will require **more of the auditor's attention** and demand that responses are performed with **greater urgency**. Evidence to satisfy significant risks may need to be **more persuasive** than otherwise required. There may also need to be **greater involvement with TCWG**. As a result, such significant risks may be considered to be **key audit matters (KAMs)**. Some ISAs may automatically direct the auditor to consider certain inherent risks to be significant (such as frauds and ISA 240) but otherwise, it is a matter of **professional judgement** taking issues such as **subjectivity** and **complexity** into account (ISA 315 (Revised 2019): paras. A219–221).

Exam focus point

ACCA has confirmed that question requirements will ask for **significant risks** to ensure that candidates are **focusing** and **prioritising risks** which are at the **upper end of the spectrum** – these will therefore be those that are of greatest **likelihood** and **magnitude**.

Essential reading

See Chapter 6 of the Essential reading for examples of the components of the risk of material misstatement.

The Essential reading is available as an Appendix of the digital edition of the Workbook.

3.1.3 The consideration of climate-related risks in an audit of financial statement

In October 2020, IAASB published a staff audit practice alert to assist auditors in the application of existing ISAs to emerging risks related to climate change. The alert is structured around the various stages of a typical audit engagement and considers how climate-related risks might affect the approach identified for individual ISAs (UK). It starts with an overview of how certain industries might be more susceptible to the direct impact of climate change (such as energy, agriculture and construction) and how others may be exposed to more indirect impacts instead (such as droughts which affect coffee harvests and thus impact entities buying and selling coffee). Management are also encouraged to consider circumstances where climate-related risks may affect the materiality of certain aspects within the financial statements.

The following table provides a summary of the stages of the audit and an overview of how it affects certain ISAs (UK):

Stage of the audit	Impact on ISAs (UK)
Risk assessment and responses to assessed risks	**ISA (UK) 315 (Revised)** requires an evaluation of how internal (eg working in an industry that is dependent on fossil fuels) and external factors (eg new regulatory commitments signed up to by governments) affect risk assessments. **ISAs (UK) 320 and 450** may need to consider those factors that are now considered material due to their significance as climate-related risks. **ISA (UK) 330** may require more persuasive evidence. **ISA (UK) 250 A** will need to consider any new laws and regulations that are climate-related.
Audit evidence	**ISA (UK) 540 (Revised)** will now need to consider the need for additional expertise in the valuation of assets such as mineral reserves and the viability of transactions based on harvests and crop yields **ISAs (UK) relating to disclosures** may require greater levels of scrutiny to comply with IFRS. **ISA (UK) 620** may also need to consider new expertise in areas such as oil or gas plant decommissioning due to regulatory change or shortened asset lives. **ISA (UK) 570** may need to consider the impact of extreme weather on the viability of an entity.
Reporting and communication with TCWG	**ISA (UK) 260** reporting will need to consider feedback on how prepared an entity is to climate-related risks. **ISA (UK) 700** may need greater scrutiny of the quality of disclosures made or the appropriateness of accounting policies related to climate risks. **ISA (UK) 701** requires an evaluation of those matters the auditor considered were of greatest significance to the audit, so climate-related risks will now need to be assessed as well. **ISA (UK) 720** requires an evaluation of the other information that is not audited: given the potential inclusion of climate-related risk disclosures here, it is possible that matters of greater significance to the future viability of the entity may not be subject to sufficient scrutiny so the auditor needs to perform this stage of the audit carefully.

 BPP

Essential reading

3.2 The auditor's approach under ISA (UK) 315 (Revised July 2020)

The auditor will use a variety of procedures as part of their risk assessment:

- **Enquiries** of appropriate individuals (including **internal audit**)
- **Analytical procedures** (including automated tools and techniques such as **data analytics**)
- **Observation** of events and activities
- **Inspection** of documents and other relevant items
- **Sharing informationfrom other sources** (such as **acceptance and continuance** procedures and the **discussions** among audit team members)

Real life example: Automated tools and techniques

ISA (UK) 315 (Revised July 2020) describes many different applications for the use of automated tools and techniques within the risk assessment process. For example:

- Remote observation tools such as **drones** could be used when inspecting certain assets
- Auditors can obtain digital downloads of accounting records and use **data analytics** techniques (ranging from spreadsheets to more complex systems) to perform analysis that assists in the **prioritisation** of significant risks of material misstatement
- The analysis of accounting records could include **journals** to identify those posted outside of normal working hours or by staff who do not normally post such items
- Entire **populations** of transactions could be **analysed** to identify situations that could indicate a **higher position on the spectrum of inherent risk** (eg account balances that are zero at the reporting date but which have seen significant transactions and journal entries during the period, suggesting possible manipulation)
- To assist the auditor, key messages from data analytics procedures are often presented using a **dashboard** (sometimes referred to as **data visualisation**) which highlights significant matters for the auditor's attention

(ISA (UK) 315 (Revised July 2020): paras. A31, A35, A137, A161 and A203)

3.2.1 The applicable financial reporting framework

The auditor needs to obtain an understanding of the **applicable financial reporting framework** (including an assessment of the suitability of the client's chosen **accounting policies**) to ensure their assessment of risk of material misstatement within the financial statements addresses all appropriate **classes of transactions, account balances** and **disclosures**.

The auditor may also need to consider the accounting implications for certain higher-risk areas, for example:

- **Revenue recognition** (eg for online retailers and resellers)
- **Industry-specific accounting principles and practices** (eg loans held by for banks or research and development in the pharmaceutical industry)
- Accounting for assets, liabilities and transactions in a **foreign currency**
- Accounting for **unusual** or **emerging issues** (eg cryptocurrency)

(ISA (UK) 315 (Revised July 2020): para. A82)

3.2.2 The entity and its environment

The auditor also needs to understand **the entity and its environment,** which can comprise the following:

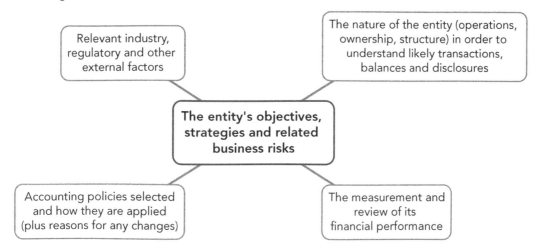

(ISA (UK) 315 (Revised July 2020): para. 19)

3.2.3 The system of internal control

This understanding also includes the entity's **system of internal control** (illustrated by the diagram below, showing the various components of internal control):

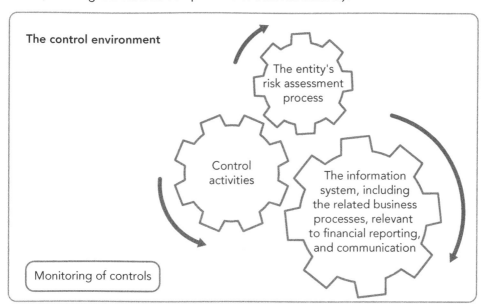

(ISA (UK) 315 (Revised July 2020): paras. 21–26)

ISA (UK) 315 (Revised July 2020) describes the work that the auditor should perform in obtaining an understanding of the various IT applications in use within an entity as well as those risks that arise from the use of IT and from general IT controls.

 Essential reading

See Chapter 6 of the Essential reading for examples of the components of internal control (found within the components of the risk of material misstatement) and the work that the auditor should undertake in relation to IT at the client.

The Essential reading is available as an Appendix of the digital edition of the Workbook.

3.3 Scepticism, scalability and standing back

As ISAs (UK) adapt over time, they introduce **new themes** that support the overall achievement of the auditor's key objectives. ISA (UK) 315 (Revised July 2020) uses the **following concepts** to ensure the auditor's identification and assessment of the risks of material misstatement is both thorough and proportionate.

3.3.1 Professional scepticism

You have met professional scepticism many times throughout your studies, but it is mentioned again here to reinforce the importance of **challenging management** and **keeping an open mind** to the **rapidly changing environment** as part of the process of identifying and assessing risks of material misstatement.

Within ISA (UK) 315 (Revised July 2020) the use of professional scepticism is discussed in terms of the auditor displaying **professional judgement** when determining whether or not a critical assessment of risk has been undertaken. It also widens the scope of any risk assessment by referring to the need to be **alert to conditions** that might indicate possible misstatements due to fraud or error. Such scepticism could include the following activities:

- Questioning evidence that appears to be contradictory
- Considering responses provided by management and TCWG
- Remaining alert to conditions that could lead to misstatements due to either fraud or error
- Evaluating evidence in the context of the risk assessment big picture (ISA (UK) 315 (Revised July 2020): paras. A12–13).

Example: Analytical procedures and professional scepticism

Data visualisation techniques may present the findings of analytical procedures, but the auditor still needs to interpret these findings using professional scepticism and identify the **core messages** that support their assessment of the risk of material misstatement.

Assume you work as the auditor for a clothing manufacturer. The company operates its own retail stores and supplies contract customers with a range of bespoke products. It also has a website that sells all product ranges.

You are inspecting the results of your firm's data analytics procedures as part of the audit of revenue and you access the following chart from the dashboard:

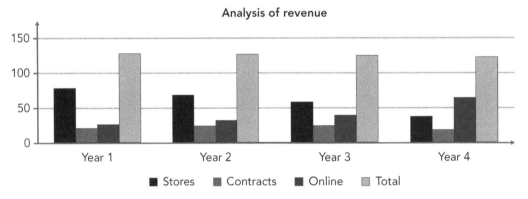

Analysis of revenue

■ Stores ■ Contracts ■ Online ■ Total

The chart suggests that the company's business model is gradually shifting from retail to online sales, which would then direct your attention towards any indications of risk from this change. You might also be inclined to consider the risks presented by IT to rise as the company's reliance on the website increases. However, you also need to conclude that the company's total revenue is falling and direct your assessment of the risk of material misstatement in this direction as well – could actual results be even worse?

3.3.2 Scalability

This is a term that is used frequently within ISA (UK) 315 (Revised July 2020) and is becoming more prevalent as the ISAs (UK) are gradually revised. Concern has been raised by IAASB that audit failure could stem from auditors performing **fewer and less thorough procedures for smaller audit clients**, regardless of the **complexity** they present to the auditor. The concept of scalability attempts to remind auditors that they should **actively consider both the size and complexity** of an audit client when determining the nature and extent of required audit procedures.

For example, although the perceived size and complexity of a larger entity would typically increase audit risk, the entity might also have rigorous controls and present far less risk to the auditor than a smaller entity with more ad hoc systems which might seem less risky, simply because of its size.

Similarly, a smaller organisation that does not have access to sophisticated control systems may still present a complex challenge to the auditor when assessing the risk of material misstatement in its financial statements.

The auditor therefore needs to use their professional judgement when assessing risk. The guidance on scalability within ISA (UK) 315 (Revised July 2020) explains that the standard is flexible enough to be applied to audits of all entities (ie scalable) regardless of size or complexity, and states the following:

'While the size of an entity may be an indicator of its complexity, some smaller entities may be complex and some larger entities may be less complex.' (ISA (UK) 315 (Revised July 2020): para. 9)

Overall, the message appears to be that auditors should approach an audit engagement **without any preconceived ideas** about the risks they are expecting to find and should apply ISA (UK) 315 (Revised July 2020) with an **open mind** and respond to the results of their risk assessment.

3.3.3 Standing back

Throughout ISA (UK) 315 (Revised July 2020) you will also find the terms **iterative** and **responsive**. These are used deliberately to reinforce the need for the auditor's identification and assessment of risks of material misstatement to be **actively considered at all stages of the process** and any **changes** or **developments** accommodated to make sure the process can **react** if new information demands it.

This is sometimes referred to as **standing back** and implies that the auditor should **pause, reflect** and **respond accordingly** if new or contradictory information emerges at any point in the process.

3.4 Additional information required?

The auditor will often need to **obtain additional information** in order to gain the required understanding of the entity, and in order to perform planned procedures. Much of the time, the auditor only has **incomplete information** about the entity being audited, and it is important to be able to recognise when more is needed. Such is the nature of real-life auditing!

AAA exams often contain a requirement to identify additional information needed in order to either understand the entity or perform a specific part of an engagement. These are often quite easy marks, and to get them, you need to:

- **Be specific** about what information you need
- State **why** you need the information

It is not necessary at this stage to speculate in too much detail about what might go wrong in each area. Questions will usually contain a little bit of information – eg that a company runs a bonus scheme for managers – but with clear gaps in it – eg how the bonuses are determined will not be stated. All you need to do is to point out this gap and say what information is needed to fill it.

Additional information does not have to be a document, but can be the reason why management has done something in the scenario, for example.

Essential reading

See Chapter 6 of the Essential reading for more detail on additional information required.

The Essential reading is available as an Appendix of the digital edition of the Workbook.

4 ISA (UK) 330 – risk response

Given that the auditor has reached ISA (UK) 330 *The Auditor's Responses to Assessed Risks*, they must now obtain **sufficient appropriate audit evidence** regarding the **assessed risks of material misstatements** through **designing and implementing appropriate responses to those risks** in order to form an opinion (ISA (UK) 330: para. 3). This is where **audit testing** starts to appear and the auditor will focus on **managing detection risk**.

ISA (UK) 330 asks for the auditor to determine whether **controls testing** is appropriate or not. The auditor always carries out some **substantive testing** but where controls are **ineffective**, these will not be tested and substantive testing will be relied upon instead.

All conclusions reached using ISAs (UK) 300, 315 and 330 must be **fully documented** to support the audit opinion.

Activity 2: Bauer

You are an audit partner attending the planning meeting for the audit of Bauer, a large technology company with two main divisions. The year end is 31 December. The first division manufactures computer hardware for use by intelligence and security agencies, and the second produces and distributes bespoke and off-the-shelf software for use on the hardware.

As part of your audit planning, you attend a meeting with Bauer's finance director, Jackie. She informs you that there have been no major changes in the business's operations during the year, but the following significant events had occurred:

(1) Owing to an unexplained improvement in the security situation in the Los Angeles area, a significant contract with the US Government for new hardware has not been renewed. This was a surprise and as a result, 100 (out of 1,000) US staff were made redundant during December.

(2) During the year, development commenced on new software for use in satellite tracking of vehicles. This has been capitalised as an intangible asset. In order to commence development, significant staff training costs were incurred.

Required

Evaluate the risks of material misstatement from items (1) and (2).   **(5 marks)**

Solution

5 The business risk approach

Business risk: 'A risk resulting from significant conditions, events, circumstances, actions or inactions that could adversely affect an entity's ability to achieve its objectives and execute its strategies, or from the setting of inappropriate objectives and strategies'. (ISA (UK) 315 (Revised July 2020), para. 12)

The business risk model is not a replacement for the traditional audit risk model but rather a vehicle, or mechanism, for the identification of audit risk, recognising that most business risks will eventually have financial consequences and, therefore, an effect on the financial statements.

In adopting a business risk approach, the auditor identifies the risks that the business itself faces, which could threaten the business from meeting its goals, aims and objectives. Once identified, the auditor is then able to identify any corresponding audit risk.

The approach allows the auditor to gain a **greater understanding of the business** and the overall risks it faces and therefore increases the likelihood of identifying the **risks of material misstatement** of the financial statements as well as being able to provide constructive business advice to aid the mitigation (through relevant controls) of such risks.

PER alert

One of the competencies you require to fulfil **Performance Objective 4** of the PER is the ability to evaluate activities in your area and identify potential risks of fraud, error or other hazards assessing their probability and impact. You can apply the knowledge you have obtained from this chapter of the Workbook to help demonstrate this competency.

Activity 3: Business risks vs audit risks

From the following scenario, identify the business risk and any corresponding audit risk.

Scenario	Business risk	Audit risk
CD Planet operates a chain of retail outlets selling chart CDs		
Mucha Pasta operates several Italian restaurants and is subject to comprehensive and stringent health and safety food hygiene legislation.		
XYZ, based in the Eurozone, trades extensively abroad in the US and invoices sales in US$.		

Business risks can be split into **three categories** to enable better identification.

5.1 Financial risk

These are the risks arising from the company's **financial activities** or the **financial consequences** of operations. Examples include the following.

5.2 Operational risk

These are the risks arising from the operations of the business, such as stock-outs, physical disasters, loss of key staff, poor brand management and loss of orders.

Essential reading

See Chapter 6 of the Essential reading for an overview of operational business risks from current and emerging trends in information technology (IT) and e-commerce.

The Essential reading is available as an Appendix of the digital edition of the Workbook.

5.3 Compliance risk

These are the risks arising from non-compliance with laws, regulations, policies, procedures and contracts (as covered in Chapter 1). Examples include the following:

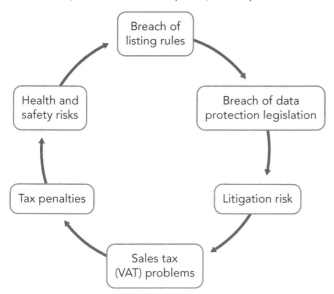

Once risks are identified, management must decide whether it **accepts** the risk or what its **control strategy** will be to manage the risk.

Management needs to be satisfied that its systems of risk management and internal controls are working properly. Internal audit can make a valuable contribution to the monitoring of risk management.

 Activity 4: Melon

Your firm has just been appointed auditor to the Melon Group, which operates a chain of fashion clothing shops for young women. The head office is based in Madrid. There are 280 shops spread across the Iberian peninsula and a further 65 shops across the European Union. The clothing is manufactured mainly in Spain and India by third-party manufacturers and fixed quantities are pre-ordered six months in advance of the season. Most of the shop buildings are held on long leases, although a small number are owned by the Group.

Approximately 40% of the shops outside the Iberian market are run on a franchise basis whereby shop fittings are supplied and installed by the Melon Group and paid for by the franchisee over five years, after which time they are replaced; the clothes are sold at a 40% discount on local retail price to the franchisees on a sale or return basis. Franchisees choose which lines of the full season's range of clothes they wish to hold, based on samples.

Required

Evaluate **FOUR** business risks and **FOUR** audit risks from the Melon Group scenario.

Solution

6 ISA (UK) 320 *Materiality in Planning and Performing an Audit*

Materiality: Misstatements, including omissions, are considered to be **material** if they, individually or in the aggregate, could reasonably be expected to influence the economic decisions of users taken on the basis of the financial statements. (ISA (UK) 320: para. 2)

An item might be deemed material due to its:

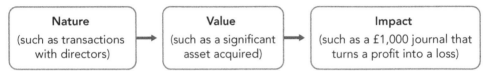

Nature	Value	Impact
(such as transactions with directors)	(such as a significant asset acquired)	(such as a £1,000 journal that turns a profit into a loss)

The level of materiality set at **planning** will always be a matter of **professional judgement**. Most audit firms set criteria for which benchmark figure to use depending on what is most appropriate. For example:

Between ½% and 1% of **revenue**	Between 1% and 2% of **total assets**	Between 5% and 10% of **profit before tax**

Example

If profit before tax is given in the question as £350,000, the lowest amount that would indicate a material misstatement in a transaction would be 5% = £17,500. Similarly, if total assets are £2 million, a misstatement in a balance of £20,000 would become material. In some cases, such as inventory, a misstatement might be directly relevant to both transactions and balances, so the auditor would use judgement to decide which of the two amounts indicated a material misstatement (clearly though, the lower amount should be used to adopt the spirit of ISA (UK) 320).

The percentage guidelines of assets, revenues and profits that are commonly used for materiality must be handled **with care**. The auditor must bear in mind the **focus** of the company being audited: for example, profit before tax might be more appropriate for a **manufacturer** judged on its performance, but revenues may be a more appropriate for a not-for-profit entity (ISA (UK) 320: para. A8).

The materiality level adopted will have an **impact** on three key areas:

(a) How many and what items to examine

(b) Whether to use sampling techniques

(c) What level of error is likely to lead to a modified audit opinion

ISA (UK) 320 also requires the calculation of **performance materiality.**

 BPP

> **Performance materiality:** The amount or amounts set by the auditor at less than materiality for the financial statements as a whole to reduce to an appropriately low level the probability that the aggregate of uncorrected and undetected misstatements exceeds materiality for the financial statements as a whole. If applicable, performance materiality also refers to the amount or amounts set by the auditor at less than the materiality level or levels for particular classes of transactions, account balances or disclosures. (ISA (UK) 320: para. 9)

Materiality levels will be determined when **planning the audit** and may need to be **revised** if new information becomes available during the audit that affects the materiality for the financial statements as a whole.

Essential reading

See Chapter 6 of the Essential reading for more detail on performance materiality.

The Essential reading is available as an Appendix of the digital edition of the Workbook.

In 2017 the FRC published **'Audit Quality Thematic Review – Materiality'** (FRC, 2017d) which considered how materiality is applied across various firms and engagements in the UK.

| |
The review covered how materiality is assessed both at the engagement level and for performance materiality. It found that in most cases, there was consistency with best practice and that firms, audit committees and standard setters are all on the right track.

However, there were also cases where materiality levels were adopted by **firms** without suitable justification and there were also cases where **audit committees** could have challenged their external auditors further on their judgment about materiality. Overall, the FRC concluded that all parties would benefit from more comprehensive guidance from **standard setters** on the subject of materiality.

7 ISA (UK) 520 *Analytical Procedures*

The auditor should apply analytical procedures as **risk assessment procedures** (ISA (UK) 315 (Revised July 2020): para. 14) to obtain an understanding of the entity and its environment and in the overall review at the end of the audit (covered further in Chapter 10).

They can also be used as a source of **substantive audit evidence** when their use is more effective or efficient than tests of details in reducing detection risk for specific financial statement assertions (covered further in Chapters 7 and 8).

Essential reading

See Chapter 6 of the Essential reading for more detail on analytical procedures.

The Essential reading is available as an Appendix of the digital edition of the Workbook.

Analytical procedures include the following type of **comparisons**, using trend analysis and reasonableness tests:

- Prior periods
- Budgets and forecasts
- Industry information
- Predictive estimates
- Relationships between elements of financial information ie ratio analysis
- Relationships between financial and non-financial information eg payroll costs to the number of employees

The following **ratios** should be considered (although you may not be able to calculate all of them – the key thing to remember is that if financial data is presented in an exam question, you must do something with it!).

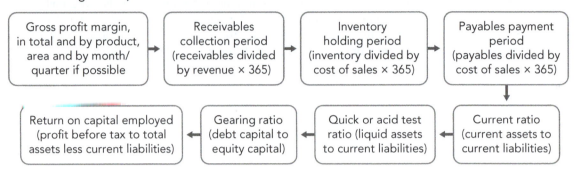

| Gross profit margin, in total and by product, area and by month/ quarter if possible | → | Receivables collection period (receivables divided by revenue × 365) | → | Inventory holding period (inventory divided by cost of sales × 365) | → | Payables payment period (payables divided by cost of sales × 365) |

| Return on capital employed (profit before tax to total assets less current liabilities) | ← | Gearing ratio (debt capital to equity capital) | ← | Quick or acid test ratio (liquid assets to current liabilities) | ← | Current ratio (current assets to current liabilities) |

Ratios mean very little when used in isolation. They should be calculated for **previous periods** and for **comparable companies**. A ratio on its own says nothing – it should **always** be **accompanied** by a **commentary** on that ratio. **For example:**

| Stating that revenue has increased by 12% will not score many, if any, marks at all, as it does not assist the auditor in planning the audit: why does it matter? | Commenting that in the context of the scenario, such a growth in revenue seems unusual as the company is in an industry that is experiencing a decline in demand, therefore should be explored further, would score most, if not all, available marks. |

The permanent file should contain a section with summarised accounts and the chosen ratios for prior years.

In addition to looking at the more usual ratios, the auditors should consider examining **other ratios** that may be **relevant** to the particular **client's business**, such as revenue per passenger mile for an airline operator client, or fees per partner for a professional office.

 BPP

Chapter summary

Planning and risk assessment

ISA (UK) 200 - audit objectives

Overall objectives of the audit

- Reasonable assurance that F/S are free from material misstatement
- Ethics, professional scepticism, professional judgement
- Sufficient appropriate audit evidence to reduce audit risk to acceptable level

Audit risk and risk of material misstatement

- AR = (IR x CR) x DR
- Risk of Material Misstatement = IR x CR
- Inherent Risk = susceptibility
- Control Risk = not prevented, detected or corrected

ISA (UK) 300 - audit planning

- Audit strategy (high level) vs audit plan (more detailed)
- Focus on important areas
- Identify and resolve potential problems
- Engagement is properly organised and managed
- Proper assignment of work
- Facilitates direction, supervision and review
- Assists in co-ordination of others (eg Internal Audit, component auditors or experts)

ISA (UK) 315 (Revised July 2020) - risk assessment

Objectives of ISA (UK) 315 (Revised July 2020)

- Identify and assess risk of material misstatement at F/S level (all assertions)
- Identify and assess risk of material misstatement at assertion level (class of transactions, account balance or disclosure)
- Inherent risks assessed along a spectrum determined by likelihood and magnitude
- Inherent risks at higher end of spectrum considered to be significant risks and prioritised
- Control risk assessment considers operating effectiveness

The auditor's approach under ISA (UK) 315 (Revised July 2020)

- Typical procedures include enquiry, analytical procedures, observation and inspection
- Acceptance and continuance information and discussions among audit team members
- Use of automated tools and techniques (including data analytics)
- Understand requirements of applicable financial reporting framework
- Consider the entity and its environment (eg industry, ownership, strategies, accounting policies etc)
- Consider internal controls (control environment, information systems, risk assessment process, monitoring and control activities)

Scepticism, scalability and standing back

- Professional scepticism - critical assessment of evidence in rapidly changing environment
- Professional judgement required (eg interpreting data analytics)
- Scalability - ISA (UK) 315 (Revised July 2020) applicable regardless of size or complexity
- Understand requirements of applicable financial reporting framework
- Risk identification and assessment is iterative and responsive, allowing opportunity to stand back and reflect

Additional information required?

Look for the gaps in the scenario and say what you need and why you need it

```
┌──────────────┐   ┌──────────────┐   ┌──────────────────┐   ┌──────────────┐
│  ISA (UK)    │   │ The business │   │  ISA (UK) 320    │   │ ISA 520 (UK) │
│  330 - risk  │   │ risk approach│   │  Materiality in  │   │ Analytical   │
│  response    │   │              │   │  Planning and    │   │ Procedures   │
│              │   │              │   │  Performing an   │   │              │
│              │   │              │   │  Audit           │   │              │
└──────────────┘   └──────────────┘   └──────────────────┘   └──────────────┘
```

ISA (UK) 330 - risk response

- Design and implement appropriate responses to risk assessment from ISA (UK) 315 (Revised July 2020)
- Controls vs substantive testing

The business risk approach

- Significant conditions that could adversely affect the entity's ability to achieve its objectives
- Complements the audit risk approach by helping to identify areas at risk of material misstatement

Financial risk

- Risks arising from the company's financial activities or the financial consequences of operations
- Examples: going concern; overtrading; credit risk; interest risk; high cost of capital; unrecorded liabilities

Operational risk

- Examples: stock-outs; physical disasters; loss of key staff; poor brand management; loss of orders

Compliance risk

- Examples: breach of data protection legislation; litigation; tax penalties; health and safety breaches

ISA (UK) 320 Materiality in Planning and Performing an Audit

- Materiality determines the relative significance or importance of a matter, depending on its nature, value or impact
- Based on the auditor's professional judgement
- Performance materiality < planning materiality levels
- Determines what to examine, how much to sample and what will affect the audit opinion

ISA 520 (UK) Analytical Procedures

- Used as risk identification and assessment procedures (PLANNING)
- Used as substantive procedures (EVIDENCE)
- Carried out as part of the overall review of the audit (COMPLETION)

BPP

Knowledge diagnostic

1. **ISA (UK) 200**

   Overall objectives of the audit are to obtain reasonable assurance that the financial statements are free from material misstatement, via audit procedures designed to reduce **audit risk** to an acceptably low level (ISA (UK) 200).

2. **Audit risk**

   Audit risk is the risk that an auditor expresses an **inappropriate opinion** on a set of financial statements. Audit risk is made up of **inherent risk, control risk (risk of material misstatement)** and **detection risk**.

3. **ISA (UK) 300**

   Audit planning aims to focus the audit on key areas, direct the auditor towards priority areas, resolve problems and allocate work efficiently (ISA (UK) 300).

4. **Risk of material misstatement**

   Risk of material misstatement is identified and assessed at both F/S and assertion levels, split between **inherent risk** (significant risks sit at higher end of spectrum) and **control risk** (operating effectiveness).

5. **Audit approach**

   Auditor's approach considers specific procedures, plus understanding the applicable financial reporting framework, the entity and its environment and internal controls.

6. **Scepticism, scalability and standing back**

   ISA (UK) 315 (Revised July 2020) includes iterative guidance on **professional scepticism, scalability** and the use of **standing back** to gauge progress and conclusions.

7. **Additional information**

   Additional information may be required to understand the entity or perform an engagement – look for the **gaps** in the scenario and explain **what** you need and **why**.

8. **ISA (UK) 330**

   The auditor will design and implement **appropriate responses to risk assessment** (ISA (UK) 330).

9. **Business risk**

   Business risks – in order to assess audit risks more effectively, auditors are now required under ISA (UK) 315 (Revised July 2020) to understand the risks that a **business** faces in three areas: financial, operational and compliance.

10. **Materiality**

    Materiality is an expression of the relative **significance** or **importance** of a particular matter in the context of financial statements as a whole – items can be material due to their nature, value or impact and the materiality chosen helps the auditor to determine what to examine, whether or not to use sampling techniques and what level of error might lead to a qualified opinion.

11. **Analytical procedures**

    Auditors can use analytical procedures, ratios and other techniques to derive evidence at various stages of the audit:

    - At the **risk assessment** stage (as per ISA (UK) 315 (Revised July 2020))
    - As part of **substantive procedures**
    - During the **overall review** at the end of the audit

 BPP

Further study guidance

Question practice

Now try the following from the Further question practice bank (available in the digital edition of the Workbook):

- Question 9 'Marsden Manufacturing' is excellent practice for evaluating significant audit risks and testing your understanding of materiality in an integrated scenario question
- Question 11 'Trendy Group' requires a comparison of business risks and audit risks for a consolidated group – make sure you can distinguish between these two types of risk as they are often confused for each other by candidates!
- Question 32 'Grissom Group' is a good representation of what you can expect to see in Question 1 of the real AAA exam where you will be asked to perform planning procedures including some form of risk assessment. The subject matter tested also covers content from a subsequent chapter so you may wish to wait until you have reached that part of your studies before attempting this question.

Further reading

There are a number of technical articles on the ACCA website written by members of the AAA examining team which are relevant to some of the topics covered in this chapter that you should read:

- *Exam technique 1 - planning questions and risk (part 1): Business Risk*
- *Exam technique 2 - planning questions and risk (part 2): Risks of Material Misstatement (RoMM) and Audit Risks*
- *Auditing in specialised industries*
- *Professional scepticism (covered in Chapter 2 but still relevant here)*
- *Audit risk*
- *Risk and understanding the entity*
- *Auditing disclosures in financial statements*

Own research

In the UK, the FRC has conducted research into various developments in the auditing profession – as an example, you could review the briefing paper on professional scepticism and see what it has to say about risk assessment:

www.frc.org.uk/auditors/audit-assurance/audit-and-assurance-research-activities

Activity answers

Activity 1: Johnson plc

> **Approach**
>
> This is really an idea-generation activity, therefore, in addition to using the limited information in the scenario, try and consider the information you have not been given but that you will need to plan this audit engagement.

Suggested solution

- **Logistics** – Assignment of staff to the audit: consider the client's locations and arrange visits where appropriate or consider using staff from other offices/countries if possible; also Johnson is listed, so it is important to consider what reporting deadlines the client is working towards.

- **Time budgets** – The audit of a large multinational will generate a significant fee but is at risk of going over budget; it is therefore important at the planning stage to prepare and communicate a time budget to the audit team and monitor this throughout the engagement.

- **Reporting** – The audit manager should consider what other reports the client may require over and above the statutory auditor's report. A large manufacturer such as Johnson is likely to produce a social and environmental report as part of the annual report; the audit manager should ascertain whether they require assurance on these issues on this report.

- **Client interface** – Consideration should be given to the method and timing of communication with the client management and/or audit committee at certain stages of the audit.

- **Preliminary materiality** – Materiality should be assessed and calculated at the planning stage (although it is likely to be based on draft figures).

- **Risk assessment** – The key aspect of the planning stage of an audit is the performance of a risk assessment. This will ensure that the work performed is focused on the important areas of the accounts.

Activity 2: Bauer

> **Approach**
>
> This activity is getting closer to exam standard – notice that the details are vague, meaning you have to consider what you don't yet know, and why any of the factors presented might lead to each risk of material misstatement. In each case, start with a possible risk and then establish why it might be misstated using your knowledge of IAS/IFRS. Although the question does not explicitly ask for them, you should be focusing on the **significant** risks of material misstatement (ie those of **greatest magnitude and likelihood**).

1. As the timing of the redundancies is towards the year end, it is important that the timing of the announcement is ascertained; if it is made before the year end, then a **provision** should be made for any redundancy costs not paid as at 31 December (IAS 37 *Provisions, Contingent Liabilities and Contingent Assets*). If the announcement is made post year end, then the costs would not be recognised until next year.

The **disclosure** of the costs should be considered, as it may be possible to treat them as an exceptional item if they meet the definition in the accounting standards (IAS 1 *Presentation of Financial Statements*).

The unexpected loss of this major contract gives rise to a potential **going concern** problem. Since only 10% of the US staff have been lost as a result, it is unlikely that this in itself would be enough to affect the going concern status of the entire business. However, this should form part of the overall assessment of going concern under ISA (UK) 570 *Going Concern*. Consideration should be given as to the reasons for the improvement in the security situation and whether similar improvements may occur in other markets.

Any of the associated transactions or balances in Bauer's financial statements related to this situation (and those in the next part of the question) should be reviewed to ensure there is no risk of material misstatement due to **fluctuating foreign exchange rates** between £ and US$ if Bauer does not report its financial statements in US$ (IAS 21 *The Effects of Changes in Foreign Exchange Rates*).

2. Close attention will need to be paid to the **software development costs** to ensure that they meet the criteria laid out in IAS 38 *Intangible Assets* and have been correctly capitalised and disclosed (see the Essential reading for Chapter 8 in the digital edition of this Workbook for more details on the criteria for appropriate research and development costs).

   It will be important to ensure that the **training costs** for the new software have not been included in the amounts capitalised. These do not represent a part of the software (which is an intangible asset) and so these training costs should be recognised as an expense when incurred.

Activity 3: Business risks vs audit risks

Approach

Candidates frequently get mixed up with these, so this activity is designed to test how you can distinguish between the things that could get in the way of an organisation achieving each of its objectives (business risks) and the areas of the financial statements that could be misstated (audit risks) from the same issue.

Suggested solution

Scenario	Business risk	Audit risk
CD Planet operates a chain of retail outlets selling chart CDs	• Overstocking of CDs resulting in inventories of ex-chart CDs • Excessive mark down and reductions in order to sell ex-chart inventories • Impact on revenues, profits and cash flows	• Identification of obsolete inventories • Valuation of inventories (possibility of NRV < cost)
Mucha Pasta operates several Italian restaurants and is subject to comprehensive and stringent health and safety food hygiene legislation.	• Breach of legislation could lead to fines, closure, bad press and costly improvement expenses • Potential impact on revenues due to impact on reputation/closure • Financial impact due to fines, legal actions and required improvements	• Provisions/contingent liability disclosure for legal action • Impact on going concern • Appropriateness of the capitalisation of improvements

Scenario	Business risk	Audit risk
XYZ, based in the Eurozone, trades extensively abroad in the US and invoices sales in US$.	• Company is exposed to exchange rate risk • Potential impact on profits and cash flows	• Correct retranslation of year-end receivables • Correct treatment of initial sale and receivable • Correct calculation, treatment and disclosure of exchange differences • Compliance with IAS 21

Activity 4: Melon

Approach

You can now start to put together what you have learned in this chapter by analysing the scenario and identifying those areas that could adversely affect the company's ability to meet its objectives (business risks) and those that could lead to material misstatement in the financial statements (audit risks). Note that there are marks now – in the exam it could be up to 3 marks for successfully evaluating an audit risk: here, you should aim for scoring up to 1 mark for identifying each risk and a further mark for explaining why it is a risk.

Suggested solution

Business risks – any four from the following:

- Foreign currency risk: Many of Melon's supplies are from India and hence cost would depend on exchange rate with the Indian rupee. Also franchisees pay 60% of local retail price to Melon, which passes currency risk to Melon where the franchisees are located outside the Eurozone (eg in the UK).

- Cash flow/financing risk: The Group bears an ongoing cash flow risk with respect to the shop fittings provided to franchisees which are not paid for until later. Given that most shop fittings will be for new franchisees, this is coupled with the business risk that those franchisees may fail.

- Leased vs owned properties: Leased properties allows the Group the flexibility to open, close or move shops, but also subjects the Group to the risks of the rental market and the potential loss of prime retail sites when the rental agreements are up for renewal. Owned properties are more secure, but are less flexible when the retail centre of a town shifts location over time.

- Fashion: The market in which Melon operates is a fast-moving one. Success depends on being at the cutting edge of latest fashions. Given that the clothes are ordered six months in advance, it is essential that Melon's research and buying department calculations are based on accurate information. Miscalculations of the market could result in large amounts of unsaleable inventories to customers or indeed to franchisees. Further, goods unsold by the franchisees can be returned to Melon, increasing its risk.

- Quality: All clothing is manufactured by third parties. Controls are necessary to ensure that the quality of goods is adequate across suppliers and consistent between suppliers and over time.

- Competitors: There are many players in the fashion market which is becoming more globalised. What in the past may have been a stable national position could quickly turn sour if a new, but established, foreign player enters the market. This needs to be regularly monitored.

- Supply issues: Unexpected supply problems could occur for Melon, a foreign investor in India, as a result of local activists criticising the use of cheaper developing world workers.

- Compliance risk: Operations in various different markets pose risks due to different regulatory and reporting requirements which must be researched and complied with.

 BPP

Audit risks – any four from the following:

- New audit client: The firm has no previous experience with this client, so the audit risk is high. This lack of familiarity could lead to potential misstatements being overlooked.

- Overseas transactions: The activities between Melon and its overseas suppliers and customers present possible risks of misstatement due to foreign currency fluctuations under IAS 21 in terms of statement of profit or loss items (such as revenues and purchases) and assets (such as inventory).

- Shop fittings and franchises: Depending on the recoverability of sums due from franchisees, there may be issues with the recognition and valuation of items in shops where a franchise may have ceased operating.

- Owned vs leased PPE: There may be a risk of misstatement in shop premises which are recorded as owned but are leased (and vice versa) meaning IAS 16 and/or IFRS 16 may not be adhered to.

- Inventory: This will be hard to value due to the volatile nature of fashion goods in general (establishing net realisable value under IAS 2, for example, may be difficult). Also, in cases where goods are returned, there may be a risk of misstatement where ownership of inventory is unclear and it is either carried incorrectly or omitted from Melon's financial statements (this could also affect revenue recognition under IFRS 15 if control of inventory is hard to establish).

7

Evidence

Learning objectives

On completion of this chapter, you should be able to:

	Syllabus reference no.
Identify and describe audit procedures (including substantive and tests of control (for both direct and indirect controls)) to obtain sufficient, appropriate audit evidence from identified sources to support the relevant assertions and disclosures.	D2(a)
Assess and describe how IT can be used to assist the auditor and recommend the use of automated tools and techniques, such as audit software, test data and other data analytics tools where appropriate.	D2(b)
Evaluate and interpret the results of data analytics tools when used during planning or evidence collection.	D2(c)
Explain the planning procedures specific to an initial audit engagement.	D1(f)
Apply the further considerations and audit procedures relevant to initial engagements.	D2(e)
Apply analytical procedures to financial and non-financial data.	D2(f)
Explain the specific audit problems and procedures concerning related parties and related party transactions.	D2(g)
Recognise circumstances that may indicate the existence of unidentified related parties and recommend appropriate audit procedures.	D2(h)
Recognise when it is justifiable to place reliance on the work of an expert (eg a surveyor employed by the audit client).	D4(a)
Evaluate the potential impact of an internal audit department on the planning and performance of the external audit.	D4(b)
Assess the appropriateness and sufficiency of the work of internal auditors and the extent to which reliance can be placed on it.	D4(c)
Recognise and evaluate the impact of outsourced functions, such as payroll, on the conduct of an audit.	D4(d)

Business and exam context

Audit evidence is a vital part of any audit. The basic issues relating to evidence are that:

- Auditors must obtain evidence to support financial statement assertions
- This evidence must be sufficient and appropriate
- Audit evidence must be documented sufficiently

Related parties are a difficult area to obtain audit evidence on. The auditor must bear in mind who the evidence is from and how extensive it is.

In special circumstances, notably the first audit, different considerations and procedures must be followed regarding opening balances.

Sometimes, the evidence the auditor requires is beyond the expertise of the auditor, and they will need to rely on the work of an expert. We also revise internal audit which you studied in some detail in your earlier auditing studies. Internal auditors provide services to the management of a company. Certain considerations arise if the external auditor intends to rely on the work of internal audit. We also consider the impact on the auditor of a client who has outsourced functions such as payroll or accounting services.

Specific audit issues examined in this subject are likely to be at a higher level than in your previous auditing exams. Therefore, the more complex evidence issues of related parties, opening balances and using the work of others are important. You should consider how they link in with specific accounting issues in Chapter 8.

These areas can be tested anywhere in the exam, in either Section A or Section B.

Chapter overview

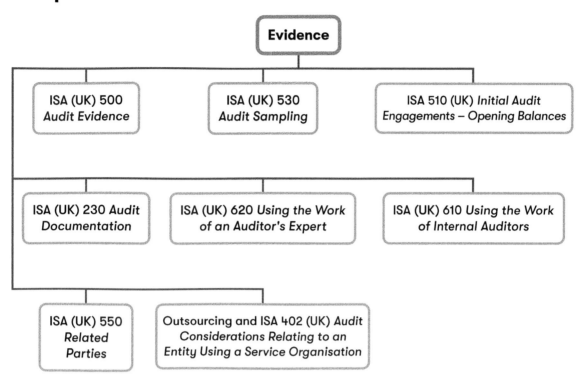

1 ISA (UK) 500 *Audit Evidence*

Audit evidence should be:

Sufficient — **Quantity** of evidence is sufficient to support the audit opinion.

and

Appropriate
- **Relevant** in supporting the financial statement assertions; and
- **Reliable**

Although the use of **assertions** helps to guide the auditor in obtaining sufficient appropriate audit evidence under ISA (UK) 500 *Audit Evidence*, the assertions themselves are defined within ISA (UK) 315 (Revised July 2020) *Identifying and Assessing the Risks of Material Misstatement* – this is to reiterate the approach that risks are assessed at both the financial statement and assertion level (ISA (UK) 315 (Revised): para. 11).

We need evidence on the validity of the financial statement assertions (essential **characteristics** for items to display in order to be included within the financial statements):

Accuracy – An accurate record of the event or transaction

Completeness – Not understated for both events/transactions and assets/liabilities

Cut off – Items have been placed in the appropriate accounting period

Accuracy, valuation and allocation – Assets and liabilities have been valued correctly

Classification – Events/transactions and assets/liabilities recorded in the proper accounts

Occurrence – Not overstated in respect of events and transactions

Presentation – All events/transactions and assets/liabilities are appropriately aggregated or disaggregated, clearly described and all related disclosures are relevant and understandable

Existence – Not overstated in respect of assets and liabilities

Rights and obligations – There is either a right or an obligation in respect of this item.

You can remember this using **ACCA COPER**.

Completeness, rights and obligations, existence, classification, accuracy, valuation and allocation and presentation relate to **assets and liabilities, and related disclosures**.

Completeness, cut off, occurrence, accuracy, classification and presentation relate **to transactions and events, and related disclosures** (ISA (UK) 315 (Revised): para. A190).

Audit evidence is obtained by performing audit tests.

- **Tests of control** – Tests to obtain audit evidence about the suitability of design and effective operation of the accounting and internal control systems
- **Substantive tests** – Tests of detail of transactions and balances, and analytical procedures, performed to obtain audit evidence to detect material misstatements in the financial statements

1.1 Procedures for obtaining evidence

The **objective** of the auditor is to design and perform audit procedures in such a way as to enable the auditor to obtain **sufficient appropriate audit evidence** to be able to draw **reasonable conclusions** on which to base the auditor's opinion (ISA (UK) 500: para. 4).

Procedures (ISA (UK) 500: paras. A10–A25)	
Inspection of assets	Inspection of assets that are recorded in the accounting records confirms **existence**, gives evidence of **valuation**, but does not confirm **rights and obligations**.
	Confirmation that assets seen are recorded in the accounting records gives evidence of **completeness**.

Procedures (ISA (UK) 500: paras. A10–A25)	
Inspection of documentation	Confirmation to documentation of items recorded in accounting records confirms that an asset exists or a transaction occurred. Confirmation that items identified in supporting documentation are recorded in accounting records tests **completeness**. Cut-off can be verified by inspecting a reverse population, that is, checking transactions recorded after the end of the reporting period to supporting documentation to confirm that they occurred **after** the end of the reporting period. Inspection also provides evidence of **valuation/measurement, rights and obligations** and the nature of items (**presentation and disclosure**). It can also be used to compare documents (and therefore test **consistency** of audit evidence) and confirm **authorisation**.
Observation	Observation involves watching a procedure being performed (for example, post opening). It is of **limited use**, as it only confirms the procedure took place when the auditor is watching.
Enquiries	Seeking information from **client staff** or **external sources**. Strength of evidence depends on knowledge and integrity of source of information.
Confirmation	Seeking **confirmation from another source** of details in the client's accounting records, for example confirmation from the bank of bank balances.
Recalculations	**Checking arithmetic** of client's records, for example adding up ledger account.
Re-performance	Re-performance is the auditor's **independent** execution of procedures or controls originally performed as part of the entity's internal control, either manually or using computer-assisted auditing techniques (CAATs). **Data analytics** is a more thorough technique where entire populations can now be audited instead of samples because of the power and capability of technology (see below for examples of how data analytics could be used by the auditor).
Analytical procedures	Analytical procedures consist of **evaluations** of financial information made by a study of plausible relationships among both financial and non-financial data. These can be used as **substantive analytical procedures** (see below for examples).

When assessing the sufficiency and appropriateness of audit evidence, auditors must consider whether the evidence is consistent. Where **contradictory evidence** is discovered, for example, where one piece of evidence suggests that a specific liability has been settled prior to the year end while another piece of evidence throws doubt on this, the auditors must perform any other procedures necessary to resolve the inconsistency (ISA (UK) 500: para. 11).

 BPP

1.1.1 Examples of data analytics routines that can be used for gathering evidence

Analysis of sales trends by product, store, month, sales operative, supplier (including margin, frequency etc) ie more detailed than traditional CAATs	Reviewing all purchases to ensure they can be traced back to a matching order, goods received note and invoice	Reviewing journals for any that have been posted outside of office hours and cross-referencing them by originator (useful for fraud or error checks)

You should stay alert to developments in this area as the use of **audit data analytics** is **evolving** at a rapid pace. Not only can larger amounts of more complex data be analysed, the introduction of **data visualisation techniques** (such as dashboards) and **artificial intelligence (AI)** mean that the auditor can now summarise data more easily and interpret the messages locked away in the data for more effectively than ever before.

Essential reading

See Chapter 16 of the Essential reading for more detail on how data analytics is changing the auditor's approach to gathering evidence. Note that there is a technical article produced by the examining team on this as well which you should read.

The Essential reading is available as an Appendix of the digital edition of the Workbook.

1.1.2 Examples of substantive analytical procedures

Simple comparisons

A simple year on year comparison could provide very persuasive evidence that an expense such as rent is correctly stated, providing that the auditor has sufficient knowledge of the business, for example knowing that the same premises have been leased year on year and that there has been no rent review.

Comparisons with estimates prepared by the auditors

A common example of this is where a business may have a large number of items of plant and machinery that are depreciated at different rates. The auditor could perform a quick calculation:

Closing balance of plant and machinery (cost)	×	Average depreciation rate

If this estimate was similar to the actual depreciation charge, it would go some way to allowing the auditor to conclude that the charge was materially correct.

Relationship between financial and non-financial information

In making an estimate of employee costs, probably for one specific department, such as manufacturing, the auditor might use information about the number of employees in the department, as well as rates of pay increases. The estimate might be:

$$\text{Prior year wages expense} \times \frac{\text{Average no. of employees current year}}{\text{Average no. of employees prior year}} \times \% \text{ pay increase}$$

If the actual expense does not make sense when compared with the estimate, explanations would need to be sought and corroborated. For example, management might explain that for several months of the year, the factory ran double shifts, so a higher proportion of hours worked were paid at higher overtime rates.

Further examination of production records for those months would be required.

If no explanation is available, then more detailed substantive testing will be required, directed towards possible misstatements, such as mis-postings, or frauds, such as payments to dummy employees. Auditors are essentially looking for enough reliable audit evidence. Audit **evidence usually indicates what is probable** rather than what is definite (it is usually persuasive rather than conclusive) so different sources are examined by the auditors. However, auditors can only give **reasonable assurance** that the financial statements are free from misstatement, so **not all sources of evidence will be examined**.

2 ISA (UK) 530 *Audit Sampling*

ISA (UK) 530 *Audit Sampling* is based on the premise that auditors do not normally examine all the information available to them, as it would be impractical to do so and using audit sampling will produce valid conclusions.

KEY
TERM

> **Audit sampling:** Involves the application of audit procedures to less than 100% of the items within a population of audit relevance such that all sampling units have an equal chance of selection in order to provide the auditor with a reasonable basis on which to draw conclusions about the entire population.
>
> **Statistical sampling:** Any approach to sampling that involves random selection of a sample, and use of probability theory to evaluate sample results, including measurement of sampling risk.
>
> **Population:** The entire set of data from which a sample is selected and about which an auditor wishes to draw conclusions.
>
> **Sampling units:** The individual items constituting a population.
>
> **Stratification:** The process of dividing a population into sub-populations, each of which is a group of sampling units, which have similar characteristics (often monetary value).
>
> **Tolerable misstatement:** A monetary amount set by the auditor in respect of which the auditor seeks to obtain an appropriate level of assurance that the monetary amount set by the auditor is not exceeded by the actual misstatement in the population.
>
> **Tolerable rate of deviation:** A rate of deviation from prescribed internal control procedures set by the auditor in respect of which the auditor seeks to obtain an appropriate level of assurance that the rate of deviation set by the auditor is not exceeded by the actual rate of deviation in the population.
>
> **Anomaly:** A misstatement or deviation that is demonstrably not representative of misstatements or deviations in a population.
>
> **Sampling risk:** Arises from the possibility that the auditor's conclusion, based on a sample, may be different from the conclusion if the entire population were subjected to the same audit procedure.
>
> **Non-sampling risk:** Arises from factors that cause the auditor to reach an erroneous conclusion for any reason not related to the sampling risk. For example, most audit evidence is persuasive rather than conclusive, the auditor might use inappropriate procedures, or the auditor might misinterpret evidence and fail to recognise an error.
>
> (ISA (UK) 530: para. 5)

Some testing procedures do **not** involve sampling, such as:

- Testing 100% of items in a population
- Testing all items with a certain characteristic (for example, over a certain value) as the selection is not representative of the population

The ISA (UK) distinguishes between **statistically based sampling**, which involves the use of random selection techniques from which mathematically constructed conclusions about the population can be drawn, and **non-statistical methods,** from which auditors draw a judgemental opinion about the population (ISA (UK) 530: para. A4). However, the principles of the ISA (UK) apply to both methods. You should be aware of the major methods of statistical and non-statistical sampling.

The auditor's judgement as to what is sufficient appropriate audit evidence is influenced by a number of factors.

- **Risk assessment**
- The **nature** of the **accounting and internal control systems**
- The **materiality** of the item being examined
- The **experience gained during previous audits**
- The auditor's **knowledge of the business** and **industry**
- The **results of audit procedures**
- The **source** and **reliability of information** available

If they are unable to obtain sufficient, appropriate audit evidence, the auditors should **consider the implications for their report**.

3 ISA (UK) 510 *Initial Audit Engagements – Opening Balances*

Auditors must make special considerations at the planning stage when they are auditing an entity for the first time, whether because the entity has never required an audit before, or because the entity has simply changed auditor.

New audits generally require a little **more work** than recurring engagements. But it is important to note that this is not because the auditor needs to do a first-time audit more thoroughly than other audits. Rather, it is because there are **specific risks** in relation to an auditor's relative **lack of knowledge** of new audit clients.

The auditor shall obtain **sufficient appropriate audit evidence** about whether the opening balances contain **misstatements** that **materially** affect the current period's financial statements by:

(a) Determining whether the prior period's closing balances have been **correctly brought forward** to the current period or, when appropriate, have been **restated**;

(b) Determining whether the opening balances reflect **the application of appropriate accounting policies**; and

(c) Performing one or more of the following:

- Where the prior year financial statements were audited, reviewing the predecessor auditor's **working papers** to obtain **evidence** regarding the opening balances;

- Evaluating whether audit procedures performed in the current period provide **evidence** relevant to the opening balances; or

- Performing **specific audit procedures** to obtain evidence regarding the opening balances.

(ISA (UK) 510: para. 6)

Essential reading

See Chapter 7 of the Essential reading for more detail on the approach to auditing opening balances.

The Essential reading is available as an Appendix of the digital edition of the Workbook.

3.1 Prior period audited by another auditor

Audit procedures:

| Review predecessor's **working papers**, considering the **professional competence** and **independence** of the predecessor auditor | **Read** the most recent set of financial statements and predecessor's auditor's report for information relevant to opening balances | If the prior period auditor's report was **modified**, pay particular attention in the current period to the matter which resulted in the modification |

3.2 Prior period not audited (ie first time being audited)

Other audit procedures need to be performed, for example:

| Collection or payment of opening **accounts receivable** or **payable** in the current period | Observation of current physical **inventory count** and **reconciliation** back to opening quantities ('roll back') | Examination of records underlying opening **non-current assets and liabilities**, including confirmation from third parties where possible |

3.3 Auditor's report

In all cases where there is a new auditor, the auditor's report **must contain an Other Matter paragraph**. This applies whether or not the audit opinion being expressed is modified. ISA (UK) 510 gives the following example of an Other Matter paragraph in this case (the example is also found in ISA (UK) 710).

Other Matter

The financial statements of the Company for the year ended December 31, 20X0 were audited by another auditor who expressed an unmodified opinion on those statements on March 31, 20X1. (ISA (UK) 510: Appendix – Illustration 1)

If there was a **modification** to the opinion and this is **still relevant** in the current period, the auditor expresses a modified opinion in this year's auditor's report in line with ISA (UK) 705 and ISA (UK) 710 (ISA (UK) 510: para. 13). Otherwise, the **opinion** would be modified under the following circumstances:

Unable to obtain **sufficient appropriate evidence** about the opening balances	Qualified 'except for' or disclaimer of opinion
Opening balances contain **material misstatements** affecting current period (either not corrected or not adequately disclosed) This includes the possibility that **accounting policies** may not be consistently applied or accounted for/disclosed properly in the new year.	Qualified 'except for' or adverse opinion
Listed auditor has **difficulty confirming opening balances**	Disclose as a Key Audit Matter in line with ISA (UK) 701

4 ISA (UK) 230 *Audit Documentation*

> **PER alert**
>
> One of the competencies you require to fulfil **Performance Objective 19** of the PER is the ability to carry out and document compliance and substantive tests and other audit work in accordance with the audit programme. You can apply the knowledge you obtain in this chapter of the Workbook to help demonstrate this competency.

In general terms, the auditor's documentation should be:

Repeat	Sufficiently **complete** and **detailed** to enable an experienced auditor with no previous connection with the audit subsequently to ascertain from them what work was performed and to support the conclusions reached.

Record	An accurate record of:

(a) The nature, timing and extent of the audit procedures performed to comply with the ISAs and applicable legal and regulatory requirements;

(b) The results of the audit procedures performed, and the audit evidence obtained; and

(c) Significant matters arising during the audit, the conclusions reached thereon, and significant professional judgments made in reaching those conclusions.

This includes the preparation of **working papers reviewed** by an appropriately senior and independent personnel.

Reasonings	The auditor's **reasoning** and **conclusions** on all significant matters requiring exercise of judgment. This helps to support the auditor's report conclusions should they require any subsequent justification (eg in response to a negligence claim).

(ISA 230: para. 8)

5 ISA (UK) 620 *Using the Work of an Auditor's Expert*

> **Auditor's expert:** An individual or organisation possessing expertise in a field other than accounting or auditing, whose work in that field is used by the auditor to assist the auditor in obtaining sufficient appropriate audit evidence. An auditor's expert may be either an auditor's internal expert (who is a partner or staff, including temporary staff, of the auditor's firm or a network firm), or an auditor's external expert.
>
> **Management's expert:** An individual or organisation possessing expertise in a field other than accounting or auditing, whose work in that field is used by the entity to assist the entity in preparing the financial statements. (ISA (UK) 620: para. 6)

Relying on the work of a management's expert is covered in ISA (UK) 500 *Audit Evidence*. When relying on the work of a management expert's work, the auditor must; evaluate the management's expert's competence, capabilities and objectivity; obtain an understanding of the expert's work, and; evaluate the appropriateness of the work as audit evidence (ISA (UK) 500: para. 8).

Reliance on an auditor's expert might be **necessary** in the following situations:

- **Valuation** of certain types of asset, eg land and buildings, precious stones
- Determination of **quantities** or **physical condition** of assets
- Actuarial **valuations** on pensions or insurance liabilities
- **Measurement** of work completed and to be completed on contracts where performance obligations are satisfied over time
- **Legal opinions** re: interpretations of agreements and regulations, or the outcome of litigation

When considering whether to use the work of an expert, the auditors should review:

- The **importance** of the matter being considered in the context of the accounts
- The **risk of misstatement** based on the nature and complexity of the matter
- The **quantity** and **quality** of other available **relevant audit evidence**

The auditor may decide to use an auditor's expert even if the entity has already used a management's expert. This could be the case if:

- The nature, scope or objectives of the management expert's work meant that it was **inadequate** for audit purposes
- The expert was **not independent enough** of management, eg management could control the expert
- The expert's **competence** and **capabilities** were not sufficient (ISA (UK) 620: para. A9)

See Chapter 7 of the Essential reading for more detail on the auditor's use of experts within the audit.

The Essential reading is available as an Appendix of the digital edition of the Workbook.

6 ISA (UK) 610 *Using the Work of Internal Auditors*

As part of their role, the external auditors will need to seek **sufficient appropriate audit evidence** in order to reach an opinion. Given the governance-related work on **internal controls** that a company's internal audit function might perform in the 21st century, there is some **logic** in the external auditor relying on this work and reducing time spent on the audit.

Considerations that the external auditor might take into account when reviewing internal audit work include:

Internal audit's **organisational status** and relevant policies and procedures. Are the internal auditors **objective**?
The **level of competence** of the internal audit function
Whether the internal audit function applies a **systematic and disciplined approach**, including **quality management** (ISA (UK) 610: para. 15)

If any of this is found to be unacceptable, the external auditor is unlikely to rely on internal audit evidence and will carry out its **own testing** instead. It may also form part of the external auditor's overall assessment of risk and the company's control environment.

See Chapter 7 of the Essential reading for further content on how to assess the internal audit function.

The Essential reading is available as an Appendix of the digital edition of the Workbook.

7 ISA (UK) 550 *Related Parties*

Central to a number of government investigations in various countries have been companies trading with organisations or individuals **other than at arm's length**. Such transactions were made possible by a degree of control or influence exercised by directors over both parties to the transactions. ISA (UK) 550 *Related Parties* covers this area.

Related party: A party that is either:

(a) A related party as defined in the applicable financial reporting framework; or

(b) Where the applicable financial reporting framework establishes minimal or no related party requirements:

    (i) A person or other entity that has control or significant influence, directly or indirectly, through one or more intermediaries, over the reporting entity;

    (ii) Another entity over which the reporting entity has control or significant influence, directly or indirectly, through one or more intermediaries; or

    (iii) Another entity that is under common control with the reporting entity through having:

        ○ Common controlling ownership;

        ○ Owners who are close family members; or

>   ◦   Common key management.
>
> (ISA (UK) 550: para. 10)

Management is responsible for the identification of related party transactions. Such transactions should be properly approved as they are frequently not at arm's length. Management is also responsible for the **disclosure** of related party transactions.

The **objectives** of the **auditor** are:

(a) Irrespective of whether the applicable financial reporting framework establishes related party requirements, to obtain an understanding of related party relationships and transactions sufficient to be able:

    (i) To recognise fraud risk factors, if any, arising from related party relationships and transactions that are relevant to the identification and assessment of the risks of material misstatement due to fraud; and

    (ii) To conclude, based on the audit evidence obtained, whether the financial statements, insofar as they are affected by those relationships and transactions:

        (1) Achieve fair presentation (for fair presentation frameworks); or

        (2) Are not misleading (for compliance frameworks); and

(b) In addition, where the applicable financial reporting framework establishes related party requirements, to obtain sufficient appropriate audit evidence about whether related party relationships and transactions have been appropriately identified, accounted for and disclosed in the financial statements in accordance with the framework.

(ISA (UK) 550: para. 9)

Activity 1: Related parties

What audit procedures should be performed to identify related parties?

Solution

During the audit, **all members** of the **audit team** should be **equally alert** for transactions which may indicate the existence of unidentified related parties. Examples include the following:

- Transactions which have **abnormal terms of trade** such as unusual prices, interest rates, guarantees and repayment terms
- Transactions which **lack a logical business reason** for their occurrence

- Transactions in which **substance differs from form**
- Transactions **processed** in an **unusual** manner
- High volume or significant transactions with **certain customers** or suppliers as compared with others
- **Unrecorded transactions** such as the receipt or provision of services at no charge

The auditor should obtain a **written representation** from management concerning the completeness of information provided concerning related parties and the adequacy of disclosures in the financial statements (ISA (UK) 550: para. 26).

Essential reading

See Chapter 7 of the Essential reading for further content on how to respond to the risks of material misstatement due to related parties.

The Essential reading is available as an Appendix of the digital edition of the Workbook.

7.1 Audit conclusions and reporting

If the auditor is unable to obtain sufficient appropriate evidence regarding related parties and transactions with such parties, this gives rise to a qualified opinion due to **insufficient or inappropriate audit evidence**.

If the auditor concludes that the disclosure of related party transactions is not adequate, this gives rise to a modified auditor's report based on **material misstatement**.

8 Outsourcing and ISA (UK) 402 *Audit Considerations Relating to an Entity Using a Service Organisation*

Outsourcing is the use of external suppliers as a source of finished products, components or services. It is also known as 'sub-contracting'.

An audit client using an external supplier in this way does not diminish the ultimate responsibility of the directors for conducting the business of the company.

Business functions that are commonly outsourced include, but are not limited to: payroll, information technology, accounting, recruitment and internal audit.

ISA (UK) 402 uses the following terms:

Service organisation: A third-party organisation (or segment of a third-party organisation) that provides services to user entities that are part of those entities' information systems relevant to financial reporting.

User entity: An entity that uses a service organisation and whose financial statements are being audited.

User auditor: An auditor who audits and reports on the financial statements of a user entity.

Service auditor: An auditor who, at the request of the service organisation, provides an assurance report on the controls of a service organisation.

Type 1 report: A report on the description and design of controls at a service organisation. It comprises:

(a) A description, prepared by management of the service organisation, of the service organisation's system, control objectives and related controls that have been designed and implemented as at a specified date; and

(b) A report by the service auditor with the objective of conveying reasonable assurance that includes the service auditor's opinion on the description of the service organisation's system, control objectives and related controls and the suitability of the design of the controls to achieve the specified control objectives.

Type 2 report: A report on the description, design and operating effectiveness of controls at a service organisation. It comprises:

(a) A description, prepared by management of the service organisation, of the service organisation's system, control objectives and related controls, their design and implementation as at a specified date or throughout a specified period and, in some cases, their operating effectiveness throughout a specified period; and

(b) A report by the service auditor with the objective of conveying reasonable assurance that includes:

(i) The service auditor's opinion on the description of the service organisation's system, control objectives and related controls, the suitability of the design of the controls to achieve the specified control objectives, and the operating effectiveness of the controls; and

(ii) A description of the service auditor's tests of the controls and the results thereof.

(ISA (UK) 402: para. 8)

A **user entity** may use a service organisation that **executes transactions** and **maintains related accountability** for them or **records transactions and processes related data** (eg a computer systems service organisation). Such an organisation may also carry out **facilities management** work or even **asset management** on behalf of a user.

Service organisations may undertake activities on a dedicated basis for one company, or on a shared basis, either for members of a single group of entities or for unrelated customers.

User auditors need to obtain sufficient, appropriate audit evidence to express an opinion on financial statements. They therefore need to consider an approach towards the parts of the audit affected by the service organisation.

8.1 Impact on audit planning

One factor that has an impact on the audit of a **user entity** is that the **user auditor** has **no direct contractual relationship** with the **service organisation** (or indeed the **service auditor**) and this may cause problems with **access** and **confidentiality**. In practical terms, however, it is in the interest of the user entity for its **service organisation** to co-operate with the user auditor, but this must still be taken into consideration when planning the audit.

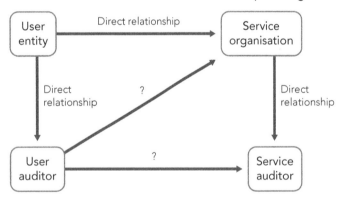

ISA (UK) 402 requires the **user auditor** to obtain an **understanding** of the nature and significance of the services provided by the service organisation, starting with the extent of the relationship between user entity and service organisation:

(a) When the services provided by the service organisation are **limited to recording and processing user entity transactions and the user entity retains authorisation and maintenance of accountability,** the user entity may be able to implement effective policies and procedures within its organisation.

(b) When the service organisation **executes the user entity's transactions and maintains accountability,** the user entity may deem it necessary to **rely on policies andprocedures at the service organisation.** In such cases, the auditor needs to design procedures that allow it to manage audit risk effectively.

The auditor needs to understand **how** a user entity uses the services of the service organisation, including:

- The nature and significance of the service provided, including the effect on the controls at the user entity
- The nature and materiality of the transactions processed or accounts/financial reporting processes affected
- The degree of interaction between the user entity and the service organisation
- The nature of the relationship between the two, including the contractual terms
- If the service organisation maintains accounting records for the user entity, whether the arrangements affect the auditors' responsibility to report concerning accounting records

Sources of information include:

- User manuals
- System overviews
- Technical manuals
- The contract/service level agreement
- Reports by the service organisations, internal auditors or regulatory authorities
- Reports by the service organisation auditor (ISA (UK) 402: paras. 9 and A1)

8.2 Obtaining evidence on the quality of a service organisations' controls

The user auditor must evaluate the controls at the user entity that relate to the service organisation and determine whether this gives the auditor sufficient understanding to provide a basis for assessing risks of material misstatement in the user entity financial statements.

If the auditor concludes that this is insufficient, they must carry out one of the following four activities.

- Obtain Type 1 or Type 2 report from the service organisation, if available
- Contact the service organisation to get specific information (with permission)
- Visit the service organisation and perform procedures to obtain the information (with permission)
- Use another auditor to perform procedures at the service organisation (with permission)

It is likely that the auditor will be able to obtain a Type 1 or 2 report, and this will be the most straightforward option. If this action is taken, the auditor needs to be sure that:

- The service organisation's auditor is competent and objective
- The standards under which the report was issued are adequate for the user entity's auditor's purposes
- The report is for an appropriate date (that is, it covers the period the user entity is reporting on)
- The evidence it is based on is sufficient and appropriate for the user entity's auditor's understanding of the internal controls
- If complementary user entity controls are relevant to the user entity, the auditor has obtained an understanding of these

8.3 Responding to assessed risks

The auditor needs to assess whether sufficient appropriate audit evidence is available from records at the user entity. If so, they should carry out **appropriate procedures** at the user entity. If not, they should carry out further audit procedures.

When the user auditor expects controls at the service organisation to be operating effectively, they must obtain evidence that this is the case, by one of the following three methods.

- Obtaining a Type 2 report, if available
- Performing test of controls at the service organisation
- Using another auditor to perform tests of controls at the service organisation

Again, obtaining a Type 2 report is the most likely option, in which case the entity auditor has to:

 BPP

- Check that the report is made up to an appropriate date
- Ensure that they have tested complimentary controls at the user entity if necessary
- Check the adequacy of the time period covered by the tests of controls and the time elapsed since those tests of controls were performed
- Ensure the tests of controls performed for the purposes of the report are relevant and provide sufficient appropriate audit evidence for the user entity auditors' purposes

The auditor must also make **enquiries of management** if they are aware or suspect any fraud, non-compliance with law and regulations or uncorrected misstatements at the service organisation that could affect the financial statements of the user entity and evaluate the impact of any matters on their procedures and report.

8.4 Reporting

The key issue to remember is that if the user auditor cannot obtain sufficient appropriate evidence about the impact of the service organisation on the user entity, the auditor must **modify** the auditor's report, as the scope of the audit has been **limited**.

Chapter summary

```
                              ┌──────────────┐
                              │   Evidence   │
                              └──────────────┘
```

ISA (UK) 500 Audit Evidence

- Evidence should be **sufficient** (enough) and **appropriate** (reliable and relevant)
- Need evidence relevant to the assertions: **ACCA COPER**
- Evidence from **tests of controls** and **substantive testing**
- Procedures: inspection; observation; enquiries, confirmation; recalculations; re-performance and substantive analytical procedures

ISA (UK) 530 Audit Sampling

- Sample selection methods:
  - Statistical
  - Non-statistical
- Evaluation of results takes cause and impact into account

ISA 510 (UK) *Initial Audit Engagements – Opening Balances*

- Ensure that all b/fwd balances are not misstated, are b/fwd correctly and that accounting policies are consistent
- Prior period **audited by another auditor:**
  - Review predecessor's working papers, read report – modified?
- Prior period **not audited** (ie first year of audit):
  - Additional procedures re: current assets and liabilities
- **Auditor's report** implications (insufficient and/or inappropriate audit evidence or material misstatement) plus OM paragraph if audited by a previous auditor)

ISA (UK) 230 *Audit Documentation*

- Repeat
- Record
- Reasoning

ISA (UK) 620 *Using the Work of an Auditor's Expert*

- May be **required** for:
  - Asset valuations
  - Actuarial valuations
  - Inventory counts
  - Stage of completion on contracts where performance obligations are satisfied over time
  - Legal opinions
- Auditor should verify the **credentials** of the expert to ensure they can be trusted as an **objective** source of audit evidence

ISA (UK) 610 *Using the Work of Internal Auditors*

- **Criteria** for assessment:
  - Organisational status (including objectivity)
  - Level of competence
  - Systematic and disciplined approach including quality management

ISA (UK) 550 Related Parties

- IAS 24 requires entities to disclose who they are related to (**related parties**) and how they have interacted (**related party transactions**).
- The auditor therefore has an obligation to obtain evidence on all related parties and associated transactions and ensure they are all disclosed in the F/S (they are **material by their nature not their size**).

Outsourcing and ISA 402 (UK) *Audit Considerations Relating to an Entity Using a Service Organisation*

- **Planning** becomes difficult due to lack of direct relationship, so need to assess significance of service organisation and their relevance to the audit
- **Audit procedures** include evidence from site visits and/or service organisation's auditor (plus Type 1 and Type 2 reports using **ISAE 3402** in Chapter 12)

 BPP

Knowledge diagnostic

1. Sufficient appropriate audit evidence

The auditor must obtain **sufficient appropriate** evidence to support the audit opinion via the assertions (ACCACOPER). Procedures for obtaining evidence need to be appropriate to the client.

2. Sampling

Auditors can use **sampling** when testing large populations – this approach requires knowing which is the best selection method (random, systematic or haphazard) and then how to **evaluate** results.

3. Opening balances

In most situations, the auditor's work in respect of **opening balances** is quite restricted. More work is required if it is a **new engagement** or if the **prior period was not audited**.

4. Documentation

Evidence should be adequately **documented** and this is usually achieved if they satisfy the three criteria: **Repeat**; **Record**; and **Reasoning**.

5. Experts

The use of an **expert** may be required in certain instances (eg valuations, opinions, measurements). The **competence** of such an expert will need to be assessed just like any other form of evidence.

6. Internal audit

The external auditor will evaluate how much it can **rely** on the work of the **internal auditor** by considering things such as **professionalism, supervision, review, judgement** and **ethical behaviour (all part of sound quality management)**.

7. Related parties

In line with IAS 24, auditors need to perform a number of tests to ensure that all **related parties and associated transactions** have been **identified** and **adequately disclosed**.

8. Outsourcing and service organisations

Outsourcing is a common practice with many companies engaging service providers to perform non-core functions, for example **internal audit, payroll, recruitment** or **IT**. Clients use these **service organisations** for transactions, maintaining records, processing data, facilities management, training and the maintenance or safe custody of assets. At the planning stage, the external auditor should assess the impact outsourced activities may have on the audit and consider performing **additional procedures** to obtain sufficient appropriate evidence.

 BPP

Further study guidance

Question practice

Now try the following from the Further question practice bank (available in the digital edition of the Workbook):

*   Question 10 'Herzog' tests risks of material misstatement and analytical procedures alongside some procedures for obtaining audit evidence.

Note. You should note the wording of the requirement to design audit procedures with a specific assertion in mind – the examining team has commented that candidates miss this and supply perfectly valid audit procedures in response to a requirement that has not been set and end up scoring zero because their answers do not reflect the stated assertion.

Further reading

There are a number of technical articles on the ACCA website written by members of the AAA examining team which are relevant to some of the topics covered in this chapter that you should read:

*   *Using the work of internal auditors*
*   *Data analytics and the auditor*
*   *Auditing in a computer-based environment*
*   *Specific aspects of auditing in a computer-based environment*
*   *Examining evidence*
*   *Audit working papers*

Own research

*   In the UK, the FRC has conducted research into how audit processes are changing – as an example, you can see how issues you have studied so far interact in the real world by accessing their reports:

    www.frc.org.uk/auditors/report-on-developments-in-audit

Activity answers

Activity 1: Related parties

> **Approach**
>
> As this is an 'idea generation' exercise, you are unlikely to come up with anything as comprehensive as the suggested solution below – however, try and think about **where** you would look to understand the auditor's objectives: understanding **who** the related parties could be and **how** they could be entering into transactions with the entity.

Suggested solution

As part of the risk assessment procedures required by ISA (UK) 315 (Revised July 2020), the auditor should gain an understanding of the entity's structure and ownership when assessing the risk of material misstatement, including related parties and their transactions (ISA (UK) 315 (Revised July 2020): para. A56).

In addition, using ISA (UK) 550 Related Parties, the auditor shall inquire of management:

- The identity of related parties including changes from prior period
- The nature of the relationships between the entity and its related parties
- Whether any transactions occurred between the parties, and if so, what
- What controls the entity has to identify, account for and disclose related party relationships and transactions
- What controls the entity has to authorise and approve significant transactions and arrangements with related parties
- What controls the entity has to authorise and approve significant transactions and arrangements outside the normal course of business

    (The auditor may have to perform risk assessment procedures in addition, in respect of the latter three points.)

- Stay alert for evidence of related party transactions when obtaining other audit evidence, in particular when scrutinising bank and legal confirmations and minutes of meetings
- If significant transactions outside the normal course of business are discovered, inquire of management the nature of the transactions and whether related parties could be involved
- Share information obtained about related parties with the audit team

(ISA (UK) 550: paras. 13–17)

The following procedures may be helpful.

- **Enquire of management** and the directors as to whether transactions have taken place with related parties that are required to be disclosed by the disclosure requirements that are applicable to the entity.
- **Review prior year working papers** for names of known related parties.
- **Review minutes** of meetings of shareholders and directors and other relevant statutory records, such as the register of directors' interests.
- **Review accounting records** for large or unusual transactions or balances, in particular transactions recognised at or near the end of the financial period.

- **Review confirmations of loans receivable** and payable and confirmations from banks. Such a review may indicate the relationship, if any, of guarantors to the entity.

- **Review investment transactions**, for example purchase or sale of an interest in a joint venture or other entity.

- **Enquire** as to the **names** of all pension and other trusts established for the benefit of employees and the names of their management and trustees.

- **Enquire** as to the **affiliation** of directors and officers with other entities.

- **Review the register of interests in shares** to determine the names of principal shareholders.

- **Enquire of other auditors** currently involved in the audit, or predecessor auditors, as to their knowledge of additional related parties.

- **Review the entity's tax returns**, returns made under statute and other information supplied to regulatory agencies for evidence of the existence of related parties.

- **Review invoices and correspondence** from lawyers for indications of the existence of related parties or related party transactions.

If risks relating to related parties and their transactions are identified, they should be treated as significant risks. Also, due to the close connection between related parties and possible fraud, the auditor must consider the overlap with ISA (UK) 240 here as well.

Skills checkpoint 2

Communication

Chapter overview

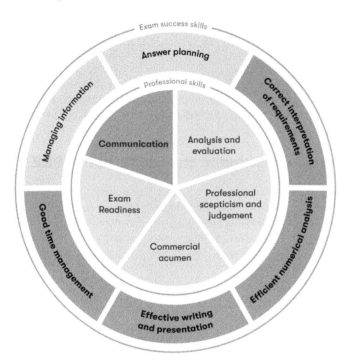

Skills checkpoint 2 – Communication

'Communication' is one of the four professional skills that have been introduced by ACCA into the AAA exam. This professional skill will only be examined in Section A of the exam as part of the compulsory 50-mark question which will test all four of the professional skills for 10 marks in total. No professional skill will ever be worth more than five marks in a question but ACCA has confirmed that you can only earn **a maximum of four marks for demonstrating professional skill in communication** within your answer to Question 1.

The wording for the professional skills at the end of a Section A question will be as follows:

> Professional marks will be awarded for the demonstration of skill in communication, analysis and evaluation, professional scepticism and judgement and commercial acumen in your answer. (10 marks)

Syllabus learning outcomes

This is how the AAA syllabus expects candidates to demonstrate the professional skill of 'communication':

- Inform concisely, objectively and unambiguously, adopting a suitable style and format, using appropriate technology.

- Advise using compelling and logical arguments, demonstrating the ability to counter argue where appropriate.
- Clarify and simplify complex issues to convey relevant information in a way that adopts an appropriate tone and is easily understood by, and reflects the requirements of, the intended audience.

How to demonstrate professional skill in 'communication'

How could you demonstrate 'communication' when attempting the Specimen exam?

In Question 1, the marks for this professional skill came from adopting the briefing notes format and structure, including the use of headings/sub-headings and an introduction. Credit was also awarded for style, language and clarity, including appropriate layout and tone of the briefing notes, suitable presentation of materiality and relevant calculations and appropriate use of the CBE tools.

In addition, marks were awarded for effectiveness and clarity of communication, whether the briefing notes are easy to follow and understand, if the answer is relevant and tailored to the scenario and ensuring the briefing notes adhere to the specific requests made by the audit engagement partner.

How were 'communication' marks awarded in the September 2022 exam?

This was the **first time** that the exam was split into 80 technical marks and 20 professional skills marks. From an analysis of the solutions and the examining team's feedback, there were few surprises in how these marks were awarded with many candidates scoring well. Remember to state in your briefing notes what you have been asked to do by the audit partner and make it clear that you are responding appropriately.

What can you do to demonstrate 'communication' when answering other questions?

ACCA has confirmed that the professional skill 'communication' will only be tested in Question 1 of the AAA exam. This is because Section A is where there is a requirement for a specific answer format to be used, which in the case of the Specimen exam was a set of briefing notes.

The good news is that answering the question and following a few simple instructions should allow you to score most, if not all, the professional marks available for demonstrating communication skills. Let's briefly consider the exam success skill of **correct interpretation of requirements** as well, using Exhibit 1 from Question 1 of the Specimen exam, to help us understand how to score the communication marks.

To: Audit Manager

From: Norma Star, Audit engagement partner

Subject: Audit planning for the Crux Group

Date: 1 July 20X5

Hello

I have provided you with some information which you should use to help you with planning the audit of our new client, the Crux Group (the Group), for the financial year ending 30 September 20X5. Based on the analysis I have done on this industry, it is appropriate for overall materiality to be based on the profitability of the Group as this is a key focus for investors and providers of finance.

I require you to prepare briefing notes for my own use, in which you:

 BPP

(a) Using the information in all exhibits, evaluate and prioritise the significant audit risks to be considered in planning the Group audit.

Note: You are NOT required to consider audit risks relating to foreign exchange transactions and balances as this will be planned separately.

(25 marks)

(b) Design the principal audit procedures to be performed on the segmental information relating to the Group's revenue.

(5 marks)

Using the information in Exhibit 4:

(c) Evaluate the matters to be considered in deciding whether Pegasus & Co should accept the engagement to provide advice on the Group's social and environmental information.

(10 marks)

Thank you.

We know from the Specimen exam marking guide that presentation of appropriate calculations (trends and materiality for example) and their significance was required in order to score here. Make sure you include the relevant calculation within your written answer: the partner's email in Exhibit 1 explains that materiality should be based on the profitability of the group, so you can state this in your answer. There are also marks for demonstrating skill in the area of 'professional scepticism and judgement' when calculating a suitable materiality threshold. Note how this is addressed by the exam success skill of **efficient numerical analysis**.

We also know from both the marking guide and the syllabus that providing an answer to each part of the requirement and the associated presentation aspects of tone, structure and format will help you to score the communication skill marks. Exam success skill **effective writing and presentation** is therefore relevant here as well but may require some explanation to put the necessary communication skills into practice.

Basically, these professional marks allow you to demonstrate an awareness of the professional nature of how the modern-day accountant should communicate, as well as to present answers in a format that is both professional and appropriate to the circumstances of the scenario.

How can you earn these professional marks? This is what the **examining team** recently suggested:

> Candidates who presented their answers in a logical and reasoned manner with sub-headings and references scored well. Again, candidates are advised to consider their exam technique in this area, for example only one concise paragraph is necessary as an introduction, not a whole page.

You should always respond according to what's been requested. The embedded email above requests answers in the format of a briefing note (a document that presents key details for someone else to be adequately briefed during a meeting). Other documents might be requested (for example reports, emails or letters) but in most cases, you will probably be briefing the audit engagement partner. You must ensure that at no point in your answer do you mention your own name - the examining team suggests the use of the name 'Audit Manager' in your answer. Suggested layouts are shown below:

Report	Briefing note/emails	Letter
Title of report	**From: A. Manager**	Sender's details
Prepared by: A. Manager	**To: Engagement Partner**	Recipient's details
Date: 2 July 20X5	**Date: 2 July 20X5**	2 July 20X5
Introduction	**Subject: re:...**	Dear Recipient,
Detailed sections and sub-sections, making use of headings and sub-headings, lists etc	Introduction (including the requirements of the question as requested by the partner in the email)	**Subject of letter**
		Details of letter, making use of headings and sub-headings, lists etc
Conclusions and	Detailed sections and sub-	Yours faithfully (if addressed

Report	Briefing note/emails	Letter
recommendations Appendices	sections, making use of headings and sub-headings, lists etc Conclusions Appendices	to 'Sir' or 'Madam') Yours sincerely (if addressed to a named individual

Skills practice

To help you develop your use of the professional skill 'communication' you should attempt Question 10 'Herzog Ltd' from the 'Further question practice' section at the back of the digital edition of the Workbook. It is a question that aims to replicate the style of Question 1 in the AAA exam.

You should also attempt Question 32 'Grissom Group' which reflects how Question 1 in the AAA exam will look. As it covers all of the professional skills and technical content up to and including group audits, you may wish to leave this question until you have covered all chapters in the Workbook.

Once you have attempted these questions, you should aim to practise this professional skill further by attempting as many questions as you can that replicate the style of Question 1 (usually testing risk assessment and other planning issues with a requirement to produce an answer in a specific style). Remember, you can attempt AAA questions from both the Workbook and the Practice and Revision Kit as well as those in the CBE software using the ACCA Practice Platform.

One final point: **good time management** is a vital exam success skill and is likely to be most important when answering Question 1 in the exam as the nature of a 50-mark question means that time overruns are common. You must also practise these questions to time if possible so you can start to understand how to produce what you want to say within the time available.

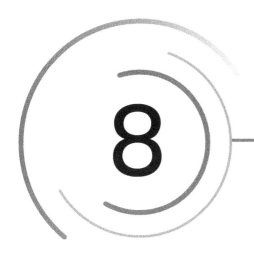

8

Evaluation and review –
matters relating to specific accounting issues

Learning objectives

On completion of this chapter, you should be able to:

	Syllabus reference no.
Design appropriate audit procedures relating to:	D3(a)

- Inventory (including standard costing systems)
- Non-current assets
- Intangible assets
- Biological assets
- Investment properties
- Assets held for sale and discontinued operations
- Financial instruments
- Accounting estimates including fair values
- Government grants
- Leases
- Impairment
- Provisions, contingent liabilities and contingent assets
- Borrowing costs
- Employee benefits
- Share-based payment transactions
- Taxation (including deferred tax)
- Related parties
- Revenue from contracts with customers
- Statement of cash flows
- Business combinations
- The effects of foreign exchange rates
- Segmental reporting
- Financial statement notes and related disclosures
- Earnings per share
- Changes in accounting policy
- Payroll and other expenses

Business and exam context

You must be able to consider four key matters in relation to items appearing in financial statements: risk, materiality, relevant accounting standards and audit evidence. In this chapter, we shall focus primarily on the last two of these, as the first two will depend more on the scenario presented in any given question.

You have previously studied the audit of a basic set of financial statements. At this level, the issues you are presented with will be more complex, but remember that key basic points apply. Bear in mind the relevant **assertions** for the financial statement items.

You need a strong knowledge of all the accounting standards you learnt up to SBR *Strategic Business Reporting* to apply in this exam.

These syllabus areas can be tested in any part of the exam: in Section A, requirements would relate to audit planning and would ask for example procedures or additional information; in Section B, requirements would relate to audit evidence and could be linked in with audit completion or current issues.

Chapter overview

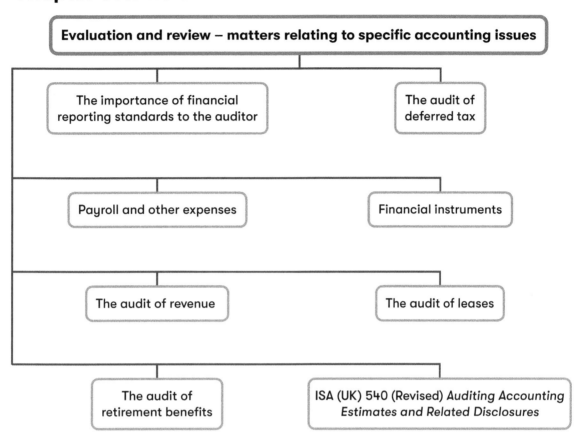

Evaluation and review – matters relating to specific accounting issues

- The importance of financial reporting standards to the auditor
- The audit of deferred tax
- Payroll and other expenses
- Financial instruments
- The audit of revenue
- The audit of leases
- The audit of retirement benefits
- ISA (UK) 540 (Revised) *Auditing Accounting Estimates and Related Disclosures*

1 The importance of financial reporting standards to the auditor

This topic deals with the matters that the auditor should consider when testing specific accounting and financial reporting issues. Remember, when faced with a complex accounting issue, the auditor should **consider** a number of different **matters** which will ensure that all relevant areas are covered. These matters could be summarised by the following process:

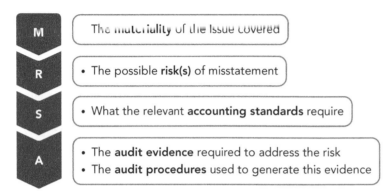

| M | The materiality of the Issue covered |

| R | • The possible **risk(s)** of misstatement |

| S | • What the relevant **accounting standards** require |

| A | • The **audit evidence** required to address the risk
• The **audit procedures** used to generate this evidence |

Important note

It will not be possible to cover all of the accounting issues mentioned in the syllabus within this topic. Some items are assumed knowledge from previous studies (such as SBR) and others will be covered during the revision phase of your studies. The skills developed in this topic can be used interchangeably between accounting issues.

Essential reading

See Chapter 8 of the Essential reading for an overview of all the relevant accounting issues and audit procedures. It is **essential that you are comfortable with this material in advance of the AAA exam**.

The Essential reading is available as an Appendix of the digital edition of the Workbook.

Let's start by looking at a straightforward illustration of how to put this approach into practice before we go into something more complex!

2 The audit of deferred tax

The auditor should obtain sufficient appropriate audit evidence that the deferred tax liability is correctly calculated.

IAS 12 *Income taxes* requires deferred tax to be calculated on the full provision basis.

Activity 1: Armstrong

You are the manager responsible for the audit of Armstrong, a start-up company producing sporting equipment for the retail market. The draft financial statements for the year ended December 20X6 show profit before taxation of £3 million and total assets of £11.6 million.

The following matters relating to deferred tax have been left for your attention.

At the year end, Armstrong had plant and equipment with a carrying amount of £3.6 million. The tax written down value of the plant and equipment was £2.1 million. (There was no deferred tax provision in the prior year as this is the first year of trade.)

The financial statements have disclosed a deferred tax provision of £450,000 based on a tax rate of 30%.

Required

In respect of the amounts relating to deferred tax in the financial statements of Armstrong, comment on:

(1)   The matters that you should consider

(2)   The evidence you should expect to find

(6 marks)

Solution

3 Payroll and other expenses

You will have already studied the audit of payroll and other expenses for your Audit and Assurance (AA) exam, so for AAA you need to remember the kinds of **procedures** that the auditor might use when assessing the risks associated with these kinds of material costs.

Taking **payroll** as an example, there are a number of **issues** to consider:

- Processing **starters** and **leavers** (and any other **changes** in people's circumstances)
- Recording the **amount of work done** (including wages, salaries and overtime)
- Calculating the **amounts to be paid** to staff and others (such as the tax authorities)
- Prompt and complete **payment** to appropriate individuals and organisations
- Accurate **records** of payments and disclosures in the financial statements

The **size**, **structure** and **complexity** of an audit client could make a big difference to the audit approach when considering payroll (and indeed any other expenses): for example, the degree of **technology** used in processing the payroll, the **ease** of being able to collect evidence and even the relative **expertise** of the staff working for the client.

As payroll could also be an **outsourced function**, the requirements of ISA (UK) 402 from Chapter 7 could come into play here as well.

Activity 2: Payroll

Considering the issues discussed above, suggest examples of typical audit procedures that could be used in the audit of payroll. Your answer should include a number of different approaches for collecting audit evidence.

Solution

4 Financial instruments

The accounting requirements for financial instruments are found in **IFRS 9** *Financial Instruments,* **IFRS 7** *Financial Instruments: Disclosure* and **IAS 32** *Financial Instruments: Presentation*. You need to be familiar with the examinable parts of these standards from your earlier FR/SBR studies.

Activity 3: Buddy plc

You are the manager on the audit of Holly Ltd; the audit team have left the following information for your attention.

In November 20X7, Holly Ltd purchased 500,000 shares in Buddy plc; this purchase gave Holly approximately 18% of the issued share capital of Buddy. The shares were purchased for £2 each and transaction costs amounted to 1% of the value of the shares. The Finance Director of Holly has stated that he has no intention of selling the shares in the near future as he doesn't like to speculate, and he sees this as a long-term investment that he may add to in the future.

The share price of Buddy at the year end was £2.25.

You should assume that the purchase price of the shares and the transaction costs are both material to the financial statements of Holly Ltd.

Required

In respect of the audit of this transaction, comment on:

(1)   The matters you would consider; and

(2)   The evidence you would expect to find.

(7 marks)

Solution

5 The audit of revenue

The audit of revenue requires an awareness of **IFRS 15** *Revenue from Contracts with Customers* which sets out the process of recognising revenue using the following five steps:

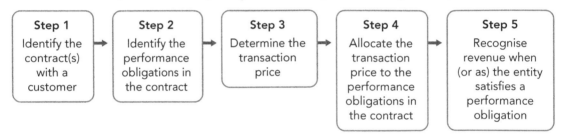

Step 1	Step 2	Step 3	Step 4	Step 5
Identify the contract(s) with a customer	Identify the performance obligations in the contract	Determine the transaction price	Allocate the transaction price to the performance obligations in the contract	Recognise revenue when (or as) the entity satisfies a performance obligation

Clearly, with so many steps to consider, including meeting the requirements of performance obligations, IFRS 15 is a very examinable area for AAA.

Activity 4: Laxman Ltd

You are an audit senior on the audit of Laxman Ltd, a wholesale seller of stationery and office products.

Recognised within revenue are a series of credit sales of inventory totalling £200,000 that took place close to the year end. Laxman Ltd continues to hold the legal title to this inventory.

Laxman Ltd holds a bank loan whose covenants impose on it a number of conditions, one of which is that its financial statements show an acid test ratio of more than one.

The following amounts are shown in Laxman Ltd's draft financial statements.

	£
Revenue	1,200,000
Current assets	1,000,000
Inventory	100,000

	£
Current liabilities	800,000

Required

Identify and explain the principal matters to consider when auditing the revenue of Laxman Ltd.

Solution

---

6 The audit of leases

IFRS 16 *Leases* defines a lease as a contract that 'conveys the right to control the use of an identified asset for a period of time in exchange for consideration' (para. 9). For **lessees**, this includes an assessment of whether the contract allows both of the following:

- The right to obtain substantially all the economic benefits from use of the identified asset
- The right to direct the use of the identified asset (known as a '**right-of-use asset**')

For a right-of-use asset (and hence lease) to be recognised, the asset should:

- Not be easily substituted by lessors; and
- Not be an exempt item, such as some intellectual property, assets related to mineral extraction, agricultural items or service contracts.

Revenue and liabilities from maintenance elements for assets must be shown separately from the lease liability within the lessee's financial statements.

A **right-of-use asset is recognised at cost**, including any fees and dismantling costs at the end of the lease term.

Depreciation is on a **straight-line basis**. Leases can be revalued if market conditions (including impairment reviews) support this.

A **lease liability** is created for all right-of-use assets – this includes all relevant financial commitments, eg the present value of lease payments not yet paid and any purchase options.

Some leased assets can be **exempt** from this accounting treatment: short-term leases (less than 12 months) and low-value assets (likely to be <£5,000) can be expensed instead.

IFRS 16 requires right-of-use assets and lease liabilities to be shown separately, either on the face of the statement of financial position (SoFP) or within the notes.

Disclosure includes:

- Depreciation charges and carrying amounts for any right-of-use assets held at the reporting date
- Interest expenses on lease liabilities
- Gains and losses from sale and leaseback transactions
- Expenses incurred on short-term and low-value leases
- Total cash outflow for leases

Disclosure is not required for leases where the information is deemed to be non-material.

Lessors follow a different approach under IFRS 16 Leases must be differentiated between 'finance leases' (where substantially all the risks and rewards of ownership are passed to the lessee, and the asset is derecognised in the lessor's financial statements once the lease terminates) and 'operating leases' (basically any other lease where the asset is held on the lessor's SoFP while income is received from the lessee) in their financial statements.

Activity 5: Leases

What would you consider to be the most significant audit risks for leases?

How would the auditor respond to some of these risks?

Solution

7 The audit of retirement benefits

IAS 19 *Employee Benefits* provides guidance on how companies should account for retirement benefit schemes. There are two types – **defined contribution** and **defined benefit** – and it is the latter type that tends to be inherently riskier as such schemes are set up to maintain funds for current and future payments to former employees and their dependants.

Consider the variables that exist in respect of such schemes:

(a) The **fund assets** are **valued** by following the market, which we know is inherently volatile.

(b) The **liabilities** of the fund can be affected by the **number** and **turnover** of qualifying employees, their **life expectancy**, the **terms** of their benefits and even future rates of pay.

In both cases, there is a risk that, from one year to the next, changes in these variables will result in a fall in assets or a rise in liabilities, or worse, both of these, which could lead to an overall deficit in the fund if not adequately managed under the terms of the standards. The auditor should obtain sufficient appropriate audit evidence that all liabilities and assets are reasonably valued, correctly accounted for and properly disclosed.

Activity 6: Jake's Pegs

You are planning the audit of Jake's Pegs, a global producer of clothes pegs and other domestic items. The company has been in existence for 35 years and is profitable. This is the first year your firm has performed the statutory audit.

The audit planning was virtually complete when the Finance Director informed you that the company operates a defined benefit pension scheme for all 750 of its employees. When challenged over the delay, the Finance Director apologised and said the scheme had 'slipped her mind'; she said she was confident that the scheme was in surplus, but she was still waiting for the actuarial report which might not be available until the week before the reporting deadline.

Required

1   What **additional** audit risks arise due to this new information regarding the pension scheme?

2   Assuming the scheme is accounted for in accordance with IAS 19, what audit procedures would you expect to carry out in respect of the pension scheme for Jake's Pegs?

Solution

8   ISA (UK) 540 (Revised) *Auditing Accounting Estimates and Related Disclosures*

The objective of the auditor is to obtain **sufficient appropriate audit evidence** about whether accounting estimates and related disclosures in the financial statements are reasonable in the context of the applicable financial reporting framework. (ISA (UK) 540: para. 11)

8.1   The nature of estimates

Right from the start of your accounting studies, you will have been aware of some of the main types of accounting estimates. **Examples** include:

*   Allowances for **receivables** or to **reduce inventories** to net realisable value

*   The assessment of useful lives for the **depreciation** of non-current assets

- Amounts set aside for **warranty provisions** or for **losses on lawsuits**

The risk of misstatement in these areas is obvious, not least because they tend to concern areas where the auditor may not possess sufficient expertise to assess them adequately themselves. If management intended to **overstate profits,** for example, they are much more likely to reduce the amount of the allowance for receivables than, say, to omit the last week's worth of supplier invoices received in the financial year.

In recent years, developments that were required to consider the accounting treatment for more complex or volatile amounts, such as **financial instruments,** have led to the need for greater scrutiny over the approach used by auditors when assessing accounting estimates.

8.2 The audit approach

ISA (UK) 540 (Revised) *Auditing Accounting Estimates and Related Disclosures* was issued in December 2018 and still emphasises the basic requirement to obtain sufficient appropriate audit evidence. However, the standard **also** requires the auditor to obtain an **understanding** of the following in relation to accounting estimates and their disclosure:

(a) **Complexity** (although in cases of simple estimates such as a publicly quoted share price, the audit approach can be scaled down accordingly)

(b) **Subjectivity** (or the reasonableness of any judgement used in arriving at an estimate)

(c) **Estimation uncertainty** (any inherent lack of precision in the measurements used)

(d) Other **inherent risk factors** that may specifically affect the generation of an estimate that goes into the financial statements (such as reliance on a standard which may be open to interpretation) - in essence, this means that a separate assessment of inherent risk is required when the auditor is considering accounting estimates

(e) An understanding of the **controls relating to accounting estimates in operation at the client**, focusing on their design, implementation and operating effectiveness (ISA (UK) 540: paras. 4, 5, 16–17)

The auditor's consideration of the **internal controls** relevant to assessing accounting estimates at a client could cover a significant amount of activities, such as the systems of **oversight and governance** in place, the use of **specialist expertise** and the role of **data** and **information systems** (ISA 540: paras. A28–4).

Once the auditor has understood these factors at the audited entity, they should respond to each of them by considering where and how they will obtain **sufficient appropriate audit evidence**. The auditor should consider the following sources of evidence in descending order:

- **Evidence from subsequent events** (such as using sales prices in the new year to assess the valuation of inventory at the reporting date)

- **Test management's own estimate** (known as 'management's point estimate') by considering the suitability of the process used by management, as well as the controls in place at the entity and the underlying data and any assumptions applied by the entity in addressing complexity, subjectivity and estimation uncertainty

- Should there be evidence that **management has failed to take account of estimation uncertainty** or that **management's point estimate cannot be relied upon,** the **auditor should consider developing their own estimate** (known as the 'auditor's point estimate', which may be either one figure or a specified range) using a process, data and assumptions that the auditor can trust (they may even consider the use of an auditor's expert in such cases) (ISA (UK) 540: paras. 18, 27–19)

8.3 Evaluation of results

The auditor must **assess** any **variances** between the estimates derived from subsequent events and management's point estimate (as well as any auditor's point estimate or range developed). They must then determine whether a **misstatement** exists in the accounting estimate and whether it could be **material** (this could relate to qualitative **disclosures** as well as the estimates themselves). Finally, the auditor considers the implications for the **auditor's report**. (ISA (UK) 540: paras. 33–36)

Essential reading

As a priority, you should note that Chapter 8 of the Essential reading really is **essential reading** for the AAA exam and covers all examinable accounting issues and audit procedures, up to and including, the knowledge that you should have learned for SBR.

The Essential reading is available as an Appendix of the digital edition of the Workbook.

Chapter summary

Evaluation and review – matters relating to specific accounting issues

The importance of financial reporting standards to the auditor

- <u>M</u>ateriality
- <u>R</u>isk of misstatement presented
- Relevant accounting <u>S</u>tandards
- <u>A</u>udit evidence and procedures

The audit of deferred tax

- IAS 12 *Income taxes*
- Full provision basis
- Amounts due to temporary differences
- Recalculation as audit evidence

Payroll and other expenses

- Consider the audit approach required in each case
- Agree work done, numbers of employees, rates of pay due and payments made

Financial instruments

- IAS 32, IFRS 7 and IFRS 9
- Valuation of instruments
- Treatment of changes in value

The audit of revenue

- IFRS 15 *Revenue from Contracts with Customers*
- 5 step process:
  - Step 1 – Identify contracts
  - Step 2 – Identify performance obligations
  - Step 3 – Determine transaction prices
  - Step 4 – Allocate prices to performance obligations
  - Step 5 – Recognise revenue on satisfaction of a performance

The audit of leases

- IFRS 16 *Leases*
- Valid right-of-use asset?
- Authorised lease?
- Any excluded assets (including low value or short term leases?)
- Verify existence of asset
- Recalculate depreciation, lease liability and interest values
- Ensure that disclosure is satisfactory

The audit of retirement benefits

- IAS 19 *Employee Benefits*
- Defined contribution and defined benefit schemes
- Fund assets are valued by the market (FV)
- Fund liabilities depend on a number of variables – assessment by actuary
- Assessment of any gains or losses on fund – amounts posted to other comprehensive income
- Fund in surplus or deficit – balance on statement of financial position

ISA (UK) 540 (Revised) *Auditing Accounting Estimates and Related Disclosures*

- Auditor needs to assess **inherent risks** associated with accounting estimates
- Specific consideration of **complexity, subjectivity** and **estimation uncertainty** as well as any evidence of **management bias**
- Audit approach:
  - Looking at events after the end of the reporting period
  - Testing how management made their own point estimate
  - Looking at relevant controls
  - Developing an auditor's point estimate to compare against

Knowledge diagnostic

1. MRSA

For AAA you need to consider the following:

- The **materiality** of the issue(s) presented
- **Risk(s)** presented by each accounting issue
- What the accounting **standard** requires
- The **audit evidence/procedures** required

2. Deferred tax

Remember that **IAS 12** requires deferred tax to be calculated on a **full provision basis** – remember how to apply the 'materiality, risk(s), standards and evidence' approach.

3. Inventory

Auditors need to be able to consider the issues surrounding inventory in line with **IAS 2** (such as **impairment**, **value** and **quantity**) especially given the material nature of such balances.

4. Financial instruments

Auditors must use their knowledge of **IAS 32**, **IFRS 7** and **IFRS 9** to ensure that this **complex area** is accounted for accurately.

5. Revenue

The audit of revenue requires the application of the 5 steps from **IFRS 15**:

- Step 1 – Identify contracts in place with customers
- Step 2 – Identify performance obligations in the contract
- Step 3 – Determine transaction prices
- Step 4 – Allocate transaction prices to performance obligations in the contract
- Step 5 – Recognise revenue on satisfaction of a performance obligation

6. Leases

You should be familiar with **IFRS 16** and be able to consider the audit risks posed:

- Is it a **right-of-use asset** that is not excluded?
- Is this a **low-value asset** or a **short-term** lease?
- Are **right of use assets and lease liability** values accurate?
- Is the accounting **disclosure** correct?

7. Pensions

Defined contribution schemes are usually straightforward but **defined benefit schemes** present more risk to auditors and companies due to the possibility of **fund assets** being outweighed by **fund liabilities**, as well as the inherently risky issue of scheme liabilities in the first place. The treatment of **actuarial gains and losses** needs to be fully understood as well – **IAS 19** is key here.

8. Accounting estimates

There are many **estimates** used in the production of a set of financial statements so the auditor needs to be comfortable with the method of their calculation. Auditors should consider **complexity**, **subjectivity** and **estimation uncertainty** associated with estimates which could lead to material misstatement (especially from **management bias**).

9. Provisions

Provisions (under **IAS 37**) require a constructive obligation, probable occurrence and a realistic estimate to be recognised – otherwise a contingent liability should be disclosed. Contingent assets should not be recognised unless virtually certain.

10. Intangible assets

Intangible assets include research and development, brands and goodwill and require professional scepticism to ensure they have not been impaired.

11. Biological assets

Biological assets (**IAS 41**) is a complex area that requires an understanding of the differences between agricultural produce and inventory for the financial statements.

12. Investment properties

Investment properties (**IAS 40**) need to be distinguished from non-current assets such as **PPE (IAS 16)**, leased assets (IFRS 16) and even **assets held for sale (IFRS 5)**.

13. Government grants

Government grants (**IAS 20**) requires an understanding of the grant conditions and an awareness of whether the grant is capital or income based.

14. Borrowing costs

Borrowing costs (**IAS 23**) should be capitalised but only in relation to qualifying activities.

15. Share-based payment

Share-based payment transactions (**IFRS 2**) can be equity and/or cash-settled but should be traced back to the contracts to ensure they do not present an audit risk.

16. Statement of cash flows

The statement of cash flows (**IAS 7**) is an important indicator of going concern but must also be audited as part of the financial statements in an audit.

17. Foreign exchange rates

The effect of foreign exchange rates under **IAS 21** requires monetary items to be translated at the closing rate, but non-monetary items to be translated at the date of the transaction.

18. Segmental reporting

Segmental reporting is covered by **IFRS 8 *Operating Segments*** and is all about disclosure of reportable segments – you need to know the criteria that identify part of the business as a reportable segment.

19. Earnings per share

Earnings per share (EPS) is required under **IAS 33** and requires disclosure of basic and diluted EPS.

20. Changes in accounting policy

Changes in accounting policy must be disclosed and applied retrospectively (but changes in accounting estimates are only applied prospectively).

21. Payroll and other expenses

Payroll and other expenses can often be a material cost, requiring an understanding of the amounts payable, the various parties involved and compliance with a number of systems, so should be prioritised for testing using a variety of techniques, including substantive, controls-based and even data analytics testing.

Further study guidance

Question practice

Now try the following from the Further question practice bank (available in the digital edition of the Workbook) where you can start to put the issues covered in this chapter into practice:

- Question 13 'Locksley' tests the audit of development expenditure and non-current assets
- Question 14 'Bainbridge' tests inventories, PPE and a convertible debenture using the MRSA approach from the chapter.
- Question 16 'Henshelwood' tests share based payment, pension costs and provisions.
- Question 17 'Keffler' tests intangibles, PPE and provisions using the MRSA approach from the chapter.
- Question 18 'Griffin' tests group accounting, going concern and laws and regulations using the MRSA approach from the chapter – however, as some of these issues relate to subsequent chapters, you may wish to leave this until you have studied them.

Further reading

There is a technical article on the ACCA website written by members of the AAA examining team which is relevant to some of the topics covered in this chapter that you should read:

- *Massaging the figures*

Own research

- In the UK, the FRC has conducted research into how audit processes are changing – as an example, you can see how issues you have studied so far interact in the real world by accessing their reports

  www.frc.org.uk/auditors/report-on-developments-in-audit

Activity answers

Activity 1: Armstrong

Approach

Questions such as these have their roots in quality management – imagine you are reviewing the work of your team and you want to make sure they have considered everything relevant to the matters described in the scenario. How will you do this?

Use the template in the solution space to apply the four stages discussed at the start of this chapter: materiality, risks and auditing standards for the matters you should consider; audit evidence and the procedures to generate them for evidence you should expect to find.

Suggested solution

1. **The matters that you should consider**

    Materiality: At 15% of profit before tax and 3.8% of total assets, the deferred tax provision is material to both the statement of profit or loss and the statement of financial position.

    Risk(s) presented:

    ○ Whether the deferred tax provision and charge are complete

    ○ Whether the deferred tax provision and statement of profit or loss charge have been properly presented and are supported by the appropriate disclosures

    ○ Whether the correct tax rate has been used

    ○ Whether the deferred tax provision has been calculated correctly

    Standards:

    ○ IAS 12 *Income Taxes* requires that deferred tax is calculated at a rate that is 'substantively enacted' and expected to apply when the deferred tax is to be settled.

    ○ IAS 12 also requires that the amount is based on accurate temporary/timing differences relating to the plant and equipment.

    ○ Disclosure needs to be made for the items forming the deferred tax provision, the movement on the liability and the major components of income tax expense.

2. **The evidence you should expect to find**

    Evidence/procedures:

    ○ Schedule of temporary/timing differences relating to the plant and equipment agreed to plant and equipment schedules and tax computations

    ○ Agreement of tax rate used (30%) to 'substantially enacted' rate of tax. (Note the rate used should be the rate substantively enacted, not merely 'announced'.)

    ○ Enquire of directors and review plant and equipment schedules and tax computation for evidence of temporary/timing differences not provided for

    ○ Recalculation of provision: Carrying amount £3.6m – written down value £2.1m = £1.5m @ 30% = £450,000

    ○ Review of disclosure in the notes to the financial statements to ensure the appropriate disclosures are made in accordance with IAS 12

Activity 2: Payroll

Approach

This is an idea generation activity, so first try and think about the various approaches that could be used by the auditor and then suggest suitable examples in each case. You may find your answers here are quite theoretical, but in a real exam question, you will obviously have a scenario to work from, so remember that application is still important when considering any audit procedures.

Suggested solution

Audit approach	Suggested audit procedures
Substantive analytical procedures (to test the population as a whole)	Compare actual payroll costs with budget and prior year amounts and investigate any variances Combine non-financial information to derive a proof-in-total (eg multiply rates of pay by the number of staff employed and investigate any variances)
Tests of detail (to test certain assertions or areas of the financial statements)	Trace a sample of new starters in the payroll back to their human resources (HR) records (occurrence) and reconcile the amounts paid to their terms and conditions (accuracy) Select a sample of leavers from HR and test subsequent payrolls to confirm they have not been included in error (occurrence) For a sample of months throughout the year, reconcile the payroll expense in the nominal ledger to the payroll expense created by the payroll system Confirm the amounts paid in payroll each month are consistent with the amounts leaving the client's bank account
Tests of control (to ensure that the payroll system can be relied upon to create reliable figures)	For a sample of months throughout the year, confirm that the payroll processed was authorised by the chief accountant For a sample of overtime payments, trace each one back to a valid authorisation, such as a signature on a timesheet For each month's statutory deductions from pay, confirm that the amounts were reviewed by a senior employee
Audit data analytics (to leverage efficient audit procedures in all of the above) **Note.** This would only be possible for clients with payroll systems that are compatible with this type of data analysis	Recalculate the entire payroll by reference to source documents such as timesheets and establishment headcounts and amounts due Recalculate the amounts due for tax and other statutory deductions throughout the year by reference to employee details and current legislative requirements Analyse the bank details used in each payroll run to search for duplicates that may indicate the existence of fraud Interrogate the payroll system for patterns to identify cases where segregation of duties is missing when processing the payroll

Activity 3: Buddy plc

Approach

This is very similar to Activity 1 ('Armstrong') but is testing your knowledge of financial instruments. Don't worry if you cannot remember everything there is to know about the accounting treatment – there are always marks available for calculating materiality and obtaining routine pieces of evidence to support assertions in the financial statements. If you need a reminder of the accounting treatment, refer to the essential reading in the digital edition of this Workbook.

Suggested solution

(1) **Matters to consider**

Materiality has already been assessed here, but in the exam, you will probably need to calculate this.

Risks presented and **standards** can be discussed at the same time. For example, the number of shares owned in Buddy is 18% – if Holly's stake was 20% (or there was evidence of significant influence) according to **IAS 28 Investment in Associates**, this would cease to be an investment and would need to be accounted for under the equity method (assuming consolidated financial statements are already being produced, which is happening here as there is a subsidiary).

If this was just an investment in shares, however, ownership of 18% of the shares in Buddy would need to be confirmed to ensure Holly has the right to carry these on the statement of financial position and be entitled to any dividends distributed.

Has Holly made the irrevocable election to hold these shares at fair value with any changes going through other comprehensive income (OCI)? If so, the **fair value of consideration plus transaction costs** would be recognised initially and any gains at year end would be recognised in OCI. If this election is **not made**, initial recognition would be at the **fair value of acquisition only** and the transaction costs would be **expensed** through profit or loss (P/L) with any fair value gains at the end of the year also being recognised in P/L.

IFRS 7 Financial Instruments: Disclosures specifies that the financial statements should disclose both the significance and the nature/extent of any risks associated with financial instruments, including an estimate of the level of market risk the shares represent to Holly.

(2) **Evidence you expect to find**

Copies of the Buddy plc share certificates in Holly's name which verify Holly's ownership of 500,000 shares in Buddy as at November 20X7.

Inspection of Buddy's statutory share records to verify Holly owns 18% of all issued shares and a review of board minutes to ascertain whether Holly holds any significant influence over Buddy.

Inspection of Holly's bank statements and cash book to confirm the transaction occurred in November 20X7.

Request a representation from the Finance Director of Holly regarding any election to treat fair value gains through OCI not P/L.

Recalculation of the payment of the purchase price (£2 × 500,000 = £1,000,000) and the transaction costs (1% × £1,000,000 = £10,000) and confirmation that the fair value initially recognised on Holly's statement of financial position matches the appropriate treatment (£1,010,000 if going through OCI; £1,000,000 if going through P/L).

Trace amounts for transaction costs through to correct locations (either as part of fair value on recognition or P/L depending on whether any election was made by Holly).

Copies of invoices or brokers' notes to corroborate the value paid (including transaction costs) plus third-party confirmation of Buddy's share price on the date of purchase (eg agree £2 per share to the quoted price in the *Financial Times* on the purchase date).

 BPP

Recalculation of the £115,000 increase in the fair value of the shares in Buddy (£2.25 × 500,000 = £1,125,000 minus £1,010,000) and a copy of any relevant working papers completed by Holly.

Reconciliation that the gain has been allocated to the correct place (OCI or P/L depending on any election made by Holly).

A copy of the journal showing the increase in value of the Buddy investment at the reporting date (eg debit financial asset, credit profit or loss) and confirmation from a third party (eg *Financial Times* again) of the share price (£2.25) at the reporting date.

A copy of the draft financial statements of Holly to ensure that the shares have been recorded as owned by Holly together with an indication of the levels of risk presented (eg market risk).

Activity 4: Laxman Ltd

> #### Approach
>
> The two principal matters to consider here are interrelated: whether IFRS 15 has been properly applied to Laxman Ltd's inventory, and whether Laxman Ltd is in breach of the conditions of its bank loan. However, remember to think outside the box a little and consider whether anything else is relevant here.

Suggested solution

Inventory

IFRS 15 states that revenue is recognised when the entity has transferred the goods to the buyer, meeting the performance obligations of the contract (IFRS 15: para. 9).

In this case, the legal transfer of title has not yet occurred and so it would therefore appear that these items should not be recognised within revenue.

However, as auditors, it will be necessary to obtain further information regarding the sale, as in accordance with IFRS 15, the transfer of legal title is not sufficient evidence that control has been transferred (and performance obligations met). It is possible, for instance, that legal title has been retained in order to protect Laxman Ltd against the possibility of non-payment by the receivable, even though, in substance, a sale has in fact occurred.

Further audit evidence must be obtained in order to form a judgement over whether IFRS 15 has been breached.

Loan condition

Laxman Ltd appears to be within the criteria laid down by the bank: it has an acid test ratio of 1.125 (= (£1,000,000 − £100,000) ÷ £800,000).

However, if the revenue recognised in respect of the inventory above has not been recognised in accordance with IFRS 15, the financial statements may need to be amended. The amendment could be by as much as £200,000 (decreasing receivables and increasing inventory) which would not affect current assets as the switch from receivables to inventory would balance itself out, but would change the acid test ratio to 0.875 (= (£1,000,000 − £300,000) ÷ £800,000).

If the conditions set by the bank have been broken, then it is likely that some negative consequence would result from this. This could range from a fine or penalty that would need to be recognised in the financial statements, to the possibility of Laxman Ltd having to repay the loan. If this were the case, it would be necessary to consider very carefully whether significant doubts exist over Laxman Ltd's ability to continue as a going concern.

Possibility of fraud

The auditor needs to consider the possibility that management has engaged in fraudulent financial reporting in respect of revenue recognition in order not to breach the conditions set by the trade organisation. If this were the case, the auditor will need to re-examine any representations it has already received from management.

Activity 5: Leases

Approach

This is simply designed to get you up to speed with IFRS 16. There is far more detail included here than required by the question, but it shows the depth of knowledge that you will need for the exam. Remember that you should always apply your IFRS knowledge to the scenario and respond accordingly.

Suggested solution

Audit risks

Audit risks for lessors

Whether a lease is an operating or finance lease – the treatment of lease repayments will vary (either receivables or income) and the asset will need to be derecognised at the end of the lease term if it is a finance lease.

Audit risks for lessees

Leases may be inappropriately recognised as leases (or not recognised when they should be) because one or more of the necessary conditions under **IFRS 16 Leases** has not been observed:

- The lessor does not have the right to substantially all the economic benefits of an identified asset.
- The asset may be easily substituted by the lessor so cannot be part of a lease agreement.
- The lessor does not have the right to direct or control the asset included in the lease.
- The conditions for recognising a 'right-of-use asset' may apply but have been ignored.

A combined contract to provide both a leased asset and servicing of the asset may not have been split into its constituent parts which could lead to incorrect recognition of the service element.

Initial recognition of the lease liability may be either incomplete or inaccurate due to some/all of the constituent elements being missed/misstated:

- The PV of the lease payments not yet paid and the discount factor used
- Any penalties for relevant early termination
- Uncertainty over any options to purchase the asset at the end of the lease term
- The agreed or implied lease term

Similarly, lease assets may be misstated due to failure to correctly account for any of the following:

- Initial fees and other charges which may have been ignored.
- Failure to account for any impairments or revaluations that have occurred during the lease term.
- Failure to account for dismantling and restoration provisions that might be required at the end of the lease term.

Assets may be treated as either short-term leases or low-value assets when they are neither (so would need to have assets and liabilities recognised on the statement of financial position).

Disclosures may be inadequate or incomplete for either lessees or lessors based on what IFRS 16 requires in each case.

Sale and leaseback agreements

Companies sometimes agree to sell assets such as land and buildings which they intend to keep on using in return for paying the new owners a fee – the sale creates either a gain or loss in the seller's financial statements when compared with the cost value of the asset on disposal. This also means that the continued use of the asset needs to be reflected in the company's accounts as a lease, so IFRS 16 needs to be followed here to create a right-of-use asset for the lessee, along with an associated lease liability.

However, this situation can be exploited by companies attempting to conceal the true purpose of an asset's disposal: sometimes, there may be an agreement for the company to repurchase the asset after a set period of time, usually for a higher price than it was sold for. When the substance of such a transaction is considered, it may appear that the initial disposal amount was, in fact, a loan and the repurchase amount is actually a repayment, and the company has simply attempted to conceal this form of financing from its financial statements.

The requirement for IFRS 16 to show all material leases as both assets and liabilities is likely to reduce the risk of this as all such leases would need to reflect IFRS 16.

Auditors need to consider whether the sale part of the agreement satisfies the requirements of **IFRS 15 *Revenue from Contracts with Customers*** – if not, the seller (who has now become lessee) needs to continue to recognise the asset they are leasing and recognise a financial liability under **IFRS 9 *Financial Instruments*** for the consideration received from the new lessor/buyer. IFRS 16 requires the IFRS 15 criteria for a sale to be met in order for the transaction to be accounted for as a sale and leaseback.

The auditor's response

Typical audit procedures

In an exam question, it is likely that there will also be a requirement to consider suitable audit procedures as the auditor's response to any of these risks, and you should therefore consider how you would obtain sufficient and appropriate audit evidence in such cases – for example:

- Obtaining copies of lease contracts to confirm the details of any agreements (including the right-of-use asset specified in the contract, evidence of exclusivity of right-of-use and the possibility of any substitute assets being introduced)

- Recalculating the amounts included at both initial recognition and subsequent measurement for right-of-use assets and associated liabilities (including lease repayments, interest rates used, initial fees paid and incentives granted)

- Verifying any conditions related to either extensions or early termination based on evidence collected from the lessee and/or elsewhere (for example, sale contracts in the case of a sale and leaseback to establish if it really is a sale)

- Verifying that a right-of-use asset cannot be either substituted or controlled by any party other than the lessee (such as from site visits, documentary evidence or enquiries)

- Obtaining copies of draft financial statements to review the level of disclosure for adequacy

Activity 6: Jake's Pegs

> **Approach**
>
> There is no mark allocation here, so you do not know the detail your answer should go into. However, in any question, carefully reading the requirement will help you: in part (1) it's just the **additional** risks that the emergence of the pension scheme creates, not the risks already present. For part (2) you should consider breaking your answer down into the main areas of the financial statements where such a pension arrangement will be reflected and the considering the work you would do to audit each part.

1 **Suggested solution**

Additional risks

The delay in informing the firm of the existence of the scheme will increase the inherent risk of the audit. This may imply that the information regarding the scheme is not fully prepared yet.

The client has withheld information regarding the scheme and claimed that it was an oversight. The pension scheme is a major part of the company's financial structure, and it is unlikely the Finance Director would forget about it. The auditor should respond to this with elevated levels of professional scepticism and consider the impact on other areas of the audit. Care should be taken before reliance is placed on representations provided by management.

The fact that the actuarial report may not be ready until late in the audit will increase the risk as the auditor may be under time pressure to complete the work inside the reporting deadline.

The impact of the scheme on the statement of profit and loss and other comprehensive income and statement of financial position will be dependent on the actuarial valuation of the scheme assets and liabilities. These are judgemental and complex areas, and the auditor may not have the expertise to audit these effectively. The audit plan should include an expectation of the need to apply ISA (UK) 620 *Using the Work of an Auditor's Expert.*

The pension scheme could have a significant detrimental impact on the statement of financial position of Jake's Pegs. The Finance Director appears confident that the scheme is in surplus, but this may be unrealistic. It is likely the scheme's assets will be held, to a large extent, in the form of shares and property, both of which might have fallen in value. This may create a significant deficit on the scheme, which is likely to be highly material to the statement of financial position. This could call into question the going concern status of the company.

2 Suggested solution

Audit procedures

The finance department at Jake's Pegs would have needed to account for the scheme in line with the standards, and this would have led to some specific steps that the auditor would need to review (covered below in the table).

General procedures

We should enquire of the directors as to the accounting policy regarding the treatment of actuarial gains and losses. The actuarial gain or loss should be recalculated by the auditor.

Specific procedures

Work undertaken by Jake's Pegs	Specific audit procedures in respect of these
Actuarial assumptions should be used to make reliable estimates of the amounts of future benefits that the scheme will have to pay out currently and in the future (eg employee turnover, sign-up rates for the scheme, mortality rates, future salary increases) in order to have an estimate of the present value of future benefit obligations.	As mentioned above, there may be some need for an expert under the terms of ISA (UK) 620 to question the specific assumptions and calculations made by the actuary. The auditor can review the logic used and the consistency of the assumptions with prior years and general market conditions. Written representations from management may be helpful here although, given the heightened level of scepticism we are deploying, this may only serve as protection in the event of unwelcome (and unspecified) audit liability claims in the future.
The **fair value** of any **scheme assets** should be established.	Review the market data used to agree the value of the fund and verify to an independent source.
Any **actuarial gains or losses** in the value of the liabilities and any difference between the return on the plan assets and the interest income calculated for the plan assets must be determined in order to agree on the amount to be recognised in the financial statements.	Such gains or losses must be recalculated and confirmation obtained from accounting records of their appropriate recognition in the financial statements.
Any **changes** that need to be made to the	Auditors should ensure that any potential

Work undertaken by Jake's Pegs	Specific audit procedures in respect of these
scheme's benefits should be accounted for appropriately.	shortfalls are adequately identified and disclosed in the financial statements.

9 Group audits and transnational audits

Learning objectives

On completion of this chapter, you should be able to:

	Syllabus reference no.
Recognise the specific matters to be considered before accepting appointment as group auditor to a group in a given situation.	D5(a)
Identify, assess and respond to risks associated with the audit of group financial statements including: • Assessment of group and component performance materiality • Assessment of aggregation risk in a given scenario • The impact of non-coterminous year ends within a group • Changes in group structure or a complex group structure	D5(b)
Identify and describe the procedures to be performed at the planning stage of an audit of group financial statements, including consideration of the role and work of component auditors.	D5(c)
Recommend and discuss the communications between the group auditor and the component auditor in a given situation.	D5(d)
Recognise the audit problems and describe audit procedures specific to a business combination, including: • The classification of investments • The determination of goodwill and its impairment • Group accounting policies • Intra-group trading • Equity accounting for associates and joint ventures • Changes in group structure, including acquisitions and disposals • Accounting for a foreign subsidiary	D5(e)
In respect of the consolidation process, identify and explain the relevant audit risks and audit procedures necessary to obtain sufficient appropriate evidence.	D5(f)
Evaluate the quality of work performed by a component auditor and assess the sufficiency and quality of the audit evidence obtained.	D5(g)

	Syllabus reference no.
Explain the responsibilities of the component auditor before accepting appointment, and the procedures to be performed in a group situation.	D5(h)
Justify the situations where a joint audit would be appropriate, including identification of additional risks and challenges associated with the engagement in a given scenario.	D5(i)
Explain the implications for the auditor's report on the group financial statements of an entity where the opinion on a component is modified in a given situation.	E3(f)
Discuss how transnational audits may differ from other audits of historical financial information (eg in terms of applicable financial reporting and auditing standards, listing requirements and corporate governance requirements).	D1(h)

Business and exam context

This is a new auditing topic for you, one which is concerned with practical difficulties of communication between auditors and the issues of language, geography and even politics.

When auditing group financial statements, as in so many other areas, the auditors require detailed accounting knowledge in order to fulfil their responsibilities.

Group audits fall into two categories:

(a) Where the same firm of auditors audits the whole group

(b) Where one firm of auditors has responsibility for the opinion on the consolidated financial statements and a different firm audits part of the group

Even where the audit of each individual company in the group is carried out by the same firm, there may be administrative complications where some audits are carried out by different branches, perhaps overseas, with different practices and procedures.

Group audits can be tested in Section A or Section B of the exam. Questions may focus on any aspect of the group audit, although auditor reporting will not be examined in Section A. Groups tend to offer plenty of suitable audit risks for AAA – consequently, it is possible that the scenario in Section A will be a group audit.

Chapter overview

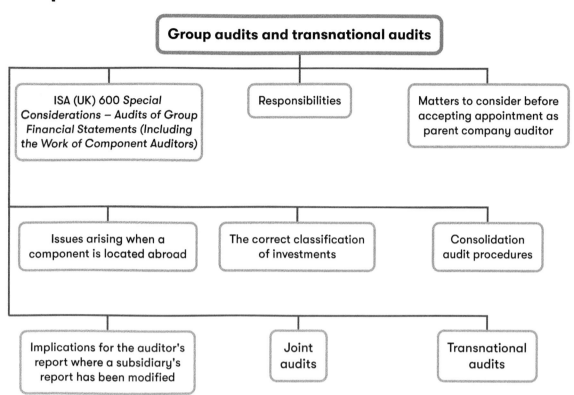

1 ISA (UK) 600 *Special Considerations – Audits of Group Financial Statements (Including the Work of Component Auditors)*

Essential reading

See Chapter 9 of the Essential reading for an overview of group accounting issues that you should have learned from your previous studies (including SBR).

The Essential reading is available as an Appendix of the digital edition of the Workbook.

As you know from your financial reporting studies, in a group situation the parent company will have to prepare its own audited financial statements, together with the audited **consolidated financial statements** incorporating **all component companies**.

> **Component:** An entity or business activity for which the group or component management prepares financial information that should be included in the group financial statements.
>
> **Component auditor:** An auditor who, at the request of the group engagement team, performs work on financial information related to a component for the group audit.
>
> **Component materiality:** The materiality level for a component determined by the group engagement team.
>
> **Group:** All the components whose financial information is included in the group financial statements. A group always has more than one component.
>
> **Group audit:** The audit of the group financial statements.
>
> (ISA (UK) 600: para. 9)

1.1 FRC Proposed ISA (UK) 600 (Revised) *Special Considerations – Audits of Group Financial Statements (Including the Work of Component Auditors)*

Issued in May 2022, this proposed standard attempts to address the issue of **audit quality** within **group audits**. This revision has been under discussion for a number of years due to its direct links to many other key standards that have been undergoing their own changes (such as ISA (UK) 315 (Revised 2020) and the suite of quality standards now in place).

Note. Due to the relatively late adoption of this revised ISA (UK), you will only be examined on the technical content of the **extant ISA (UK) 600** in the **UK version exam**. However, **knowledge of the revisions** from the **FRC Proposed ISA (UK)** will also be expected. The ACCA examining team has confirmed that you will be able to use either the extant ISA (UK) 600 or the proposed ISA (UK) 600 (Revised) in your answers should it be examined. It is therefore recommended that you learn this content (especially **aggregation risk** which is covered below and which is now part of the syllabus learning outcomes) and can apply it to the scenario.

Specific **areas of interest** from this Exposure Draft of ISA (UK) 600 (Revised) include the following:

*   Ongoing emphasis of the importance of **professional scepticism** and the need to **apply all ISAs (UK) across the whole of the group audit process**
*   Reinforcement of the importance of **identifying and assessing risks of material misstatement in the group financial statements** and responding appropriately via **suitable audit procedures** (emphasising the **involvement** of the group auditor in any work undertaken by a component auditor)
*   Reiterating that **aggregation risk** (the risk that the aggregate of uncorrected and undetected misstatements exceeds F/S materiality) is more likely to be increased within a group audit, especially if the size and/or complexity of the group and its components increases

 BPP

- As a result of the need to **manage aggregation risk** across a variety of different components, the ISA (UK) will move away from the classification of certain components as significant components and will instead expect group auditors to deploy **professional judgement** and use **component performance materiality** to respond appropriately to audit risk across the consolidated F/S
- **Enhanced communication** between all parties involved in a group audit (such as the group engagement partner, group engagement team and component auditors) will therefore be necessary
- New guidance will also be added on **testing controls** across the group and improved guidance on how to respond to any **restrictions** that might apply to people or information
- There will also be further details of aspects that apply to the group audit in the areas **communication** across the engagement team (including any component auditors) and **auditdocumentation**

(FRC, 2022c)

2 Responsibilities

The **group auditor** has sole responsibility for the opinion on the group financial statements. In most countries, this responsibility is not diminished by reliance on the work of any **component auditors**, who are a source of evidence only and are not referred to within the group auditor's report. There will be a **group engagement team** led by the **group engagement partner** who will be responsible for the performance of the group audit and providing an auditor's report on the group financial statements.

The group auditor must decide how much **reliance** they will place on the work performed by the **component auditor**. In order to do this, they will consider the qualifications, experience, competence, ethical standpoint and resources of the component auditors.

ISA (UK) 600 states that if a component company is audited by a component auditor and is deemed by the group auditor either to be so **significant in size or to pose a significant risk of material misstatement**, they can stipulate:

- That **further audit procedures** must be carried out; and
- The **extent** that the component auditor is involved (if at all).

The group auditor may not be able to access all the information it needs about components or component auditors, because of laws relating to confidentiality or data privacy, for example. The effect on the group audit opinion depends on the **significance of the component**.

If the **component is not significant**, then it may be sufficient just to have a complete set of financial statements, the component auditor's report, and information kept by group management.

If the **component is significant**, then it is possible that there will be an **inability to obtain sufficient appropriate audit evidence** about the component, in which case the audit opinion is either **qualified** or a **disclaimer of opinion** is issued. In this instance, it would also be impossible to comply with ISA (UK) 600's requirement to be involved with the work of the component auditor (for significant components), which would also lead to an inability to obtain sufficient appropriate audit evidence.

Generally, the group auditor should have the **right** to ask the component auditors for all reasonable information and explanations required to form their audit opinion. ISA (UK) 600 states that the component auditors should **co-operate** with the group auditor. In the UK, the Companies Act 2006 forces UK companies to provide all such information as the group auditor requires.

2.1 Significant components

Significant component: A component identified by the group engagement team: (a) that is of individual significance to the group, or (b) that, due to its specific nature or circumstances, is likely to include significant risks of material misstatement of the group financial statements. (ISA (UK) 600: para. 9(m))

ISA (UK) 600 states that a significant component can be identified by using a **benchmark** (ISA (UK) 600: para. A5). If component assets, liabilities, cash flows, profit or turnover (whichever is the most appropriate benchmark) **exceed 15% of the related group figure**, then the auditor may judge that the component is a **significant component.**

If a component is financially significant to the group financial statements, then the group engagement team or a component auditor will perform a full audit based on the component materiality level.

The group auditor should be involved in the assessment of risk in relation to significant components. If the component is otherwise significant due to its nature or circumstances, the group auditors will require **one** of the following.

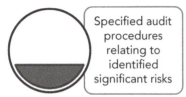 Specified audit procedures relating to identified significant risks

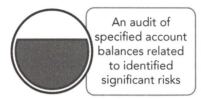 An audit of specified account balances related to identified significant risks

 A full audit using component materiality

Components that are not 'significant components' will be subject to analytical procedures at a group level – a full audit is not required for the purpose of the group audit/consolidated financial statements.

2.2 The component auditor

2.2.1 Understanding the component auditor

ISA (UK) 600 requires the group engagement team to obtain an **understanding** of the component auditor. This involves an assessment of the following.

(a) Whether the component auditor is **independent** and understands and will comply with the ethical requirements that are relevant to the group audit

(b) The component auditor's **professional competence**

(c) Whether the group engagement team will be **involved in the work of the component auditor** to the extent that it is necessary to obtain sufficient appropriate audit evidence

(d) Whether the component auditor operates in a **regulatory environment** that actively oversees auditors

2.2.2 Involvement with the component auditor

The extent of **involvement** by the group auditor at the planning stage will depend on the:

- Significance of the component
- Risks of material misstatement of the group financial statements
- Extent of the group auditor's understanding of the component auditor

The basic rule is that **where the component is significant, the group auditor must be involved in the component auditor's work**.

The **component auditor** should consider whether there might be any **restrictions** on them providing the group auditor with access to information, such as laws relating to **confidentiality** or data privacy. It should be borne in mind that in general, the component auditor is **not normally obliged to co-operate** with the group auditor (unless they are operating in a jurisdiction which requires them to do so). In practice, this means that the same audit firm will often be appointed as auditor of the group and its significant components.

2.2.3 Assessing the component auditor

For all companies in the group, the group auditor is required to perform a **review of the work done by the component auditor**. This is normally achieved by reviewing a report or questionnaire completed by the component auditor which highlights the key issues which have been identified during the course of the audit. The effect of any uncorrected misstatements and any instances where there has been an inability to obtain sufficient appropriate audit evidence should also be

 BPP

evaluated. On the basis of this review, the group auditor then needs to determine whether any additional procedures are necessary. These may include:

- Designing and performing further audit procedures. These may be designed and performed with the component auditors, or by the group auditor.
- Participating in the closing and other key meetings between the component auditors and component management
- Reviewing other relevant parts of the component auditors' documentation

2.2.4 Communicating with the component auditor

The group engagement team shall **communicate its requirements to the component auditor** on a timely basis. This communication shall set out the work to be performed, the use to be made of that work and the form and content of the component auditor's communication with the group engagement team (ISA (UK) 600: para. 40).

The group engagement team shall **request the component auditor to communicate matters** relevant to the group engagement team's conclusion with regard to the group audit (ISA (UK) 600: para. 41).

2.2.5 Communicating with group management and those charged with governance

ISA (UK) 600 identifies the following as matters which should be communicated to group management.

- Material deficiencies in the design or operating effectiveness of group-wide controls
- Material deficiencies that the group engagement team has identified in internal controls at components that are judged to be significant to the group
- Material deficiencies that component auditors have identified in internal controls at components that are judged to be significant to the group
- Fraud identified by the group engagement team or component auditors or information indicating that a fraud may exist

Where a component auditor is required to express an audit opinion on the financial statements of a component, the group engagement team will request group management to inform component management of any matters that they, the group engagement team, have become aware of that may be significant to the financial statements of the component. If group management refuses to pass on the communication, the group engagement team will discuss the matter with those charged with governance of the group. If the matter is still unresolved, the group engagement team shall consider whether to advise the component auditor not to issue the auditor's report on the component financial statements until the matter is resolved.

2.2.6 Communication with those charged with governance of the group

The following matters should be communicated to those charged with governance of the group.

- An overview of the type of work to be performed on the financial statements of the component
- An overview of the nature of the group engagement team's planned involvement in the work to be performed by the component auditors on significant components
- Instances where the group engagement team's evaluation of the work of a component auditor gave rise to a concern about the quality of that auditor's work
- Any limitations on the group audit, for example, where the group engagement team's access to information may have been restricted
- Fraud or suspected fraud involving group management, component management, employees who have significant roles in group-wide controls or others where fraud resulted in a material misstatement of the group financial statements

Activity 1: Communication

Communication is a two-way process. This is especially true in the context of the dialogue between the group auditor and the component auditor.

Required

1   Suggest some of the requirements that the group auditor would communicate to the component auditor.

2   Suggest some of the matters that the component auditor needs to tell the group auditor.

Solution

_____

2.3 Illustration of a simple group

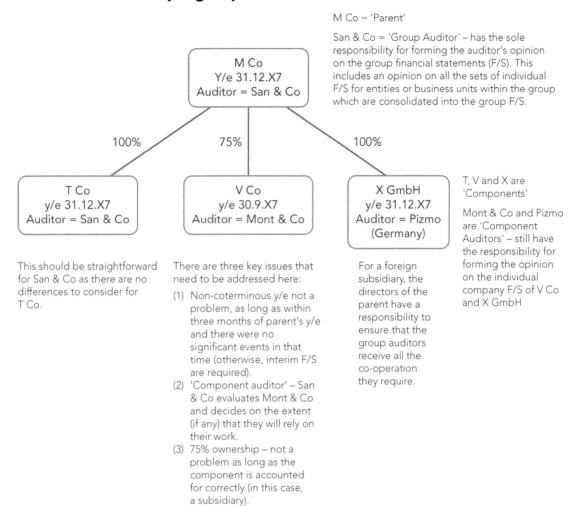

M Co = 'Parent'

San & Co = 'Group Auditor' – has the sole responsibility for forming the auditor's opinion on the group financial statements (F/S). This includes an opinion on all the sets of individual F/S for entities or business units within the group which are consolidated into the group F/S.

M Co
Y/e 31.12.X7
Auditor = San & Co

100% 75% 100%

T Co
y/e 31.12.X7
Auditor = San & Co

V Co
y/e 30.9.X7
Auditor = Mont & Co

X GmbH
y/e 31.12.X7
Auditor = Pizmo
(Germany)

T, V and X are 'Components'

Mont & Co and Pizmo are 'Component Auditors' – still have the responsibility for forming the opinion on the individual company F/S of V Co and X GmbH

This should be straightforward for San & Co as there are no differences to consider for T Co.

There are three key issues that need to be addressed here:

(1) Non-coterminous y/e not a problem, as long as within three months of parent's y/e and there were no significant events in that time (otherwise, interim F/S are required).

(2) 'Component auditor' – San & Co evaluates Mont & Co and decides on the extent (if any) that they will rely on their work.

(3) 75% ownership – not a problem as long as the component is accounted for correctly (in this case, a subsidiary).

For a foreign subsidiary, the directors of the parent have a responsibility to ensure that the group auditors receive all the co-operation they require.

Other considerations

Are any of the components immaterial? If so, obtain draft financial statements from them and perform an analytical review only. If this review suggests any errors exist, more detailed work will be needed.

Have there been any **changes** to the group structure? Changes such as acquisitions, disposals (or even part-disposals) are required under ISA (UK) 600 para. A12 as part of understanding the group. Is the **going concern** status of any component dependent on the parent's ongoing support? If so, a letter of support or comfort letter should be obtained by the auditor.

Given the nature of most consolidated groups in the 21st century, the group auditor's job is extremely **complex** and likely to be subject to a number of risks not faced during the audit of the parent company alone:

(a) Understanding the **structure of the group**, paying close attention to any **changes** and the risk of 'hidden' or 'shell' companies, as discovered during the Enron scandal

(b) Consideration of **group-wide controls** (controls designed, implemented and maintained by group management over group financial statements) to ensure there are no inherent problems in the audit

(c) The fact that their group opinion is often **based upon the work of others** and as such, this demonstrates significant audit risk

Consequently, **great care** must be taken when deciding whether or not to **accept** such work.

3 Matters to consider before accepting appointment as parent company auditor

Taking factors from Section 2 into account, the group auditor should consider whether or not their participation is sufficient to be able to act as the group auditor. For this purpose, the group engagement partner **must obtain an understanding of the group before acceptance** (ISA (UK) 600: para. 12) which should include the following:

- The **materiality** of the portion of the financial statements which the group auditor audits (and therefore, by implication, **the proportion that they do not audit**)
- The group auditor's degree of **knowledge** regarding the business of the components
- The **risk** of material misstatements in the financial statements of the components audited by the component auditor(s)
- The ability, where necessary, to perform **additional procedures** to enable them to act as group auditors
- The nature of the group auditor's **relationship** with the firm acting as component auditor

Under ISA (UK) 600, the group auditor will consider the following:

- The **quality of work** from **component auditors**;
- The ability of the group auditor to get involved with component auditors to obtain **sufficient appropriate audit evidence** if necessary; or
- The availability of **information on consolidation from the client**.

If the group auditor has **concerns** about any of these issues and are unlikely to be able to deliver anything other than a disclaimer of opinion, they should **not** consider either **accepting or continuing** with the engagement (ISA (UK) 600: para. 13).

4 Issues arising when a component is located abroad

When a component is located abroad a number of potential difficulties could arise such as the following:

Different accounting policies might be used in the foreign country. The component accounts must be brought into line with the accounting policies used by the parent company in order to consolidate properly. The group auditor will use the checklist mentioned above to determine the accounting policies used.

There may be **cultural problems** unique to the country in which the component operates. The group auditor will need to be sensitive to these during dealings with the component auditors. **Language problems** might also arise.

There may be issues in existence which are **specific to the country** in which the component operates. For example, some countries are subject to hyperinflation; accounts produced in these circumstances will need to be adjusted prior to consolidation with the parent. If the component is located in a developing country, there may be aspects of business infrastructure missing (eg education, technology or even anti-bribery legislation). Factors such as these will need to be identified for each component and tackled as appropriate during the audit.

5 The correct classification of investments

Essential reading

See Chapter 9 of the Essential reading for an overview of Associates and Joint Ventures that you should have learned from your previous studies (including SBR).

The Essential reading is available as an Appendix of the digital edition of the Workbook.

You know from your accounting studies that an investment is treated as a **subsidiary** when the parent company has **control** over that company. Where **significant influence** is held, the investment is treated as an **associate**. It is important that the degree of control exercised by the parent company is tested by the group auditor.

The auditor needs to consider how an investment fits into the activities of the group. They should **review board minutes** for evidence of the degree of influence exercised by the parent. They should also discuss the matter with the parent directors.

The existence of **other significant shareholders** may indicate that the parent company has little **influence**. The auditor should check the register of members to determine the level of shareholding and potential influence held by other shareholders.

The auditor should also consider how easy it is to obtain **information** about another company. This could also be an indicator of significant influence.

6 Consolidation audit procedures

There are a number of procedures that should be performed by the group auditor:

- Confirming the balances extracted from the financial statements of each component prior to their inclusion on the consolidation schedule
- Reviewing the disclosures necessary for the group accounts, such as related parties
- Gathering evidence appropriate to the various consolidation adjustments

Essential reading

See Chapter 9 of the Essential reading for an overview of the problems with consolidations and associated audit procedures that you should have learned from your previous studies (including SBR).

The Essential reading is available as an Appendix of the digital edition of the Workbook.

Activity 2: Consolidation

What are the major types of consolidation adjustment required for group financial statements?

Solution

Goodwill is calculated in accordance with **IFRS 3 *Business Combinations*,** to provide more transparency of the value of **non-controlling interests (NCI).** The standard allows measurement of NCI, either at share of subsidiary net assets or fair value (FV). The latter results in 100% of goodwill on acquisition analysed between parent and NCI elements for consolidation.

FV is used to determine assets and liabilities for these calculations. Share price on acquisition is used for the FV of the NCI. The overall approach the auditor should follow for determining FV can be summarised as follows:

- Obtain an understanding of the entity's process for determining FV
- Identify and assess the risks of material misstatement at the assertion level
- Perform audit procedures on the data used to develop the FV
- Evaluate whether the FV measurements have been properly determined

Activity 3: Wolf plc

You are the group auditor for Bad Ltd and are currently reviewing the consolidation adjustments for goodwill in respect of the acquisition of Wolf plc. Bad Ltd acquired 7½ million of the 10 million ordinary shares in Wolf plc for £12 million. At the time of acquisition, the FV of Wolf plc's net assets was £10 million and the share price was £1.50 each. Bad Ltd operates a policy of valuing NCI at fair value.

Required

Calculate goodwill on the acquisition of Wolf plc and explain the principal audit procedures you would perform on the goodwill calculation schedule.

£'000

Consideration transferred

NCI

Sub-total

Net assets acquired

Goodwill

NCI at FV

NCI at share of net assets

Goodwill attributable to NCI

Goodwill attributable to Bad Ltd shareholders

Goodwill attributable to NCI shareholders

Total goodwill

Solution

What happens if a group disposes of one or more components?

Activity 4: Saul Group

It is 1 July 20X5. You are an audit manager in Will & Co that is responsible for the audit of the Saul Group (the Group) which consists of a parent company and a number of wholly owned subsidiaries all operating in the publishing industry. Your firm audits all components within the Group, which has a reporting date of 30 September 20X5. You are planning the audit of the Group and the following events have been flagged as priority planning matters:

(1) On 31 March 20X5, the Group disposed of all shares owned in one subsidiary, Mabel Ltd, in order to generate cash for ongoing product development.

(2) On 30 June 20X5, the Group decided to dispose of its interest in Neve Co, a subsidiary that is responsible for all of the Group's operations in a sub-continent called Amaria where sales have recently been badly affected by a major conflict among several neighbouring countries.

Required

As part of your planning for the audit of the Group, describe the matters that your firm will need to consider in relation to the disposals of Mabel Ltd and Neve Co, and recommend suitable audit procedures to address these matters.

Solution

7 Implications for the auditor's report where a component's report has been modified

In a group situation, **materiality** and **risk** must be assessed in the context of the group as a whole. The group auditor must consider the materiality of any modifications to a component's auditor's report in relation to the whole of the consolidated financial statements.

This can lead to situations where a **component** may have a **material qualification** that has **no impact on the group opinion** which would then remain unmodified. Similarly, a **pervasive** modification in a component's auditor's report may only have a **material impact** on the group opinion.

Ultimately the decision as to the impact of a modification to a component's auditor's report on the consolidated opinion is a matter of **judgement** for the group auditor. Where the group auditor concludes that **adequate evidence** about the work of the component auditor cannot be obtained and has been unable to perform sufficient additional procedures with respect to that component, they should consider the **implications** for the auditor's report. A subsequent modification in these circumstances would be on the grounds of **insufficient inappropriate audit evidence**.

8 Joint audits

A joint audit means an audit where two or more auditors are responsible for an audit engagement and jointly produce an auditor's report to the client.

Reasons for joint audits

Two or more firms could act as joint auditors for the following reasons:

(a) In a new **acquisition**, the parent may insist that their auditor acts jointly with those of the new subsidiary.

(b) A company operating from widely **dispersed locations** may find it useful to have joint auditors.

(c) **Foreign subsidiaries** may need to employ local audit firms to satisfy the laws of the country in which they operate. These local auditors may act jointly with the group auditors.

 BPP

(d) Some companies may prefer to use **local accountants**, while at the same time, enjoying the wider range of services offered by a large national firm.

Before accepting appointment as a joint auditor, it will be necessary to consider the **experience** and **standards** of the other firm.

The allocation of work between the firms needs to be agreed and the auditors should agree whether joint or separate engagement letters will be sent.

Both firms must sign the auditor's report, and both are responsible for the whole audit. They are **jointly liable** in the event of litigation. Such joint audits can therefore be seen to be complex to manage and potentially expensive.

Real life example: Joint audits in practice

In the wake of high-profile 21st century corporate collapses that included Carillion and BHS, the UK government has been under pressure to introduce reforms to the way that audits are undertaken. There has been no shortage of consultation and opinion on what is needed, and in May 2022, the government's plans for revamping the audit regime were unveiled. Some of the proposals had been recommended by previously commissioned reports: for example, in 2018, the Kingman Review had called for the Financial Reporting Council (FRC) to be replaced by a regulator with more wide-ranging powers, and it is anticipated that the Audit, Reporting and Governance Authority (ARGA) will fulfil this role in the UK from 2025. Recommendations made around the same time by the Brydon Review and Competitions and Markets Authority (CMA) were also considered, including the creation of a separate auditing profession, but the government concluded that not all proposals could be implemented as it attempted to find a middle-ground between greater regulatory control to avoid further scandals and avoiding bureaucracy in order to encourage greater economic prosperity.

One of the measures that did make the cut was the need for audits of the top 350 UK listed companies to be conducted using 'challenger' firms from outside of the 'Big Four' of Deloitte, EY, KPMG and PwC in an attempt to remove some of these firms' dominance and thus improve audit quality. It has also been observed that with so little competition in this field, should one of the Big Four no longer be able to provide audit services to clients, the entry barriers for firms outside of the Big Four are considered detrimental to increasing quality through competition.

The UK government refers to this approach as 'managed shared audits' but this is an example of how joint audits could be seen in practice, where the Big Four firm takes the lead and the smaller challenger firm can be allocated subsidiaries more appropriate to their size.

Since committing to this new approach, the proposals have not received the response the UK government was after. Some critics suggest that these arrangements would lead to duplicated work and higher fees, with estimates of the additional audit fees for this approach topping £1 billion over the next ten years, raising questions over what benefit this additional cost will bring to the people being asked to pay for them. Big Four firms appear sceptical that the approach will work in practice, while some challenger firms have expressed a preference for completing smaller audits on their own as opposed to helping out on larger engagements.

Considering the learning outcome for this part of the syllabus, candidates are going to be expected to consider when such an approach would be considered appropriate and what additional risks and challenges joint audits would bring. There are clearly some benefits to introducing more competition to the audit market by allowing fresh ideas to be introduced, improving innovation, and disrupting the status quo, but the risk that work could be duplicated (or worse, left by one firm to be dealt with by the other and ignored), plus the additional costs involved, make this approach challenging to implement.

9 Transnational audits

A transnational audit means an audit of financial statements which are, or may be, relied upon **outside the entity's home jurisdiction** for purposes of significant lending, investment or regulatory decisions. This will include audits of all financial statements of companies with listed equity or debt and other public interest entities which attract particular public attention because of their size, products or services provided.

The growth in such transnational engagements has led to a number of issues that clients are more aware of in the 21st century:

(a) Variations in **audit approaches** and the role of regulators across different jurisdictions has led to variable degrees of engagement quality.

(b) The incomplete nature of ISA adoption worldwide has led to **variations** in audit approach.

(c) **Cultural differences** worldwide have also led to different audit approaches.

In response to this trend towards globalisation and the issues associated with transnational audits, a **Forum of Firms (FOF)** was created, initially by the 'Big Four' firms but now with over 20 member firms.

To support and provide guidance to the FOF the IAASB has set up the **Transnational Auditors Committee**.

Specific responsibilities of the TAC include the following:

- Identifying audit practice issues. When the issues suggest changes in auditing or assurance standards may be required, recommending to the appropriate IFAC standard-setting boards that the issue be reviewed.

- Providing a forum to discuss 'best practices' in areas including quality management, auditing practices, independence, and training and development.

- Proposing members to the IFAC Regulatory Liaison Group and identifying qualified candidates to serve on IFAC standard-setting boards.

- Acting as a formal conduit for interaction among transnational firms and international regulators and financial institutions with regard to audit quality, systems of quality management, and transparency of international networks.

Chapter summary

Group audits and transnational audits

ISA (UK) 600 *Special Considerations – Audits of Group Financial Statements (Including the Work of Component Auditors)*

- **Group auditor:** Sole responsibility for audit opinion on group financial statements
- **Group engagement team** performs the group audit
- **Component auditor:** Used as a source of evidence only - need to be assessed for quality and reliability
- Group auditor can request **further work** on a component if component is of significant size and/or risk (with or without component auditor's involvement)
- Need to consider **issues** such as non-coterminous year-ends (<3 months = adjust for significant events only; >3 months = interim F/S) and part ownership
- Group auditor requires from component auditor(s):
  - Independence requirements
  - Areas of special interest in the component
- Component auditor requires questionnaire of timetables
- Responsibilities from group auditor

Responsibilities

- Parent company produces own financial statements, audited by own auditor
- Components in a group include:
  - Division
  - Branch
  - Subsidiary
  - Joint Venture
  - Associate
- Group accounts audited by parent company auditor
- Subsidiary accounts audited by component auditor

Matters to consider before accepting appointment as parent company auditor

- Materiality of components not audited by group auditor
- Knowledge of business of components not audited
- Risk of components not audited:
  - Ability to perform additional procedures
  - Nature of relationship with component auditors
  - Group auditor may consider that if insufficient and/or inappropriate evidence is available – Disclaimer – continue or decline?

Issues arising when a component is located abroad

- Different accounting policies
- Cultural problems
- Language problems
- Country specific problems

The correct classification of investments

- Control = subsidiary
- Significant influence = associate
- Auditor must look for evidence of who is actually in control (eg board minutes, correspondence etc)

Consolidation audit procedures

- Calculation of goodwill and any impairments
- Cancellation of any inter-company balances
- Provisions for unrealised profits
- Fair Value (FV) adjustments
- Retranslation of F/S from overseas components
- Correct value of components in parent F/S

```
┌─────────────────────────┐        ┌──────────┐          ┌──────────────┐
│ Implications for the     │        │  Joint   │          │ Transnational│
│ auditor's report where   │        │  audits  │          │    audits    │
│ a subsidiary's report    │        └──────────┘          └──────────────┘
│ has been modified        │
└─────────────────────────┘
```

- Group auditor must assess materiality for the group as a whole
- The degree of modification (material or pervasive) may be different in the component auditor's report than for the group
- Group auditor uses judgment to decide whether or not there is a material impact or a lack of sufficient/appropriate audit evidence

- Why?
  – New acquisition
  – Dispersed location
  – Foreign subsidiaries
  – Client choice
- Need to consider standards and experience of other firm
- Joint liability
- Impacts on the profession?

- Audits where the F/S may be relied on in a different country to where the entity is based
- Different approaches and regulations have led to varying levels of audit quality
- Forum of Firms (Big Four plus others)
- IAASB – Transnational Auditors Committee (TAC):
  – Identifying audit practice issues
  – Discussing best practice
  – Membership of IFAC committees
  – Formal conduit for promoting interaction between firms

Knowledge diagnostic

1. ISA (UK) 600

Group auditors are responsible for the audit of the parent company and group financial statements, while **component auditors** are responsible for the opinion on component financial statements. The group auditor can ask for **more work** to be done by the component auditor or even discount with their opinion if risk of material misstatement dictates. Remember that you need to be aware of the contents of the recent Exposure Draft (FRC Proposed ISA) on ISA (UK) 600 (Revised).

2. Acting as the group auditor

Auditors must consider whether or not they are happy to **accept or continue** in such engagements such as, for example, when there are concerns over the amount known about this audit or the **risk of misstatement on audits not covered by them**.

3. Overseas components

Issues arising when a component is located abroad are often of a very practical nature and can impact on the auditor's ability to perform the tasks necessary for the audit opinion.

4. Correct classification of components

The correct classification of investments is key to how group financial statements are presented – Subsidiary vs Associate vs Joint venture vs Investment.

5. Consolidation and goodwill

Auditors need to be able to calculate the **consolidation adjustments** required for the consolidated accounts, including **goodwill** based on the correct **FV** of the group's assets and liabilities.

6. Reporting issues

Depending on the **size** and **nature** of any component modification, the impact may range from immaterial to pervasive.

7. Joint audits

In some cases, there may be a need for more than one audit firm to act as group auditor and each has to be aware of the issues before agreeing to act.

8. Transnational audits

As the impact and financing of consolidated groups become **more global**, the auditing profession has set up an **FOF** supported by the IAASB to address the needs of how best to provide consistent quality and approaches.

Further study guidance

Question practice

Now try the following from the Further question practice bank (available in the digital edition of the Workbook):

- Question 19 'Annabella' tests audit planning in a group context, including the audit procedures required to test a consolidation.

- Questions 11 'Trendy Group' and 18 'Griffin' also cover groups, although they have been set for earlier chapters – make sure you revisit these in the context of what you have learned here.

- Question 32 'Grissom Group' is a good representation of what you can expect to see in Question 1 of the real AAA exam where you might be asked to perform planning procedures in the context of a group audit engagement. Note that this question also tests all four professional skills, so you may wish to refer to the skills checkpoints before attempting this question.

Further reading

There is one technical article written by the AAA examining team that you will find relevant to this chapter. It is available for you to read on the ACCA website:

- Group audits

Own research

- Find a copy of a set of financial statements for a consolidated group and review them for the various disclosures made by both management and auditors to see what such an engagement actually includes.

- Use the following link to read up on the Transnational Auditors Committee (TAC) and the Forum of Firms (FOF):

  www.ifac.org/who-we-are/committees/transnational-auditors-committee-forum-firms

 BPP

Activity answers

Activity 1: Communication

Approach

This is an opportunity for you to consider some very practical points about the dialogue between group auditors and component auditors. Pretend that you are the group auditor and you know nothing about the firm on whose work you will be relying: What do you need to know in order to be able to trust them?

Consider:

(1)   What you need the component auditor to either know or confirm to the group auditor; and

(2)   What you really need to know about the outcome of the audit that the component auditor has conducted on your behalf.

Suggested solution

These communications to the component auditor would include:

1.   A request that the component auditor confirms their co-operation with the group engagement team

2.   The ethical requirements that are relevant to the group audit and in particular, independence requirements

3.   In the case of an audit or review of the financial information of the component, component materiality and the threshold above which misstatements cannot be regarded as clearly trivial to the group financial statements

4.   Identified significant risks of material misstatement in the group financial statements, due to fraud or error that are relevant to the work of the component auditor; the group engagement team requests the component auditor to communicate any other identified significant risks of material misstatement and the component auditor's responses to such risks

5.   A list of related parties prepared by group management and any other related parties of which the group engagement team is aware; component auditors are requested to communicate any other related parties not previously identified

Suggested solution

This communication by the component auditor often takes the form of a memorandum, questionnaire or report of work performed and includes the following:

1.   Whether the component auditor has complied with ethical requirements that are relevant to the group audit, including independence and professional acceptance

2. Whether the component auditor has complied with the group engagement team's requirements

3. Identification of the financial information of the component on which the component auditor is reporting

4. Information on instances of non-compliance with laws and regulations that could give rise to material misstatement of the group financial statements

5. A list of uncorrected misstatements of the financial information of the component (the list need not include items that are below the threshold for clearly trivial misstatements)

6. Indicators of possible management bias

7. Description of any material deficiencies identified in internal control over financial reporting at the component level

8. Other significant matters that the component auditor communicated or expects to communicate to those charged with governance of the component, including fraud or suspected fraud involving component management, employees who have significant roles in internal control at the component level or others where the fraud resulted in a material misstatement of the financial information of the component

9. Any other matters that may be relevant to the group audit or that the component auditor wishes to draw to the attention of the group engagement team, including exceptions noted in the written representations that the component auditor requested from component management

10. The component auditor's overall findings, conclusions and opinion on the component's financial statements

Activity 2: Consolidation

Approach

This should be idea-generation again – you should get used to the need to recall certain items rapidly as this may happen in the real exam. Consider what you have learned about consolidations from FR and SBR and then consider what adjustments you have completed when attempting questions for these subjects!

Suggested solution

- The calculation of any goodwill, including any impairment reviews as appropriate
- Cancellation of intra-group balances and transactions, such as dividends
- Provisions for unrealised profits resulting from intra-group transactions
- Fair value adjustments on assets and liabilities
- Retranslation of financial statements for overseas components
- The correct value of any components included in the parent company's financial statements

Activity 3: Wolf plc

Top Tips

Calculations of NCI at the year end will require this acquisition figure plus any share of identifiable net assets. Review the essential reading in the digital edition of this Workbook for fuller details of ISA (UK) 600 and IFRS 3 and how to calculate this schedule. Once you have the numbers, work your way down each line and consider what evidence you could seek to back each one up.

Suggested solution

	£'000
Consideration transferred	12,000
Non-controlling interest (2.5m shares × £1.50 per share)	3,750
Sub-total	**15,750**
Net assets acquired	(10,000)
Goodwill (difference)	**5,750**
Non-controlling interest at fair value (above)	3,750
Non-controlling interest at share of net assets (25% × £10m FV)	2,500
Goodwill attributable to NCI (difference)	**1,250**
Goodwill attributable to Bad Ltd shareholders (balancing figure)	4,500
Goodwill attributable to NCI shareholders (above)	1,250
Total goodwill (above)	**5,750**

Principle audit procedures

- Obtain a copy of the goodwill calculation from Bad Ltd and recalculate to ensure accuracy.
- Confirm the consideration of £12 million to a broker's invoice and Bad Ltd's bank statements.
- Confirm Bad Ltd's ownership of the shares, the date of the transaction and the number of shares owned by inspecting copies of the share certificates.
- Confirm the share price paid on the date of transfer using a third-party source (eg Bloomberg).
- Obtain working papers confirming the fair value of £10 million for Wolf plc's net assets.
- Confirm the total number of ordinary shares in existence for Wolf plc.
- Confirm choice of correct accounting treatment by reading board minutes for adoption of IFRS 3.

> **Tutorial note.** Should you be asked to design suitable audit procedures in respect of an acquisition, in addition to those listed above, you could discuss seeking confirmation of the board's approval for the acquisition by obtaining copies of the relevant board minutes, recalculating any amounts used in the accounting treatment, challenging any of the assumptions used in the process of determining fair values, and evaluating the process used to acquire the new component (such as whether any due diligence was required and whether any necessary loan financing has been appropriately accounted for).

Activity 4: Saul Group

> **Approach**
>
> This question reflects the type of thing you could see in the exam – the context of various organisations, some supporting information for detail, and a specific requirement. To stand a good chance of scoring well here, you need to remember that your answers should prioritise the impact of these events on the planning of the group audit, so the group financial statements should be your primary focus. You will also need to remember how to account for disposals and discontinued operations in a group, so make sure you have referred to the relevant parts of the Essential reading for Chapter 8 and 9 if you are unsure of any of the accounting standards.

Mabel Ltd

Matters to consider

IFRS 5 *Non-current assets held for sale and discontinued operations* is the relevant standard for disposals. For Mabel Ltd, this should be a straightforward process of identifying all of the assets and liabilities that related to Mabel Ltd at 31 March 20X5 and confirming that they have not been included in the statement of financial position for the Group at 30 September 20X5.

The income and expenditure of the Group should reflect all of the activity relating to Mabel Ltd up to 31 March 20X5 when the company ceased to be part of the Group. Disclosures relating to the disposal of Mabel Ltd will also need to be reviewed to confirm that they showed Mabel Ltd's activity as a discontinued operation under IFRS 5. There will also be a group profit or loss on disposal, calculated as the disposal proceeds less Mabel Ltd's net assets at 31 March 20X5 less any goodwill remaining relating to Mabel Ltd; this will also be disclosed in the group statement of profit or loss and other comprehensive income as a discontinued operation.

> **Tutorial note.** The investment in Mabel Ltd has been disposed of and will therefore be removed from the financial statements of the parent and a gain or loss on disposal recognised in the parent's financial statements. However, the question is only asking for the impact on the group audit, so comments about the parent's financial statements would not be required.

Audit procedures

- Obtain copies of the Group board minutes confirming the decision to dispose of Mabel Ltd, including agreement that the date of disposal was 31 March 20X5, the amount of consideration that was agreed and the method of payment (cash and/or paper, whether immediate, deferred or contingent etc).

- Obtain copies of all relevant sale documentation for the disposal of Mabel Ltd (such as contracts and/or invoices).

- Confirm the correct receipt of any funds paid by reference to the relevant bank account and cash book. Reconcile the correct treatment of any other form of disposal proceeds (for example, shares to the relevant share certificates and an estimate of their value).

- Inspect draft copies of the consolidated financial statements for any deferred or contingent consideration and confirm consistency with relevant sale documentation.

- Recalculate the group profit or loss on disposal of Mabel Ltd.

- Inspect the Group consolidation workings to ensure that the assets and liabilities of Mabel Ltd have not been included in the group statement of financial position at 30 September 20X5.

- Recalculate the income and expenditure of Mabel Ltd on a pro-rata basis and reconcile these amounts to the group statement of profit or loss and other comprehensive income, confirming their disclosure as discontinued operations.

> **Tutorial note.** Other sensible audit procedures that address the disposal should be rewarded provided they are relevant to Mabel Ltd and the Group.

Neve Co

Matters to consider

Compliance with IFRS 5 will be especially important here because although Neve Co is going to be disposed of, the disposal does not yet appear to have happened. (However, it still might before the end of the reporting period, so the auditor should remain alert to this throughout the planning process.) Should the disposal occur shortly after the reporting date, it is likely that it will represent a non-adjusting event under IAS 10 *Events after the reporting period* and will therefore require disclosure in the consolidated financial statements of the Group.

IFRS 5 allows items classified as 'held for sale' to be presented separately in the financial statements, but only if they meet the criteria stipulated by IFRS 5. Non-current assets held for sale should be measured at the lower of their carrying amount at the date they classified as 'held for sale' and fair value less costs to sell, with any resultant impairment losses recognised in the group statement of profit or loss and other comprehensive income, and no further depreciation should be recognised on these assets after 30 June 20X5 (assuming the IFRS 5 criteria have been satisfied).

Underpinning all of this is the need to confirm that the disposal of Neve Co satisfies the criteria laid down by IFRS 5. A discontinued operation is a component that has either been disposed of or is classified as 'held for sale' and which represents a separate major line of business or geographical area of operations and is part of a single co-ordinated plan to dispose of a separate major line of business or geographical area of operations. Neve Co appears to satisfy these criteria, given that it is a separate component of the group and deals with the Group's publishing activities in Amaria, which is an area where the Group is keen to cease trading. Neve Co also needs to be available for immediate sale in its present condition and the sale must be highly probable.

In order to determine compliance with these criteria, the auditor needs to answer the following questions by performing the following procedures:

Questions	Audit procedures
Is the management of the Group committed to the sale of Neve Co?	Obtain copies of board minutes that confirm the decision to dispose of the Group's interest in Neve Co.
Is there an active plan to locate a buyer for Neve Co?	Discuss progress on the sale process with the management of the Group and seek evidence that the sale is actively occurring (for example, confirming that a firm or other agency has been appointed to proceed with the sale of Neve Co).
Is Neve Co being marketed at a fair price?	Inspect documentation associated with determining the sales value of Neve Co and consider the appropriateness of the value in comparison with similar businesses.
Will the sale of Neve Co be completed by 30 June 20X6?	Discuss progress on the sale of Neve Co with management and any sales agents as appropriate.
Are the plans to dispose of Neve Co likely to change?	Obtain written representations from the management of the Group to confirm the decision to dispose of Neve Co is not likely to be changed.

Audit procedures

- Obtain draft copies of the consolidated financial statements of the Group and confirm that the disclosure requirements of IFRS 5 have been met for Neve Co (for example, separate disclosure on the statement of financial position and any revaluation gains or losses and post-tax profits disclosed separate to continuing operations in the statement of profit or loss and other comprehensive income, separate cash flows, separate earnings per share (EPS) calculations for Neve Co etc).

- Compare the draft consolidated financial statements for the year ending 30 September 20X5 with the prior year to confirm all assets and liabilities and income and expenditure relating to Neve Co have been removed from the appropriate lines.

 BPP

- Obtain valuation information for Neve Co and confirm the carrying amount with the most recent set of audited financial statements.

- Review the calculations used to calculate the fair value less costs to sell for Neve Co and confirm the reasonableness of the assumptions used in relation to any impairment or other market factors.

- Confirm that depreciation has not been charged on any non-current assets associated with Neve Co after 30 June 20X5.

- Deploy suitable levels of professional scepticism to ensure that the accounting entries used to reflect Neve Co as a discontinued operation are not manipulated in order to make the company look more attractive and hence increase its sales value

---

Tutorial note. Other sensible audit procedures that address the requirements of IFRS 5 and other disposal arrangements should be rewarded provided they are relevant to Neve Co and the Group.

10

Completion

Learning objectives

On completion of this chapter, you should be able to:

	Syllabus reference no.
Design audit procedures designed to identify subsequent events which may require adjustment to, or disclosure in, the financial statements of a given entity.	E1(a)
Evaluate indicators that the going concern basis may be in doubt and recognise mitigating factors.	E1(b)
Recommend audit procedures, or evaluate the evidence that might be expected to be available and assess the appropriateness of the going concern basis in given situations.	E1(c)
Assess the adequacy of disclosures in financial statements relating to going concern and explain the implications for the auditor's report with regard to the going concern basis.	E1(d)
Apply analytical procedures for the purposes of evaluation and review and evaluate the results in the context of other audit evidence.	E2(a)
Assess whether an engagement has been planned and performed in accordance with professional standards.	E2(b)
Evaluate whether reports issued are appropriate in the relevant circumstances.	E2(c)
Evaluate as part of the final review the matters (eg materiality, risk, relevant accounting standards) and audit evidence to confirm if sufficient and appropriate evidence has been obtained.	E2(d)
Evaluate the use of written representations from management to support other audit evidence.	E2(e)
Justify the review procedures which should be performed in a given assignment, including the need for an engagement quality review and the appropriateness of the review performed.	E2(f)
Recommend appropriate additional procedures or actions required following review of the assurance work.	E2(g)
Describe the importance of the role of the engagement quality reviewer.	E2(h)

	Syllabus reference no.
Evaluate the appropriateness of the engagement quality reviewer in a given scenario, recommending further actions which may be taken within the firm.	E2(i)
Describe appropriate audit procedures relating to: (xxi) Events after the end of the reporting period	D3(a)
Explain how the auditor's responsibilities for corresponding figures, comparative financial statements and 'other information' are discharged.	D3(b)
Discuss the courses of action available to an auditor if a material inconsistency or material misstatement exists in relation to other information, such as contained in the integrated report.	E3(h)

Business and exam context

Towards the end of an audit, a series of reviews and evaluations are carried out. You should be familiar with them from your previous auditing studies.

We start with the **overall review** which is undertaken on the financial statements as a whole and the review of misstatements and potential misstatements. The section then discusses the details of a **quality management review of an individual audit**.

Often the auditors will have to rely on **written representations** about related parties and other issues. Written representations are subjective evidence, and the auditor must proceed with caution when dealing with them. The auditor conducts reviews of the period between the period end and the signing of the auditor's report **(subsequent events)** and of the **going concern** presumption.

The issue of **comparatives** is also discussed. The auditor has different responsibilities for corresponding figures and for comparative information. Finally, the auditor must review **other information** to establish whether it contradicts the financial statements. The detailed procedures and requirements are discussed in Section 4.

Going concern is a particularly important audit review which could be relevant in risks or evidence questions. Bear in mind the links with planning, knowledge of the business and analytical procedures. **Subsequent events, corresponding figures** and **other information** could also come up in an exam question in the context of auditor's reports.

Questions in syllabus sections E – G can only be examined in Section B of the exam, and will not be part of the audit planning question. It is theoretically possible that events after the reporting period could be examined in Section A of the exam, but this is very unlikely.

Chapter overview

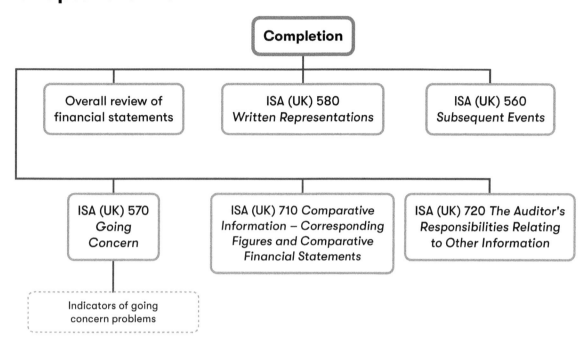

1 Overall review of financial statements

1.1 ISA (UK) 220 (Revised) *Quality Management for an Audit of Financial Statements*

PER alert

One of the competencies you require to fulfil **Performance Objective 20** of the PER is the ability to review the performance of an audit, ensuring the process has been undertaken effectively and that all work undertaken is accurate and complete and that sufficient evidence has been obtained. You can apply the knowledge you have obtained from this chapter of the Workbook to help demonstrate this competency.

At the completion stage, the auditor performs an overall review of all work done to obtain reasonable assurance that the audit complies with professional standards and all applicable legal and regulatory requirements, and that the auditor's report issued is appropriate in the circumstances (ISA (UK) 220 (Revised): para. 11).

Under ISA (UK) 220 (Revised) the engagement partner has overall responsibility for managing and achieving quality within an audit engagement (in the UK, the engagement partner is a key audit partner). In order to achieve this quality, the standard applies the firm-wide approach from ISQMs (UK) 1 and 2 to each audit engagement in the following areas:

- Leadership responsibilities for managing and achieving quality on audits
- Relevant ethical requirements, including those related to independence
- Acceptance and continuance of client relationships and audit engagements
- Engagement resources
- Engagement performance
- Monitoring and remediation
- Taking overall responsibility for managing and achieving quality
- Documentation

Engagements undertaken for listed entities and other entities that might either present certain quality risks to the firm or be subject to certain legal or regulatory requirements shall have an objective **engagement quality review** performed, which evaluates significant judgements and conclusions reached by the engagement team in the context of professional standards and the applicable legal and regulatory framework. This review should be conducted by an individual with suitable competence and capabilities, plus appropriate independence and authority, and is completed before the auditor's report is dated by the engagement partner. The guidance on engagement quality reviews from ISA (UK) 220 (Revised) is supported by ISQMs (UK) 1 and 2 which is covered in more detail in Chapter 4.

Essential reading

See Chapter 10 of the Essential reading for more detail on ISA (UK) 220 (Revised). Remember that we have already covered a lot of the firm-level detail of quality management in Chapter 4.

The Essential reading is available as an Appendix of the digital edition of the Workbook.

1.2 ISA (UK) 520 *Analytical Procedures*

Relevant trends and ratios are **recalculated** by the auditor at the completion stage in order to ensure the consistency of the final version of the financial statements with the evidence that has been collected during the audit.

Examples of the areas that the analytical procedures at the final stage must cover:
Important accounting ratio
Related items
Changes in products and/or customers
Price and mix changes
Wages changes
Variances
Trends in production and sales
Changes in material and labour content at production
Other statement of profit or loss expenditure
Variations caused by industry or economic factors

The analytical procedures performed at the completion stage are no different from those performed elsewhere in the audit process. The only difference is that by this time, the auditor should know enough about the client to be able to point to evidence explaining the issues highlighted by the analytical review.

If the auditor finds a previously unrecognised risk of material misstatement at this stage, then it will have to revise its assessment of audit risk. This may affect materiality, for example, and may mean that further audit evidence is needed in certain areas.

PER alert

One of the competencies you require to fulfil **Performance Objective 19** of the PER is the ability to evaluate evidence collected, demonstrating professional scepticism, investigating areas of concern and ensuring documentation is complete and all significant matters and areas of judgement are highlighted. You can apply the knowledge you gain from this chapter of the Workbook to help demonstrate this competency.

1.3 ISA (UK) 450 (revised) *Evaluation of Misstatements Identified during the Audit*

By the end of the audit, there may be a number of misstatements that have been identified as a result of the auditor's procedures (including **disclosures** where details could have been either omitted or misstated and which could indicate **fraud**). Those that are clearly **trivial** will be ignored, while those that the client has already **agreed to amend** will be reviewed to ensure this has occurred. What about any remaining misstatements though?

The auditor must consider the impact on the financial statements of **uncorrected misstatements**, especially those that are not individually material, because in **aggregate**, their cumulative effect may become material (ISA (UK) 450: para.11). The auditor needs to evaluate these misstatements and differentiate between those that are **factual misstatements** (those that are clearly misstated), **judgemental misstatements** (those relating to accounting policies or estimates) and **projected misstatements** (which cannot be quantified specifically) (ISA (UK) 450: para. A6).

Should the **aggregate** of uncorrected misstatements **start to become material**, then the auditor can either perform **further procedures** or request management to **adjust the financial statements**. Ultimately, this could lead to a **modification of the audit opinion** if corrections are not made, so it is essential to discuss this with those charged with governance. However, if any reference to misstatements could be considered to represent **tipping off** (for example, if the misstatement related to NOCLAR or, more specifically, money laundering) legal advice should be sought by the auditor before proceeding any further (ISA (UK) 450 (revised): para. 8).

During this stage of the audit, materiality may **change** due to adjustments made by management, so the auditor should be alert to the risk that some misstatements may now become material.

The **summary of uncorrected misstatements** will not only list misstatements from the current year, but also those from the previous year(s). This will allow misstatements to be highlighted which are reversals of misstatements in the previous year, such as in the valuation of closing/opening inventory. **Cumulative** misstatements may also be shown, which have increased from year to year. It is normal to show both the statement of financial position and the statement of profit or loss and other comprehensive income effect, as in the **example** given here.

Schedule of uncorrected misstatements

	20X2				20X1			
	Statement of profit or loss		Statement of financial position		Statement of profit or loss		Statement of financial position	
	Debit	Credit	Debit	Credit	Debit	Credit	Debit	Credit
	£	£	£	£	£	£	£	£
(a) ABC Co receivable unprovided	10,470			10,470	4,523			4,523
(b) Opening/ closing inventory undervalued*	21,540			21,540		21,540	21,540	
(c) Closing inventory undervalued		34,105	34,105					
(d) Opening unaccrued expenses								
Telephone*		453	453		453			453
Electricity*		905	905		905			905
(e) Closing unaccrued expenses								
Telephone	427			427				
Electricity	1,128			1,128				
(f) Obsolete inventory write off	2,528			2,528	3,211			3,211
Total	36,093	35,463	35,463	36,093	9,092	21,540	21,540	9,092
*Cancelling items	21,540			21,540				
		453	453					
		905	905					
	14,553	34,105	34,105	14,553				

2 ISA (UK) 580 *Written Representations*

The **objectives** of the auditor under ISA (UK) 580 are:

(a) To **obtain appropriate representationsfrom management** and, where appropriate, those charged with governance that they believe that they have fulfilled their **responsibility** for the preparation of the financial statements and for the completeness of the information provided to the auditor

(b) To **support other audit evidence** relevant to the financial statements or specific assertions in the financial statements by means of written representations if determined necessary by the auditor or required by other ISAs (UK)

(c) To **respond appropriately** to written representations provided by management and, where appropriate, those charged with governance, or if management or, where appropriate, those charged with governance do not provide the written representations requested by the auditor (ISA (UK) 580: para. 6)

2.1 If the client refuses to provide representations

If the responsible party refuses to provide requested representations, this constitutes 'insufficient/inappropriate audit evidence' **leading to a disclaimer of opinion** (this would also be the case if there was doubt over management's integrity) (ISA (UK) 580: paras. 19–20).

2.2 Contents of a typical letter of representation

- Responsibilities for preparing the financial statements, including significant assumptions
- Related party relationships and transactions
- Events subsequent to the date of the financial statements
- The effects of uncorrected misstatements (and confirmation that they are not material)
- Confirmation that access has been granted to all information
- All transactions have been recorded in the accounting records
- All information in relation to fraud or suspected fraud that management is aware of
- Known instances of non-compliance or suspected non-compliance with laws and regulations

3 ISA (UK) 560 *Subsequent Events*

Subsequent events are defined as 'both events occurring between the period end and the date of the auditor's report and facts discovered after the date of the auditor's report' (ISA (UK) 560: para. 5). Such events can be either those that have an effect on the financial statements or those that do not (**adjusting** or **non-adjusting events** as per IAS 10 *Events After the Reporting Period*).

BPP

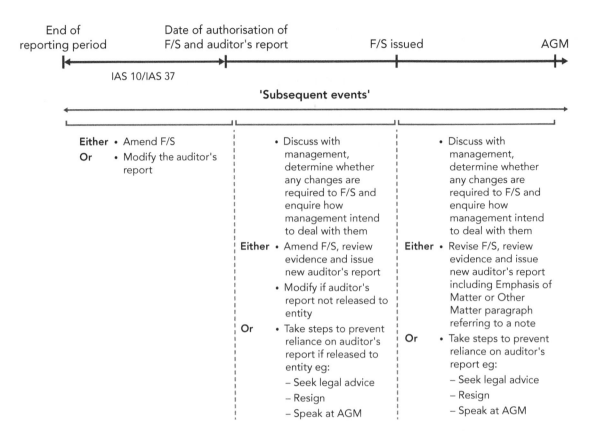

End of reporting period	Date of authorisation of F/S and auditor's report	F/S issued	AGM

IAS 10/IAS 37

'Subsequent events'

Either • Amend F/S

Or • Modify the auditor's report

• Discuss with management, determine whether any changes are required to F/S and enquire how management intend to deal with them

Either • Amend F/S, review evidence and issue new auditor's report

• Modify if auditor's report not released to entity

Or • Take steps to prevent reliance on auditor's report if released to entity eg:
  – Seek legal advice
  – Resign
  – Speak at AGM

• Discuss with management, determine whether any changes are required to F/S and enquire how management intend to deal with them

Either • Revise F/S, review evidence and issue new auditor's report including Emphasis of Matter or Other Matter paragraph referring to a note

Or • Take steps to prevent reliance on auditor's report eg:
  – Seek legal advice
  – Resign
  – Speak at AGM

Activity 1: Subsequent events

What procedures should the auditor perform just prior to signing the auditor's report to ensure there are no unidentified material subsequent events that require adjustment or disclosure in the financial statements?

Solution

Essential reading

See Chapter 10 of the Essential reading for more detail on subsequent events, especially how audit procedures can vary depending on where you are in the subsequent events timeline.

The Essential reading is available as an Appendix of the digital edition of the Workbook.

4 ISA (UK) 570 *Going Concern*

4.1 Management and auditor responsibilities

Management	• Assess entity's ability to continue as a going concern and present the financial statements accordingly. • The assessment should cover at least 12 months from the date of the financial statements (the auditor shall request that directors extend their assessment if this period is not covered).
Auditor	• Consider the appropriateness of management's use of the going concern basis of accounting (even if the local GAAP does not require it). • Consider if there are material uncertainties threatening the client's going concern status that need to be disclosed (ISA (UK) 570: para. 9).

4.2 Indicators of going concern problems

Financial	Operational	Other
• Net liability or net current liability position • Inability to pay payables on due dates • Arrears/discontinuance of dividends • Fixed-term borrowings approaching maturity without realistic prospects of renewal or repayment • Withdrawal of financial support by receivables and other payables • Negative operating cash flows • Adverse key financial ratios • Substantial operating losses or significant fall in value of cash generating assets • Inability to comply with terms of loan agreements • Change from credit to cash on delivery transactions with suppliers • Inability to obtain financing for essential new product	• Management intentions to liquidate entity or to cease operations • Shortage of supplies • Emergence of highly successful competitor • Loss of key management without replacement • Loss of major market, franchise, licence, or principal supplier • Labour difficulties or shortages of important supplies	• Uninsured or underinsured catastrophes when they occur • Non-compliance with capital or other statutory requirements • Pending legal or regulatory proceedings that may, if successful, result in claims that are unlikely to be satisfied • Changes in legislation or government policy expected to adversely affect the entity

Financial	Operational	Other
development or other essential investments		

The auditor should **evaluate** the assessment made by management using a variety of techniques:

Analysing and discussing cash flow, profit and other forecasts with management
Analysing and discussing the entity's latest available **interim financial statements**
Reading the terms of debentures and loan agreements and determining whether any have been breached
Reading minutes of the meetings of shareholders, those charged with governance and relevant committees for reference to financing difficulties
Enquiring of the entity's legal counsel regarding **litigation and claims**
Confirming the existence, legality and enforceability of arrangements to provide or maintain financial support with related and third parties and **assessing** the **financial ability** of such parties to **provide additional funds**
Evaluating the entity's plans to deal with **unfilled customer orders**
Performing audit procedures regarding subsequent events to identify those that either mitigate or otherwise affect the entity's ability to continue as a going concern
Confirming the existence, terms and adequacy of **borrowing facilities**
Obtaining and reviewing reports of **regulatory actions**
Determining the adequacy of **support for any planned disposal of assets** (ISA (UK) 570: paras. 12, A8)

4.3 Auditor's report implications

> Going concern assumption appropriate, but a material uncertainty exists

If the material uncertainty is **adequately disclosed**, the auditor should express an **unmodified opinion**, but add a separate paragraph called '**Material uncertainty related to going concern**' which also states that the auditor's opinion is not modified in this respect.

If there is **inadequate disclosure**, the auditor expresses a **qualified** or **adverse opinion**.

> Going concern assumption inappropriate

The auditor should express an **adverse opinion** if the financial statements have been prepared on a going concern basis when this is no longer appropriate for the entity. Assuming an **alternative accounting treatment** is applied appropriately (such as on a **break-up basis**) an **Emphasis of Matter paragraph** could be used to draw attention to this.

> Management unwilling to make or extend an assessment

This would represent insufficient or inappropriate audit evidence and would lead either to a **qualified** or **disclaimer of opinion**, depending on the severity of the circumstances.

Going concern and the auditor's report are covered in more detail in Chapter 11 *Reporting*.

5 ISA (UK) 710 *Comparative Information – Corresponding Figures and Comparative Financial Statements*

According to ISA (UK) 710 para. 6, comparative information can be of two types:

(a) **Corresponding figures**: Where amounts and disclosures for the preceding period are included as part of current period financial statements

(b) **Comparative financial statements**: Where amounts and disclosures for the preceding period are included **separately** as an entire statement for comparison purposes

The auditor's opinion relates to the current period financial statements **as a whole,** so corresponding figures are not separately identified. The auditor should obtain sufficient appropriate evidence that **accounting policies** used are **consistent** with those of the current period and that the **amounts agree** to those presented in the prior period (ISA (UK) 710: para. 7).

The extent of any **additional audit procedures** and the **impact on the auditor's report** all depend on whether the prior period financial statements were audited and, if so, by whom.

5.1 Preceding period financial statements were NOT audited by our firm

For **both** corresponding figures and comparative financial statements:

The preceding period F/S were audited by another firm	The preceding period F/S were not audited
If there is no legal prohibition from using one, an 'Other Matter' paragraph states: • That the F/S were audited by another auditor • The opinion issued plus any modifications • The date of that report	This can be stated in an 'Other Matter' paragraph.

In each case, audit procedures from **ISA (UK) 510** for agreeing **opening balances** then apply.

5.2 Preceding period financial statements were audited by our firm

For **corresponding figures**, there are two separate scenarios that need to be considered:

There was no modification to the preceding period F/S audit opinion, but a material issue with these figures is identified during the audit of the current period:	There was modification to the preceding period F/S audit opinion in relation to the corresponding figures:
• If the issue is **resolved** in the current year's corresponding figures, the auditor's report remains **unmodified** (an Emphasis of Matter paragraph may be used here). • If the issue remains **unresolved** in the corresponding figures, the auditor's opinion is modified in line with the issue's nature and extent.	• If the issue is now **resolved** in the current year's corresponding figures, the auditor's report remains **unmodified** in this respect. • If the issue remains **unresolved** in the corresponding figures, the auditor's opinion is modified in line with the issue's nature and extent.

For **comparative financial statements**, the auditor should separately identify each period reported on within the auditor's report. If the opinion on that period has changed since the original opinion was issued, an **'Other Matter'** paragraph should be used to explain why.

6 ISA (UK) 720 *The Auditor's Responsibilities Relating to Other Information*

The auditor is required to give an opinion as to whether the financial statements give a true and fair view.

BPP

The annual report containing the audited financial statements will also include **other information** which the auditor may be required to report on as a separate engagement, such as:

(a)   The directors' or management's report, including names of directors

(b)   Financial summaries, ratios or highlights

(c)   Employment data

(d)   Selected quarterly data

(e)   An integrated report

6.1   Material misstatements

The auditor must **read the other information** and be alert for material inconsistencies:

*   Between the other information and the financial statements; and/or

*   Between the other information and the auditor's knowledge obtained during the audit.

If any such material inconsistency appears to exist, the auditor shall **discuss this with management** and conclude whether there is a **material misstatement** in either the other information or the financial statements, or if the **auditor's understanding** of the entity and its environment needs to be updated (ISA (UK) 720: para. 16).

In any event, inconsistencies between the other information and the financial statements should always be **communicated to those charged with governance.**

Amendment necessary to	Auditor response if uncorrected
Audited financial statements	Consider **further audit procedures** as required by ISAs (UK) and the effect (if any) on the **auditor's report**. Evaluate the misstatement(s) in line with **ISA (UK) 450**.
The other information	**Understand the issue** (an expert may be required) and **ask management to revise the other** information if it still requires restatement (if they refuse, ask those charged with governance). If still not corrected, consider the **impact on the auditor's report** (see below) or **withdraw** from the engagement.
Auditor's understanding	Respond in line with other ISAs (UK) (such as ISA (UK) 315).

6.2   Reporting other information in the auditor's report

The auditor's report will always include a separate section on other information, but how it is presented will vary depending on the circumstances (highlighted for key differences).

When the **other information contains no material misstatement:**

Other Information

Management is responsible for the other information. The other information comprises the [information included in the X report, but does not include the financial statements and our auditor's report thereon.]

Our opinion on the financial statements does not cover the other information and we do not express any form of assurance conclusion thereon.

In connection with our audit of the financial statements, our responsibility is to read the other information and, in doing so, consider whether the other information is materially inconsistent with the financial statements or our knowledge obtained in the audit or otherwise appears to be materially misstated. If, based on the work we have performed, we conclude that there is a material misstatement of this other information, we are required to report that fact. We have nothing to report in this regard.

The other information **may not be available to the auditor**, so the following is used instead:

Other information

Management is responsible for the other information. The other information comprises the [information included in the X report, but does not include the financial statements and our auditor's report thereon]. The X report is expected to be made available to us after the date of this auditor's report.

Our opinion on the financial statements does not cover the other information and we do not express any form of assurance conclusion thereon.

In connection with our audit of the financial statements, our responsibility is to read the other information identified above when it becomes available and, in doing so, consider whether the other information is materially inconsistent with the financial statements or our knowledge obtained in the audit or otherwise appears to be materially misstated. ~~If based on the work we have performed, we conclude that there is a material misstatement of this other information we are required to report that fact. We have nothing to report in this regard~~.

There may be cases where the auditor is able to conclude that **there is a material misstatement to the other information** and it has **not been corrected by management**. In such cases, the section on other information is **moved up the auditor's report** to a position **immediately after the 'Basis for opinion' section (above key audit matters)**:

There may be cases where the auditor is able to conclude that **there is a material misstatement to the other information** and it has **not been corrected by management**. In such cases, the section on other information is **moved up the auditor's report** to a position **immediately after the 'Basis for opinion' section (above key audit matters)**:

Other information

Management is responsible for the other information. The other information comprises the [information included in the X report, but does not include the financial statements and our auditor's report thereon.]

Our opinion on the financial statements does not cover the other information and we do not express any form of assurance conclusion thereon.

In connection with our audit of the financial statements, our responsibility is to read the other information and, in doing so, consider whether the other information is materially inconsistent with the financial statements or our knowledge obtained in the audit or otherwise appears to be materially misstated. If, based on the work we have performed, we conclude that there is a material misstatement of this other information, we are required to report that fact. ~~We have nothing to report in this regard~~. As described below, we have concluded that such a material misstatement of the other information exists.

[Description of the material misstatement of the other information.]

Chapter summary

```
┌─────────────────┐
│   Completion    │
└─────────────────┘
```

Overall review of financial statements

- **ISA (UK) 220 (Revised):** Overall review of work undertaken to confirm compliance with standards, laws and regulations. Application of ISQM (UK) 1 and 2 by engagement partner, including engagement quality review (EQR) if required
- **ISA (UK) 520:** Final **analytical procedures** to confirm consistency with audit evidence
- **ISA (UK) 450:** Evaluation of misstatements identified during the audit – consider **uncorrected misstatements** (especially their **aggregate** impact on the F/S) and establish which are **factual, judgmental** and **projected** misstatements

ISA (UK) 580
Written Representations

- Objectives of **auditor** under ISA (UK) 580:
  - Obtain **written representations** from management (or those **charged with governance**) that they have fulfilled their **responsibilities** for preparing F/S and supplying all necessary **information**
  - **Support audit evidence** obtained by written representations if more detail is required (eg related parties, subsequent events, fraud, NOCLAR, uncorrected misstatements etc)
  - **Respond appropriately** when representations are provided (or when they are not but should be!)

ISA (UK) 560
Subsequent Events

- Period up to auditor's report
- Period after report is signed

 BPP

ISA (UK) 570 *Going Concern*

- **Responsibilities?**
  - **Management:** Assess ability to continue as a going concern.
  - **Auditor:** Consider appropriateness of use of going concern basis of accounting – if uncertainties exist but are disclosed, the **auditor's report** should be **modified** (*see overleaf*).

Indicators of going concern problems
- Financial
- Operational
- Other

ISA (UK) 710 *Comparative Information – Corresponding Figures and Comparative Financial Statements*

- Corresponding figures
- Comparative financial statements

ISA (UK) 720 *The Auditor's Responsibilities Relating to Other Information*

- **Material inconsistencies** between (i) items audited within F/S, (ii) items presented outside the F/S and not audited ('Other Information') and/or (iii) the auditor's knowledge obtained during the course of the audit – which one needs correction?
- **Discuss with management** to establish whether there is material misstatement or if the auditor's understanding of the entity needs to be updated:
  - (i) **Amendment required to F/S?** Consider further audit procedures and possible modified opinion if not amended
  - (ii) **Amendment required to 'Other Information'?** Understand, request revision – if not corrected, either withdraw or **modify report** (*see overleaf*)
  - (iii) **Auditor's understanding inadequate?** Respond in line with ISAs (UK) (such as ISA (UK) 315).

 BPP

Knowledge diagnostic

1. Overall review

Overall review of financial statements will determine whether or not **appropriate accounting policies** have been used, if information published is **compatible with audit findings,** if disclosure is adequate and if information **complies** with all statutory and regulatory requirements. The stage of the audit just before the opinion is signed is crucial and the auditor must perform a **final quality management review.** This review will also involve an evaluation of any **misstatements identified during the audit** to ensure the correct treatment of any that remain **uncorrected.**

2. Representations

Representations from those responsible for the financial statements are used to **supplement** the opinion where no other evidence exists. There are procedures for obtaining them and auditors must be aware of what to do if these representations are either not provided or lead to further questions.

3. Subsequent events

Auditors need to be aware of any subsequent events (**adjusting or non-adjusting**) that may occur either before or after they issue their auditor's report to ensure they still give the right opinion in light of these events.

4. Going concern

Both **management** and **auditors** have responsibilities regarding **going concern,** but auditors should be mindful of any issues that indicate possible going concern problems in any financial, operational or other areas of the business.

5. Corresponding figures and comparatives

Auditors need to be aware of the implications for their auditor's reports if there are issues with either **corresponding figures** or **comparative financial statements** in the financial statements.

6. Other information

As well as the audited accounts, the auditor has to be aware of any **other information** within the financial statements and ensure that it is both consistent and factually correct. In the event of any **material misstatements** or **cases where the auditor's understanding of the entity and its environment needs to be updated,** the auditor must determine what requires amendment and how best to act.

Further study guidance

Question practice

Now try the following from the Further question practice bank (available in the digital edition of the Workbook):

- Question 20 'Bestwood Electronics' tests theory and application related to subsequent events.
- Question 21 'Bingham Engineering' tests your knowledge of going concern and how you might apply certain procedures when reaching any conclusions about the going concern status of an entity.
- Question 22 'Lambley Properties' tests your ability to apply your knowledge of written representations to a more complex scenario.

Further reading

There are some technical articles on the ACCA website written by members of the AAA examining team which are relevant to some of the topics covered in this chapter that you should read:

- *Evaluation of misstatements*
- *Completing the audit*
- *Going concern*

Own research

Obtain a copy of a recent set of financial statements for an organisation and find as many real-life examples of the following issues discussed in this chapter as you can:

- Going concern
- Other information
- Subsequent events
- Corresponding figures

Activity answers

Activity 1: Subsequent events

Approach

This is revision from AA – what would you do if you wanted to be as sure as you could that there are no issues still outstanding when you sign the auditor's report?

Suggested solution

- Review procedures management has established to ensure that subsequent events are identified.

- Read minutes of board meetings, shareholder meetings and audit committees that have taken place since the year end.

- Obtain and review the latest available interim financial statements and/or management accounts, budgets and other related management reports.

- Enquire of the entity's legal counsel concerning litigation and claims.

- Enquire of management as to whether any subsequent events have occurred which might affect the financial statements.

Reporting

Learning objectives

On completion of this chapter, you should be able to:

	Syllabus reference no.
Determine the form and content of an auditor's report and assess the appropriateness of the contents of an auditor's report containing an unmodified opinion.	E3(a)
Recognise and evaluate the factors to be considered when forming an audit opinion in a given situation, including the effects of uncorrected misstatements, and justify audit opinions that are consistent with the results of audit procedures.	E3(b)
Critically appraise the form and content of an auditor's report in a given situation.	E3(c)
Assess whether or not a proposed audit opinion is appropriate.	E3(d)
Advise on the actions which may be taken by the auditor in the event that a modified auditor's opinion is issued.	E3(e)
Recognise when the use of an emphasis of matter paragraph, other matter paragraph and KAM disclosure would be appropriate and recommend and justify the content of each.	E3(g)
Critically assess the quality of a report to those charged with governance and management.	E4(a)
Advise on the content of reports to those charged with governance and management in a given situation.	E4(b)

Business and exam context

At this level, you are not only expected to know what the audit opinion is and how it is presented, but are also required to determine audit opinions and also assess the appropriateness of an audit opinion formed by another person.

In this chapter we shall also consider the form of the auditor's report, the criticism that it receives and whether it enables an auditor to express properly a true and fair view. Recent developments are considered, dwelling in detail on the inclusion of key audit matters in some auditor's reports. We shall also look at the auditor's requirements in relation to reporting to those charged with governance.

Auditor reporting questions at this level tend to be challenging, but 'do-able', particularly if you have practised similar questions and have established a step-by-step approach to questions on forming an auditor's opinion. You are very likely to encounter a question on auditor's reports in Section B of the exam, and are guaranteed a question on syllabus Section E (covering completion, subsequent events and going concern, and reporting).

Chapter overview

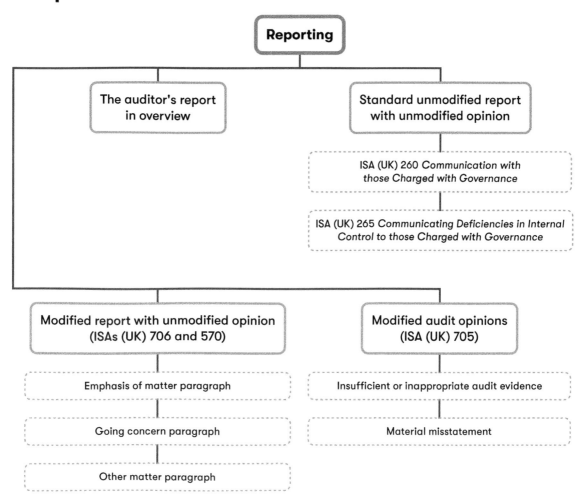

1 The auditor's report in overview

The **primary objective** of the audit is to express an **opinion** on the **truth** and **fairness** of the financial statements. The format of the basic auditor's report is laid down in **ISA (UK) 700 *Forming an Opinion and Reporting on Financial Statements***. This is supported by **ISA (UK) 701 *Communicating Key Audit Matters in the Independent Auditor's Report*** and **FRC *Bulletin: Illustrative Auditor's Reports on United Kingdom Private Sector Financial Statements***.

> ### PER alert
>
> One of the competencies you require to fulfil **Performance Objective 20** of the PER is the ability to prepare auditors' reports in accordance with relevant standards on auditing, or equivalent standards, and applicable regulations and legislations. You can apply the knowledge you obtain in this chapter of the Workbook to help demonstrate this competency.

2 Standard unmodified report with unmodified opinion

Here is a **standard unmodified report**, as given in the FRC Bulletin (FRC, 2021: Appendix 5).

INDEPENDENT AUDITOR'S REPORT

Opinion

We have audited the financial statements of [XYZ Limited] (the 'parent company)' and its subsidiaries (the 'group') for the year ended [*date*] which comprise [*specify the titles of the primary statements*] and notes to the financial statements, including significant accounting policies. The financial reporting framework that has been applied in the preparation of the group financial statements is applicable law and UK adopted international accounting standards. The financial reporting framework that has been applied in the preparation of the parent company financial statements is applicable law and United Kingdom Accounting Standards, including Financial Reporting Standard 101 *Reduced Disclosure Framework* (United Kingdom Generally Accepted Accounting Practice).

In our opinion:

- The financial statements give a true and fair view of the state of the group's and of the parent company's affairs as at [date] and of the group's [profit/loss] for the year then ended.
- The group financial statements have been properly prepared in accordance with UK adopted international accounting standards.
- The parent company financial statements have been properly prepared in accordance with United Kingdom Generally Accepted Accounting Practice.
- The financial statements have been prepared in accordance with the requirements of the Companies Act 2006.

Basis for opinion

We conducted our audit in accordance with International Standards on Auditing (UK) (ISAs (UK)) and applicable law. Our responsibilities under those standards are further described in the Auditor Responsibilities for the Audit of the Financial Statements section of our report. We are independent of the group and the parent company in accordance with the ethical requirements that are relevant to our audit of the financial statements in the UK, including the FRC's Ethical Standard as applied to listed public interest entities, and we have fulfilled our other ethical responsibilities in accordance with these requirements. We believe that the audit evidence we have obtained is sufficient and appropriate to provide a basis for our opinion.

Our approach to the audit

[Overview of the scope of the parent company and group audits]

Key Audit Matter	How our scope addressed this matter
Key audit matters are those matters that, in our professional judgment, were of most significance in our audit of the financial statements of the current period and include the most significant assessed risks of material misstatement (whether or not due to fraud) we identified, including those which had the greatest effect on the overall audit strategy, the allocation of resources in the audit and directing the efforts of the engagement team. These matters were addressed in the context of our audit of the financial statements as a whole, and in forming our opinion thereon, and we do not provide a separate opinion on these matters.	
[Key audit matter title] [Description of each key audit matter in accordance with ISA (UK) 701 (Revised November 2019). The significant judgements made by the engagement team with respect to each key audit matter should be explained. The auditor should include a description of the most significant assessed risks of material misstatement, a summary of their response and any key observations arising in relation to those risks.]	[Explanation of how the scope addressed each key audit matter and was influenced by the auditor's application of materiality.]

Our application of materiality

[Explanation of how the auditor applied the concept of materiality in planning and performing both the parent company and group audits. This is required to include the threshold used by the auditor as being materiality for both the group and parent company financial statements as a whole, as well as the threshold used by the auditor as being performance materiality but may include other relevant disclosures. The significant judgements made by the auditor in determining both of these thresholds should also be explained.]

Conclusions relating to going concern

In auditing the financial statements, we have concluded that the directors' use of the going concern basis of accounting in the preparation of the financial statements is appropriate. Our evaluation of the directors' assessment of the group's and parent company's ability to continue to adopt the going concern basis of accounting included [Explanation of how the auditor evaluated management's assessment and the key observations arising with respect to that evaluation].

Based on the work we have performed, we have not identified any material uncertainties relating to events or conditions that, individually or collectively, may cast significant doubt on the group's and parent company's ability to continue as a going concern for a period of at least twelve months from when the financial statements are authorised for issue.

Our responsibilities and the responsibilities of the directors with respect to going concern are described in the relevant sections of this report.

Other Information

The other information comprises the information included in the annual report other than the financial statements and our auditor's report thereon. The directors are responsible for the other information contained within the annual report. Our opinion on the financial statements does not cover the other information and, except to the extent otherwise explicitly stated in our report, we do not express any form of assurance conclusion thereon. Our responsibility is to read the other information and, in doing so, consider whether the other information is materially inconsistent with the financial statements or our knowledge obtained in the course of the audit, or otherwise appears to be materially misstated. If we identify such material inconsistencies or apparent material misstatements, we are required to determine whether this gives rise to a material misstatement in the financial statements themselves. If, based on the work we have performed, we conclude that there is a material misstatement of this other information, we are required to report that fact.

We have nothing to report in this regard.

 BPP

Opinions on other matters prescribed by the Companies Act 2006

In our opinion the part of the directors' remuneration report to be audited has been properly prepared in accordance with the Companies Act 2006.

In our opinion, based on the work undertaken in the course of the audit:

- The information given in the strategic report and the directors' report for the financial year for which the financial statements are prepared is consistent with the financial statements; and
- The strategic report and the directors' report have been prepared in accordance with applicable legal requirements

Matters on which we are required to report by exception

In the light of the knowledge and understanding of the group and the parent company and their environment obtained in the course of the audit, we have not identified material misstatements in the strategic report or the directors' report.

We have nothing to report in respect of the following matters in relation to which the Companies Act 2006 requires us to report to you if, in our opinion:

- Adequate accounting records have not been kept by the parent company, or returns adequate for our audit have not been received from branches not visited by us; or
- The parent company financial statements and the part of the directors' remuneration report to be audited are not in agreement with the accounting records and returns; or
- Certain disclosures of directors' remuneration specified by law are not made; or
- We have not received all the information and explanations we require for our audit.

Responsibilities of directors

As explained more fully in the directors' responsibilities statement [set out on page ...], the directors are responsible for the preparation of the financial statements and for being satisfied that they give a true and fair view, and for such internal control as the directors determine is necessary to enable the preparation of financial statements that are free from material misstatement, whether due to fraud or error. In preparing the financial statements, the directors are responsible for assessing the company's ability to continue as a going concern, disclosing, as applicable, matters related to going concern and using the going concern basis of accounting unless the directors either intend to liquidate the company or to cease operations, or have no realistic alternative but to do so.

Auditor Responsibilities for the audit of the financial statements

Our objectives are to obtain reasonable assurance about whether the financial statements as a whole are free from material misstatement, whether due to fraud or error, and to issue an auditor's report that includes our opinion. Reasonable assurance is a high level of assurance but is not a guarantee that an audit conducted in accordance with ISAs (UK) will always detect a material misstatement when it exists. Misstatements can arise from fraud or error and are considered material if, individually or in the aggregate, they could reasonably be expected to influence the economic decisions of users taken on the basis of these financial statements.

The extent to which our procedures are capable of detecting irregularities, including fraud, is detailed below:

[Explanation as to what extent the audit was considered capable of detecting irregularities, including fraud.]

A further description of our responsibilities is available on the FRC's website at:

https://www.frc.org.uk/auditors/audit-assurance/auditor-s-responsibilities-for-the-audit-of-the-fi/description-of-the-auditor%E2%80%99s-responsibilities-for

This description forms part of our auditor's report.

Other matters which we are required to address

We were appointed by [state by whom or which body the auditor was appointed] on [date] to audit the financial statements for the period ending [date]. Our total uninterrupted period of engagement is [X] years, covering the periods ending [date] to [date].

The non-audit services prohibited by the FRC's Ethical Standard were not provided to the group or the parent company and we remain independent of the group and the parent company in conducting our audit.

[Indicate any services, in addition to the audit, which were provided by the firm to the group that have not been disclosed in the financial statements or elsewhere in the annual report.]

Our audit opinion is consistent with the additional report to the audit committee.

[Signature]

Gurvinder Das (Senior Statutory Auditor)

For and on behalf of ABC LLP, Statutory Auditor

[Address][Date]

2.1 ISA (UK) 260 *Communication with those Charged with Governance*

In addition to reporting to shareholders, the external auditor is expected to communicate matters of **audit importance** to those charged with governance (TCWG) – usually the directors, but this could be an **audit committee** as well, so the auditor should establish **to whom they must report**. This should be an ongoing, two-way dialogue and is initiated at the engagement stage to avoid any omissions, as well as **how** (in writing) and **when** (described in the ISA (UK) as 'timely').

In the UK, auditors should take into account **how well** they think the audit committee has communicated to the board, matters which the auditor itself communicated to the audit committee.

Auditors must remember, however, that communicating matters relating to **money laundering** or **other illegal acts** to the entity might be considered to be **tipping off** so they should therefore consider obtaining **legal advice** in such circumstances (ISA (UK) 260: para. 7).

The **items to be communicated** relate to the **auditor's responsibilities** as part of the audit and information relevant to the audit, such as **independence**, **scope** and **timing**, as well as any **issues arising** from the audit. This is sometimes referred to as the **report to management** and includes **significant findings** from the audit, such as views about the chosen **accounting policies**, **difficulties** encountered **during the audit** and any other matters relevant to the **oversight of the financial reporting purpose**.

2.2 ISA (UK) 265 *Communicating Deficiencies in Internal Control to those Charged with Governance and Management*

This standard deals with any **specific internal control issues** identified to ensure they are communicated promptly for the right action to be taken. The issues communicated are only those identified **during the course of the audit** as **necessary to the creation of the financial statements under review**: they are not an assessment of the overall adequacy of the accounting and internal control systems currently operated by management.

Deficiencies are classified as **significant** if they warrant the attention of TCWG. Findings are usually presented along with **recommendations** and a **timescale**.

2.3 ISA (UK) 701 *Communicating Key Audit Matters in the Independent Auditor's Report*

If the auditor has a responsibility to report **matters of audit significance** under ISAs (UK) 260 and 265, why are key audit matters (KAMs) included in the auditor's report? **ISA (UK) 701 requires the auditor to determine KAMs** from the matters communicated to TCWG and, having already formed an opinion on the financial statements, **communicate those matters to shareholders and other users of the financial statements** by describing them in the auditor's report before reporting them as KAMs to TCWG.

The auditor should keep appropriate documentation of all KAMs: they are defined as being those matters that, in the auditor's professional judgement, were **of most significance** in the audit of the financial statements of the current period. They are **required for all listed entity auditor's reports** and are part of the standard unmodified report (so they are not the same as Emphasis of Matter or Other Matter paragraphs and do not lead to a modification of the auditor's opinion).

 BPP

Identifying such matters requires the auditor to use **professional judgement** – for example:

- **Material, complex** or **subjective** items, especially any associated misstatements
- Matters where the auditor encountered **difficulty** or required **extra audit effort**
- Areas where audit procedures were **difficult to apply** or where **several issues converged**

It should be obvious that KAMs are **audit matters**, not just difficult areas of financial reporting. The decision-making framework looks like this:

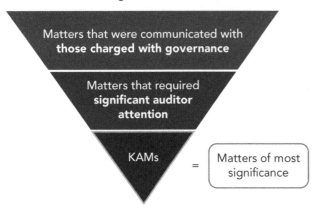

Source: IAASB Determining and Communicating Key Audit Matters (IAASB, 2016b)

KAMs should be disclosed within the 'Key audit matters' section of the auditor's report stating **why** they were assessed as KAMs, **how** they were addressed during the audit and the **note** from the financial statements where more detail is supplied by the audited entity.

The ISA (UK) states that the **description** should contain:

A description of the **most significant assessed risks** of material misstatement (whether or not due to fraud)
A summary of the **auditor's response** to those risks
Where relevant, **key observations** arising with respect to those risks

(ISA (UK) 701: para. 13–1)

The ISA (UK) also requires the report to state how the auditor **identifies** KAMs while planning the audit, including the materiality level used, and an overview of the scope of the audit, including how materiality affected the assessment of KAMs (ISA (UK) 701: para. 16–1).

If it is felt that disclosure would compromise the need for **confidentiality** (eg in cases of money laundering) or if the law precludes it, the auditor can choose not to communicate specific KAMs.

It is extremely unlikely that there will be **no KAMs** from an audit but if this is the case, there is still a section headed 'Key audit matters' stating that there are none. **Going concern uncertainty** is not treated as a KAM as that would have its own section if required within a modified auditor's report (see below).

Essential reading

See Chapter 11 of the Essential reading for further details of how the auditor's report has become more informative over recent years, including the perceived benefits of using KAMs and the FRC's experiences of using extended auditor's reports in the UK. You will also find details of where the Companies Act 2006 specifically applies to the UK auditor's report, as well as how the external auditor communicates their findings to those charged with governance and management.

The Essential reading is available as an Appendix of the digital edition of the Workbook.

3 Modifications to the auditor's report

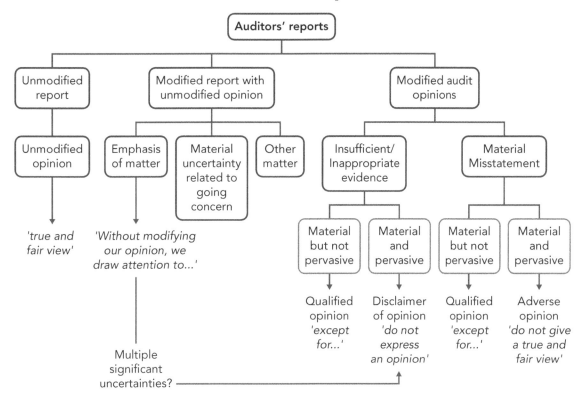

Note. The ISAs do not specifically use the terms '**modified report**' or '**unmodified report**' but you will find they are often used to help clarify certain situations, including those when the auditor's report has some form of **additional communication** (such as the use of a **going concern** or **emphasis of matter paragraph**) but the audit opinion remains unmodified. In addition, remember that the term '**present fairly**' can be used **instead of 'true and fair view'** when expressing an unmodified opinion on the financial statements.

4 Modified report with unmodified opinion

4.1 ISA (UK) 706 *Emphasis of Matter Paragraphs and Other Matter Paragraphs in the Independent Auditor's Report*

In the auditor's opinion, it may be **necessary** to **draw users' attention** to matters presented **within the financial statements** or **other information** in the annual report that are of such importance they are **fundamental to users' understanding** of either the financial statements or the rest of the audit including the report.

An '**Emphasis of matter**' paragraph draws users' attention to issues that are **adequately disclosed within the financial statements** that they **need to see** in order to understand them properly, such as:

- Uncertainties relating to future outcomes of exceptional litigation or regulatory action (where there are multiple uncertainties, the auditor may feel it is appropriate to express a disclaimer of opinion instead – however, '**Emphasis of matter**' **paragraphs are not used to address going concern uncertainties**, as a separate section of the auditor's report is used to communicate such matters – see below)

- Early application of new accounting standards

- A major catastrophe that has had, or continues to have, a significant effect on the entity's financial position

- If a new auditor's report is issued (such as when ISA (UK) 560 *Subsequent Events* applies)

It is important to understand the **distinction** between **KAMs** (matters of most significance to the audit) and **emphasis of matter paragraphs** (fundamental to users' understanding of the financial statements). Emphasis of matter paragraphs should not be used as a substitute for any required KAMs, while **KAMs that are fundamental to users' understanding** of the financial statements should be **prioritised within the KAMs section** of the auditor's report. Similarly, matters that **did not require significant auditor attention** but which may still be **fundamental to users' understanding** of the financial statements should form part of an emphasis of matter paragraph (ISA (UK) 706: paras. A1–3).

The additional paragraph should be added immediately **after the basis for opinion paragraph** in the auditor's report, using the heading **'Emphasis of matter'** including **full details** of the matter and the **location** within the financial statements which explains the issue further. It is up to the auditor's judgement whether to place the Emphasis of Matter paragraph **before or after the 'Key audit matters' section**.

The paragraph states that the auditor's **opinion** is **not modified in respect of this matter** – the use of such a paragraph **must only occur** if the matter in question has been **adequately treated and disclosed** in the financial statements and the auditor is in agreement with this.

An **'Other matter'** paragraph draws users' attention to issues **outside the scope of the financial statements** (so therefore items not addressed by 'Emphasis of matter' paragraphs) and can include anything else that users need to know about the audit, such as:

- Issues related to **ISA (UK) 510** *Initial Engagements – Opening Balances*
- Items relating to the conduct of the audit (eg being unable to withdraw as auditor)
- Disclosure or comment required by laws, regulations or local GAAP

Other Matter paragraphs must not refer to KAMs as other matters are by definition beyond the scope of the audited financial statements. Similarly, **ISA (UK) 720** *The Auditor's Responsibilities Relating to Other Information* regarding **other information** does not make use of an 'Other matter' paragraph either, as this is referred to within a separate section of the auditor's report.

The additional paragraph is headed **'Other matter'** and shall be included **after the basis for opinion paragraph**, after **any 'Emphasis of matter' paragraph** and after the **'Key audit matters' section**.

4.2 Modification of the auditor's report due to going concern issues

In order to be able to adequately **form a conclusion on the entity's going concern status**, the auditor should **corroborate** the board's own robust assessment of the entity's emerging and principal risks (ISA (UK) 570 (Revised): para. 16–1) and determine whether they want to add or draw attention to anything related to the entity's going concern status (ISA (UK) 570 (Revised): para. 24–1) including the possibility of any form of **management bias** (ISA (UK) 570 (Revised): para. 18–1). The standard now requires the auditor to communicate more formally on these matters in the auditor's report (ISA (UK) 570 (Revised): para. 21–1) including an overview of the **work done** and the **conclusions reached**: this is illustrated in the standard unmodified report at the start of this chapter by the section titled **'Conclusions relating to going concern'**.

In previous sections of these materials, we also learned that if there was a **material uncertainty related to going concern** but the use of the going concern assumption was still appropriate, as long as the disclosure made by the audited entity was deemed adequate by the auditor, an unmodified opinion could be issued but a **separate disclosure** was required within the auditor's report.

This appears **immediately after the 'Basis for opinion' section**: remember that any uncertainty related to going concern is not a KAM and does not get reported by an Emphasis of matter paragraph.

The following is an illustration of what this section of a modified auditor's report would look like (taken from **ISA (UK) 570** *Going concern*):

Material Uncertainty Related to Going Concern

We draw attention to Note 6 in the financial statements, which indicates that the Company incurred a net loss of ZZZ during the year ended 31 December 20X1 and, as of that date, the Company's current liabilities exceeded its total assets by YYY. As stated in Note 6, these events or conditions, along with other matters as set forth in Note 6, indicate that a material uncertainty exists that may cast significant doubt on the Company's ability to continue as a going concern. Our opinion is not modified in respect of this matter.

Essential reading

See Chapter 11 of the Essential reading for more detail on the reporting of material uncertainties related to going concern, key audit matters and emphasis of matter paragraphs.

The Essential reading is available as an Appendix of the digital edition of the Workbook.

Activity 1: Spot the ball

On the proforma, indicate where the following items would appear on a modified auditor's report:

(1) A **misstatement of the other information** presented within the document containing the financial statements

(2) A **material uncertainty related to going concern** adequately disclosed in the financial statements

(3) An **Emphasis of matter paragraph** explaining an uncertainty related to ongoing litigation

(4) An **Other matter paragraph** explaining that the prior year financial statements were audited by another firm

INDEPENDENT AUDITOR'S REPORT

Opinion

Basis for opinion

Key audit matters

Other information

Responsibilities of management and those charged with governance for the financial statements

Auditor's responsibilities for the audit of the financial statements

Report on other legal and regulatory requirements

Signed

5 Modified audit opinions

5.1 ISA (UK) 705 *Modifications to the Opinion in the Independent Auditor's Report*

There are **three types of modified opinion** that the auditor can issue (depending on the **cause** or **nature of the matter** giving rise to any modification and the **impact** or **pervasiveness** of that matter on the financial statements):

(a) A qualified opinion

(b) An adverse opinion

(c) A disclaimer of opinion

From ISA (UK) 705 para. 5a, the term '**pervasive**' has the following **definitions**:

The matters giving rise to any modifications:

Are **not confined** to **specific elements**, accounts or items of the financial statements;
If so confined, represent or could represent a **substantial proportion** of the financial statements; or
In relation to disclosures, are **fundamental** to users' understanding of the financial statements.

The types of modification can be summarised as follows by considering the **judgements** required by the auditor in two key respects – **nature (cause)** and **pervasiveness (impact)**:

Nature of matter giving rise to the modification	Auditor's judgement about the pervasiveness of the effects or possible effects on the financial statements	
	Material but not pervasive	**Material and pervasive**
Financial statements are materially misstated (The term 'Disagreement' is used in the UK)	**Qualified opinion** ('except for the effects of the matter described in the basis for qualified opinion section...')	**Adverse opinion** ('because of the significance of the matter discussed...the financial statements do not give a true and fair view...')
Inability to obtain sufficient appropriate audit evidence (The term 'Limitation on scope' is used in the UK)	**Qualified opinion** ('except for the possible effects of the matter described in the basis for qualified opinion section...')	**Disclaimer of opinion** ('we do not express an opinion ...because of the significance of the matter described...')

5.2 Material misstatements

The circumstances leading to a modification due to material misstatement could include:

- The **appropriateness** of selected accounting policies (either inconsistent with the applicable financial reporting framework or those that do not lead to fair presentation)
- The **application** of selected accounting policies (through either inconsistency or error)
- The appropriateness or adequacy of **disclosures** in the financial statements

5.3 Inability to obtain sufficient appropriate audit evidence

The circumstances leading to a modification due to being unable to obtain sufficient appropriate audit evidence are as follows:

- Circumstances **beyond the control of the entity** (such as the loss of records in a fire)

- Circumstances relating to the **nature or timing of the auditor's work** (eg the auditor being appointed after the date of counting physical inventory stocks)
- Limitations on the scope of the audit **imposed by management** (such as management denying access to third parties for external confirmations)

Essential reading

See Chapter 11 of the Essential reading for illustrations of the wording used when the auditor's opinion is modified.

The Essential reading is available as an Appendix of the digital edition of the Workbook.

5.4 Modifications within the report when the audit opinion is modified

When the auditor has to issue a **modified opinion**, the 'Basis for opinion' section should provide a description of the matter giving rise to the modification, the **details** of any **corrections** required (only possible with misstatement due to being able to quantify such issues, or recommend the required disclosure) or the **uncertainty** remaining (by definition, usually unquantifiable). This should be titled 'Basis for qualified/adverse/disclaimer of opinion' and follows the opinion paragraph.

Similarly, for modified opinions, the **opinion paragraph** should be titled 'Qualified/Adverse /Disclaimer of opinion' and should use the relevant modification terminology depending on the opinion chosen.

5.4.1 Actions when an auditor's opinion is modified

When a modified opinion is likely, the auditor should consider the following implications:

TCWG need to be informed of any such issue and the reason for it (allowing TCWG opportunity to respond)	**External consultation** with regulators or others may be required	**Management integrity** may be called into question (including any representations supplied) meaning an EQR is required	**Possible withdrawal** from the engagement (and seek legal advice?)

Activity 2: Santa plc

You are an audit partner. Your firm carries out the audit of Santa plc, a listed company. Because the company is listed, you have been asked to perform a second partner review of the audit file for the year ended 31 December 20X3 before the audit opinion is finalised. Reported profit before tax is £2.35 million and total assets are £9.5 million.

You have read the following note from the audit file.

'Debt: Rudolph Ltd

There is a debt outstanding from Rudolph Ltd, a limited liability company, from January 20X3 in respect of a vehicle developed by Santa to Rudolph's own specification. Rudolph has disputed the quality of the vehicle and also does not agree that it was made completely to the specification. The company has submitted the dispute with Santa to arbitration, in accordance with its contractual agreement. Rudolph was a major customer up until the time of the dispute, often accounting for 50% of sales ledger total. It has not placed any orders with Santa in 20X3 or 20X4, preferring a French supplier which is Santa's only real competitor in the European market.

The directors of Santa are confident that at arbitration Rudolph will be required to pay the full bill, which is in the region of £1 million. They state that the quality of the machine is irrefutable and that any amendments to the specification were only safety improvements. The arbitral decision, which is not subject to appeal, is expected after the date of the AGM. Given their confidence, the directors of Santa have refused to refer to the dispute in the financial statements.

Given that the outcome of this arbitration is by no means certain, the potential overstatement of the debt is material and the permanent loss of Rudolph's custom could affect the going concern opinion, the following modification to the auditor's report is proposed:

Disagreement on Accounting Policies – Inappropriate Accounting Method – Adverse opinion

No allowance has currently been made for the impairment of an outstanding debt from Rudolph in respect of a dispute over a contract which has currently been submitted to arbitration, which, in our opinion, is not in accordance with International Financial Reporting Standards. An allowance of £1 million should be made in respect of this debt. Accordingly, receivables, profit for the period and retained earnings should be reduced by £1 million. Also, due to its significance, this allowance should have been disclosed separately in accordance with IAS 1 *Presentation of Financial Statements*.

In our opinion, because of the effects of the matters discussed in the preceding paragraph, the financial statements do not give a true and fair view of the financial position of Rudolph Ltd as of 31 December 20X3, and of its financial performance and its cash flows for the year then ended in accordance with International Financial Reporting Standards.'

Required

Comment on the appropriateness of the proposed audit opinion, and critically appraise the form and content of the proposed auditor's report, recommending improvements where necessary.

Note. You are **not** required to redraft the extracts from the auditor's report. **(8 marks)**

Solution

Essential reading

See Chapter 11 of the Essential reading for further details of how to critically appraise an auditor's report.

The Essential reading is available as an Appendix of the digital edition of the Workbook.

Chapter summary

```
                                    ┌─────────────────┐
                                    │    Reporting    │
                                    └─────────────────┘
```

The auditor's report in overview

- ISAs (UK) 700 and 701
- FRC Bulletin: Compendium of illustrative auditor's reports

Standard unmodified report with unmodified opinion

Key contents:
- Title – independent auditor's report
- Addressee
- Opinion
- Basis for opinion
- Key audit matters
- Other information
- Responsibilities
- Legal and regulatory
- Signature
- Date

ISA (UK) 260 Communication with those Charged with Governance
- ISA (UK) 260 addresses points made in the report to management – matters of audit importance (eg adjustments required, disagreements over treatment)
- ISA (UK) 260 also defines those charged with governance (TCWG) at engagement stage

ISA (UK) 265 Communicating Deficiencies in Internal Control to those Charged with Governance
ISA (UK) 265 ensures that any specific internal control weaknesses identified during the audit are brought to the attention of those charged with governance and not subject to management bias.

Modified report with unmodified opinion (ISAs (UK) 706 and 570)

Emphasis of matter paragraph
- Opinion is unmodified
- Draws attention to uncertainty disclosed in F/S (not G/C)

Going concern paragraph
- Opinion is unmodified
- Draws attention to going concern (G/C) issues only

Other matter paragraph
- Opinion is unmodified
- Draws attention to issues outside of F/S

Modified audit opinions (ISA (UK) 705)

Insufficient or inappropriate audit evidence
- If material to F/S but not pervasive, issue a **Qualified opinion** ('*except for*')
- If unable to form an opinion (both material and pervasive) issue a **Disclaimer of opinion** ('*we do not express an opinion*')

Material misstatement
- If material to F/S but not pervasive, issue a **Qualified opinion** ('*except for*')
- If misstatement is so severe (both material and pervasive) issue an **Adverse opinion** ('*the F/S do not give a true and fair view*')

Knowledge diagnostic

1. Reports and opinions

Auditors' reports are the only tangible output produced by the auditor; it is therefore very important that the **opinion** expressed is appropriate in the circumstances and the **report** follows the correct approach.

2. Standard auditor's report

The basic auditor's report uses ISAs (UK) 700, 701 and 720 to produce a **standardised report format** depending on the **jurisdiction** applied. ISAs (UK) 260 and 265 cover points made in the report to management.

3. Modifications to the auditor's report

It is important that you understand the **different modifications** that can be made to the standard auditor's report, including forms of **additional communication**.

4. Emphasis of matter and other matter paragraphs

To ensure that the users of financial statements are not misled, additional information is required such as **Emphasis of matter** (drawing attention to matters adequately disclosed within the financial statements) and **Other matter** (anything outside the scope of the financial statements) paragraphs and disclosure of **going concern** uncertainties.

5. Modified audit opinions

The auditor has to decide on the **nature** and **pervasiveness** of any matters that lead to opinions such as **qualified**, **adverse** or a **disclaimer** of opinion. Such matters can relate to material misstatements ('disagreement' in the UK) or insufficient/inappropriate audit evidence ('limitations on scope' in the UK)

Further study guidance

Question practice

Now try the following from the Further question practice bank (available in the digital edition of the Workbook):

- Question 12 'Illuminations' tests theory and application related to appointments and opening balances, so should be viewed as good revision of what you have covered so far.
- Question 15 Recognition' requires you to think about what's really happening and consider the implications for the auditor's report.
- Question 23 'Maple' is a more traditional question testing fraud as well as your knowledge of reporting.
- Question 24 'Petrie' blends together a number of syllabus areas but requires you to know the impact on the auditor's report and opinion.

Further reading

There is one technical article on the ACCA website written by members of the AAA examining team which is relevant to some of the topics covered in this chapter that you should read:

- *Auditor's reports to those charged with governance*

Own research

Obtain a copy of a recent set of financial statements for an organisation and find as many real-life examples of auditor's reports as you can.

 BPP

Activity answers

Activity 1: Spot the ball

> **Approach**
>
> Find the relevant content for each element of the auditor's report in the Workbook and the work out where it should go on the proforma for each of the four situations outlined.

Suggested solution

INDEPENDENT AUDITOR'S REPORT

Opinion

Basis for opinion

Material uncertainty related to going concern – after the 'Basis for opinion' section.

Emphasis of matter paragraph – before or after 'Key audit matters' (if used) depending on severity and likely to be below any going concern issue.

Misstatement in the other information – below 'Basis for opinion' but above 'Key audit matters' and likely to be below any Emphasis of Matter paragraph.

Key audit matters

Emphasis of matter paragraph – before or after 'Key audit matters' (if used) depending on severity and likely to be below any going concern issue.

Other matter paragraph – after the 'Basis for opinion' and 'Key audit matters' (if used) and then after any Emphasis of Matter paragraph.

~~Other information~~

(**Misstatement in the other information** – this will **not** appear here any longer.)

Responsibilities of management and those charged with governance for the financial statements

Auditor's responsibilities for the audit of the financial statements

Report on other legal and regulatory requirements

Signed

Note. 'Key audit matters' is presented here as best practice, although it is only required for listed entities.

Activity 2: Santa plc

> **Approach**
>
> You should work your way through the scenario and challenge every statement made – is it consistent with the rest of the information presented here? Does it conform with the approach that we know an auditor's report should follow? Is the opinion appropriate under the circumstances? Are there any other issues here that we need to pick up outside the auditor's report that might be relevant?

 BPP

Suggested solution

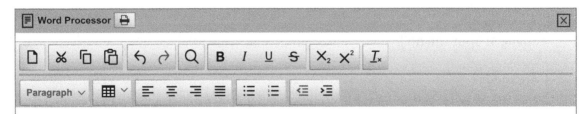

Allowance for receivables

The receivables balance for the year is potentially overstated by £1 million, depending on the outcome of arbitral proceedings. The amount is material, being 43% of profit and 11% of total assets, and any settlement by which the price is reduced by more than 10% would be **material** to the statement of profit or loss:

Profit before tax = £2.35 million. Materiality = (say) 5% of PBT.

5% × £2.35m = £117,500 which is nearly 12% of contract price (£1,000,000)

The outcome of the arbitration does not appear certain, despite the directors' feelings on the subject. It is clear that they did make amendments to the specification, albeit for what they saw as the right reasons, and therefore, as auditor we must be aware of the possibility that this price will be materially reduced, rendering the reported debt overstated.

In these circumstances, an allowance for the impairment of the debt should be made to some extent. We should take advice from the company's legal advisers as to whether they estimate the price will be reduced at arbitration, and if so, by how much (suitable comments about IAS 37 Provisions, Contingent Liabilities and Contingent Assets could be made here).

If Santa's directors refuse to make any necessary allowance in the financial statements, the auditor's opinion should be modified on the grounds of **material misstatement** due to this lack of allowance as has been suggested on the audit file. However, this opinion should probably only be a **qualified** rather than an adverse opinion as suggested on the audit file as, although it would be material, it does not appear to be pervasive to the financial statements, but rather confined to one item.

Inappropriate paragraph headings, contents and placement

The proposed auditor's report shows almost all the right content but is presented in the wrong order – the opinion section needs the heading **'Qualified Opinion'** and should be positioned at the start of the auditor's report. However, the company referred to within the opinion section should be 'Santa plc', not 'Rudolph Ltd'.

The details of the various disagreements represent the basis of that opinion and should therefore be presented in the next section, headed **'Basis for qualified opinion'**. However, reference to IAS 37 Provisions, Contingent Liabilities and Contingent Assets should be made here to explain the reasons for the allowance that should be made against receivables.

IAS 1 disclosure

If a material allowance against this debt is required, as discussed above, separate disclosure will be required in respect of it in the notes in accordance with IAS 1 *Presentation of Financial Statements*. Again, if the directors fail to amend the financial statements to reflect this **disclosure**, the auditor's report should be modified on the grounds of **material misstatement** due to this lack of disclosure. Again, this is not pervasive to the financial statements, so a **qualified** opinion, rather than the suggested adverse opinion, would be appropriate.

Going concern

While the outcome of the arbitration might not in itself affect the going concern basis of the company, irretrievable loss of a major customer (representing half of the company's revenue) could have seriously detrimental effects and does at least need to be considered by the auditor.

Hopefully the audit team has reviewed the going concern position of the company and this is all documented on file and has, if necessary, been disclosed in the financial statements. If these events present a material uncertainty for Santa, the auditor's report might also have to be modified.

There could be sufficient uncertainty about the company's future to warrant an additional paragraph from the auditor called **'Material uncertainty related to going concern'** placed after the 'Basis of opinion' section where the auditor would set out the fact that such a material uncertainty existed. If **sufficient disclosure** had been made about this uncertainty by directors, the auditor would use this to draw attention to this disclosure note within the financial statements and state that the opinion was not modified in that respect. However, if **insufficient disclosure** were given, the auditor would address this within the 'Basis of opinion' section of the auditor's report and **qualify** the auditor's opinion on the grounds of lack of disclosure.

Events after the reporting period

The arbitral decision is not expected until after the AGM, when the financial statements will have been issued to members. However, although the IAS 10 *Events After the Reporting Period* time frame for adjustments finishes when the financial statements are authorised for issue, the **auditor's duty** in respect of subsequent events continues under ISA (UK) 560 *Subsequent Events*. An early decision before the financial statements are authorised for issue would directly impact the financial statements and might require **further amendment** and a **change in the audit opinion**. A decision after that date may require the financial statements to be **reissued** and the auditor may need to seek legal advice as to possible actions if the directors refuse to do so.

Skills checkpoint 3

Professional scepticism and judgement

Chapter overview

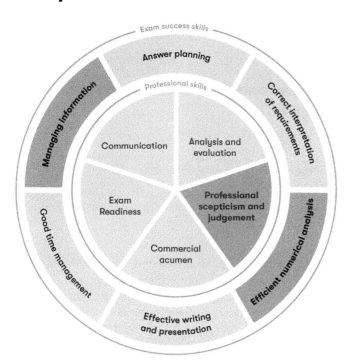

Skills checkpoint 3 – Professional scepticism and judgement

'Professional scepticism and judgement' is one of the four professional skills that have been introduced by ACCA into the AAA exam. This professional skill will be examined in Section A of the exam as part of the compulsory 50-mark question which will test all four of the professional skills for 10 marks in total.

This professional skill may also be examined in Section B, which consists of two compulsory scenario-based 25-mark questions, each of which allocates five marks to professional skills.

Each Section B question will contain a minimum of two professional skills: 'analysis and evaluation' plus 'professional scepticism and judgement' and/or 'commercial acumen'. Section B questions will state which of these professional skills are being tested.

No professional skill will ever be worth more than five marks in a question.

Syllabus learning outcomes

This is how the AAA syllabus expects candidates to demonstrate the professional skill of 'professional scepticism and judgement':

- Explore the underlying reasons for issues, applying an attitude of a questioning mind, beyond what is immediately apparent from the usual sources and opinions available and demonstrate the ability to be to alert to, and identify, conditions which might indicate misstatements or the existence of fraud or error.
- Question contradictory information or facts, opinions, assertions and the reliability or inherent bias of information presented, by seeking corroboratory or additional information to either support or reject its acceptance.
- Challenge and critically assess the information and evidence presented, or decisions made, to reach a conclusion on whether sufficient and appropriate evidence has been obtained on which to base the audit opinion.
- Demonstrate appropriate professional judgement, including the application of appropriate auditing, accounting and ethical standards, to draw conclusions and make informed decisions about the courses of action which are appropriate in the context of the engagement.

How to demonstrate professional skill in 'professional scepticism and judgement'

How could you demonstrate 'professional scepticism and judgement' when attempting the Specimen exam?

This professional skill was examined in all three questions on the Specimen exam and marks appear to have been awarded if candidates could demonstrate three main aspects to this skill:
- Challenging and critically assessing information, including any missing information or additional information which should have been supplied
- Determining and justifying a suitable materiality level, appropriately and consistently applied
- Appropriately applying professional judgement to draw conclusions and make informed decisions

A word on the importance of drawing a conclusion. For example, where a question asks you to explain the impact on the auditor's report, students sometimes hedge their bets and put two different options. To score these marks, you need to choose one and conclude why. For ethical questions you might need to conclude whether or not to accept an engagement, rather than just explaining the threats. A lot of students forget to do this – you have been told now!

How were 'professional scepticism and judgement' marks awarded in the September 2022 exam?

This was the first time that the exam was split into 80 technical marks and 20 professional skills marks. From an analysis of the solutions and the examining team's feedback, the following additional points should be noted:
- In **Question 1**, candidates were told how materiality was to be assessed (using profit before tax) but answers still needed to calculate a threshold in order to allow the effective prioritisation of risks of material misstatement.
- The typical range of materiality amounts based on profit before tax is 5%–10% so candidates needed to calculate both and then decide whether to use 10% (if they considered this to be a lower risk audit due to the firm's familiarity with the client) or drop to 5% (to reflect the changes explained in the exhibits).
- The solutions concluded that as both assessments of risk were valid, materiality should occupy the middle ground and a figure of 7.5% of profit before tax would be applied to items when evaluating and prioritising the risks of material misstatement.

There is clearly no right answer as long as you justify the materiality threshold used in your answer, but you should remember to base your threshold on appropriate assumptions for the scenario if no indication on materiality is given.

What can you do to demonstrate 'professional scepticism and judgement' when answering other questions?

In some respects, you are fortunate that both 'professional scepticism' and 'professional judgement' are already examinable under the syllabus learning outcomes that cover the technical aspects of AAA. Consequently, you should already be on the lookout for issues that require challenge, critical assessment and judgement in areas such as ethics, risk assessment and reporting.

The ACCA has also commented that displaying professional judgement is necessary when prioritising risks along the spectrum of inherent risk as required by ISA (UK) 315 (Revised), which reinforces the message that correctly answering the technical aspects of the question will help you score the relevant professional skills marks. (However, please note that risk prioritisation has already been covered in the Skills Checkpoint on demonstrating 'analysis and evaluation'.)

However, it is still important that you can demonstrate these professional skills because they could very easily be required in all aspects of the 21st century accountant's role. Consequently, we will take a look at the skill 'professional scepticism and judgement' in the context of two exam success skills.

When **managing information**, it is important that you respond appropriately to everything presented in the scenario as it is not put in there by accident! The AAA examining team will have considered how they want each question to look, including the positioning of certain pieces of information.

In the Audit and Assurance (AA) exam, for example, you are presented with a scenario and each issue is documented logically and sequentially, with very little in the way of 'interference' to confuse you. However, in the AAA exam, you will need to look around the scenario more carefully – although there should not be much in the way of 'interference' you may still need to piece together the facts a little more to see the whole picture. The very nature of the CBE is a good illustration of this: you may have to marry up points from separate Exhibits to gain a proper understanding of the entity in the question, which again is part of 'analysis and evaluation'.

Here are two illustrations of where 'professional scepticism and judgement' might help you when managing information:

- An Exhibit containing the draft financial statements for the entity might show a bank overdraft, while a separate Exhibit containing an overview of the entity might provide details of the agreed overdraft limit – if the two are very close, it could indicate that the entity might have manipulated the reported amount to avoid alerting the auditors or that the company may be in breach of its debt covenant and could face further sanctions.
- You may be told something about the company in the CBE main screen (for example, it is a listed entity or a new audit client for your firm) but which is not mentioned anywhere else, so if you miss it, you may make assumptions in your analysis that are not valid.

You should always ask yourself **why** something has been included in the question and be prepared to challenge any statements made for inconsistency. Remember that the instructions in the requirement(s) will usually point you towards certain Exhibits so make sure you take note of any instructions you have been given.

Efficient numerical analysis is essential if financial statement extracts and other forms of financial or non-financial data is presented in a scenario (especially Question 1 of the AAA exam). Basically, if data is presented, you will need to do something with it – it is not there for either decoration or distraction! The use of suitable analytical procedures will be required in such cases and you can then work out from the results whether there is anything that doesn't quite fit or raises more questions.

Here are some illustrations of where 'professional scepticism and judgement' might help you when analysing data:

- Inconsistent ratios when compared with non-financial information: for example, if the number of branches operated by a retailer has fallen during the year of audit, why has revenue increased?
- If budget, market or industry data is supplied, you should be on the lookout for any inconsistencies with reported information in the scenario and be prepared to challenge them

 BPP

- Certain judgemental aspects of the financial statements might require a second look: a goodwill figure that hasn't changed from one year to the next; a depreciation charge that implies a longer lifetime for an asset than the supporting data in an Exhibit might require; or a revaluation that is inconsistent with the other assets in a particular category.

Remember that the financial statements you are given in a question are always draft amounts and as such are always subject to some kind of audit risk. You need to use the skills of 'professional scepticism and judgement' to find out where!

Skills practice

To help you develop your use of the professional skill 'professional scepticism and judgement' you should attempt Question 23 'Maple Ltd' from the 'Further question practice' section at the back of the digital edition of the Workbook. It is a question that tests both your ability to challenge information and reach appropriate conclusions.

You should also attempt Question 32 'Grissom Group' which reflects how Question 1 in the AAA exam will look. As it covers all of the professional skills and technical content up to and including group audits, you may wish to leave this question until you have covered all chapters in the Workbook.

12

Audit-related services and other assurance services

Learning objectives

On completion of this chapter, you should be able to:

	Syllabus reference no.
Describe the nature of audit-related services, the circumstances in which they might be required and the comparative levels of assurance provided by professional accountants and distinguish between: • Audit-related services and an audit of historical financial statements • An attestation engagement and a direct engagement.	F1(a)
Describe the main categories of assurance services that audit firms can provide and assess the benefits of providing these services to management and external users.	F1(b)
Describe the level of assurance (reasonable, high, moderate, limited, negative) for an engagement depending on the subject matter evaluated, the criteria used, the procedures applied and the quality and quantity of evidence obtained.	F1(c)
Specific assignments • Due diligence • Review of interim financial information For each of the other assignments listed above:	F2
Define and describe the purpose of each type of assignment and analyse the appropriate level of assurance which may be offered by a professional firm in relation to these assignments.	(a)
Evaluate the matters to be considered before accepting the engagement, including any ethical and professional considerations.	(b)
Plan the assignment, applying professional scepticism, to gather suitable evidence and provide an appropriate level of assurance in line with the objectives of the assignment.	(c)
Discuss the level of assurance that the auditor may provide and explain the other factors to be considered in determining the nature, timing and extent of examination procedures.	(d)
Describe and recommend appropriate substantive, examination or investigative procedures which can be used to gather sufficient and	(e)

	Syllabus reference no.
appropriate evidence in the circumstances.	
Analyse the form and content of the professional accountant's report for an assurance engagement as compared with an auditor's report.	F5(a)
Discuss the effectiveness of the 'negative assurance' form of reporting and evaluate situations in which it may be appropriate to modify a conclusion.	F5(c)

Business and exam context

In this chapter we look at audit-related services and other assurance services.

Audit-related services include review engagements, such as interim financial information reviews and due diligence reviews. We consider the differences between the external audit and audit-related services.

Assurance services are also considered in this chapter, and we examine the different levels of assurance that can be provided on such engagements. In particular we look at risk assessments, performance measurement and value for money audits. Finally in this chapter we look at the ways in which companies are using IT in their organisations and how this affects business risks.

Assurance and audit-related services are very important areas for auditors in practice. Questions in this area may come up in Section B of the exam. Although the only two examinable documents for the AAA–UK exam included in this chapter are ISRE (UK) 2410 *Review of Interim Financial Information Performed by the Independent Auditor of the Entity* and ISAE (UK) 3000 *Assurance Engagements other than Audits or Reviews of Historical Financial Information* the principles discussed throughout could still be applied in an exam question, so you should make sure you are familiar enough with them to know them in overview.

Chapter overview

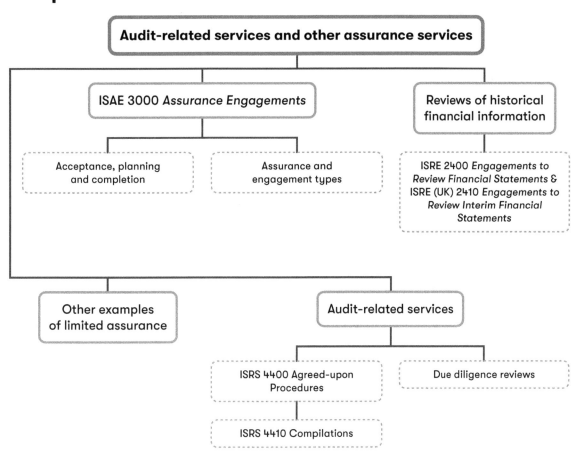

1 Introduction to assurance and audit-related services

> **Assurance engagement:** Where a professional accountant (or 'practitioner') evaluates or measures a subject matter that is the responsibility of another party against suitable criteria and expresses an opinion which provides the intended user with a level of assurance about the subject matter. It is implied that such an opinion requires evidence to be reached and a report to communicate it.

Professional firms may not just be asked for assurance reports – they can also be engaged to deliver a number of **audit-related services**, providing varying amounts of assurance (if any at all) depending on the engagement. Audit-related services allow firms to use their skills to support their clients in any way possible and include **reviews, agreed-upon procedures** and **compilations**.

2 ISAE 3000 *Assurance Engagements*

ISAE 3000 provides standards for assurance engagements **other than audits or reviews of historical financial information**. In substance, many of the requirements are similar to those required for an audit or a review, including the need for **professional scepticism**.

In the UK, ISAE (UK) 3000 *Assurance Engagements other than Audits or Reviews of Historical Financial Information* was issued in 2020 to ensure the relevant ethical guidance from both the FRC Ethical Standard and the practitioner's own professional institute is adhered to when providing non-audit services to public interest entities (the ISAE (UK) states that for other entities the guidance is voluntary unless other FRC guidance states otherwise).

Acceptance, planning and completion

Before accepting such an engagement, the practitioner needs to meet the requirements of both the **IESBA Code of Ethics** (and the **FRC Ethical Standard** in the UK) and **ISQM (UK) 1**, which includes agreeing on the **terms** of the engagement with the client and confirming these in an engagement letter. Effective **planning** is required as with an audit. The **appropriateness** of the **subject matter** and the **suitability** of the **criteria to be used in the engagement** should be assessed: such criteria must be relevant, complete, reliable, neutral and understandable. Sufficient appropriate **evidence** is required on which to base the conclusion. **Documentation** of matters significant in providing evidence to support the assurance **conclusion** and **report** is also required to show that the engagement was performed in accordance with ISAE (UK) 3000.

Elements of an assurance engagement

In order to qualify as an assurance engagement, the practitioner will confirm during acceptance and the agreement of terms that it exhibits **all** the following **elements**:

(a) A **three-party relationship** involving:

    (i) A **practitioner**

    (ii) A **responsible party**

    (iii) **Intended users** (ie the person(s) for whom the report is prepared)

(b) An appropriate **subject matter**

(c) Suitable **criteria**: ie the benchmarks used to evaluate or measure the subject matter

(d) Sufficient appropriate **evidence**

(e) A written assurance **report** (providing either **reasonable** or **limited** assurance)

The **subject matter** under review can vary enormously:

(a) **Physical characteristics**, such as the capacity of a facility

(b) **Performance** of an entity: this could include **performance indicators** both **internally** and **externally** required, such as those produced within an **integrated report** or as part of **public sector governance** (covered separately in these materials) as well as **formal** or **informal**, **financial** and **non-financial** performance, such as the requirement to secure **value for money** (VfM) often against budgets or targets

(c) The operation and reliability of **systems** and **processes**: for example, an entity's **internal controls** (as seen in AA) or controls over specific **IT systems**

Activity 1: KPIs

Suggest **FOUR** non-financial key performance measures (KPIs) that a manufacturing business could use internally that a practitioner could be asked to report on in an assurance engagement.

Solution

Activity 2: IT risks

What risks are a business exposed to as a result of unreliable IT systems?

Solution

There are a number of engagements where assurance may still be given but where a different ISAE applies:

(a) **Prospective financial information** where the practitioner reviews planned financial performance of an entity (**ISAE 3400** *The examination of prospective financial information* is covered separately in these materials).

(b) **Due diligence** of any potential business change (covered later in this topic).

(c) **Assurance reports on service organisations** – ISAE 3402 *Assurance reports on controls at a service organisation* provides guidance for practitioners who have been asked to report on the quality of controls in place at a service organisation which provides financial reporting information on an outsourced basis for an audited client (these reports can be produced on either a 'Type 1' or 'Type 2' basis and are covered in Chapter 7 when **ISA (UK) 402** *Audit considerations relating to an entity using a service organisation* is discussed).

2.1 Assurance provided

2.1.1 Reasonable assurance

Reasonable assurance engagement: The objective of a **reasonable assurance engagement** is to reduce assurance engagement risk to an acceptably low level as the basis for a **positive** form of expression of the practitioner's conclusion.

For example, in the case of assurance on effectiveness of internal controls, the report would be worded: 'In our opinion internal control is effective, in all material respects, based on XYZ criteria.'

2.1.2 Limited assurance

Limited assurance engagement: The objective of a **limited assurance engagement** is to reduce assurance engagement risk to a level that is acceptable as the basis for a **negative** form of expression of the practitioner's conclusion.

For example, 'Based on the work described in this report, **nothing** has come to our attention that causes us to believe that internal control is **not effective**, in all material respects, based on XYZ criteria.'

2.2 Engagement type

2.2.1 Attestation engagement

Attestation engagement: In an **attestation engagement**, the **client** measures or evaluates the underlying subject matter against the necessary criteria and prepares the outcome subject matter information, about which the **practitioner** provides assurance of whether or not it is free from material misstatement. The auditor's report on the financial statements is an illustration of this (except that auditors' reports obviously fall outside the scope of ISAE (UK) 3000).

For example, 'In our opinion, the financial statements present fairly, in all material respects...'

2.2.2 Direct reporting engagement

Direct reporting engagement: In a **direct reporting engagement**, the **practitioner** measures or evaluates the underlying subject matter against the criteria, the outcome of which is the subject matter information, and the **practitioner** then **also** issues an assurance conclusion on that subject matter information. This may involve performing **additional tasks** during or after the assurance process which, alongside the **independence** brought by the practitioner, enhances the assurance given – this is what distinguishes a direct reporting engagement from a compilation engagement where typically no assurance is given (compilations are covered later in this topic). Using a Type 2 report on a service organisation as an illustration.

For example, 'In our opinion, internal control is effective, in all material respects, based on XYZ criteria.'

2.3 Form and content of reports

ISAE (UK) 3000 does not stipulate a standardised format for the report. Different wording will have to be used depending on the engagement. The report should include the following basic elements as a **minimum**:

(a) A title that clearly indicates that the report is an independent assurance report
(b) An addressee
(c) An identification and description of the subject matter information and, when appropriate, the subject matter

(d) Identification of the criteria
(e) Where appropriate, a description of any significant inherent limitation associated with the evaluation or measurement of the subject matter against the criteria
(f) When the criteria are available only to specific intended users/relevant only to a specific purpose, a statement restricting the use of the assurance report to those users/that purpose
(g) A statement to identify the responsible party and to describe the responsible party's and the practitioner's responsibilities
(h) A statement that the engagement was performed in accordance with this ISAE (UK), ISQM (UK) 1 and the relevant ethical authority in place (this will be the FRC Ethical Standard in the UK, plus any requirements from an institute's own Code of Ethics and, if more demanding, the provisions of the IESBA Code of Ethics)
(i) A summary of work performed
(j) The practitioner's conclusion
(k) The assurance report date
(l) The signature, name of the firm or practitioner, and a specific location

(ISAE (UK) 3000: para. 69)

3 Reviewing historical financial information

ISAE (UK) 3000 does not cover audits or reviews of historical financial information – this is because there are different types of historical financial information produced and different types of clients who require some form of assurance on this information. You already know that **reasonable assurance** is expressed in a **positive manner** for **audits** which are governed by ISAs (UK) covered elsewhere on this course, but what about situations when an audit is **not required** but a **limited form of assurance** is still desired by a client?

Limited assurance engagements are increasingly **popular** for entities **exempt from audit** which still value the **benefit** that such an engagement can bring – these so-called 'mini-audits' are carried out either on an ad hoc basis or using the standards explained below. **Audited entities** can also have such engagements completed for them by their auditor to supply additional information to various stakeholders **in advance of the audit**: for example, listed entities may require reviewed financial statements to be submitted to the stock market for an initial assessment of the company's most recent full year performance.

3.1 ISRE 2400 *Engagements to Review Historical Financial Statements*

As with any assurance engagement, the practitioner should ensure that they are able to **accept** the engagement in line with the **IESBA Code of Ethics**, that the **terms** of the engagement are agreed in a **signed engagement letter** and that the engagement will be **planned** and **performed** in line with **ISQM (UK) 1**, with an attitude of **professional scepticism** recognising that circumstances may exist which cause the financial statements to be **materially misstated** or not in line with the **applicable financial reporting framework**.

The practitioner should obtain **sufficient appropriate evidence** to support their conclusion primarily through **enquiry** and **analytical procedures** (ISRE 2400: para.7).

The **review report** is usually addressed to the **directors** of the company (not to the shareholders) to indicate who has requested this engagement to be performed. The conclusion delivered within this review will enable the practitioner to state that **nothing** has come to their attention that causes them to believe that the historical financial statements contain **material misstatement** and are not prepared in accordance with an applicable financial reporting framework (ie **limited** assurance).

As with an audit, such a conclusion can be **modified** depending on the nature and extent of the issue(s) identified, with such modifications requiring an explanatory **basis** paragraph immediately preceding the conclusion. In the same way, **Emphasis of matter** and **Other matter paragraphs** can be added if appropriate (ISRE 2400: paras. 87 and 90, Appendix).

3.2 ISRE (UK) 2410 *Review of Interim Financial Information Performed by the Independent Auditor of the Entity*

As entities become more accountable to their various stakeholders, the need for **timely** and **reliable** financial information increases, especially at certain times of their reporting period (such as **retailers** who need to report **peak trading** figures). ISRE 2410 provides guidance for assurance engagements where the subject matter does not contain historical financial information for a full reporting period. Broadly speaking, it follows the same approach as ISRE 2400, primarily using **enquiry** and **analytical procedures** to deliver a conclusion but is specifically applicable to engagements carried out the by the entity's auditor, who will have access to information that another practitioner would not (in such cases, ISAE (UK) 3000 or ISRE 2400 would probably be used by these other practitioners).

Note. ISRE (UK) 2410 was issued in 2021 to provide clarity on the scope of this kind of review. It is logical that users of a review of interim information might form their own conclusions about the entity's going concern status. However, this type of limited assurance review work can never generate the evidence required to reach such a conclusion under ISA (UK) 570 (Revised) so the FRC is managing users' expectations by specifying exactly what ISRE (UK) 2410 can and cannot be used for.

The UK listing rules do not mandate the review of interim financial information, but if a review is completed, it must comply with ISRE (UK) 2410 and the review report must be published.

Essential reading

See Chapter 12 of the Essential reading for illustrations of the reports produced under ISRE 2400 and ISRE 2410.

The Essential reading is available as an Appendix of the digital edition of the Workbook.

4 Audit-related services

Reviews of historical financial information using both ISRE 2400 and ISRE 2410 provide a degree of assurance and are sometimes referred to as audit-related services to differentiate them from the more general types of assurance that we saw earlier in this topic. However, not all audit-related services offer assurance.

4.1 ISRS 4410 *Compilation Engagements*

Practitioners may be asked to **produce subject matter information** and **report** on how this matches the criteria used to assess such subject matter. In other instances (most notably the **preparation of financial statements for small entities**) the practitioner produces the subject matter but **does not provide any assurance** as once complete, no procedures to verify the information are carried out – it is simply a demonstration of the practitioner's accounting skills.

4.2 ISRS 4400 (Revised) *Agreed-upon Procedures Engagements*

Practitioners may also be asked to perform **specific procedures** that have been **agreed upon** by both the practitioner and the engaging party. The practitioner will **complete** these agreed-upon procedures (AUP) and **communicate** their **findings** in a **report**. As the report only confirms the procedures that were agreed upon and subsequently performed, **no assurance is given** and the engaging party and the intended users are left to draw their **own conclusions**.

Examples of AUP engagements could include **fraud investigations** or situations where **increased accountability** is necessary for entities claiming **grants** or **other funding**. Both **forensic**

accounting and **forensic auditing** engagements could also be considered to be AUP engagements, but they are covered separately in this Workbook.

4.3 Due diligence reviews

> **Corporate finance services:** A broad range of restructuring services that can be provided to an entity which support any proposed changes in the entity's corporate strategy. (For example, identifying potential purchasers or targets for acquisition, forecasting, advising on any necessary capital financing arrangements and even acting as an intermediary in negotiating such arrangements.)
>
> **Due diligence:** Sometimes referred to as a transaction-related service, this is a specific type of engagement which covers investigations of entities identified as possible acquisitions or disposal targets with a view to providing information relevant to the entity's acquisition or disposal decision.

Note. ACCA has observed that candidates frequently mistake due diligence for corporate finance and vice versa – these definitions are provided for clarification and show that while due diligence work may be included as part of the broad range of restructuring services that come under the corporate finance umbrella, a due diligence engagement is focused on evaluating other entities as part of a possible transaction.

Due diligence reviews are a specific type of review engagement. A typical due diligence engagement is where a practitioner is engaged by one company planning to **take over** another to identify the material **risks** associated with the transaction (including a review of all the **assumptions** underlying the purchase) in order to ensure that the acquirer has all the necessary facts. This is important when determining purchase price. Similarly, due diligence can also be requested by sellers.

It may include some or all of the following aspects.

Financial due diligence (a review of the financial position and obligations of a target to identify such matters as covenants and contingent obligations)	**Environmental** due diligence (environmental, health and safety and social issues)	**Regulatory** due diligence (review of the target's level of compliance)

Operational and **IT** due diligence (extent of operational and IT risks, including quality of systems, associated with a target business)	**People** due diligence (key staff positions under the new structure, contract termination costs and costs of integration)

Due diligence work is primarily limited to **enquiry** and **analytical procedures**.

A typical due diligence review could include enquiries into:

- **Assets/liabilities**, in order to **value** the company
- **Management's representations** about the company, which may need to be substantiated by evidence
- **Structure**, including how the target is owned and constituted and what changes will be necessary
- **Acquisition planning**, looking at potential benefits/drawbacks of the acquisition (eg synergies with the acquirer's business, or potential economies of scale)
- **Financial health**, based on a detailed examination of past financial statements and an analysis of the existing asset base
- **Credibility of the owners**, directors and senior managers, including validation of the career histories of all the main players in the business
- **Future potential**, reflected in the strengths of its products or services and the probability of earnings growth over the medium to long term

- **Assessment of the risk** to the acquiring business, in terms of its markets, strategy and likely future events
- **The business plan**, in terms of how realistic it is, how solid the assumptions used are and how well it conveys the potential

Due diligence can sit in a number of **engagement categories** because it can be performed as any of the following.

- As a review of historical financial information (limited assurance)
- As an assurance engagement (limited assurance)
- As agreed-upon procedures (no assurance)

There is no international standard on due diligence engagements, so in practice the engagement would be conducted in accordance with whichever standard best fits the particular engagement being conducted – perhaps ISRE 2400, ISAE (UK) 3000 or ISRS 4400.

Note that although due diligence uses the techniques of a review engagement, it is **unlikely** that **any assurance** will be provided. It is normally a report of factual findings such as agreed-upon procedures.

Essential reading

See Chapter 12 of the Essential reading for more detail on each of these engagements.

The Essential reading is available as an Appendix of the digital edition of the Workbook.

Chapter summary

Audit-related services and other assurance services

ISAE 3000 *Assurance Engagements*

Acceptance, planning and completion
- Agree terms of engagement
- Planning – as an audit
- Assess appropriateness of subject matter and criteria
- Obtain sufficient appropriate evidence
- Documentation
- Conclusion and reporting

Assurance and engagement types
- **Elements** of an assurance engagement:
  - 3 party relationship
  - Subject matter
  - Criteria
  - Evidence
  - Written report
- **Reasonable 'positive'** assurance: ('...*in our opinion, the F/S show a true and fair view...*')
- **Limited 'negative'** assurance: ('...*nothing has come to our attention to suggest the F/S do not show a true and fair view...*')
- **Attestation based** – client measures the subject matter and the practitioner provides a conclusion
- **Direct reporting** – the practitioner both measures the subject matter and provides a conclusion

Reviews of historical financial information

ISRE 2400 *Engagements to Review Financial Statements* & ISRE (UK) 2410 *Engagements to Review Interim Financial Statements*
- Report to directors
  - Primarily enquiry and analytical review
- Limited assurance expressed negatively:
  - 'nothing has come to the auditor's attention that the statements do not show a true and fair view'

Other examples of limited assurance

- ISAE 3400 *The Examination of Prospective Financial Information* (see Chapter 13)
- ISAE 3402 *Assurance Reports on Controls at a Service Organisation* (see Chapter 7)

Audit-related services

ISRS 4400 Agreed-upon Procedures
- Factual findings
- Examples are fraud investigations, verifications of claims for funding and forensic audits (see Chapter 14)
- No assurance given as the practitioner just reports what they have done (ie performing the agreed-upon procedures)

ISRS 4410 Compilations
- Producing subject matter information
- Examples are often accounts preparation for smaller clients
- No assurance given as the practitioner just reports what they have done (effectively a test of their skills)

Due diligence reviews
- Provision of advice to purchasing company in a transaction
  - Financial
  - Operational and IT
  - People
  - Regulatory
  - Environmental
- Ensures acquirer has all necessary facts
- Usually enquiry and analytical review only
- Normally no assurance given

Knowledge diagnostic

1. Non-audit engagements

Non-audit engagements can still offer some **assurance**, depending on the nature of work undertaken, or they may be classed as **audit-related** with either **limited** or **no assurance** granted at all.

2. Assurance engagements

Any engagement can be an assurance engagement provided it satisfies the elements of an assurance engagement as laid down in **ISAE (UK) 3000**. The subject matter reviewed can vary enormously (including **prospective financial information** and **reviews of service organisations**).

3. Different types of assurance

Engagements are planned and conducted in a similar manner to the external audit: assurance reported can be either **reasonable** or **limited** and engagements can be either **attestation** or **direct reporting**.

4. Reviews

Only a **limited (negative) level of assurance** is provided due to a review consisting mainly of **enquiries** and **analytical review** – this could be a full year (ISRE 2400) or interim review (ISRE (UK) 2410).

5. No assurance provided?

There are many **additional services** an audit firm can offer their clients. Some of these engagements provide **no assurance at all** and involve the auditor using their skills to perform **agreed-upon procedures (ISRS 4400)** or a **compilation (ISRS 4410)** of financial statements.

6. Due diligence

Due diligence engagements are used for a variety of purposes, so their nature and the level of assurance granted (if at all) can vary too.

Further study guidance

Question practice

Now try the following from the Further question practice bank (available in the digital edition of the Workbook):

- Question 25 'Aquinas' only presents a limited amount of information, so you are going to need to work hard for the marks, but it is a good opportunity to test the theory in this chapter.
- Question 26 'Audit' is also light on detail, but is still a good opportunity to practise something unusual which you may not expect to see in the AAA exam.

Further reading

At the time of writing there are currently no technical articles relevant to this chapter on the ACCA website, but you should continue to look out for any by accessing the website regularly: www.accaglobal.com/an/en/student/exam-support-resources/professional-exams-study-resources/p7/technical-articles.html

Own research

Enter the term 'due diligence' into an online search engine – you should be presented with a range of technical and commercial examples of this kind of engagement – read as many as you can to get a better flavour for this topic.

Activity answers

Activity 1: KPIs

Approach

The secret to success here is to remember that this is a manufacturing business, so you need to recommend key performance indicators (KPIs) relevant to a factory or workshop with its own cost structure, where labour and/or technology is used to turn raw materials into finished goods.

Suggested solution

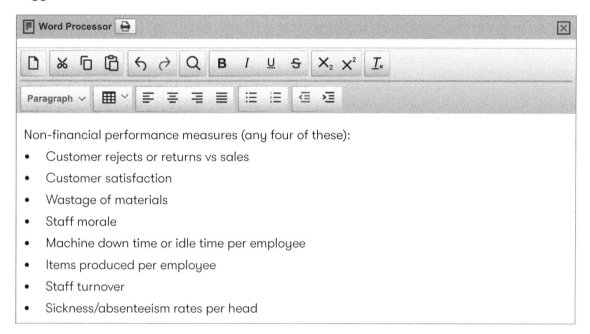

Non-financial performance measures (any four of these):

- Customer rejects or returns vs sales
- Customer satisfaction
- Wastage of materials
- Staff morale
- Machine down time or idle time per employee
- Items produced per employee
- Staff turnover
- Sickness/absenteeism rates per head

Activity 2: IT risks

Approach

Again, this is a very practical activity that requires a logical solution – even if you do not work for a business like Amazon, eBay or Facebook, you can probably imagine could go wrong with their IT systems (however unlikely) and the impact that each issue could have.

Suggested solution

Businesses are exposed to the following risks if their systems are unreliable:

- Assets are misappropriated or tampered with.
- They are at risk of being unable to trade with their customers (eg service interruption) leading to customer dissatisfaction and loss of customers to a competitor.
- Systems are damaged and shut down.

- Data is tampered with and unauthorised amendments made.
- Confidential data is stolen.
- Data protection legislation is not complied with (eg GDPR in the UK and beyond) leading to fines, loss of reputation and possibly going concern problems.

13

Prospective financial information (PFI)

Learning objectives

On completion of this chapter, you should be able to:

	Syllabus reference no.
Specific assignment • Prospective financial information For the assignment listed above:	F2
Define and describe the purpose of this assignment and analyse the appropriate level of assurance which may be offered by a professional firm in relation to this assignment.	(a)
Evaluate the matters to be considered before accepting the engagement, including any ethical and professional considerations.	(b)
Plan the assignment, applying professional scepticism, to gather suitable evidence and provide an appropriate level of assurance in line with the objectives of the assignment.	(c)
Discuss the level of assurance that the auditor may provide and explain the other factors to be considered in determining the nature, timing and extent of examination procedures.	(d)
Describe and recommend appropriate substantive, examination or investigative procedures which can be used to gather sufficient and appropriate evidence in the circumstances.	(e)
Discuss the content of a report for an examination of prospective financial information.	F5(b)

Business and exam context

Reporting on prospective financial information (PFI) is covered by ISAE 3400 *The Examination of Prospective Financial Information*.

Forecasts are of significant interest to users. Some would say that PFI is of more interest to users of accounts than historical financial information (HFI) which, of course, auditors report on in the external audit.

This is an area in which the auditors can therefore provide an alternative service to audit, in the form of a review or assurance engagement. This chapter looks at the factors that the auditor should think about when taking on such an engagement. The basis for this chapter has been laid in Chapter 12 but, in this chapter, we consider issues specific to PFI.

PFI can only be examined in Section B of the exam. The difficulties of reporting on PFI could be examined in an exam question. Section B questions can easily be set in the context of a PFI assignment.

Chapter overview

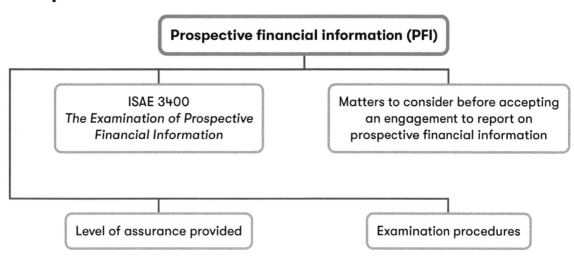

1 ISAE 3400 *The Examination of Prospective Financial Information*

1.1 Terminology

Prospective financial information means financial information based on assumptions about events that may occur in the future and possible actions by the entity (ISAE 3400: para. 3).

Auditors are regularly engaged to provide assurance on prospective financial information.

Prospective financial information can be of two types (or a combination of both).

> **Forecast:** Prospective financial information based on assumptions as to future events which management expects to take place and the actions management expects to take (best-estimate assumptions).
>
> **Projection:** Prospective financial information based on hypothetical assumptions about future events and management actions, or a mixture of best-estimate and hypothetical assumptions. (ISAE 3400)

There are two other terms commonly associated with prospective financial information:

> **Hypothetical illustration:** Prospective financial information based on assumptions about uncertain future events and management actions which have not yet been decided on.
>
> **Target:** Prospective financial information based on assumptions about the future performance of the entity. (ISAE 3400: paras. 4–5)

Listed companies should have procedures that allow them to generate reliable prospective financial information (PFI), compare it to market expectations, publish it when necessary and subsequently report actual performance against it.

Activity 1: PFI examples

PFI has a key role for businesses in terms of providing information to third parties as well as an internal management tool. Can you think of some examples of different types of PFI?

Solution

2 Matters to consider before accepting an engagement to report on PFI

Before deciding to accept such an engagement, the audit firm should also consider the following.

(a) The **intended use** of the information. For example, is it intended for internal or external use?

(b) Whether the information will be for **general** or **limited distribution**.

(c) The nature of the **assumptions** on which the information is based.

(d) The **information** to be included.

(e) The **period covered** by the information (ISAE 3400: para. 10)

The auditor should not accept, or should withdraw from, an engagement when the assumptions are clearly unrealistic or when the auditor believes that the prospective financial information will be inappropriate for its intended use (ISAE 3400: para. 11).

3 Level of assurance provided

Due to the nature of PFI, the audit firm will be unable to conclude on whether the results forecast will be achieved. Also there may be insufficient evidence available to conclude that the assumptions are free from material misstatement. Therefore, the audit firm can generally only provide a **limited level of assurance**.

The audit firm will normally provide negative assurance. This means they will state that '**nothing has come to their attention**' which causes them to believe that the assumptions are **not** a reasonable basis for the forecast.

Example of an unmodified report on a forecast

REPORT TO....

We have examined the forecast in accordance with the International Standard on Assurance Engagements applicable to the examination of prospective financial information. Management is responsible for the forecast including the assumptions set out in Note X on which it is based.

Based on our examination of the evidence supporting the assumptions nothing has come to our attention which causes us to believe that these assumptions do not provide a reasonable basis for the forecast. Further, in our opinion the forecast is properly prepared on the basis of the assumptions and is presented in accordance with International Financial Reporting Standards.

Actual results are likely to be different from the forecast since anticipated events frequently do not occur as expected and the variation may be material.

AUDITOR

Date

Address

(ISAE 3400 (revised): para.28)

The auditor can express a qualified (material misstatement or insufficient/inappropriate audit evidence) opinion if he believes:

(a) The presentation and disclosure of the PFI is not adequate

(b) One or more of the assumptions do not provide a reasonable basis for the PFI

4 Examination procedures

The auditor should obtain sufficient appropriate evidence as to whether:

* Management's **assumptions** on which the PFI is based are **not unreasonable**
* The information is **properly prepared** on the basis of the assumptions
* The information is **properly presented** and all material assumptions are **adequately disclosed**
* The PFI is prepared on a **consistent basis** with historical financial statements, using appropriate accounting policies

The auditor should obtain **sufficient knowledge** of the business to be able to evaluate whether the assumptions are justified. The historical information will be used as a yardstick to assess the assumptions underlying the information.

In carrying out their review of the accounting bases and calculations for forecasts, and the procedures followed by the company for preparing them, the **main points** which the reporting accountant will wish to consider include:

Whether the forecast under review is based on forecasts regularly prepared for the purpose of management, or whether it has been separately and specially prepared for the specific purpose	Where forecasts are regularly prepared for management purposes, the degree of accuracy and reliability previously achieved, and the frequency and thoroughness with which estimates are revised	Whether the forecast under review represents the management's best estimate of results which they reasonably believe can and will be achieved rather than targets which the management have set as desirable
The extent to which forecast results for expired periods are supported by reliable interim accounts	The details of the procedures followed to generate the forecast and the extent to which it is built up from detailed forecasts of activity and cash flow	The extent to which profits are derived from activities having a proven and consistent trend and those of a more irregular, volatile or unproven nature
How the forecast takes account of any material extraordinary items and prior year adjustments, their nature, and how they are presented	Whether adequate provision is made for foreseeable losses and contingencies and how the forecast takes account of factors which may cause it to be subject to a high degree of risk, or which may invalidate the assumptions	Whether working capital appears adequate for requirements (normally this would require the availability of properly prepared cash flow forecasts) and, where short-term or long-term finance is to be relied on, whether the necessary arrangements have been made and confirmed

The auditor should confirm the **arithmetical accuracy** of the forecast and the supporting information and whether forecast statements of financial position and statements of cash flows have also been prepared (as these help to highlight arithmetical inaccuracies and inconsistent assumptions).

The auditor should also obtain **written representations** from management regarding the intended use of the information, the completeness of significant assumptions and management's acceptance of its responsibility for the PFI.

Activity 2: Prism

Prism, a public company, is one of the world's leading suppliers of fast-moving consumer goods. The company is looking to increase its operations in Eastern Europe and requires some additional finance.

You are the manager of a firm of Chartered Certified Accountants and have been approached by Paul Robinson, the Chief Executive of Prism. He is trying to obtain some additional finance from the bank and they have asked that he obtain an independent review of the figures that have been produced to support the loan application.

Statement of profit or loss

	Forecast 20X4	Actual 20X3
	£m	£m
Revenue	47.6	40.9
Cost of sales	(33.3)	(30.7)
Gross profit	14.3	10.2

	Forecast 20X4	Actual 20X3
	£m	£m
Profit on disposal of investment	1.0	0.6
Other expenses	(5.3)	(4.6)
Profit before tax	10.0	6.2

Statement of financial position

	Forecast 20X4	Actual 20X3
	£m	£m
Non-current assets		
Property, plant and equipment	14.9	10.9
Intangible assets	22.1	25.0
Investments	–	2.3
	37.0	38.2
Current assets		
Inventories	5.6	4.1
Receivables	9.1	7.3
Cash	2.5	2.4
	17.2	13.8
	54.2	52.0
Equity		
Share capital	5.3	5.3
Revaluation surplus	3.2	3.2
Retained earnings	9.8	8.3
	18.3	16.8
Non-current liabilities	18.1	18.3
Current liabilities	17.8	16.9
	54.2	52.0

Required

Describe the audit work that a professional certified accountant would perform on the forecast statement of profit or loss and statement of financial position.

Solution

Chapter summary

Prospective financial information (PFI)

ISAE 3400
The Examination of Prospective Financial Information

Distinction between:
- A forecast (based on events and assumptions expected to occur)
- A projection (based on expectations and hypothetical assumptions)
- A hypothetical illustration (based on decisions not yet made eg 'flying kites')
- A target (based on possible future performance of an entity)

Matters to consider before accepting an engagement to report on prospective financial information

- Intended use
- General vs limited distribution
- Nature of assumptions
- Information to be included
- Period covered by PFI

Level of assurance provided

- Due to nature of engagement likely to be limited (negative) assurance
  '...nothing has come to our attention...'
- An opinion (effectively reasonable positive assurance) that the forecast has been prepared in line with the assumptions and relevant reporting framework

Examination procedures

- Limited assurance comes from approach – usually enquiry and analytical review
- Auditor should obtain sufficient appropriate evidence that:
  - Management assumptions are not unreasonable
  - Information is properly prepared on the basis of the assumptions
  - Information is properly presented and assumptions disclosed
  - PFI is prepared on basis consistent with historical financial statements (eg accounting policies; activity rates etc)

Knowledge diagnostic

1. Prospective financial information (PFI)

PFI relates to any financial data prepared based on assumptions relating to **future** events or actions. Such PFI can relate to **forecasts, projections, hypothetical illustrations** and **targets**.

2. Acceptance

Auditors must consider some additional factors before accepting an engagement to report on PFI, such as who the information is for and what it is to be used for.

3. Level of assurance given (assumptions)

In practice the level of assurance given in a PFI engagement will always be **limited**, expressed in a **negative form**, for the **reasonableness of the assumptions**.

4. Level of assurance given (preparation)

However, the level of assurance given in a PFI engagement for the **application of those assumptions** will always be reasonable, expressed in a **positive form (ie an opinion)**.

5. Evidence

The type of audit work performed will, in the main, be restricted to **enquiry** and **analytical review** – enough to ensure sufficient appropriate evidence exists for whatever report is required.

Further study guidance

Question practice

Now try the following from the Further question practice bank (available in the digital edition of the Workbook):

- Question 27 'Verity' which is essential exam-standard question practice for the contents of this chapter.

Further reading

At the time of writing there are currently no technical articles relevant to this chapter on the ACCA website but you should continue to look out for any by accessing the website regularly: www.accaglobal.com/an/en/student/exam-support-resources/professional-exams-study-resources/p7/technical-articles.html

Own research

When you are next at work, ask someone in a position of authority whether your employer has ever created forecasts or business plans – why were they required, were they ever reviewed by anyone and were they successful?

Activity answers

Activity 1: PFI examples

> **Approach**
>
> This is a practical exercise in thinking about why PFI would be required and who would benefit from it. Try and consider both internal and external stakeholders for this kind of information.

Suggested solution

Prospective financial information can include financial statements or one or more elements of financial statements and may be prepared:

(1) As an internal management tool, for example, to assist in evaluating a possible capital investment; or

(2) For distribution to third parties in, for example:

    (i) An annual report to provide information to shareholders, regulatory bodies and other interested parties

    (ii) A document for the information of lenders which may include, for example, cash flow forecasts

Activity 2: Prism

> **Approach**
>
> This is definitely exam-standard and demonstrates a key piece of advice – if financial information is presented in a question, you need to do something appropriate with it. However, what will you do here? The solution is laid out in three categories: (i) general procedures over the creation of the PFI; (ii) profit or loss items, which should be considered in terms of the story of how the company's fortunes are going to change; and (iii) the financial position and what it will be in a year's time.
>
> Consider what you have been told and how likely it is that the company will either continue as it is or will change from the figures presented.
>
> Finally, remember that performing analytical procedures is important, but you must do more than just say 'Revenue has increased' – you need to work out whether such an increase is reasonable, whether other factors would support this, whether you need further information to understand this increase etc.

Suggested solution

General procedures

1. Meet with Paul to determine the process for preparing the forecast information.

2. Identify and document internal controls over the process. Consider the role played by the Internal Audit department.

3. Obtain backing schedules for the information, cast and ensure they are numerically accurate.

4. Review the accounting policies used and ensure they are consistent with previous periods.

5. Discuss the need to produce a full statement of profit or loss, taking account of the proposed tax, interest and dividend payment.

6. Produce a letter of engagement.

7. Obtain management representation with regard to the completeness and accuracy of information and assumptions used. This should also contain a statement that it is management's responsibility to produce the information.

Statement of profit or loss

1. I would compare the forecast revenues for the year with those in the previous audited financial statements. Challenge Paul's assumption that revenue will increase by 17%.

2. Agree the increase to contracts, review the management accounts for the start of the year: do they show an increase in revenue?

3. Consider the likelihood of such an increase in revenue by reviewing the performance of similar companies in the same sector and reviewing the wider economic climate.

4. Obtain a detailed analysis of revenue and cost, perform a detailed analytical review and discuss the unusual movements with Paul or other relevant directors of Prism.

5. Compare the gross profit margin with that achieved in the past. The forecast shows an increase of 5% – how has this been achieved? Is it a realistic expectation?

6. I would compare the level of expenses with those in prior year. Certain expenses should be fixed and remain static. Others will vary according to revenue levels. Any significant fluctuations would be investigated further.

7. Review the expected profit on disposal of investment to supporting documentation and recalculate it.

Statement of financial position

1. I would confirm the value of non-current assets to the most recent audited accounts. Possible impairment of assets will be discussed with the directors.

2. I would recalculate depreciation for each period and compare the accounting policies against those used in previous financial statements.

3. I would calculate the age of inventories, receivables and payables and compare them with past financial statements. Any significant variations would be investigated further.

4. Discuss with management the possibility of obtaining equity finance.

5. Calculate key ratios and compare them year on year, such as ROCE, asset turnover, current asset and quick asset ratios. Review any current bank agreements and confirm that bank covenants are not breached.

6. Discuss the need to include any provisions for contingencies, such as warranties.

7. I would agree the cash figure and the level of overdraft and loans to agreements with the banks and financial institutions.

BPP

Skills checkpoint 4

Commercial acumen

Overview

Skills checkpoint 4 – Commercial acumen

'Commercial acumen' is one of the four professional skills that have been introduced by ACCA into the AAA exam.

This professional skill will be examined in Section A of the exam as part of the compulsory 50-mark question which will test all four of the professional skills for 10 marks in total.

This professional skill may also be examined in Section B, which consists of two compulsory scenario-based 25-mark questions, each of which allocates five marks to professional skills.

Each Section B question will contain a minimum of two professional skills: 'analysis and evaluation' plus 'professional scepticism and judgement' and/or 'commercial acumen'. Section B questions will state which of these professional skills are being tested.

No professional skill will ever be worth more than five marks in a question.

Syllabus learning outcomes

This is how the AAA syllabus expects candidates to demonstrate the professional skill of 'commercial acumen':

- Demonstrate awareness of any wider external factors or implications, in a given scenario, for the audit engagement, audit firm or audit client

- Recognise key issues and limitations, and consider the plausibility, and the practical or commercial implications, of recommendations made in the context of the engagement and audit firm
- Show insight and perception in understanding the wider implications and impact of implementing relevant recommendations and demonstrate acumen in arriving at suitable conclusions

How to demonstrate professional skill in 'commercial acumen'

How could you demonstrate 'commercial acumen' when attempting the Specimen exam?

In Question 1, professional marks were awarded for demonstration of this skill as follows:
- Audit procedures are practical and plausible in the context of the Crux Group
- Use of effective examples and/or calculations from the scenario to illustrate points or recommendations
- Recognition of the appropriate commercial considerations of the audit firm

In Question 2, professional marks were awarded for demonstration of this skill as follows:
- Inclusion of appropriate recommendations regarding the additional quality management procedures required by the firm
- Appropriate recognition of the wider implications on the engagement, the audit firm and the company

'Commercial acumen' was not examined in Question 3 of the Specimen exam.

How were 'commercial acumen' marks awarded in the September 2022 exam?

This was the first time that the exam was split into 80 technical marks and 20 professional skills marks. From an analysis of the solutions and the examining team's feedback, commercial acumen could have been displayed (and credit awarded via professional marks) for appreciating the link between matters expressed within the scenario:
- Explaining why certain **business risks** were important to the company in Question 1
- Suggesting that reducing the costs on the audit in Question 2 may be an indication that the audit fee was set at too low a level (ie **lowballing**)
- The wider implications for an organisation with such poor cash flow as that seen in Question 3 (hence the increased risk of **management bias** in the cash flow forecast)

What can you do to demonstrate 'commercial acumen' when answering other questions?

When you analyse both the syllabus and the marking guide for commercial acumen' the **keyword**s that keep appearing are as follows:
- Wider awareness
- Plausibility
- Practical or commercial
- Insight and perception
- Appropriate

As well as considering the commercial impact of certain factors on the firm in an exam question, the organisations featured in scenarios and exhibits may operate in a variety of different sectors or industries and you will therefore be expected to display commercial acumen when considering the factors that are relevant to these organisations as well. For example:

- **Private sector organisations** are mainly interested in profit, but may also be focused on growth, market share or even just survival, so the assessment of relevant business risks will be rewarded (but no prioritisation of business risks will be required).
- Other profit-oriented private sector organisations might operate in **regulated industries** where the correct treatment of intangibles such as licences become more critical to their going concern status.
- **Not-for-profit organisations** may have a different focus, such as charities where the focus is on fund-raising and cost control.
- **Public sector organisations** will be different again, focusing on their social objectives and any other funding constraints.

Clearly, 'commercial acumen' is more nuanced than the other professional skills and so you will need to think carefully when answering a question where it is included in the list of skills being examined. Experience of how to answer questions and experience in the real world must form part of your approach to such questions.

In some ways, 'commercial acumen' is the equivalent of charisma: if you need to ask what it is, you probably don't possess it. However, you can start to develop a form of radar to help you identify situations where 'commercial acumen' might need to be displayed in your answer. We will use two exam success skills to illustrate what we are talking about by suggesting some common pitfalls. Overall, you need to consider the bigger picture, the logical risks involved from a course of action and how things are inter-connected.

Firstly, let's look at **answer planning**. Questions on non-audit engagements can be quite technical – for example, the specific matters to be considered before accepting an engagement to review prospective financial information (PFI) – but they may also be based on the examining team's technical articles. You can access technical articles written by the examining team online (available from the ACCA website) which will help you to build a plan.

Questions on topics like this can also be more applied and require sound commercial awareness and common sense to score well. A previous exam question was set in the context of a company which would only receive substantial government funding if it achieved targets in three specific areas, one of which was 'accidents in the workplace'. The following requirement relates to this:

(ii)   **Describe the procedures to verify the number of serious accidents in the year.**

(4 marks)

The examining team reported that for this question:

'Many candidates seemed to think that the auditor has access to absolutely any kind of evidence that they could wish for. Common sources of evidence referred to included:

- The private medical records of employees

- Police reports on 'dangerous' incidents

- Hospital admissions data

- Interviews with ambulance drivers/paramedics/doctors

- Death certificates

'Candidates need to appreciate that although the auditor will have access to books and records held by their client, they will not be able to access external and possibly highly confidential information as a means to gather evidence. The above examples show of a lack of commercial, or even, common sense.'

Next, we will consider the **correct interpretation of requirements**. It is vital that you read the data in the scenario and then consider the requirements of the question in that context. All too often, candidates read the requirements and then produce an answer to the question they think has been asked or the question they think they can answer, not the actual question itself.

Consider the following question from a recent exam sitting:

Your audit client, Mulligan Co, designs and manufactures wooden tables and chairs. The directors want to secure a loan of $3 million in order to expand operations and have approached LCT Bank for the loan. The bank's lending criteria stipulate the following:

'Loan applications must be accompanied by a detailed business plan, including an analysis of how the finance will be used. LCT Bank need to see that the finance requested is adequate for the proposed business purpose. The business plan must be supported by an assurance opinion on the adequacy of the requested finance.'

Your firm has agreed to review the business plan and to provide an assurance opinion on the completeness of the finance request. A meeting will be held tomorrow to discuss this assignment.

(a)   Identify and explain the matters … that should be discussed at the meeting … (8 marks)

What matters should be discussed at this meeting? Issues of an acceptance nature perhaps: 'Do we want the work?'; 'Are we competent to act?'; or even, 'Have we got the necessary resources?' Maybe issues of a client acceptance nature might also be appropriate here, such as, 'Is this client legitimate?'

Reading the scenario is vital – the following comes from the AAA examining team's report:

'The vast majority of answers to requirement (a) stated that at the meeting they would discuss 'whether we are competent to take on the work'. Surely this is not something you would raise at a meeting with your client having just agreed to do the work…

'Many candidates (also) wanted to discuss at the meeting matters such as, 'Do we have the experience to perform the work?' Again, I would think that the client would be surprised to learn that you may not be knowledgeable enough to conduct the assignment, especially considering that you are the auditor of their business. I would urge candidates to stop and think and consider if the matters they are suggesting discussing at the meeting… fit in with the scenario provided.'

You do at least have a clue when 'commercial acumen' will matter because it will be mentioned in the requirement that there are certain professional skills that answers should demonstrate, so keep an eye on these and tailor your approach accordingly.

Skills practice

To help you develop your use of the professional skill 'commercial acumen' you should attempt Question 27 'Verity Ltd' from the 'Further question practice' section at the back of the digital edition of the Workbook. Once you have attempted this question, you should aim to practise as many questions as you can from both the Workbook and the Practice and Revision Kit as well as those in the CBE software using the ACCA Practice Platform.

You should also attempt Question 32 'Grissom Group' which reflects how Question 1 in the AAA exam will look. As it covers all of the professional skills and technical content up to and including group audits, you may wish to leave this question until you have covered all chapters in the Workbook.

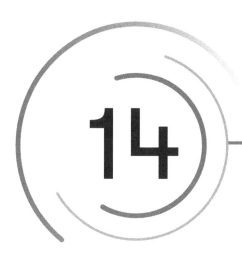

14

Forensic audits

Learning objectives

On completion of this chapter, you should be able to:

	Syllabus reference no.
Specific assignment • Forensic audits For the assignment listed above:	F2
Define and describe the purpose of this assignment and analyse the appropriate level of assurance which may be offered by a professional firm in relation to this assignment.	(a)
Evaluate the matters to be considered before accepting the engagement, including any ethical and professional considerations.	(b)
Plan the assignment, applying professional scepticism, to gather suitable evidence and provide an appropriate level of assurance in line with the objectives of the assignment.	(c)
Discuss the level of assurance that the auditor may provide and explain the other factors to be considered in determining the nature, timing and extent of examination procedures.	(d)
Describe and recommend appropriate substantive, examination or investigative procedures which can be used to gather sufficient and appropriate evidence in the circumstances.	(e)

Business and exam context

In the current globalised business world, there is an increasing demand for forensic services. Audit and assurance professionals are well-placed to provide these. This chapter introduces forensic accounting and auditing and discusses its applications in practice and continues with a look at investigative procedures and evidence.

This topic is often examined in a very practical way. It is important to have an understanding of the framework, but case study questions will involve the application of procedures similar to those used in traditional audits of financial statements. Some specific knowledge is required of basic definitions, but otherwise the application of audit-style procedures is used. Questions on forensics may only come up in Section B of the exam.

Chapter overview

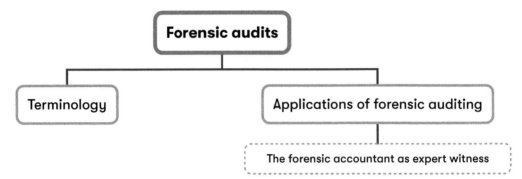

Forensic audits

Terminology

Applications of forensic auditing

The forensic accountant as expert witness

 BPP

1 Terminology

KEY TERM

Forensic auditing: (The process.) Relates to the **procedures** followed by the firm and can be defined as gathering, analysing and reporting on data, in a pre-defined context, for the purpose of finding facts and/or evidence in the context of financial/legal disputes and/or irregularities and giving preventative advice in this area.

Forensic investigation: (An example of a forensic auditing engagement.) Applies similar procedures to a forensic audit but is carried out for specific civil or criminal cases. Such cases could involve fraud or asset tracing in money laundering cases.

Forensic accounting: (The skills involved.) Involves undertaking a financial investigation in response to a particular event, where the findings of the investigation may be used as evidence in court or to otherwise help resolve disputes.

2 Applications of forensic auditing

The range of assignments in this area is vast, so to give specific definitions for each is not always practicable. In a publication of the Chartered Professional Accountants of Canada, *Standard practices for investigative and forensic accounting engagements* (November 2006), the following definition is established.

Investigative and forensic accounting engagements are those that:

(a) Require the application of professional accounting skills, investigative skills, and an investigative mindset

(b) Involve disputes or anticipated disputes, or where there are risks, concerns or allegations of fraud or other illegal or unethical conduct (CPA Canada (2006): p2)

Forensic audit and accounting is a rapidly growing area. The major accountancy firms all offer forensic services, as do a number of specialist companies. The demand for these services arises partly from the increased expectation of corporate governance codes for:

Company directors to take seriously their responsibilities for the prevention and detection of fraud (for example, to quantify the extent of the losses

Governments concerned about risks arising from criminal funding of terrorist groups

Otherwise, in a case where an auditor or accountant is being sued for **negligence**, both parties may wish to employ forensic accountants, either to investigate the standard of work performed or to establish the losses suffered by the plaintiff.

Insurance companies often engage forensic accountants to verify and report on the amounts of losses suffered by a claimant where there is a dispute between the claimant and the company.

2.1 The forensic accountant as an expert witness

Due to the nature of this work, forensic accountants will very often be called as **expert witnesses** in civil or criminal cases. This is a very important function, and some jurisdictions have specific rules governing their duties.

For example, in England and Wales, experts have a duty to exercise reasonable skill and care to those instructing them, and to comply with any relevant professional code of ethics. **However**, when they are instructed to give or prepare evidence for the purpose of civil proceedings, they have an overriding **duty to help the court** on matters within their expertise. This duty **overrides** any obligation to the person instructing or paying them. Experts must not serve the exclusive interest of those who retain them.

The **Forensic Science Regulator** has produced guidance for experts in England and Wales to follow when producing reports for criminal prosecutions. The main contents are outlined below.

 Expert reports should contain the following:

(a) Statements regarding the objectivity of the expert and that no conflicts of interest exist

(b) Confirmation that any fees are not paid on a contingent basis

(c) Acknowledgement that the expert's duty is to the court and not the party who engaged them to give evidence

(d) An overview of the sources of information used in creating the report

(e) Confirmation that the expert has complied with the relevant Code of Conduct in producing the evidence used in the case

(f) A declaration of the following:

    (i) That they are an expert in their field

    (ii) Their qualifications and experience

    (iii) That the contents of their report are true to the best of their knowledge

    (iv) Acknowledgment that any false statements may lead to their prosecution

    (v) Name, signature, date and occupation

(Forensic Science Regulator, 2019)

Ethical implications of acting as a witness in a case related to an audit client

It is possible that a professional accountant might be asked to give evidence related to an audit client in a court or tribunal. Such work may fall into one of two categories:

(a) As a **witness of fact**, giving evidence based on direct knowledge of facts or events – should this evidence include judgements or conclusions based on professional expertise, it will not create any threats to independence

(b) As an **expert witness**, the professional accountant provides evidence, including their opinion on certain matters, based on their expertise as opposed to facts or events - should those matters relate to acting as an expert witness on behalf of an audit client, an **advocacy threat** is created

The extent of this advocacy threat, and whether it could be mitigated will depend on the following issues:

- If the firm was appointed by the court or tribunal (and not the audit client) the threat is considered acceptable

- If the firm was appointed as part of a class action and the involvement of any audit clients is minimal (no more than 20% of the group involved and not taking any kind of leadership role) the threat is considered acceptable

- If neither of these conditions applies, the firm cannot act as expert witness for a public interest entity audit client

- For audit clients that are not public interest entities, the firm can act as long as the expert witness has not been an audit team member

(IESBA Code: paras. 607.7-8, R607.9)

Essential reading

See Chapter 14 of the Essential reading for further information on planning and conducting a forensic audit engagement.

The Essential reading is available as an Appendix of the digital edition of the Workbook.

Activity 1: Sam Seel

You are a manager in an audit firm with a small team dedicated to forensic investigations. You have been approached by the Finance Director of SL Ltd to perform an investigation into a fraud perpetrated by a purchase ledger clerk.

You have ascertained the following.

The fraud came to light after another employee drew attention to the activities of the purchase ledger clerk, Sam Seel. Initial investigations have identified that Sam had been paying money into his own bank account by raising false invoices and paying them through SL Ltd's purchase ledger. The fraud had gone undetected for an unknown amount of time because SL Ltd's controls only require invoices in excess of £1,000 to be authorised by a senior member of staff. Invoices below this amount are processed and authorised for payment by the relevant purchase ledger clerk.

SL Ltd is a very large company with revenue in excess of £100m and operates in the construction industry. Sam Seel joined the finance department nine months ago and has since been suspended from duties pending this investigation.

The Finance Director has requested that your firm perform such procedures as necessary to quantify the extent of the loss suffered by the business.

Required

1   In the context of the ACCA's fundamental ethical principles, what factors should you take into account before accepting this engagement?

2   Assuming you accept the engagement, what specific procedures would you perform to allow you to quantify the loss suffered by SL Ltd?

Solution

Chapter summary

```
                    ┌─────────────────────┐
                    │   Forensic audits   │
                    └─────────────────────┘
                              │
            ┌─────────────────┴─────────────────┐
    ┌───────────────┐              ┌──────────────────────────────────┐
    │  Terminology  │              │ Applications of forensic auditing │
    └───────────────┘              └──────────────────────────────────┘
```

- **Forensic auditing** is the process of gathering, analysing and reporting on data, in a pre defined context, for the purpose of finding facts and/or evidence in the context of financial/legal disputes and/or irregularities and giving preventative advice in this area.
- **Forensic investigation** applies similar procedures to a forensic audit but is carried out for specific civil or criminal cases. Such cases could involve fraud or asset tracing in money laundering cases.
- **Forensic accounting** involves undertaking a financial investigation in response to a particular event, where the findings of the investigation may be used as evidence in court or to otherwise help resolve disputes.

- **Fraud investigations:**
  Used to quantify the possible amount lost, for example.
- **Negligence cases:**
  To establish the standards of work actually done.
- **Verification of insurance claims:**
  In the event of dispute between claimant and company.

The forensic accountant as expert witness

The accountant's duty to help the court overrides any duty owed to clients who may have paid for their services.

 BPP

Knowledge diagnostic

1. Forensic engagements

Auditors are increasingly being called upon to use their skills in forensic work. Engagements in this area can include **forensic auditing, forensic investigations** and **forensic accounting.**

2. Examples of forensic engagements

The work can involve **fraud investigations, evidence gathering** where an auditor is being sued for negligence or performing work for insurance companies to **verify customer claims.**

3. Acting as expert witness

Due to the nature of the work, it is likely the forensic accountant will be called to a court of law as an **expert witness** and care must be taken to ensure that this function is fulfilled in the appropriate way.

Further study guidance

Question practice

Now try the following from the Further question practice bank (available in the digital edition of the Workbook):

*   Question 28 'Painswick Ltd' is further practise of the content introduced here and the skills required if a question on forensics comes up in the exam.

Further reading

There is one technical article on the ACCA website, written by members of the AAA examining team, which is relevant to some of the topics covered in this chapter that you should read:

*   *Forensic auditing*

Own research

*   There are plenty of accounting firms that offer forensic audit services – compare what they do and see if there are any significant differences in their approach.
*   There are many other resources online that can help this subject come to life: try this as an example of what forensic audit can include:

    corporatefinanceinstitute.com/resources/knowledge/accounting/what-is-a-forensic-audit/

Activity answers

Activity 1: Sam Seel

Approach

This requirement has two parts: for the first part, you need to list the five fundamental ethical principles (hopefully not a struggle, but refer back to Chapter 2 in this Workbook if you can't remember them all!) before you consider how each one could be compromised by accepting this engagement.

For part 2 you should try and visualise the fraud and explore everything that Sam could have been connected with to see how far it has spread throughout SL. Remember to make your procedures active, explaining what you will be doing, why and how – this will make for a thorough answer.

Suggested solution – ethical factors

Integrity

SL Ltd has been a victim of fraud perpetrated by at least one of its own staff. It appears that this is isolated to one junior member of staff. Despite this, prior to accepting the engagement, we should consider the risk that the fraud was assisted by more senior members of staff or that there is a weak control environment which could call into question the integrity of some or all of the senior staff at SL Ltd. If we feel there is a significant risk of our own integrity being compromised, we should not accept the engagement.

Objectivity

Should this case come to court in the future, there is a very real chance staff from our firm could be called as an expert witness. We would need to consider our relationship with the client and whether that would restrict our ability to provide testimony to the court in an objective manner. An expert witness should seek to provide evidence independently, regardless of the interests of their client.

Professional competence and due care

As with any engagement, we should consider our ability to perform the engagement with the required level of expertise and competence. Our firm has a forensic department (albeit a small one), so it is likely that we have performed similar engagements in the past. We should note, however, that SL Ltd is a construction company and we would need to carefully consider whether we have sufficient knowledge of the business and the industry to perform a meaningful investigation.

Confidentiality

As with all other engagements, this will carry a duty of confidentiality to SL Ltd. However, this will be overridden should we be called to court as an expert witness, and we should inform SL Ltd of this in the engagement letter. Additionally, this is likely to be a sensitive investigation and we should discuss the levels of secrecy required while we are at the client's premises.

Professional behaviour

There is a chance that this case could enter the public domain in a court case that could be relatively high profile. We should be careful to conduct ourselves in a professional manner and do nothing that brings our firm or the profession into disrepute, particularly if we are called as an expert witness.

Suggested solution – procedures

- Enquire of the Purchasing Manager as to the contracts/jobs for which Sam Seel dealt with the invoices.

- Perform an analytical review on purchases for contracts/jobs that Sam wasn't involved in to identify any unusual trends that may imply the fraud is more widespread.

- Inspect **all** (materiality is not relevant) invoices that Sam dealt with below £1,000. Be alert for invoices to suppliers not on the company's approved list or purchase ledger for the previous year. (Sam was only employed for nine months.) Unusual suppliers should be contacted to confirm their existence; where the supplier cannot be verified, the invoice should be listed as being fraudulent.

- Perform an analytical review of all invoices dealt with by Sam in excess of £1,000. Consider any unusual trends in purchasing costs, margins and so on compared to the prior year. Unexplained fluctuations could indicate more extensive fraud and collusion with senior staff.

- Depending on the results of this analytical review, select a sample of invoices greater than £1,000 and ensure the existence of the suppliers as above.

15 Social and environmental auditing and the auditing aspects of insolvency

Learning objectives

On completion of this chapter, you should be able to:

	Syllabus reference no.
Plan an engagement to provide assurance on integrated reporting (performance measures and sustainability indicators).	F3(a)
Describe the difficulties in measuring and reporting on economic, environmental, social and sustainability information and give examples of performance measures and sustainability indicators.	F3(b)
Describe substantive procedures to detect potential misstatements in respect of socio-environmental and sustainability matters.	F3(c)
Discuss the form and content of an independent verification statement of an integrated report or sustainability information.	F3(d)
Explain the auditor's main considerations in respect of social and environmental matters and how they impact on entities and their financial statements (eg impairment of assets, provisions and contingent liabilities).	D3(c)
Explain the meaning of, and describe the procedures involved in, placing a company into voluntary or compulsory liquidation or administration.	F4(a)
Explain the consequences of liquidation or administration for a company and its stakeholders.	F4(b)
Advise on the differences between fraudulent and wrongful trading and the consequences for company directors.	F4(c)
Examine the financial position of a company and determine whether it is insolvent.	F4(d)
Identify the circumstances where administration could be adopted as an alternative to liquidation, and explain the benefits of administration compared to liquidation.	F4(e)
Explain and apply the priority for the allocation of company assets.	F4(f)

Business and exam context

In this chapter we start by investigating the impact of social and environmental issues on assurance services.

Increasing importance is being placed on social and environmental issues in business. Recent years have seen a substantial weight of environmental legislation passed, which puts a significant burden of compliance on companies. The danger of non-compliance (fines, bad publicity, going concern) is an aspect of the environmental risk which companies face.

Such cases of non-compliance can become significant and we will also look at how auditors can be involved: shareholders and creditors sometimes look to blame auditors for not having warned them of a business becoming insolvent. A company which is heading towards insolvency can often be saved, using a variety of legal protections from creditors until the problem is sorted out. Unfortunately, many companies cannot be saved. Liquidation, sometimes called 'winding up', is when a company is formally dissolved and ceases to exist.

The topics in this chapter may be examined as part of a Section B question, and are unlikely to be more than a sub-section of a question as opposed to being the subject of a full question. However, it is unlikely that a whole question would be set on insolvency, or that it would be examined at every sitting.

You have previously studied insolvency in LW Corporate Law (formerly Paper F4). Much of the material here will be familiar from that subject, but will be examined at a higher level. For AAA you will be required to apply your knowledge and use your judgement to a much greater degree than before.

Chapter overview

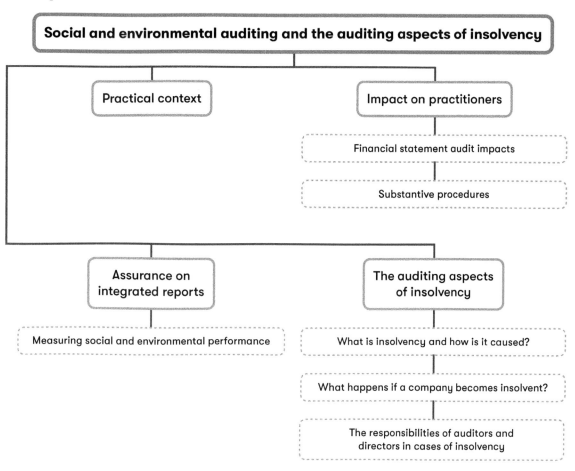

1 Practical context

Activity 1: Social and environmental factors

The importance of social and environmental factors is increasingly recognised by the business community. Many businesses now have specific policies governing their relationship with their employees, society and the environment.

Required

What factors have led to the rapid growth in business awareness of these issues?

Solution

The difficulties in measuring and reporting on economic, environmental, social and sustainability information

You already know that the auditor's job (among others) is to report on the financial statements of an entity. This includes the assessment of the risk of material misstatement, an evaluation of sufficient appropriate audit evidence and communication of an appropriate opinion. The process of auditing this financial information is tightly regulated by laws and regulations, professional standards and other forms of best practice. Clearly, we also know that this is a challenging task!

However, stakeholders don't just require an understanding of the financial position, performance and prospects of an entity: they also want to know about its environmental, social and sustainability credentials too. Although there is plenty of best practice, there is no definitive approach, although there are plenty of examples of best practice that can be considered.

Later in this chapter, we will discuss how integrated reports address this need. For now, let's start by considering some examples of performance measures and sustainability indicators, how challenging they can be to both measure and report on and then suggest some areas which might be more prone to misstatement. We will then go on to consider how to verify this kind of information along with the possible form and content of an independent verification statement on sustainability information.

Examples of performance measures and sustainability indicators

Sustainability is likely to be a term you have met before, but in case you are uncertain what it means, here is one of the most famous definitions from the 1987 **United Nations (UN) Brundtland Commission.**

> **Sustainability:** Meeting the needs of the present without compromising the ability of future generations to meet their own needs (UN, 2021).

There is no shortage of approaches to illustrate sustainability. In 2015, the UN adopted a series of **UN sustainable development goals (SDGs)** that illustrated how the world could put this definition of sustainability into practice. The following diagram shows these 17 UN SDGs:

The **OECD** (2021) has also published a series of more than 200 key performance indicators (KPIs) on the environment and sustainable development, including data that covers the following:

- Air and climate (such as pollution levels and CO_2 or other greenhouse gas emissions)
- Biodiversity (such as data on threatened species as a proportion of all species)
- Environmental policy (such as environmental taxes raised and other green policies adopted)
- Forest resources (such as rates of tree felling)
- Materials (such as mineral extraction rates)
- Waste (both household and business tonnages)
- Water (including water wastage and sewage treatment rates)

They are presented in alphabetical order on the OECD website as a way of acknowledging that there is no one area that should dominate, a theme that the UN SDGs have stressed as well: they are all important themes and dealing with them requires making some tough choices. You will find that if you conduct more research on this topic, there are many more methodologies in existence.

The challenge of measuring and reporting on performance measures and sustainability indicators

The main challenge for organisations is to decide how to provide visibility of their own environmental and sustainability position and performance in the context of the various methodologies and KPIs in place. Every organisation will leave its own environmental footprint, depending on what it does and how it does it. Significant resource is now being deployed in order to produce information that answers the question of how good a corporate citizen an organisation really is.

Once decisions have been taken about how to present an organisation's sustainability credentials, the next challenge is to implement ways of recording this footprint, agreeing on a series of suitable metrics and KPIs, putting in place accurate recording mechanisms for them and then compiling the results in a way that can be used in an ongoing way to set targets, chart progress and inform strategy.

Real life example

BBC Future Planet: counting carbon

The BBC website Future Planet (BBC, 2020) shares stories that are designed to help readers understand how to make the world a more sustainable place. At the end of each article published online, there is an estimate of the carbon emissions from that particular story – the publishers explain that this is provided in order to make carbon emissions more transparent so everyone attached to the article is aware of how much carbon is involved in the article itself.

This estimate is based on two things: (i) the carbon emissions associated with any travel that the author may need to undertake in order to produce the article, and (ii) the energy required to provide the article in a digital format for the reader. As part of describing the methodology involved, Future Planet explains that a range of values is provided due to the varied activities that go into creating their content and the inherent complexities of the estimation techniques involved. For the article on how and why they count carbon, this range is 1.2g to 3.6g CO_2 per pageview: to put this into context, it is usually estimated that boiling a kettle emits around 7g CO_2.

Reading an article about reducing carbon emissions that actually creates carbon emissions might seem counter-intuitive but Future Planet maintains that this transparency and visibility will help to start the process of finding solutions that can reduce these carbon emissions.

(Source: BBC Future Planet (2020) *Why and how does Future Planet count carbon?* BBC website)

Are there areas that are prone to misstatement?

Having considered some of the KPIs that could be used, the risk of misstatement seems real. Measurement may be complicated, requiring expensive equipment and expertise that may be in scarce supply. Estimation may be necessary if dealing with significant volumes of data, some of which may be prone to a degree of subjectivity (for example, the quality of environmental strategies adopted or the definition of an endangered species).

Being sceptical, it is unlikely that an organisation is going to present itself in anything other than a favourable light, not least because this is still not an area which is governed by laws and regulations in the same way as financial reporting. However, the ongoing importance of sustainability does mean that scrutiny is now becoming more thorough. In a previous chapter we saw that assurance engagements were fast becoming popular among organisations where the benefits outweighed the costs. It is likely that some kind of review will assist an organisation in its attempts to present a materially true and fair reflection of its sustainability position and performance.

Real life example

Adidas Annual Report 2020

Sportswear manufacturer Adidas produces a non-financial statement in line with German legislation. The report contains all aspects of the company's operations not explicitly covered by the audited financial statements. As well as the UN SDGs, Adidas uses the Global Reporting Initiative or GRI to help compile this report. The company also uses a materiality-based approach to consider the most relevant information that should be presented. Note that it includes social issues as well as those related to the environment or sustainability.

The non-financial statement consists of data and other information on environmental issues, including sustainable materials (such as eradicating plastic bags in all parts of its supply chain) as well water consumption, carbon footprint and wastage in its supply chain. Here are some other sustainability examples:

- Adidas has pledged to source 100% of its most common production material, polyester, from recycled sources by the year 2024: in 2020, the amount of recycled polyester in its apparel and footwear ranges was 71%.

- All of the company's cotton is considered sustainable (in other words, it comes from a process that reduces the use of pesticides and promotes more efficient water and land use)

- The company also has supply chain targets for water, waste chemicals and energy usage that require achievement by the year 2025, including carbon neutrality for corporate and own-retail sites.

The non-financial statement also contains data and other information on the following:
- Product safety and integrity (in other words, avoiding defective and dangerous products)
- Human rights, including fair labour conditions across suppliers and the supply chain
- Employee-related issues such as wages, development, training and diversity
- Customer satisfaction
- Anti-bribery and corruption practices
- Tax

How to verify this kind of information

There is no legal requirement to audit this non-financial information but Adidas appointed KPMG in Germany to undertake an independent limited assurance engagement, using ISAE 3000 (Revised) as the basis for a review of the method of preparation and the underlying data of the 2020 non-financial statement. This was a separate engagement to the audit of the financial statements which was also conducted by KPMG.

Independent verification statement on sustainability information

In summary, the limited assurance report by KPMG regarding the Adidas non-financial statement contains the following:
- A statement of the work carried out and the legislation in place
- Management's responsibility for preparing the non-financial statement
- The practitioner's responsibility for expressing a conclusion under ISAE 3000 (Revised) in relation to the preparation of the statement using enquiries and analytical procedures relating to the process for reporting and the supporting data
- Confirmation that the work was undertaken by the firm in line with appropriate independence and quality requirements
- A conclusion that nothing has come to the practitioner's attention that would cause them to believe that the non-financial statement has not been complied with in line with the appropriate legislation

(Source: paraphrased from content found within Adidas Annual Report 2020)

Essential reading

You can learn more about the difficulties in measuring social and environmental performance in Essential reading, as well as how the public sector is responding to this increasing awareness in social and environmental factors by referring to the content which summarises the 2021 CIPFA report *Evolving climate accountability: A global review of public sector environmental reporting*.

The Essential reading is available as an Appendix of the digital edition of the Workbook.

2 Impact on practitioners

Social and environmental issues cannot be ignored by external auditors. Potential impacts on their work may arise from:

| The application of environmental **laws** and **regulations** during the audit | The operation of processes that may cause **pollution** or the use of **hazardous substances** | The holding of an interest in **land and buildings** that have been **contaminated** by previous occupants |

| Dependence on a **major customer segment** whose business is threatened by **environmental pressures** | The voluntary reporting of any initiatives undertaken by an organisation to address social or environmental **concerns** of **stakeholders** (such as **integrated reporting**) |

2.1 Financial statement audit impacts

Auditors do not necessarily have a specific knowledge of environmental or social matters. However, in planning the audit, they should obtain sufficient knowledge of the business (under **ISA (UK) 315 (Revised July 2020)** *Understanding the Entity and its Environment*) to understand the social and environmental events, transactions and practices (**ISA (UK) 250A** *Consideration of Laws and Regulations in an Audit of Financial Statements*) that may have a significant effect on the financial statements or the audit and respond appropriately to them (**ISA (UK) 330** *Risk Response*).

2.1.1 Substantive procedures

The auditor may perform substantive testing to obtain evidence in relation to social and environmental matters. Below are some **suggested procedures**: it is not intended that all of the procedures will be appropriate in every case (in many cases, the auditor may judge it unnecessary to perform any of these procedures and may apply others instead) so overall, **common sense** and **commercial awareness of the scenario** should play a part here.

Documentary review

(a) Review **minutes** from meetings of directors, audit committees, or any other subcommittees of the board specifically responsible for environmental matters.

(b) Read **publicly available information** regarding any existing or possible future environmental matters.

Where relevant, consider:

- **Reports** by **environmental experts** about the entity, such as site assessments, due diligence investigations or environmental impact studies
- **Internal audit reports** and other internal reports dealing with environmental matters
- Reports issued by, and correspondence with, **regulatory** and **enforcement agencies**
- **Publicly available registers** or **plans** for the restoration of soil contamination
- **Environmental performance reports** issued by the entity
- Correspondence with the entity's **lawyers**

(c) Obtain **written representations** from management that it has considered the effects of environmental matters on the financial statements, and that it:

- Is not aware of any **material liabilities** or **contingencies** arising from environmental matters, including those resulting from illegal or possibly illegal acts;
- Is not aware of environmental matters that may result in a material **impairment** of assets; or
- If aware of such matters, has **disclosed** to the auditor all related facts.

Asset impairments (IAS 36)

(a) Enquire about any planned changes in capital assets, for example, in response to **changes** in **environmental legislation** or **business strategy** and their impact on the valuation of those assets or the company as a whole.

(b) For any asset impairments related to environmental matters that existed in **previous periods**, consider whether the **assumptions** underlying a write down or related carrying values **continue to be appropriate**.

Liabilities, provisions and contingencies (IAS 37)

(a) Enquire about policies and procedures operated to **identify** liabilities, provisions or contingencies arising from environmental matters.

(b) Enquire about **events** or **conditions** that may give rise to liabilities, provisions or contingencies arising from environmental matters, for example:

- **Penalties** or **possible penalties** arising from breaches of social or environmental laws and regulations; **or**

- **Claims** or **possible claims** for environmental damage.

(c) For property abandoned, purchased, or closed during the period, enquire about requirements or intentions for **site clean-up and restoration**.

(d) For property sold during the period (and in prior periods) enquire about any **liabilities** relating to environmental matters retained by contract or by law.

(e) For liabilities, provisions, or contingencies related to environmental matters, consider whether the **assumptions** underlying any **estimates** continue to be appropriate.

(f) Review the adequacy of any **disclosure** of the effects of environmental matters on the financial statements, especially in relation to **going concern (ISA (UK) 570)**.

2.1.2 FRC Staff Guidance - Auditor responsibilities under ISA (UK) 720 in respect of climate-related reporting by companies required by the Financial Conduct Authority (February 2022)

Under UK law, most listed entities are now required to make a formal statement regarding their compliance with the Task Force on Climate-Related Financial Disclosures (TCFD) recommendations in respect of their climate-related disclosures. Non-compliance with the TCFD recommendations is an option but does require formal disclosure of the reasons for departure from the framework. This **TCFD compliance statement** is another example of the **comply-or-explain** approach used by regulators to improve transparency in corporate reporting.

The TCFD framework is structured as follows:

Governance

The organisation's governance around climate-related risks and opportunities

Strategy

The actual and potential impacts of climate-related risks and opportunities on the organisation's businesses, strategy and financial planning

Risk management

The processes used by the organisation to identify, assess, and manage climate-related risks

Metrics and targets

The metrics and targets used to assess and manage relevant climate-related risks and opportunities

The largest UK companies are now required to report climate-related financial information as **TCFD aligned disclosures** using the TCFD framework. The UK government expects to mandate this across all companies by 2025.

Under **ISA (UK) 720**, auditors are required to read **other information** included in a client's annual report and then report accordingly on its consistency with the audited financial statements and any other knowledge obtained during the course of the audit. This FRC Staff Guidance has been published to clarify the responsibilities of the auditor regarding clients' TCFD aligned disclosures and the TCFD compliance statement because their classification as other information is not always obvious under UK law and reporting requirements.

In summary:

- The TCFD **compliance statement** is **other information** because there is a requirement under the listing rules to include this comply-or-explain disclosure in the company's annual report
- If the TCFD **compliance statement** is included in the company's Directors' Report, Strategic Report or Corporate Governance Statement, it will also be considered to be **statutory other information**
- TCFD **aligned disclosures** are only considered to be **other information** if they appear in the annual report
- TCFD **aligned disclosures** will be considered to be both **other information** and **statutory other information** if they are included within the company's Directors' Report, Strategic Report or Corporate Governance Statement

The Staff Guidance also clarifies the auditor's responsibilities under ISA (UK) 720 for **Streamlined Energy and Carbon Reporting (SECR)** disclosures made by their clients. Under this initiative, most large UK companies are now required to publicly disclose their UK energy use and carbon emissions within their Directors' Report or via cross reference to the Strategic Report. Consequently, these SECR disclosure would be considered to be both **other information** and **statutory other information** under ISA (UK0 720.

3 Assurance on integrated reports

Increasingly, practitioners are being asked to provide **assurance** on (and even **produce**) **reports** for clients that explain more fully their **responsibilities** to their various **stakeholders**. This includes a blend of **financial** and **non-financial information**, covering areas such as **governance**, **sustainability** and **remuneration**. The term used to describe such a report is **integrated reporting**.

3.1 Planning and performing an engagement to review an integrated report

The process of planning and performing any engagement follows a number of key steps, so when reviewing an integrated report, the practitioner will consider the following:

1 **Acceptance issues** – Does the engagement present any ethical issues (such as fee dependency, self-review, competence to act and required experience) or risks (such as liability or reputation factors)?

2 **Quality management** – Policies and procedures within the firm to manage the engagement

3 **Agreeing the terms of the engagement** via an engagement letter (this may need to be very specific, given the non-statutory nature of such integrated reports)

4 **Planning** – This will depend on the engagement but risk assessment and collecting evidence will need to be considered (see next section)

5 **Conclusions and reporting** – There is no required format as long as the terms of reporting and concluding are agreed in the engagement letter

3.1.1 Measuring social and environmental performance

While such engagements are a good source of revenue for many assurance firms, they do present **challenges**, as very often the **outputs** that need to be reported on are either **difficult to measure** (eg emissions of a pollutant) or **intangible** in nature (eg impact on the local community).

It is therefore accepted that measuring social and environmental performance is **difficult**, so when planning this kind of engagement, the practitioner will need to consider either **how** to **validate** the measurements made by the client, or **how** they can **measure** the information themselves. Understandably, this could affect acceptance (but conversely, this may make those firms that choose to specialise in providing this kind of engagement very sought after).

 Essential reading

See Chapter 15 of the Essential reading for more detail on measurement difficulties.

The Essential reading is available as an Appendix of the digital edition of the Workbook.

The following types of measures may be used:

*   **Direct** – For example, kilograms (kg) of contaminant emitted
*   **Relative** – For example, kg of contaminant emitted per kg of product manufactured
*   **Indexed** – Measured over a period of time to identify longer-term trends
*   **Aggregated** – Information of the same type, but from different sources expressed as a combined value (for example, volume of waste recycled or employees supported by training)
*   **Weighted** – Information modified by applying a factor relating to its significance

Examples of **specific indicators** included in environmental and social elements of integrated reports on which the auditor may be asked to provide assurance include:

*   Toxic gas emissions
*   Energy usage, recycling levels and progress against waste reduction targets (such as reducing packaging)
*   Average wage levels vs minimum wage
*   Employee satisfaction and/or staff turnover levels
*   Customer complaints
*   Financial assistance to charitable organisations
*   Investment in infrastructure, such as schools and roads

3.1.2 IAASB Discussion Paper on integrated reporting

In August 2016, the IAASB **released the** Discussion Paper, *Supporting Credibility and Trust in Emerging Forms of External Reporting: Ten Key Challenges for Assurance Engagements*.

The paper introduced a new piece of jargon for us to consider now within social and environmental reporting: EER, **E**merging forms of **E**xternal **R**eporting. The issue debated by the IAASB was credibility and trust, and how best to achieve this with EER (both in terms of its creation and the assurance that can be provided on it).

One of the key issues is that the external auditor's opinion does **not** include EER as it is part of the 'Other information' reviewed under ISA (UK) 720. While there is a strong overlap with existing assurance services (especially the audit, where credibility and trust are enhanced) **flexibility** is required to meet the ongoing needs of stakeholders as this EER is not legally required but clearly still has great significance.

In conclusion, some other form of engagement to provide assurance on this EER is required, but determining exactly how to arrive at the desired level of assurance is not straightforward – hence the core of the paper: the 'Ten Key Assurance Challenges':

Ten key assurance challenges
Determining the scope of an EER assurance engagement, which can be **complex**
Evaluating the **suitability of criteria** in a consistent manner
Addressing **materiality** for diverse information with little guidance in EER frameworks
Building assertions for subject matter information of a diverse nature
Lack of maturity in governance and internal control over EER reporting processes
Obtaining assurance with respect to **narrative information**
Obtaining assurance with respect to **future-oriented information**
Exercising **professional scepticism** and **professional judgement**
Obtaining the **competence** necessary to perform the engagement
Communicating effectively in the assurance report

(IAASB, 2016: pp 34–39)

Following a period of **consultation** with many different stakeholders, IAASB issued a **Feedback Statement** in January 2018 which delivered the following messages:

- There should be greater awareness of the **limitations of ISA 720** among stakeholders so they can decide on the best way of providing assurance on EER alongside the audit opinion
- While the use of a **specific standard** to provide assurance consistently on EER is favoured (probably ISAE 3000 as mentioned in Chapter 12) it should still reflect the fluid nature of such reporting and should therefore **not be too specific or rigid**
- Respondents felt that the **top three assurance challenges** from the original list of ten were suitable criteria, materiality and the form of reporting that should be used
- While this is still an evolving area of reporting, EER will **inevitably grow in significance** as more stakeholders get on board and this growth will drive the way that EER should be both created and reviewed (IAASB, 2018: pp 5–14)

3.1.3 Non-authoritative guidance on applying ISAE 3000 (Revised) to Extended External Reporting (EER) assurance engagements

In April 2021, the IAASB published this non-authoritative guidance to support practitioners that perform assurance engagements using ISAE 3000 (Revised) for entities that publish financial and non-financial information that fits the category of Extended External Reporting (EER – while the name is slightly different, this is effectively the same EER as mentioned above). In issuing this guidance, the IAASB aimed to support the credibility of any assurance provided on EER which would in turn lead to enhanced credibility and trust in the underlying EER information in the eyes of its intended users.

Examples of the EER information given in this guidance includes:

- An integrated report
- A US SEC form 10-K
- A UK strategic report
- Other specific quantitative or qualitative, financial or non-financial information on matters ranging from greenhouse gases, value for money or corporate social responsibility

The need for guidance stems from the varied and diverse nature of the EER – it could be voluntarily produced or part of a legal or regulatory framework. It could be based on criteria specified by external organisations or regimes or could use criteria developed by the reporting entity. The EER information may be published or presented as a video and subject to the internal controls in place at the reporting entity. As a result of the broad spectrum of work that such an engagement might entail, the guidance complements the existing advice in ISAE 3000 (Revised) to allow it to be applied successfully in the following areas:

(a) Applying appropriate competence and capabilities

(b) Exercising professional scepticism and professional judgement

(c) Determining preconditions and agreeing the scope of an EER engagement

(d) Considering the entity's process to identify reporting topics

(e) Determining the suitability and availability of criteria

(f) Consideration of process used to prepare the EER information

(g) Using assertions

(h) Obtaining evidence

(i) Considering the materiality of misstatements

(j) Addressing qualitative EER information

(k) Addressing future-oriented EER information

(l) Communicating effectively in the Assurance report

(IAASB, 2021: contents pages, paras. 1-20)

Note how familiar the process is by comparison to other engagements that you are familiar with. However, remember that while the concept of providing assurance to any kind of subject matter might be fairly universal, the specific nature of the process of designing suitable procedures to obtain sufficient and appropriate evidence for this EER is what makes this guidance necessary.

3.1.4 Auditing integrated reports

Auditors may be engaged to produce an independent verification statement on an integrated report. This is an assurance report and would therefore need to be performed in line with the guidance contained in ISAE (UK) 3000 *Assurance engagements other than audits or reviews of historical financial information* (covered in detail in Chapter 12 of this Workbook).

This could be either a direct or an attestation engagement, with the practitioner presenting the integrated report themselves (direct), or providing a report on information presented by the entity.

Practitioners in this area face many of the difficulties outlined above in relation to the audit of public sector performance information. The measurement of financial or even physical capital is relatively unproblematic because these areas may be readily subject to quantification. But intellectual, human and social capital are much more difficult to present objectively; their measurement involves a good deal of judgement. It is therefore difficult to see how an assurance engagement on an integrated report could offer much more than **limited assurance**, sticking as much as possible to the factual assertions made by the report and wording its conclusion negatively.

Essential reading

See Chapter 15 of the Essential reading for a reminder of how the various capitals are used within the International Integrated Reporting Framework.

The Essential reading is available as an Appendix of the digital edition of the Workbook.

Activity 2: Integrated reporting

1   What are the perceived benefits from an entity's point of view of paying for assurance on its integrated report?

2   What would you expect to be the key contents of the practitioner's conclusion on an integrated report?

Solution

4 The auditing aspects of insolvency

4.1 What is insolvency and how is it caused?

It is important to distinguish between a company being **insolvent** and a company experiencing **liquidity** problems.

> **Insolvency:** The inability of a company to pay its debts as they fall due.
>
> **Illiquidity:** The inability of a company to readily obtain cash from its assets in order to meet obligations.

Illiquidity is a shortage of cash (and assets that can readily be converted into cash), so that a company may not be able to pay its creditors (payables). **Liquidity generally refers to current assets and liabilities.**

Insolvency is not just a shortage of **cash**. It is more long term or fundamental than illiquidity. Insolvency could be thought of as a shortage of **assets** so that, even if all a company's assets were sold, it would still not be enough to pay its debts. **The main symptom of insolvency is a position of net liabilities in the statement of financial position.**

Example

	Illiquid Ltd		Insolvent Ltd
	£		£
Non-current assets	100,000	Non-current assets	50,000
Inventory	30,000	Inventory	5,000
Cash	5,000	Cash	500
Payables	(60,000)	Payables	(60,000)
Net assets	75,000	Net assets	(4,500)

Illiquid Ltd has positive net assets and is solvent. But it does not have enough cash and inventory to pay its payables and is therefore illiquid.

Insolvent Ltd is **both insolvent and illiquid**. It does not have **enough cash and inventory** to pay its payables. But more than this, even if it **sold its non-current assets,** it still would not be able to pay its payables. It is therefore **insolvent**.

A company can become insolvent for a number of reasons. Two of the most common are **overtrading** and a long-term **lack of profitability**.

A company that is **overtrading** in the effort to grow quickly may be able to overcome its liquidity problems in the short term by raising new finance. However, if it is unable to raise sufficient finance, it runs the risk of becoming insolvent.

If a company is not profitable in the long term, then it will eventually run down its statement of financial position so that it is unable to trade and pay its debts.

The **cause** of a company's insolvency may be an **indicator** of its future. If a company is fundamentally unable to make a profit, it is likely that the best thing is for it to be **wound up**. But if a company is able to make a profit in the long term, then it makes sense to try to **save it**. Examples of this might include companies insolvent because of overtrading, or companies which are not solvent as a whole but which have profitable elements within them.

4.2 What happens if a company becomes insolvent?

Reflecting these two basic possibilities, the two alternatives facing an insolvent company are **liquidation** and **administration**.

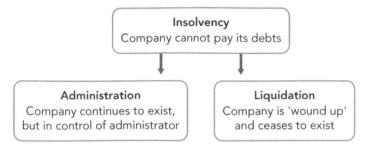

A company which is heading towards insolvency can often be saved. **Administration** offers a company a variety of legal protections from creditors until the problem is sorted out. The directors of a company can get into a lot of trouble if they carry on trading through a company in serious financial difficulties, and their actions result in creditors being defrauded. Specifically, there is a risk of being convicted of fraudulent trading (a criminal offence), or more likely **wrongful trading**.

Administration does not mean carrying on as if everything is normal. It can mean seeking help from the court or a qualified **insolvency practitioner** to put a plan together to save the company and get it out of its bad financial position.

Unfortunately, many companies cannot be saved, and the members and directors are forced to take the other alternative, to stop operating the business through the company. **Liquidation**, sometimes called 'winding up', is when a company is formally dissolved and ceases to exist.

Various methods of achieving liquidation are covered in this Workbook. Note, though, that a company does not have to be in financial difficulty to be liquidated.

4.3 The responsibilities of directors and auditors in cases of insolvency

When a company is insolvent, the directors must take steps to ensure that the creditors are protected and must consider the interests of shareholders and other stakeholders. This might mean applying for the company to be put into administration, appointing an insolvency practitioner **or asking auditors for advice**.

Directors do not normally have any personal liability for the debts of the company, but there are some exceptions: where **fraudulent or wrongful trading** has taken place.

Once an insolvency practitioner has been appointed, they will assess the reasons for the insolvency. It is at this point that any fraudulent or wrongful trading would come to light. If this has happened then liquidators can apply to the court for an order that those responsible (usually the directors) are liable to repay all, or some specified part, of the **company's debts**.

4.3.1 Fraudulent trading

This is a **criminal offence**, where the business of a company in liquidation has been carried on with **intent to defraud creditors** or for any fraudulent purpose. Offenders are liable to imprisonment or a fine (Companies Act 2006, s.993).

If the liquidator considers that there has been fraudulent trading, they should apply to the court for an order that those responsible are liable to make good to the company all or some specified part of the company's debts.

There is also a **civil offence** of the same name under s.213 of the Insolvency Act 1986 but it only applies to companies which are in liquidation. Under this offence, courts may declare that **any persons** who were knowingly parties to carrying on the business in this fashion shall be liable for the debts of the company.

Various rules have been established to determine **what is fraudulent trading**.

- Only persons who **take the decision** to carry on the company's business in this way, or play some active part, are liable.
- 'Carrying on business' can include a single transaction and also the mere payment of debts as distinct from making trading contracts.
- The offence relates not only to **defrauding creditors** but also to carrying on a business for the purpose of any kind of fraud: *R v Kemp 1988*.

Under the civil offence, if the liquidator considers that there has been fraudulent trading, they should apply to the court for an order that those responsible are liable to make good to the company all or some specified part of the **company's debts**.

4.3.2 Wrongful trading

The problem which faced the creditors of an insolvent company before the introduction of 'wrongful trading' was that it was exceptionally difficult to prove in court. A **civil liability** for 'wrongful trading' was therefore introduced. If a director is found guilty of wrongful trading, they can be ordered to 'make a contribution' to the company's assets.

The difference between wrongful and fraudulent trading is that for wrongful trading it is **not necessary to prove intent**. A director is guilty of wrongful trading if they **knew**, or should have known, that there was **no reasonable prospect** that the **company** could have **avoided** going into **insolvent liquidation**, but did not **then take sufficient steps** to **protect creditors**.

Directors will be liable if the liquidator proves the following.

- The director(s) of the insolvent company **knew**, or **should have known**, that there was **no reasonable prospect** that the **company** could **have avoided going into insolvent liquidation**. This means that directors cannot claim they lacked knowledge if their lack of knowledge was a result of failing to comply with Companies Act requirements, for example preparation of accounts: *Re Produce Marketing Consortium Ltd 1989*.
- The director(s) did not take **sufficient steps** to minimise the potential loss to the creditors.

Directors will be deemed to know that the company could not avoid insolvent liquidation if that would have been the conclusion of a **reasonably diligent person** with the **general knowledge, skill and experience** that might reasonably be expected of a person carrying out that particular director's duties. If the director has greater than usual skill, then they will be judged with reference to their own capacity.

4.3.3 Auditors and insolvency

The auditor has **no direct responsibility** if a company it audits becomes insolvent. However, auditors do need to understand what insolvency is, and what the effect might be if an audit client becomes insolvent. In particular, auditors may be called on by company directors to provide **advice** in the event of companies experiencing financial difficulties. Auditors must be in a position to determine the **level of financial difficulty** faced by a client, to explain and recommend the various options available to management, and explain the consequences of liquidation or administration.

When a company becomes insolvent, the auditor sometimes gets the blame for not having alerted shareholders and creditors to its difficulties sooner, and to any doubts that might have existed about it being a **going concern**. This criticism is often rooted in the familiar **expectations gap** between the public's high expectations of auditors, and what they are actually required to do by law (and by ISAs (UK)).

As we saw in Chapter 3, if an auditor is negligent then they may have a liability to the client's shareholders or to other third parties. If the auditor should have identified going concern problems at the time of the audit but did not do so, they might be accused of **professional negligence**. Just being negligent, though, is not of itself enough for there to be a lawsuit against the auditor. The claimant also needs to prove that a **duty of care** existed; that this duty of care was **breached**; and that this breach caused the injured party a **loss**.

The *Caparo* judgement, in particular, established that the auditor owes a duty of care to the company (the shareholders as a body) only. Investors or potential investors would have to prove that the auditor had taken on a contractual relationship with them, to the effect that the auditor was recommending the accounts to them for a specific purpose. This makes it quite difficult for negligence claims to be made against auditors.

Auditors are able to reduce the risk of being found guilty of negligence by way of a **liability limitation agreement**. The Companies Act 2006 allows this, subject to some restrictions.

- Agreement can only stand for one year – must be **replaced annually**
- Liability can only be limited to what is **fair and reasonable**
- Agreement must be **approved by the members** and publicly **disclosed** in the accounts or directors' report

Real life example

During 2018, there were allegations of fraud leading to going concern worries for UK-based coffee shop and cake maker Patisserie Valerie. Concerns were raised when funding shortfalls, including secret overdrafts of nearly £10 million, were discovered, leading to emergency funding from the company's biggest investor to stay in business. The company was put into administration and is now trading as a significantly smaller business. These accounting irregularities were investigated by the FRC, who also investigated the work of Patisserie Valerie's auditors, Grant Thornton. The FRC investigation was focused on the financial statements for the years 2015, 2016 and 2017. In 2021, the FRC fined Grant Thornton and the audit engagement partner for their failure to conduct the audit in accordance with auditing standards. At the time of writing, the FRC investigation into the company's accounting irregularities is still ongoing. Clearly, the role of the auditor in a company maintaining its going concern status is significant. (BBC, 2021)

4.3.4 Going concern – IAS 1

In the UK, IAS 1 requires financial statements to be prepared on a going concern basis, except where:

An entity is being liquidated and has ceased trading	The directors have no realistic alternative but to cease trading or liquidate the business

In these circumstances, the **directors have an option** to prepare financial statements on a **basis other than that of a going concern**. One reason for this is that financial statements prepared on a **break-up or liquidation basis** do **not provide** users with much **useful information**, such as on financial adaptability and cash generation ability. (IAS 1: para. 25)

The directors have an obligation to **assess** whether there are **significant doubts** about an entity's ability to continue as a **going concern** when preparing financial statements.

IAS 1 suggests that directors should review the following factors:

4.3.5 Going concern – ISA (UK) 570

Audit of going concern was covered in detail in Chapter 10 of this Workbook. Auditors' assessments of going concern have long been a contentious area, particularly if a client becomes insolvent shortly after having received an unmodified audit report. ISA (UK) 570 para. 9 sets out the auditor's key objectives in relation to going concern. These can be summarised as:

- To **obtain evidence** on management's assumption of going concern
- To **conclude** whether a **material uncertainty** exists that may cast **significant doubt** over going concern
- To determine the implications for the **auditor's report**

In the event of a client becoming insolvent, it will be important for the auditor to have kept appropriate working papers in line with ISA (UK) 230 *Audit Documentation*. This would be useful if the auditor were to find themselves in court later on!

The auditor needs to consider going concern while planning the audit, during the audit, and when concluding and forming the audit opinion. The implications of going concern problems for the audit opinion are summarised in the following table.

Is the entity a going concern?	Financial statements	Auditor's report
Significant doubt	• Prepared on going concern basis • Contain adequate disclosures	'Material uncertainty related to going concern' section (ISA (UK) 570: para. 22)
Significant doubt	• Prepared on going concern basis • Do not contain adequate disclosures	Qualified or adverse opinion (ISA (UK) 570: para. 23)
No – going concern assumption not appropriate	• Prepared on going concern basis	Adverse opinion (ISA (UK) 570: para. 21)

4.3.6 Impairment of assets

If a company is experiencing going concern issues, then some of its assets may be impaired. The auditor needs to test whether the **IAS 36 criteria** have been complied with. At the **planning** stage of the audit, the auditor should look for indicators of impairment. If there are any, then it should ask to see management's impairment review. (The auditor does not need to do an impairment review themselves – this is management's responsibility.) This impairment review then needs to be audited to verify that it is in line with IAS 36.

If **management** has **not** conducted an **impairment review,** then the **auditor's report** may need to be **qualified** (disagreement). Note that this does not necessarily mean that the assets are misstated – the fact that management has not conducted an impairment review at all is grounds for qualification in relation to IAS 36.

IAS 36 was covered in Chapter 8, but here is a quick recap.

- An asset is impaired when its **carrying amount** is greater than its **recoverable amount**.
- The recoverable amount is the higher of **value in use** and **fair value** less costs to sell.
- If value in use cannot be estimated for an individual asset, then it should be estimated for its suitability as a **cash-generating unit**.

4.3.7 Provisions

A company experiencing going concern problems is likely to want to make provisions. These should be audited for compliance with IAS 37, covered in Chapter 8. The following examples are relevant to a company in financial difficulty.

- **Onerous contracts** – provide for the present value of the obligation
- **Restructuring** – for a provision to be made there must be a **detailed formal plan** and a **valid expectation** in those affected
- **Cannot provide** for future operating losses

Provisions are a **risky** area to audit, but are even more so for a client with going concern problems. The number of provisions required is likely to increase with the chance of the company becoming insolvent.

4.3.8 Using an expert

It may be necessary to use an auditor's expert. ISA (UK) 620 *Using the Work of an Auditor's Expert* is relevant here, and was covered in Chapter 7. This might apply to the accounting issues identified above as follows.

> **Going concern.** The auditor could consider using an **insolvency expert** to assess whether the entity can trade as a going concern (although this is not often done in practice).

> **Provisions.** It might be necessary to use a **legal expert** to interpret legal documents, for instance in assessing the value of an **onerous contract**.

ISA (UK) 620 requires an auditor to assess:

- Whether it is necessary to use an auditor's expert
- Competence and objectivity of the auditor's expert
- The auditor's expert's scope of work
- The actual work of the auditor's expert

In the case of **impairment**, it is more likely that a **management's expert** will have been used by the entity, for example to value properties, or as part of a value in use calculation. ISA (UK) 500 *Audit Evidence* requires the auditor to:

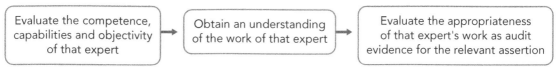

Evaluate the competence, capabilities and objectivity of that expert → Obtain an understanding of the work of that expert → Evaluate the appropriateness of that expert's work as audit evidence for the relevant assertion

 ## Essential reading

See Chapter 15 of the Essential reading for a reminder of content that you have previously studied on liquidation, administration and the allocation of company assets.

The Essential reading is available as an Appendix of the digital edition of the Workbook.

Chapter summary

Social and environmental auditing and the auditing aspects of insolvency

Practical context

- Increased importance – why?
  - Social and environmental issues now politically and economically important
  - Growth of ethical investors, consumers and employees
  - Increase in social and environmental legislation affecting businesses
  - Increased amounts of sustainability information being used to highlight growing climate crisis

Impact on practitioners

- Affects auditors through:
  - Application of environmental laws and regulations
  - Potential pollution by client
  - Contamination of land and buildings on statement of financial position
  - Dependence on major market affected by environmental issues
  - Greater use of voluntary reporting to satisfy stakeholders

Financial statement audit impacts

- No specific knowledge of environmental matters required
- Should obtain sufficient knowledge of the business to understand impact on audit

Substantive procedures

- **General:** Board minutes, reports, media etc
- **Assets:** Impairments and changes in asset usage policy.
- **Liabilities, provisions and contingencies:** Restructuring, fines and penalties, estimates
- **Disclosure:** Sufficient for stakeholders?

 BPP

Assurance on integrated reports

- **Additional assurance engagements** – no formal structure for reports
- **Integrated reports** use the six capitals: Financial; Manufactured; Human; Intellectual; Natural; Social

Measuring social and environmental performance

- Types of measurement:
  - Direct (eg kg emitted)
  - Relative (eg kg per capita)
  - Indexed (eg over a period)
  - Aggregated
  - Weighted
- Items for measurement include gas/liquid emissions, waste amounts, staff turnover, customer complaints and even donations to charity

The auditing aspects of insolvency

What is insolvency and how is it caused?

- Illiquidity is a shortage of cash to pay debts
- Insolvency is a shortage of assets to cover liabilities
- Insolvency is usually caused by either overtrading or having an unprofitable business

What happens if a company becomes insolvent?

- A company can be placed into administration and run until its future can be determined – this could be either saving it or liquidating it
- A company without a future may require liquidation anyway – this can happen either voluntarily (brought about by members or creditors) or as a compulsory liquidation (usually as a result of either being unable to pay its debts or being judged as just and equitable)
- The official receiver is appointed by the court to wind up a company going into liquidation – one of the activities carried out will be allocating company assets in line with any charges or other liabilities owed

The responsibilities of auditors and directors in cases of insolvency

- Directors can be found guilty of either wrongful trading (where they should have known insolvency was a risk but continued anyway) or fraudulent trading (which can be either a criminal or a civil offence)
- Auditors have no legal responsibility but should be aware of case law and the impact on the audit of going concern, impairments, provisions and the need for additional expertise where appropriate

Knowledge diagnostic

1. Social and environmental issues

Social and environmental issues are now of **critical importance** to the vast majority of businesses, customers and employees and therefore cannot be ignored.

2. Impact on the audit

The auditor must have an understanding of the **impact** of these issues on their work, as social and environmental issues can generate significant **risks** for audits. (Although auditors do not have to be experts, they should respond to any significant risks with **appropriate substantive procedures**.)

3. Integrated reports

Stakeholders are demanding **accountability** from businesses and increasingly, they are responding by producing **social** and **environmental information** as part of an **integrated report**. In many cases, the auditor will provide **assurance** on this information although the precise nature of this information can vary enormously.

4. Insolvency

A company is **insolvent** when it **cannot pay its debts as they fall due**. In reality, auditors are frequently blamed for shareholder losses in insolvencies. They may be **liable** if they have been professionally **negligent**. An auditor must therefore consider the effects of insolvency on a company's financial statements.

5. Liquidation

Liquidation is the **dissolution** or **'winding up'** of a company. There are three methods of **liquidation: compulsory, members' voluntary** and **creditors' voluntary**. Compulsory liquidation and creditors' voluntary liquidation are proceedings for insolvent companies, and members' voluntary is for solvent companies.

6. Carrying out the liquidation

A **liquidator** must be an authorised, qualified insolvency practitioner. Once **insolvency procedures** have commenced, share trading must cease, the company documents must state that the company is in liquidation and the directors' power to manage ceases.

7. Winding up

A winding up is **voluntary** where the decision to wind up is taken by the company's members, although, if the company is insolvent, the creditors will be heavily involved in the proceedings. In order to be a members' winding up, the directors must make a **declaration of solvency**. It is a criminal offence to make a declaration of solvency without reasonable grounds. When there is no declaration of solvency there is a **creditors' voluntary winding up**.

8. Compulsory liquidation

There are **seven statutory reasons** for the compulsory liquidation of a company, which can all be found in the Insolvency Act 1986. A **dissatisfied member** may get the court to wind the company up on the **just and equitable ground**. The differences between compulsory and voluntary liquidation are associated with **timing**, the **role** of the **official receiver, stay of legal proceedings** and the **dismissal of employees**.

9. Administration

An **administrator** is appointed primarily to try to rescue the company as a going concern. A company may go into administration to carry out an established plan to save the company. Some parties – **secured creditors** and **directors** and the **members** by resolution – can appoint an administrator without a court order. Various parties can apply for **administration** through the court.

10. Effects of administration

The **effects** of administration depend on whether it is effected by the **court** or by a **floating chargeholder**, to some degree. The administrator has **fiduciary duties** to the company as its agent, plus some legal duties. The administrator must either **propose a rescue plan**, or state that the **company cannot be rescued**. The administrator takes on the **powers** of the directors. Administration can last up to **12 months**.

11. Allocating company assets

Administration has been found to have many advantages for the **company**, the **members** and the **creditors**. Liquidators' costs are usually paid first, followed by fixed chargeholders, preferential creditors, floating chargeholders and lastly unsecured creditors.

Further study guidance

Question practice

Now try the following from the Further question practice bank (available in the digital edition of the Workbook):

- Question 29 'Rank' is further practice of acceptance and procedures for a non-audit engagement – in this case, a social and environmental report for an ethical company.
- Question 30 'Mantis' tests how well you can explain the issues surrounding administration and the different forms of liquidation in use in the UK.

Further reading

There are technical articles on the ACCA website written by members of the AAA examining team which are relevant to some of the topics covered in this chapter that you should read:

- *The assurance of social, environmental and sustainability information (part 1)*
- *The assurance of social, environmental and sustainability information (part 2)*
- *Audit and insolvency*

Own research

- Try and find some real-life examples of social and environmental reports – have they been reviewed and if so, what did the review report contain?
- For an example of what an integrated report could look like, why not have a look at what ACCA has done?

  https://annualreport.accaglobal.com/mediaLibrary/other/english/ACCA-Integrated-Report-2020.pdf

- Sustainability reporting is fast becoming one of the most important issues for any organisation - in relation to AAA, you should consider the challenges faced by both preparers of financial statements, including how they reflect best practice on environmental, social and governance (ESG) matters within their annual report, and auditors of financial statements who now need to adapt in order to be able to continue to provide the necessary levels of assurance that stakeholders demand.

  As part of your own ongoing research, try and stay up to date with two key areas:

  - the **Taskforce on Climate-related Financial Disclosures** (**TCFD**) which provides a framework for how organisations should disclose climate change matters within their annual report under the headings governance, strategy, risk management and metrics and targets (this disclosure framework is already a requirement for listed entities in the UK and is expected to widen its scope in the coming months)

  - The broader landscape containing the various **ESG and sustainability reporting frameworks** is constantly evolving – for example, back in 2021, the International Integrated Reporting Council (IIRC) and the Sustainability Accounting Standards Board (SASB) merged to form an organisation called the Value Reporting Foundation (VRF), although the methodology for integrated reporting has not changed. During 2022, the VRF and another organisation (the Climate Disclosure Standards Board or CDSB) were absorbed into the IFRS Foundation and became the International Sustainability Standards Board (ISSB) to oversee the use of sustainability-related disclosure standards within financial reporting

  At the time of publication, two new climate-related reporting standards were the subject of consultation via exposure drafts: IFRS S1 General Requirements for Disclosure of Sustainability-related Financial Information and IFRS S2 Climate-related Disclosures. You can monitor the progress of how these standards will help our understanding of sustainability and climate-related risks and opportunities by visiting the ISSB website:

  https://www.ifrs.org/groups/international-sustainability-standards-board/

Activity answers

Activity 1: Social and environmental factors

> **Approach**
>
> You will definitely have covered content related to social and environmental issues in your studies so far (both ACCA and others) so this activity should be a way of summarising what you know. Remember to consider your answer by thinking: 'Social and environmental issues have become more important to business in recent years because...' and proceed from there.

Suggested solution

Social issues – family-friendly issues such as **parental leave** and **flexible working conditions** for parents, guardians and carers – have become more important now due to changes in society.

There has been a growth in the importance of **the environment** as a political and economic issue – climate change (which has major social aspects to it), plus the importance of sustainability and the impact of the environment on business (fuel costs and climate change issues etc).

This has led to the growth of so-called **ethical consumers, investors and employees**. These key groups are now very selective about who they will purchase goods from, which companies they invest in and who they will work for. Food miles are more important now than ever before, as is the role of plastic carrier bags (now to be charged for in many jurisdictions to reduce their adverse environmental impact).

As a result of this, **businesses** are keen to be seen to be engaging with **key stakeholder groups** and demonstrating a commitment to ethical, social and environmental behaviour. This, in turn, helps to attract and retain customers and employees.

From an alternative perspective there has been, in many countries, a growth in the volume of domestic and supra-national **legislation** regulating the behaviour of businesses in these areas. This leads to penalties and fines in certain jurisdictions for breaches of social issues (working time directive, discrimination policies etc) and environmental legislation (Environment Agency in the UK).

Social and environmental issues have **evolved** over time and made us look at things in a different way. Consider the coal industry: a coal mining company's financial statements will include the costs of employee wages, plant and machinery used, licences and future dismantling costs. The coal industry is usually seen as bringing economic benefits to society, through providing energy to consumers and employment for workers.

But the costs of the coal industry to the social and natural environment may be much more widespread than this. The environmental impact of the coal industry as a whole includes the following factors, which are not part of financial statements:

- **Land use**. Mining radically changes the landscape, eg by eliminating vegetation, changing soil profiles and stopping current land uses.
- **Waste management**. Burning coal (eg to make electricity) creates ash, much of which must be stored in the ground, which both uses up land and creates a potential hazard to communities.

- **Wildlife.** Mining damages wildlife principally by changing or destroying habitats, which can result in the depletion or total extinction of species from affected areas.
- **Air pollution.** Coal is the largest contributor to the man-made increase of carbon dioxide (CO_2) in the atmosphere, which is associated with climate change.

Activity 2: Integrated reporting

Approach

As integrated reporting is such an evolving issue, you should be prepared for it to form part of a discussion-style question (such as that seen on the specimen exam for AAA). Consequently, this is excellent practice for you to consider the benefits of having an assurance report reviewed (remember to do this from the perspective of the entity creating the integrated report).

When answering the second part of this question, think about the contents of an auditor's report and any other reports that you have seen so far in AAA and then consider what might be most appropriate to use in the context of an integrated report.

1 **Suggested solution**

Perceived benefits of assurance work on integrated reports include:

- The assurance report adds credibility to the data reported.
- It reassures investors by promoting transparency (and may improve stock market price).
- There is added prestige of having the information audited.
- It gives a competitive advantage over those whose reports are not audited.
- It identifies areas of weakness which can be addressed.
- It may be a requirement for trading with some companies/countries or governments.
- Social and environmental performance is taken more seriously, which in turn will improve performance and (hopefully) reduce costs.

2 **Suggested solution**

Contents of the practitioner's reported conclusions

- Note of the objectives of the review
- Opinion (if the engagement was agreed-upon procedures rather than assurance, there will be no opinion given)
- Basis on which the opinion (if any) has been reached
- Work performed
- Limitations (if any) to the work performed
- Limitations (if any) to the opinion given

Note. There is **no specific guidance** on the contents of a practitioner's conclusion on an integrated report on social and environmental issues; the above points represent the **minimum** you should expect to see included. The International Integrated Reporting Framework (denoted by the term <IR>) supported by ACCA is a voluntary scheme that suggests the areas where companies might wish to report on their social and environmental credentials in a combined format with other financial and non-financial performance. It is likely that you will have already met integrated reporting (for example, as part of your studies for Strategic Business Leader).

16 Current issues

Learning objectives

On completion of this chapter, you should be able to:

	Syllabus reference no.
Discuss current developments in auditing standards including the need for new and revised standards and evaluate their impact on the conduct of audits.	G2(a)
Discuss current developments in business practices, practice management and audit methodology and evaluate the potential impact on the conduct of an audit and audit quality.	G2(b)
Discuss the proposed changes to the audit profession and critically evaluate the implications of these changes for companies and audit firms and their impact on audit process and quality.	G2(c)
Discuss current developments in emerging technologies, including big data and the use of automated tools and techniques such as data analytics, and sustainability reporting and the potential impact on the conduct of an audit and audit quality.	G2(d)
Discuss the impact of significant global events on audit practice.	G2(e)

Business and exam context

At this level in your studies you are expected to be familiar with current developments affecting the audit and assurance profession. Currently, many of these relate to international regulation.

You must read *Student Accountant* and the wider professional press to keep up to date with these.

You may be asked to discuss current developments and must be prepared to argue for or against any new proposals from the point of view of either a preparer or user of assurance reports.

Chapter overview

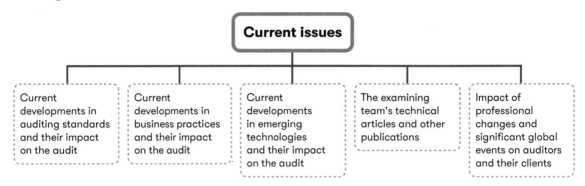

Current issues

- Current developments in auditing standards and their impact on the audit
- Current developments in business practices and their impact on the audit
- Current developments in emerging technologies and their impact on the audit
- The examining team's technical articles and other publications
- Impact of professional changes and significant global events on auditors and their clients

 BPP

1 Current issues

Syllabus section G on current issues may be examined in Section A or B as appropriate. The topic of current issues is unlikely to form the basis of any question **on its own** but instead, will be **incorporated** into the Case Study or either of the Section B questions, dependent on question content and the topical issues affecting the profession at the time of writing.

For example, Question 3 part (a) of the previous specimen exam contained this requirement following a comment made by the IESBA on the subject of auditors performing non-audit work:

'Discuss the changes made to the Code in relation to non-assurance services and evaluate the arguments for and against auditors providing non-assurance services to audit clients. (8 marks)'

Clearly, producing a sound answer to this would require the following:

Awareness of the current changes made to the IESBA Code – you can get this from reading Chapter 16 of the Essential reading (found in the digital edition of this Workbook) and from keeping an eye on the ACCA's website for any recent technical articles written by the examining team for AAA.

Good technique for writing solutions using all the elements of the requirement:
- A discussion of the changes
- Arguments in favour
- Arguments against
- An overall conclusion

Use the 'Further Question Practice' at the back of the Workbook to work on your technique (available in the digital edition of this Workbook).

Overview of current issues covered in Essential reading

By now, you will probably have realised that when something is classified as Essential reading, it is because you really need to know about it! Within the Essential reading section for this chapter on current issues, we have compiled a series of updates that reflect the priorities of the profession. The following table summarises the content that you need to be able to understand and discuss if required in the exam.

Categories of current issue	Content covered
Technology	The impact of digital solutions has been felt all across the world and the auditing profession is no different. You need to know what advances there are in terms of technology (such as audit data analytics) and how this kind of technology is revolutionising the way that audits are being conducted. You also need to know how various regulatory bodies are responding to the challenges and opportunities from this technological change.
IAASB	As the global standard-setting body for the auditing profession, the IAASB is always on the lookout for areas of practice that require some form of adaptation or evolution as a response to real-world events. Within this section you will find details of any exposure drafts as well as ongoing developments in key areas such as professional scepticism and audit quality.
IESBA	As the profession evolves over time, so does the system designed to monitor its ethical credentials. This is especially important in the context of how stakeholders perceive both

Categories of current issue	Content covered
	audits and auditors in areas such as fees, non-audit engagements and independence.
FRC	As the UK regulator of reporting, auditing and corporate governance (for the time being at least) the FRC is responsible for setting the tone for UK stakeholders. Current issues that you need to be aware of include audit quality and the impact of climate change.
UK and beyond	Finally, this is where you will find some of the most dynamic issues facing the profession in the UK and beyond: what are the stories that are influencing the profession, how and why might audits change in the future as a result and who will be setting the tone for such change?

Essential reading

See Chapter 16 of the Essential reading for further details of all the relevant current issues that ACCA and BPP think you need to be aware of to be prepared for the AAA exam.

The Essential reading is available as an Appendix of the digital edition of the Workbook.

Chapter summary

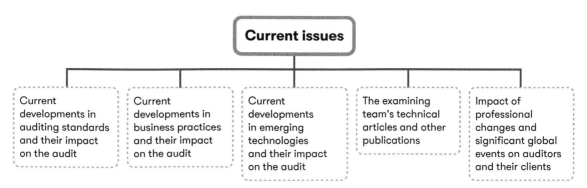

Knowledge diagnostic

1. Essential reading

It is essential that you access the material from the Essential reading section, available in an Appendix of the digital edition of the Workbook, for all the information relevant to this part of the syllabus.

2. ACCA technical articles

You must keep accessing the ACCA website for any last-minute technical articles published that might be examined.

Further study guidance

Question practice

Now try the following from the Further question practice bank (available in the digital edition of the Workbook):

- Question 31 'Merger of audit firms' – there is no way of knowing what (if any) current issues the exam will contain, but you should get used to being able to discuss things in this manner.

Further reading

There is one technical article on the ACCA website written by members of the AAA examining team which is relevant to some of the topics covered in this chapter that you should read:

- *Auditing disclosures in financial statements*

Own research

- You **must** keep reading the business press and a quality news source for regular updates on what is relevant to the auditing and accountancy profession.
- You also **must** keep up to date with any last-minute technical articles published by the ACCA AAA examining team in case they are tested in your exam.

Skills checkpoint 5

Exam Readiness

Overview

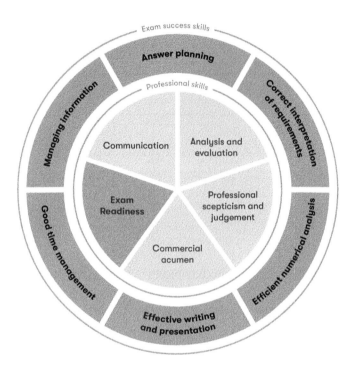

Skills checkpoint 5 – Exam readiness

Having covered the technical aspects of the syllabus and the four professional skills, you now need to make sure that you know how to use the **computer-based exam (CBE) software** so you are fully prepared for the AAA exam.

The syllabus for AAA contains four learning outcomes related to **employability and technology skills** which we will now explore in the context of the CBE with reference to the relevant **professional skills** and **exam success skills** which were covered in the introductory section of the Workbook.

You should start to familiarise yourself with the CBE software as soon as possible – in order to do this you should access the ACCA's Practice Platform via the **AAA study support resources** on the ACCA website where you will find a number of previous exam questions that can be attempted as a CBE.

Use computer technology to efficiently access and manipulate relevant information

This supports the following exam success skills: **1. Managing information** and **3. Answer planning**.

Introduction and instructions

Instructions (1 of 4)
The instructions displayed below are representative of those displayed in the live exam. Where t
General Instructions
- In the specimen exam, the instruction screens are not timed however in the live exam they
- In the live exam, the stated exam time will automatically start once the 10 minute period ha
- A copy of the instruction screens can be accessed at any time during the exam by selectinç

Introduction
The specimen exam indicates how the live exam will be st
You should use the specimen exam to become familiar wi

The Workspace
- Your exam consists of a number of questions. Each question is presented in a workspace.

The first thing you will see when you load up a CBE is an introduction followed by a series of instructions on how to use the CBE software. The instructions in the ACCA Practice Platform also explain where it differs from the CBE software used in the live AAA exam: at the time of writing, this included some **minor differences** in the look and functionality of PDFs used in certain Exhibits and the process for copying and pasting into spreadsheet responses. You are **strongly advised** to access these resources as soon as possible so you are familiar with the look and feel of the CBE.

Workspace

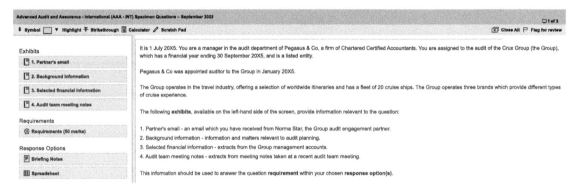

Once you have started the CBE and are in Question 1, you should note the various elements of the workspace:

- Introductory information – this helps you to understand your role and the information that you will need to access in order to answer the question, such as today's date and background about the client
- Exhibits – these contain more detailed information about the client necessary to answer the question. In Question 1, there will also be an Exhibit that contains the embedded email from the audit engagement partner that explains the specific tasks you are required to perform
- Requirement(s) – these will vary depending on the question but will specify what you are required to do and may direct you to specific exhibits
- Response option(s) – there will be a word processor option (in the example of the workspace shown above, it is labelled 'Briefing notes') where you will type your answer. Some questions may also offer you the option to use a spreadsheet as well. We will look at how these response options work in more detail later in this skills checkpoint)

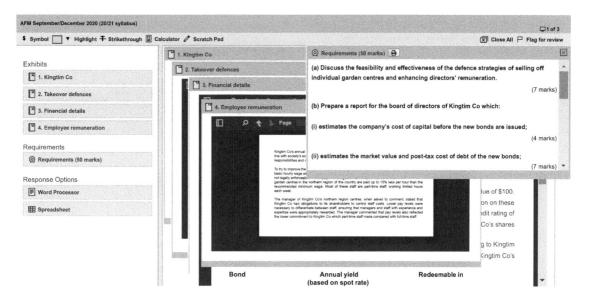

You will probably have observed that with up to four Exhibits, at least one requirement and at least one response option, the screen will start to get very cluttered. In order to help you manage all this information you can re-arrange how each of these windows looks on screen. They are both mobile and can be re-sized: you just need to get used to how they move and how you can arrange them.

It is also important that you scroll all the way down and across each Exhibit to ensure you have seen all of the contents of the Exhibit. It's likely to be a case of trial and error using the ACCA Practice Platform in order to become more familiar with how to plan and produce your answer.

Note. When arranging your workspace, there is a 'close all' option which closes all open windows, but if you use this you will lose anything you have entered into the calculator.

Work on relevant response options, using available functions and technology, as required by the workspace

This supports the following exam success skills: **4. Efficient numerical analysis** and **3. Answer planning.**

Response options

All questions will have a **word processor** response option and some (usually Question 1) may also offer you the opportunity of using a **spreadsheet** option as well. Some requirements might specify that a response option is used to answer that part of the question, but otherwise you should use the one that works best for you (in the AAA exam, this will probably be the word processor option).

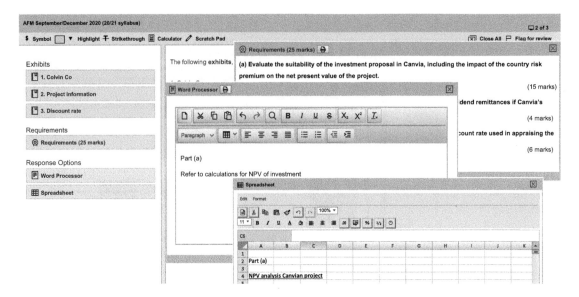

Within the workspace and response options, you will find a number of functions that will help you plan your answer, such as highlighting and formatting text, undo and redo and copy and paste.

As you will have noticed in the instructions at the start of the CBE, there are many functions and formulae that can be used in the spreadsheet, so you are advised to start using it as soon as possible in order to see what it can (and can't) do. This will help with the professional skill of analysis and evaluation.

For AAA, it's likely that the spreadsheet option will only be used in Question 1 when you are most likely to need to perform analytical procedures on financial statement data presented in an Exhibit. You can then copy and paste from the Exhibit into the spreadsheet and perform your analysis there.

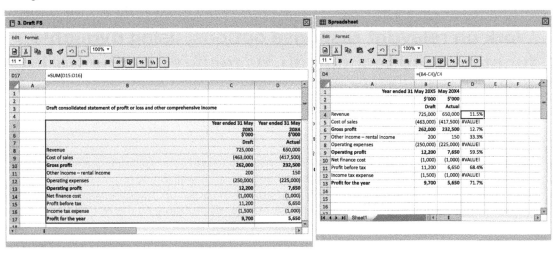

Be careful if the source data contains brackets as they may not work with your formulae. In the example above the left-hand window is the Exhibit with the financial statement data and the right-hand window is a spreadsheet response option where the financial statement data has been copied and pasted. Adding a formula in column D to calculate the percentage change between the two years works, but not for items copied over with brackets, so you may need to "cleanse" the data in order to analyse it.

Other workspace functions

If you want to make rough notes while you are planning your answer, you may be able to use pen and paper, depending on where you are sitting your CBE. Alternatively, you can use the **scratchpad** function embedded within the workspace. However, you should remember that the contents of the scratchpad **will not be marked**, so unless you copy anything important from the scratchpad and paste it into a response option, it will not be included in your final answer.

Consequently, we recommend that you plan your answer in the word processor response option and develop it as you go along.

The workspace also contains a **calculator** function (you can use your own but it must not have the ability to enter and store data).

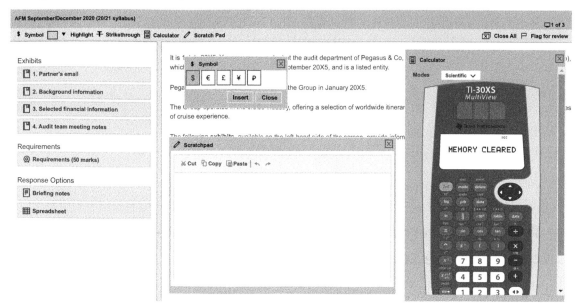

Navigate windows and computer screens to create and amend responses to exam requirements, using the appropriate tools

This supports the following exam success skills: **1. Managing information**, **2. Correct interpretation of requirements** and **3. Answer planning**.

Requirements and response options

By now, you should be starting to feel more comfortable toggling between the various elements of the CBE – the exhibits, the requirement(s) and your response option(s). Remember that although the scratchpad function is available, you should start to make rough notes in the response option when planning your answer and then replace them as you address the requirement in more detail and start developing your final answer. We also recommend that you copy the requirement(s) into the word processor response option to help with the structure of your answer (plus it means that you can then close the requirement window which helps to remove unnecessary onscreen clutter).

Navigation tools

What about switching between questions? This can be done by accessing the **navigator** function on the bottom right-hand corner of the workspace:

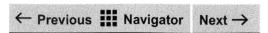

If you feel you need to move on but haven't finished what you wanted to say (perhaps you're stuck or you are concerned about time) the navigator gives you the option to flag it for review at a later stage to make sure that you haven't forgotten about it. There is also a help function which provides an overview of the instructions for both the workspace and the exam itself.

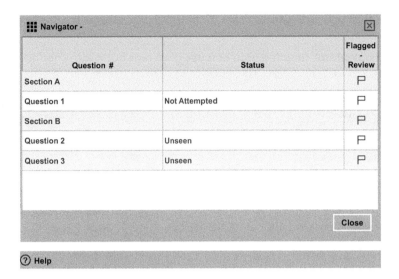

Present data and information effectively, using the appropriate tools

This supports the following exam success skills: **5. Effective writing and presentation** and **6. Good time management**.

Make use of questions available in the ACCA Practice Platform – they will help to familiarise you with the various elements of the CBE and how you can make use of them when answering questions. The formatting functionality in the word processor response option will help you to produce a more professional-looking answer, especially in Question 1 where the professional skill of communication is examined.

There is no timer on the ACCA Practice Platform so you should keep track of each part of each question, how long it should be taking you and when you need to move on to the next part.

Although there are syllabus outcomes on employability and technology skills, demonstration of these skills won't specifically attract marks in the same way that you are rewarded for technical and professional skills. However, just like in the workplace, familiarity with the technology that you are given in the CBE will help you score the marks you need to successfully answer all of the questions in the CBE.

Index

The entity and its environment, 111

The system of internal control, 111

Third parties, 46

Those charged with governance, 231

Tipping off, 5

Tolerable misstatement, 135

Tolerable rate of deviation, 135

Transnational audits, 195

True and fair view, 233

Type 1 report, 141

Type 2 report, 141

U

UN SDGs, 301

UN sustainable development goals, 301

United Nations (UN) Brundtland Commission, 300

User auditor, 141

User entity, 141

V

Value Reporting Foundation, 320

VRF, 320

W

Witness of fact, 288

Wrongful trading, 311, 312

BPP

Bibliography

ACCA (2008) *Technical Factsheet 84* [Online]. Available at:
www.accaglobal.com/content/dam/ACCA_Global/Technical/fact/technical-factsheet-84.pdf
[Accessed 11/2022]

ACCA (2012) *Obtaining professional work* [Online]. Available at:
www.accaglobal.com/content/dam/acca/global/PDF-
members/2012/2012p/professional_work.pdf [Accessed 11/2022]

ACCA (2019) *Student accountant* [Online]. Available at:
www.accaglobal.com/ie/en/student/sa.html [Accessed 11/2022]

ACCA (2022) *Code of Ethics and Conduct* [Online]. Available at:
https://www.accaglobal.com/gb/en/about-us/regulation/rulebook/code-of-ethics-and-
conduct.html [Accessed 11/2022]

Adidas (2021) *Annual Report 2020* [Online]. Available at: https://www.adidas-
group.com/media/filer_public/af/5a/af5a09d6-aacc-49d7-bddb-f3677a71248f/adidas_ar20_en.p
df [Accessed 11/2022]

BBC [2018] *UK accountancy firms face major overhaul under new plans* [Online]. Available from:
www.bbc.co.uk/news/business-46591575 [Accessed 11/2022]

BBC Future Planet (2020) *Why and how does Future Planet count carbon?* [Online]. Available at:
https://www.bbc.com/future/article/20200131-why-and-how-does-future-planet-count-
carbon?ocid=ww.social.link.email [Accessed 11/2022]

BBC (2021) *Grant Thornton fined £2.3m for Patisserie Valerie scandal* [Online]. Available at:
https://www.bbc.co.uk/news/business-58671915 [Accessed 11/2022]

BEIS (2021) *Restoring trust in audit and corporate governance: proposals on reforms*
(Consultation) [Online]. Available at: https://www.gov.uk/government/consultations/restoring-
trust-in-audit-and-corporate-governance-proposals-on-reforms [Accessed 11/2022]

BEIS, DLUHC & Lord Callanan (2022) *Audit regime overhaul to help restore trust in big business*
[Online]. Available at: https://www.gov.uk/government/news/audit-regime-overhaul-to-help-
restore-trust-in-big-business [Accessed 11/2022]

CIPFA (2021) *Evolving climate accountability: A global review of public sector environmental
reporting* [Online]. Available at: https://www.cipfa.org/home/protecting-place-and-
planet/sustainability-reporting [Accessed 11/2022]

Competition and Markets Authority (CMA) (2018) *CMA launches immediate review of audit sector*
[Online]. Available at: www.gov.uk/government/news/cma-launches-immediate-review-of-audit-
sector [Accessed 11/2022]

Competition and Markets Authority (CMA) (2018a) *CMA proposes reforms to improve competition
in audit sector* [Online]. Available at: https://www.gov.uk/government/news/cma-proposes-
reforms-to-improve-competition-in-audit-sector [Accessed 11/2022]

CPA Canada (2006) *Standard practices for investigative and forensic accounting engagements*
[Online]. Available at: https://www.muskratfallsinquiry.ca/files/P-00244.pdf[Accessed 11/2022]

FATF (2013) *Politically exposed persons (recommendations 12 and 22)* [Online]. Available at:
www.fatf-gafi.org/media/fatf/documents/recommendations/Guidance-PEP-Rec12-22.pdf
[Accessed 11/2022]

Forensic Science Regulator (2019) *Expert Report Guidance: FSR-G-200, Issue 3* [Online]. Available
at:
assets.publishing.service.gov.uk/government/uploads/system/uploads/attachment_data/file/7963
87/Statement_and_Report_Guidance_Appendix_Issue_3.pdf [Accessed 11/2022]

FRC (2009b) *Developments in Corporate Governance Affecting the Responsibilities of Auditors of
UK Companies* [Online]. Available at: www.frc.org.uk/getattachment/32fdf84b-1cd5-4cea-b416-
24cd24afae4a/Bulletin-2009-4-Developments-in-Corporate-Governance-Dec-2009.pdf
[Accessed 11/2022]

FRC (2014) *Guidance on risk management, internal control and related financial and business reporting* [Online]. Available at: www.frc.org.uk/getattachment/d672c107-b1fb-4051-84b0-f5b83a1b93f6/Guidance-on-Risk-Management-Internal-Control-and-Related-Reporting.pdf [Accessed 11/2022]

FRC (2015b) *Audit Quality Inspections, Annual Report 2014–15* [Online]. Available at: www.frc.org.uk/getattachment/d83b5d16-de6f-4fb0-b230-f5de62989daf/AQR-2014-15-Annual-Report-final.pdf [Accessed 11/2022]

FRC (2015c) *Extended Auditor's Reports: a review of experience in the first year* [Online]. Available at: www.frc.org.uk/getattachment/561627cc-facb-431b-beda-ead81948604e/Extended-Auditor-Reports-March-2015.pdf [Accessed 11/2022]

FRC (2016b) *Developments in audit 2015/16: An Overview (July 2016)* [Online]. Available at: www.frc.org.uk/Our-Work/Publications/FRC-Board/Developments-in-Audit-2015-16-Overview.pdf [Accessed 11/2022]

FRC (2016c) *Conduct Committee* [Online]. Available at: www.frc.org.uk/About-the-FRC/FRC-structure/Conduct-Committee.aspx [Accessed 11/2022]

FRC (2016d) *FRC Structure* [Online]. Available at: www.frc.org.uk/about-the-frc/structure-of-the-frc [Accessed 11/2022]

FRC (2016fe) *Guidance on Audit Committees* [Online]. Available at: www.frc.org.uk/getattachment/6b0ace1d-1d70-4678-9c41-0b44a62f0a0d/Guidance-on-Audit-Committees-April-2016.pdf [Accessed 11/2022]

FRC (2016j) *Extended Auditor's Reports: a further review of experience* [Online]. Available at: www.frc.org.uk/getattachment/76641d68-c739-45ac-a251-cabbfd2397e0/Report-on-the-Second-Year-Experience-of-Extended-Auditors-Reports-Jan-2016.pdf [Accessed 11/2022]

FRC (2017a) *Audit Thematic Review – Firms' Audit Quality Control Procedures and Other Audit Quality Initiatives* [Online]. Available at: www.frc.org.uk/getattachment/f42bfdea-4582-4c49-b8dc-fbf85faf78b8/Audit-Quality-Thematic-Review-control-procedures-March-2017.pdf [Accessed 11/2022]

FRC (2017d) *Audit Quality Thematic Review: Materiality* [Online]. Available at: www.frc.org.uk/getattachment/4713123b-919c-4ed6-a7a4-869aa9a668f4/Audit-Quality-Thematic-Review-Materiality-(December-2017).pdf [Accessed 11/2022]

FRC (2018) *Developments in Audit 2018* [Online]. Available at: www.frc.org.uk/getattachment/5e1ac2d1-f58c-48bc-bb91-1f4a189df18b/Developments-in-Audit-2018.pdf [Accessed 11/2022]

FRC [2018c] *Audit Quality Thematic Review – Other Information in the Annual Report* [Online]. Available at: www.frc.org.uk/getattachment/7afae1fe-75c8-43fc-9f60-3f2a78b438a9/AQR-Thematic-Review-Other-Information-in-the-Annual-Report-Dec-2018.pdf [Accessed 11/2022]

FRC (2019) *Audit Quality – Practice Aid for Audit Committees* [Online]. Available at: https://www.frc.org.uk/getattachment/68637e7a-8e28-484a-aec2-720544a172ba/Audit-Quality-Practice-Aid-for-Audit-Committees-2019.pdf [Accessed 09/2022]

FRC (2019b) *Feedback Statement and Impact Assessment: Post Implementation Review of the 2016 Auditing and Ethical Standards* [Online]. Available at: www.frc.org.uk/getattachment/676ac0a0-554c-4c89-ac48-33b6c020ed70/;.aspx [Accessed 11/2022]

FRC [2019c] *Glossary of terms – ethics and auditing* [Online]. Available at: www.frc.org.uk/getattachment/d4968a74-15d1-47ce-8fc4-220ae3536b06/Glossary-of-Terms-(Auditing-and-Ethics)-(Updated-Jan-2020).pdf [Accessed 11/2022]

FRC [2020] *ISAE (UK) 3000 (July 2020) Assurance Engagements Other Than Audits or Reviews of Historical Financial Information* [Online]. Available at: www.frc.org.uk/getattachment/2dc92f3e-df64-47d8-a9de-0292795fc8c3/ISAE-(UK)-3000-Jul-2020.pdf [Accessed 11/2022]

FRC [2020] *Audit Quality Thematic Review – Audit Quality Indicators (May 2020)* [Online]. Available at: www.frc.org.uk/getattachment/f116f7d7-94d8-4c82-94b2-ba24e3b195eb/AQTR_AQI_Final.pdf [Accessed 11/2022]

FRC [2020] *Audit Quality Thematic Review – The Use of Technology on the Audit of Financial Statements (March 2020)* [Online]. Available at: www.frc.org.uk/getattachment/1c1478e7-3b2e-45dc-9369-c3df8d3c3a16/AQT-Review_Technology_20.pdf [Accessed 11/2022]

FRC (2020) *FRC Climate Thematic: Audit* [Online]. Available at: https://www.frc.org.uk/getattachment/ab63c220-6e2b-47e6-924e-8f369512e0a6/Summary-FINAL.pdf [Accessed 11/2022]

FRC (2021) *ISRE (UK) 2410: Review of interim financial information performed by the independent auditor of the entity* [Online]. Available at: https://www.frc.org.uk/getattachment/08bac29d-781a-44bc-bd54-ef2a9bef1edd/Revised-ISRE-(UK)-2410-Final.pdf [Accessed 11/2022]

FRC (2021) *ISA (UK) 240 (Revised May 2021) The auditor's responsibilities relating to fraud in an audit of financial statements* [Online]. Available at: https://www.frc.org.uk/getattachment/e48499f2-b69b-4f45-8bef-762583eab1cd/ISA-(UK)-240-Final.pdf [Accessed 11/2022]

FRC (2021) *Bulletin: Illustrative auditor's reports on United Kingdom private sector financial statements* [Online]. Available at: https://www.frc.org.uk/getattachment/7a8874ec-a22d-422b-a0fd-81c7493519ab/Bulletin-Illustrative-Statutory-Auditor-s-Reports-20210823.pdf [Accessed 11/2022]

FRC (2022) Staff Guidance - Auditor responsibilities under ISA (UK) 720 in respect of climate-related reporting by companies required by the Financial Conduct Authority [Online]. Available at: https://www.frc.org.uk/getattachment/b6e1b51c-4dc8-413f-8a83-ae051e4d000e/FRC-Staff-Guidance-Auditor-responsibilities-under-ISA-(UK)-720-in-respect-of-climate-related-reporting.pdf [Accessed 10/2022]

FRC (2022b) Professional judgement guidance [Online]. Available at: https://www.frc.org.uk/getattachment/fff79ba1-3b5a-4c04-8f1e-eb8df3aacd40/FRC-Professional-Judgement-Guidance_June-2022.pdf [Accessed 10/2022]

FRC (2022c) Proposed ISA (UK) 600 (Revised) *Special Considerations – Audits of Group Financial Statements (Including the Work of Component Auditors)* [Online]. Available at: https://www.frc.org.uk/getattachment/482ee6c7-46e3-4123-a8df-0d0a6051d11f/Proposed-ISA-(UK)-600-May-2022.pdf [Accessed 10/2022]

IAASB (2009) *Emerging Practice Issues Regarding the Use of External Confirmations in an Audit of Financial Statements* [Online]. Available at: www.ifac.org/publications-resources/staff-audit-practice-alert-emerging-practice-issues-regarding-use-external-co [Accessed 11/2022]

IAASB (2015) *Auditor Reporting—Illustrative Key Audit Matters* [Online]. Available at: www.ifac.org/publications-resources/auditor-reporting-illustrative-key-audit-matters [Accessed 11/2022]

IAASB (2016) *Discussion Paper, Supporting Credibility and Trust in Emerging Forms of External Reporting* [Online]. Available at: www.ifac.org/publications-resources/discussion-paper-supporting-credibility-and-trust-emerging-forms-external [Accessed 11/2022]

IAASB (2018) *Feedback Statement Prepared by the Staff of the IAASB: Exploring the Growing Use of Technology in the Audit, with a Focus on Data Analytics* [Online]. Available at: www.ifac.org/system/files/publications/files/Data-Analytics-Feedback-Statement.pdf [Accessed 11/2022]

IAASB (2018a) *Feedback Statement, Supporting Credibility and Trust in Emerging Forms of External Reporting: Ten Key Challenges for Assurance Engagements* [Online]. Available at: www.ifac.org/system/files/publications/files/IAASB-EER-Feedback-Statement_0.pdf [Accessed 11/2022]

IAASB (2019) *Introduction to ISA 315 (Revised 2019) Identifying and Assessing the Risks of Material Misstatement* [Online]. Available at: www.ifac.org/system/files/publications/files/IAASB-Introduction-to-ISA-315.pdf [Accessed 11/2022]

IAASB (2020) *Exposure Draft - Proposed International Standard on Auditing 600 (Revised) Special Considerations – Audits of Group Financial Statements (Including the Work of Component Auditors)* [Online]. Available at: www.iaasb.org/publications/proposed-international-standard-auditing-600-revised-special-considerations-audits-group-financial [Accessed 11/2022]

IAASB (2020) *Fact Sheet – Introduction to ISRS 4400 (Revised) Agreed-Upon-Procedures Engagements* [Online]. Available at: www.ifac.org/system/files/publications/files/ISRS-4400-Revised-Fact-Sheet-final.pdf [Accessed 11/2022]

IAASB (2020) *ISRS 4400 (Revised) Agreed-Upon-Procedures Engagements* [Online]. Available at: www.ifac.org/system/files/publications/files/ISRS-4400-Revised-Agreed-Upon-Procedures-final.pdf [Accessed 11/2022]

IAASB (2020) *Non-authoritative support material related to technology: Audit documentation when using automated tools and techniques* [Online]. Available at: www.ifac.org/system/files/publications/files/FINAL-Non-Authoritative-Support-Material_Audit-Documentation-When-Using-Automated-Tools-And-Techniques.pdf [Accessed 11/2022]

IAASB (2020) *Non-authoritative support material related to technology: frequently asked questions (FAQ)— The use of automated tools and techniques when identifying and assessing risks of material misstatement in accordance with IAS 315 (Revised 2019)* [Online]. Available at: https://www.ifac.org/system/files/publications/files/IAASB-Technology-FAQ-Automated-Tools-Techniques.pdf [Accessed 11/2022]

IAASB (2020) *The consideration of climate-related risks in an audit of financial statement* [Online]. Available at: https://www.ifac.org/system/files/publications/files/IAASB-Climate-Audit-Practice-Alert.pdf [Accessed 11/2022]

IAASB (2020) *Non-authoritative support material related to technology: frequently asked questions (FAQ)— The use of automated tools and techniques in performing audit procedures* [Online]. Available at: https://www.ifac.org/system/files/publications/files/IAASB-FAQ-Automated-Tools-Techniques.pdf [Accessed 11/2022]

IAASB (2021) *Proposed Amendments to the IAASB's International standards: Conforming and Consequential Amendments to the IAASB's Other Standards as a Result of the New and Revised Quality Management Standards* [Online]. Available at: https://www.ifac.org/system/files/publications/files/IAASB-Conforming-Amendments-Quality-Management.pdf [Accessed 11/2022]

IAASB (2021) *Non-Authoritative Guidance on Applying ISAE 3000 (Revised) to Extended External Reporting (EER) Assurance Engagements* [Online]. Available at: https://www.ifac.org/system/files/publications/files/IAASB-Guidance-Extended-External-Reporting.pdf [Accessed 11/2022]

IAASB (2021) *Addressing risk of overreliance on technology arising from the use of automated tools and techniques* [Online]. Available at: https://www.ifac.org/system/files/publications/files/IAASB-Automated-Tools-Techniques-FAQ.pdf [Accessed 11/2022]

IAASB (2021) *Discussion paper: Fraud and going concern in an audit of financial statements* [Online]. Available at: https://www.ifac.org/system/files/publications/files/IAASB-Discussion-Paper-Fraud-Going-Concern.pdf [Accessed 11/2022]

IAASB (2022) *Frequently asked questions August 2022: Reporting going concern matters in the auditor's report* [Online]. Available at: https://www.ifac.org/system/files/publications/files/IAASB-Going-Concern-Frequently-Asked-Questions.pdf [Accessed 09/2022]

IBM (2018) *The Four V's of Big Data* [Online]. Available at https://www.researchgate.net/figure/IBM-Four-Vs-of-Big-Data_fig1_320799079 [Accessed: 11/2022]

ICAEW (2016b) *Framework for Resolving Ethical Problems* [Online]. Available at: www.icaew.com/en/technical/ethics/framework-for-resolving-ethical-problems [Accessed: 11/2022]

IESBA (2012) *Responding to a Suspected Illegal Act* [Online]. Available at:
www.iaasb.org/system/files/publications/files/IESBA-Code-of-Ethics-Illegal-Acts-Exposure-
Draft.pdf [Accessed 11/2022]

IESBA (2016) *Responding to Non-Compliance with Laws and Regulations* [Online]. Available at:
www.ifac.org/publications-resources/responding-non-compliance-laws-and-regulations
[Accessed 11/2022]

IESBA (2019) *Exposure Draft – Proposed Revisions to the Code to Promote the Role and Mindset
Expected of Professional Accountants* [Online]. Available at:
www.ifac.org/system/files/publications/files/IESBA-Exposure-Draft-Role-and-Mindset.pdf
[Accessed 11/2022]

IESBA (2020) *Exposure Draft – Proposed revisions to the fee-related provisions of the code*
[Online]. Available at: www.ifac.org/system/files/publications/files/FINAL-IESBA-ED_Proposed-
Revisions-to-the-Fee-related-Provisions-of-the-Code_0.pdf [Accessed 11/2022]

IESBA (2020) *Exposure Draft – Proposed revisions to the non-assurance services provisions of the
code* [Online]. Available at: www.ifac.org/system/files/publications/files/FINAL-IESBA-ED-
Proposed-Revisions-to-the-NAS-Provisions-of-the-Code.pdf [Accessed 11/2022]

IESBA (2020) *Revisions to the Code to Promote the Role and Mindset Expected of Professional
Accountants* [Online]. Available at: https://www.ifac.org/system/files/publications/files/Final-
Pronouncement-Role-and-Mindset_0-1.pdf [Accessed 11/2022]

IESBA (2021) *2020 Handbook of the International Code of Ethics for Professional Accountants*
[Online]. Available at: https://www.ifac.org/system/files/publications/files/IESBA-English-2020-
IESBA-Handbook_Web-LOCKED.pdf [Accessed 11/2022]

IESBA (2021) *Revisions to the Code Addressing the Objectivity of an Engagement Quality Reviewer
and Other Appropriate Reviewers* [Online]. Available at:
https://www.ifac.org/system/files/publications/files/Final-Pronouncement-Objectivity-of-
Engagement-Quality-Reviewer-and-Other-Appropriate-Reviewers.pdf [Accessed 11/2022]

IESBA (2021) *Revisions to the Fee-related Provisions of the Code* [Online]. Available at:
https://www.ifac.org/system/files/publications/files/Final-Pronouncement-Fees.pdf [Accessed
11/2022]

IESBA (2021) *Revisions to the Non Assurances Services Provisions of the Code* [Online]. Available
at: https://www.ifac.org/system/files/publications/files/Final-Pronouncement-Non-Assurance-
Services.pdf [Accessed 11/2022]

IESBA (2021) *Non-assurance services (NAS) - Mapping table - Comparison of extant and revised
provisions* [Online]. Available at: https://www.ifac.org/system/files/publications/files/Mapping-
Table-Comparison-Extant-Versus-Final-Provisions-Non-Assurance-Services-final.pdf [Accessed
11/2022]

IESBA (2022) *Revisions to the definitions of Listed Entity and Public Interest Entity in the Code*
[Online]. Available at: https://www.ifac.org/system/files/publications/files/IESBA-Final-
Pronouncement_Listed-Entity-and-Public-Interest-Entity.pdf [Accessed 10/2022]

IFAC (2010) ISAE 3400 *The examination of prospective financial information* [Online]. Available at:
https://www.ifac.org/system/files/downloads/b013-2010-iaasb-handbook-isae-3400.pdf
[Accessed 10/2022]

IFAC (2017) *Toward enhanced professional skepticism: Observations of the IAASB-IAESB-IESBA
Professional Skepticism Working Group* [Online]. Available at: www.iaasb.org/publications-
resources/toward-enhanced-professional-skepticism [Accessed 11/2022]

IIRC (2013) *The international IR framework* [Online]. Available at: integratedreporting.org/wp-
content/uploads/2015/03/13-12-08-THE-INTERNATIONAL-IR-FRAMEWORK-2-1.pdf [Accessed
11/2022]

Norton (2019) *Norton Cyber Safety Insights Report* [Online]. Available at:
now.symassets.com/content/dam/norton/campaign/NortonReport/2020/2019_NortonLifeLock_C
yber_Safety_Insights_Report_Global_Results.pdf?promocode=DEFAULTWEB [Accessed 11/2022]

O'Dwyer, M. and Pickard, J (2022) *Cost of UK plan to break Big Four stranglehold rises to £1bn* [Online]. Available at: https://www.ft.com/content/347e5dbb-c8e1-4cd0-8989-93fba1f935d4 [Accessed 11/2022]

OECD (2021) *OECD environmental data and indicators* [Online]. Available at: https://www.oecd.org/env/indicators-modelling-outlooks/data-and-indicators.htm [Accessed 11/2022]

PCAOB (2016) *Mission and vision* [Online]. Available at: pcaobus.org/About/History/Pages/default.aspx [Accessed 11/2022]

TAC (2010) *Who we are* [Online]. Available at: www.ifac.org/who-we-are/committees/transnational-auditors-committee-forum-firms [Accessed 11/2022]

UN (2021) *Academic impact: Sustainability* [Online]. Available at: https://www.un.org/en/academic-impact/sustainability [Accessed 11/2022]

UN (2021) *The 17 Goals* [Online]. Available at: https://sdgs.un.org/goals [Accessed 11/2022]

UK Law

Companies Act 2006 [Online]. Available at: www.legislation.gov.uk/ukpga/2006/46/contents [Accessed 11/2022]

Open Parliament Licence v3.0: www.nationalarchives.gov.uk/doc/open-government-licence/version/3/ [Accessed 11/2022]

US Law

Sarbanes-Oxley Act 2002 [Online]. Available at: www.sec.gov/answers/about-lawsshtml.html#sox2002 [Accessed 11/2022]

Corporate governance code

FRC (2018) *FRC UK Corporate Governance Code* [Online]. Available at: www.frc.org.uk/getattachment/88bd8c45-50ea-4841-95b0-d2f4f48069a2/2018-UK-Corporate-Governance-Code-FINAL.pdf [Accessed 11/2022].

FRC Audit and Assurance Standards and Guidance

FRC (2022) *Current auditing standards* [Online]. Available from: www.frc.org.uk/auditors/audit-assurance/standards-and-guidance/current-auditing-standards [Accessed 11/2022].

International Financial Reporting Standards

IFRS Foundation (2021) *IFRS* [Online]. Available at: eifrs.ifrs.org [Accessed 11/2022].

International Sustainability Standards Board

IFRS (2022) *IFRS Foundation work plan* [Online]. Available at: https://www.ifrs.org/projects/work-plan/ [Accessed 11/2022]

International Audit and Assurance Standards Board guidance

IAASB (2018) *Publications* [Online]. Available from: www.ifac.org/system/files/publications/files/IAASB-2018-HB-Vol-1.pdf [Accessed 11/2022].

FRC Ethical Standard

FRC (2019) *Revised Ethical standard 2019* [Online]. Available from: www.frc.org.uk/getattachment/601c8b09-2c0a-4a6c-8080-30f63e50b4a2/Revised-Ethical-Standards-2019-Updated-With-Covers.pdf [Accessed 11/2022].

Tell us what you think

Got comments or feedback on this book? Let us know.
Use your QR code reader:

Or, visit:
https://bppgroup.fra1.qualtrics.com/jfe/form/SV_9TrxTtw8jSvO7Pv

Need to get in touch with customer service?

www.bpp.com/request-support

Spotted an error?

www.bpp.com/learningmedia/Errata